Seeing Justice

Seeing Justice

*Witnessing, Crime, and Punishment
in Visual Media*

MARY ANGELA BOCK

OXFORD
UNIVERSITY PRESS

OXFORD
UNIVERSITY PRESS

Oxford University Press is a department of the University of Oxford. It furthers
the University's objective of excellence in research, scholarship, and education
by publishing worldwide. Oxford is a registered trade mark of Oxford University
Press in the UK and certain other countries.

Published in the United States of America by Oxford University Press
198 Madison Avenue, New York, NY 10016, United States of America.

© Oxford University Press 2021

Library of Congress Cataloging-in-Publication Data
Names: Bock, Mary Angela, author.
Title: Seeing justice : witnessing, crime, and punishment in visual media /
Mary Angela Bock.
Description: New York, NY : Oxford University Press, [2021] |
Includes bibliographical references and index.
Identifiers: LCCN 2021000058 (print) | LCCN 2021000059 (ebook) |
ISBN 9780190926984 (paperback) | ISBN 9780190926977 (hardback) |
ISBN 9780190927004 (epub)
Subjects: LCSH: Mass media—Social aspects—United States. | Social justice—
United States. | Photojournalism—Social aspects—United States. |
Criminal justice, administration of—United States. | Visual sociology—United States.
Classification: LCC HN90.M3 B625 2021 (print) |
LCC HN90.M3 (ebook) | DDC 302.23—dc23
LC record available at https://lccn.loc.gov/2021000058
LC ebook record available at https://lccn.loc.gov/2021000059

DOI: 10.1093/oso/9780190926977.001.0001

1 3 5 7 9 8 6 4 2

Paperback printed by Marquis, Canada
Hardback printed by Bridgeport National Bindery, Inc., United States of America

For David,
who knew it was possible before I did.

For the most part we do not first see, and then define, we define first and then see.

—Walter Lippmann, *Public Opinion*, 1922

Contents

Preface

In 2020, it took eight minutes and forty-six seconds to move the world. The video of George Floyd dying, losing breath, crying out for his mother as his body strains for oxygen under the weight of officer Derek Chauvin's knee, ignited protests on behalf of Black lives across the United States and around the world. Protesters took to the streets to call for defunding or even abolishing police. Corporations promised to improve hiring practices. Congress debated a police reform bill. Statues have been pulled down and murals painted on streets.

How much of the moment will lead to real change? As of this writing, it is not clear. Photographic imagery made an impact on the public conversation, but that impact is contingent and mutable. Professional and social media users renarrativized the video repeatedly into stories that served their individual interests. In fact, some viewers even suggested that Floyd's death had been staged.

The George Floyd case encapsulates much of the ground this book covers: the evidentiary value of photographic imagery, the contingency of its image meaning, the perpetual battles over narratives that use images and the nature of spectacle. Yes, the video inspired calls for change. As of this writing, significant policy changes are still being debated. I hope this book might explore the reasons why.

This book was not inspired by the George Floyd video, nor any other of the many clips currently in circulation that are shaping public discourse about crime, punishment, and justice. In fact, this book started germinating before social media put video production in the hands of everyday users, and long before I became an academic. I remember when the seed fell: the day that local basketball star Allen Iverson appeared in court in Philadelphia on a domestic violence charge. My task, as the field producer, was to make sure that the five photographers assigned to the courthouse remained at their posts in order to shoot the perp walk. Five photographers. There were seven on the roster at that time of day, so this meant that the majority of our visual team was assigned to the Criminal Justice Center: two out front, one on each side, one at the back.

And me.

I was instructed to make sure everyone stayed at their assigned post, but because it was ninety degrees out, and because no one wants to be the photographer who misses a shot, my real work that day turned out to be holding position for each photographer when they needed a bathroom break and buying bottled water for everyone. Have I mentioned that at that stage in my career I'd had more than fifteen years in TV news? That I'd started my journalism career as a sixteen-year-old small-town newspaper reporter? Yet here I was, circling the block-sized building all day on perp walk patrol.

The shot we finally got was through an SUV's window. Iverson had been allowed to drive in and drive out of the facility's underground garage, and the veteran TV photographer assigned to that side of the building obtained about three seconds of video in which Allen Iverson was visible through the SUV's windows. Five photographers, a full shift: all for three seconds of video of an already very famous man. Philadelphians already knew what Allen Iverson looked like, so why did we need this incredible effort? Why was this considered such a victory in the newsroom?

Much of my academic research career has been devoted to answering questions like these, in practical and theoretical terms. The project at hand combines them and asks, "What is the role of visual media in shaping public discourse about criminality, justice, right, and wrong?" How and why are visual messages created, and what—or more pointedly—whose purposes do they serve? Digitization is changing the visual media ecology, and today people are able to speak to power in unprecedented ways. This book was written during a time of extraordinary change and describes the opportunities and problems associated with this revolution.

Several strands of scholarship offer guidance for this book. I rely heavily on Michel Foucault's expansive work about power, knowledge, and discourse, as well as his examination of social discipline's relationship with surveillance. I am further indebted to the work of Stuart Hall, who was influenced in part by Foucault, for his critical theorization of media (and whose encoding and decoding model is especially relevant in the social media era), and Walter Fisher's narrative paradigm, which emphasizes the persuasive power of storytelling. Guy DuBord's notion of the "spectacle" and Jean Baudrillard's extension of the simulacra help connect disciplinary surveillance with mass media. Other scholars, including Erving Goffman, Nicholas Mirzoeff, Pierre Bourdieu, Barbie Zelizer, Paul Messaris, David Altheide, Nick Couldry, and my mentor, Klaus Krippendorff, have helped untangle the web of social and technological interactions that form the criminal justice media ecosystem. Perhaps unexpectedly, feminist theory must be considered in research on photography, for its emphasis on the role of the body in social interaction. Photojournalism, after all, engages the body in ways that word-based reporting does not. I could not have performed my role at the Criminal Justice Center from an air-conditioned distance. This is not to say that writers do not use their bodies to work, but that news photography makes essential use of the body in the various social contexts under study here.

This is not a book about images. It is about the processes by which visual messages are made, and by whom, for a particular purpose. Throughout this book I argue that social actors struggle over the construction of visual messages in embodied and discursive ways, and that digitization has vastly expanded the encoding capabilities of everyday citizens, allowing them to add visibility to their expression of democratic voice, even as the ethical rules for visual expression are inchoate. This argument is based on assumptions long held by visual scholars: that images are constructions and their meaning is contingent. The constructed nature of photographs tends to be eclipsed by faith in the camera's accuracy, and the work of human actors—who use their bodies in time and space to cover events—tends to be occluded by media organizations lauding the documentary perfection of a camera's output.

Images present and an essential (if not ultimate) manifestation of power over narrative. In large part, to control the image is to control the story. Part of that effort entails controlling the practices of photojournalists on the ground in real time, a concept I have named "embodied gatekeeping," those corporeal and discursive practices connected to the control of visual media production. Whether in the form of laws that prevent news photography in courtrooms, attorneys attempting to shield their clients from perp walks, or activists who walk at night to monitor police activity, embodied gatekeeping provides a useful construct for analysis, not because such restrictions may annoy visual journalists (which is, of course, the case) but because such restrictions have an impact on the eventual image constructed.

Seeing justice is more than a metaphor. For millennia, humans have sized up situations and each other using visual cues. The law is a linguistic abstraction. Justice is physical. It is material. Its narratives are experienced emotionally and persuasively, and occasionally erroneously. This is where injustice lurks nearby, for human perception is not nearly as reliable as believed, and notions of justice are tangled in stereotypes, biased expectations, and ideology. News organizations both help and hinder as intermediaries in the process because of their own institutional motivations. Digital media and mobile technologies have enabled unprecedented bottom-up participation in the visual conversation. Yet while we have more information than ever, specifically more visual information than ever, we don't necessarily *know* much more. The jaw-dropping disparities in our justice system in terms of race, gender, and class are evidence enough that there is much work to do.

This project would not be possible without the support of my husband, David Alan Schneider, who made it possible for me to pursue a PhD and never wavered in his belief in my abilities. Rosemary and Emily Carlson, my daughters, have always given me good reason to carry on. My parents, Rosalie and Joe, have patiently listened to my tales of woe throughout my academic career, and I know somewhere my mom still has some of the early "books" I wrote with a crayon tucked in a file somewhere.

I am forever indebted to my mentor, Klaus Krippendorff, who introduced me to new, productive ways of thinking about the world and who never failed to show me kindness even when faced with my clumsiest academic efforts. I am grateful to students who worked with me on some of the foundational research: Melissa Suran, Laura Marina Boria González, Ever Figueroa, and Kyser Lough, who combed through the archives of hanging photos so I could just deal with the "good stuff." My colleagues at the University of Texas at Austin, Kutztown University, the Annenberg School for Communication at the University of Pennsylvania, and the visual communication community at large have also helped me theorize and make sense of my research. I must also acknowledge the support and intellectual influence of Paul Messaris, who died during the year I wrote this book. I started researching perp walks during my very first semester at Penn in his graduate class. I was lucky to have learned from him.

Finally, I must thank each and every photographer I've ever worked with, interviewed, and questioned in the course of my research. Without you, there'd be nothing to see, nothing to talk about, nothing to learn.

1

Playing with Fire

Scene one: I am wearing a skirted suit, high heels, and stockings, and I am crawling around the floor of the Polk County (IA) Courthouse under a table to connect cables and electrical cords. We are covering a trial, with a camera inside the courtroom and a video distribution system in the hallway so that the TV reporters can work without distracting the jury.

Scene two: I am at a crime scene with a photographer, and a police officer tells us we must turn off the camera. I explain that this is a public space and we are on public ground, so we are allowed to shoot video. The officer insists that we move across the street. I soon learn from a seasoned photographer that instead of arguing with authorities, it's simpler to appear to comply by taking the camera off one's shoulder—but continue rolling tape.

Scene three: I am watching an experienced newspaper reporter learn how to produce a short feature video for the web. He sets up the camera to interview a public relations officer, then takes it down and gets down on one knee to interview a child. He then takes the camera off the tripod to collect some other shots for the story. Wiping sweat off his brow, he looks at me and says, "This is hard work."

News work is always a sweaty, messy, and contentious process, and photojournalism is especially so. The end product often appears so clean and well focused, the video stories so seamless, that it is easy to disregard the work that produced them. In fact, journalism usually encourages the audience to disregard that work in order to perpetuate the belief that the camera's output is "truth." Consider, then, the messiness of news work in the context of the criminal justice system, with its complex of social, technological, and material relationships, as it constructs our understanding of how we are supposed to behave in a civilized society—and what happens when we do not. The digital age adds yet another ingredient to the mix: media made by everyday people.

Seeing Justice. Mary Angela Bock, Oxford University Press. © Oxford University Press 2021.
DOI: 10.1093/oso/9780190926977.003.0001

The result is a confusing polarity: images are being presented as factual evidence even as they are debated as complex constructions that must be understood in context. Millions more people are able to account for their lives using visual communication while the norms and ethics for doing so are embryonic.

This book attempts to make sense of the debate as it reflects the patterns of today's visual ecology. It examines the way images about justice are created, contextualized, and distributed, and how different social actors vie for control of those processes. Historically, two institutions, the press and the criminal justice system, have operated symbiotically to visually represent criminal justice, constituting what might be considered a form of what Mirzoeff calls a "complex of visuality."[1] Images traveled a somewhat linear and predictable path from event to audience, contextualized and recontextualized by social actors within varied institutional frameworks. Today, however, digital media allow for images to bypass institutional processes en route to a worldwide audience. The democratization of image production has enabled important counternarratives from marginalized groups that are leveraging the power of mimesis to their cause. This democratization of access to the tools of visual community also creates opportunities for propagandists with mischievous, if not mendacious, intent.

This chapter outlines the theoretical foundation for the book, first by describing what is special about images, how they are made meaningful, and why they are especially useful in the construction of ideological messages— the reason social actors work so hard to control their construction and use in narrative. Here and throughout the book, I draw from this foundation to argue that social actors struggle over the construction of visual messages in embodied and discursive ways, and that digitization has vastly expanded the encoding capabilities of everyday citizens, allowing them to add visibility to their expression of democratic voice even as the ethical rules for visual expression are inchoate. Studying the process by which images are created and then used in discourse allows for a clearer understanding of their influence in the digital public sphere, and further offers insight into ways the system— and its visual messaging—might be different.

Harnessing Light's Power

We have privileged the sense of sight over others as we navigate the world. To see is to know; think of how we even use the phrase "I see," to mean, "I understand." Our eyes provide us not only with information about what is in our field of view, but where it is in relation to the body. We use vision to interpret our environment and move through it. Images, whether moving or still, help us to navigate the world at large. Today, much of what we see is not natural, but constructed imagery. We are beset by a flood of visual information about the social world. This "bain d'images" is at times overwhelming, compelling, and controversial. We spend so much time with screens (by one estimate, eleven hours a day) that it is conceivable that someday we'll spend a majority of our time viewing mediated images rather than the world around us.[2] A hallmark of modernity, visual messaging entertains, sells, and teaches. In this postmodern, digital world, visual communication has shifted from professional production to a more democratic sphere, a move that has significantly changed the way we understand and use images as evidence. Photographic imagery is used as "proof" in more spaces than ever before at the very moment when digital democratization casts those images in doubt.

Our reliance on vision for knowledge is in large part a matter of biology, something researchers call "visual primacy" or the "picture superiority effect." Our brains process images more quickly than words, and images trigger our fear and memory centers more powerfully than words.[3] Images act as sites of memory in the public and private spheres.[4] Eye-tracking research has found that visual information guides the way people move through a newspaper.[5] When faced with mixed messages in which the words say one thing but the visuals another, the human brain accepts the image.[6] Experimental research has shown that viewers have a hard time detecting photo fakery, and even subjects who are "visually literate" are influenced by enhanced advertising photography.[7] Visual primacy is so strong it operates even when viewers are reminded of the fact that advertising images are enhanced[8] or misleading.[9]

Whether still or moving, the phenomenology of images contributes to their interpretation. Images are compelling in part because of their kinesthetic cues. As Mirzoeff theorized, there is more to visuality than what stimulates the optic nerve: it is a form of knowing based on all the senses.[10] When politicians are photographed from below, they look regal; when we encounter a full-frame face-to-face portrait, our mirror neurons (which engage our sociality) are engaged.[11] What scholars often ignore, however, is the phenomenology of their creation; the connection between practice and meaning. Shooting the regal perspective usually requires a photographer to *literally* position themselves beneath the subject; shooting a bird's-eye view involves *physically* rising above a scene. The rising use of video camera drones has inspired fresh conversations about embodied perspective, what Astrid Gynnild called "robot witnessing," for the way a machine performs these actions.[12]

Faces are particularly compelling and augment the phenomenological dimension of photographs.[13] We have, according to evolutionary anthropology, an innate need to read faces and to "sort out" friend and foe.[14] Visual information in the form of nonverbal communication dominates our conversations, and certain human expressions are not only universal but perceived more forcefully than language.[15] Visual primacy and the strength of image memory mean that stereotypical images are particularly pernicious for their durability.[16] Scientists are only beginning to understand the power of mirror neurons, which react to the nonverbal cues of other people, affect our cognition.[17] In short, images can trigger our emotions more quickly, and with greater force, than words can compel us to reason. They are emotionally compelling, persuasive, and memorable.

Images and Justice

It's no surprise, therefore, that those in power have historically worked to leverage images to their favor. Pyramids, monuments, cathedrals, crowns, sculptures, coins, and flags, marked with symbols of royalty or religion, are just a few examples of visual representations of power. Literal images support metaphorical, public images of power, and as Machiavelli advised, "It is not essential that a Prince should *have* all the good qualities which I have enumerated above, but it is most essential that he should *seem* to have them."[18] Modern leaders have become adept at crafting visual messaging so as to *seem* to have those good qualities.[19]

Because visual communication combines the literal and symbolic, it easily fuels myth, not only because signs are quickly and easily understood, but because human beings are prone to visual primacy. That is, when a visual message conflicts with a verbal one, people tend to believe what they see.[20] Edelman recounted a political example from the 1980s, when Leslie Stahl took a phone call from a leader of Ronald Reagan's presidential reelection campaign, believing he would complain about her story, which listed the failed promises from the president's first term.[21] Instead, according to the story, he thanked her, saying that no one heard her critique, they only saw the celebratory scenes.

The criminal justice system similarly harnesses visual messaging to construct its mythology. Architecture predates photography but remains an important mode for communicating judicial authority. Courthouses are placed in the center of many American towns as a sign of their importance. Resnik, Curtis, and Tait used the term "icons of the state" to describe modern courthouses and the way their architecture symbolizes judicial independence.[22] Inside, the courtrooms resemble churches, with benches that mimic pews. Judges, jurors, and attorneys work behind a bar or rail that separates them from the public.[23] High ceilings, oversized light fixtures, and classic woodwork are all elements designed to visually demand reverence for the rule of law. Attorneys furnish their offices with leather and finished wood, and display shelves of richly colored law books with gilded titles to visually convey their status. Legal symbols are ubiquitous and immediately recognizable in such spaces. The Roman goddess Justitia is depicted wearing her blindfold, because law should prevail without regard for the social standing of the people involved.[24] She also holds the scales, symbolizing the two sides of an argument, and a sword that wields the state's power. More recently, the shield-shaped badge is an immediately recognizable icon for policing. A more provocative symbol has also emerged recently, the thin-blue-line American flag, connoting not policing so much as support for police in refutation of their critics.

The role of visuality in social control goes beyond iconography, and the evolution of professional policing and photography are historically intertwined. In keeping with Weber's definition of state as "the human community that within a defined territory . . . (successfully) claims the monopoly of the legitimate force for itself," it follows that if a democratic state is to hold its monopoly on violence, it must hold the faith of its citizens.[25] Weber's definition is useful not only for its emphasis on legitimate force, but his use of the phrase "human community" for the state, which includes all the human actors in such institutions as the criminal justice system, law enforcement agencies, penal institutions, and so on. Historically this community—the state—has used displays of violence, or spectacles of the scaffold, to frighten citizens into submission.[26] Today the images might work in either direction, with shows of force of public relations videos depicting officers rescuing ducklings; the tool, in this case, is the image, a critical part of police work.[27]

Imbalanced viewing, or being able to surreptitiously watch, is particularly powerful. Those in power are able to watch from behind a metaphorical curtain and fashion that curtain in ways that reinforce faith in their legitimacy.

This unilateral power energizes today's surveillance society.[28] Surveillance scholars have examined the way contemporary cameras are used for social control.[29] Roy Coleman argued that increased use of surveillance in modern cities may help authorities identify criminals, but can also exacerbate social inequality, providing a "a condemnatory gaze on the powerless."[30]

Scholars from a variety of perspectives have pointed to the connection between visuality and police power. In one of the earliest instances, the French (military) posted photographs of Communards dead in their coffins as a warning to any other potential rebels.[31] Wanted posters started as a form of public relations for the newly formed US Federal Bureau of Investigation.[32] Tagg and Sekula described the way photography became a policing tool, exploiting faith in the camera to cultivate ideas about classifying human beings.[33] Mug shots, for instance, arose as much from a belief in physiognomy as a need to document arrestees.[34]

Visual representations are increasingly important to the legal realm, an institution that historically has rested authority in language.[35] Legal scholarship attends to the visual in terms of constitutional law (regarding, for instance, the right to film public events in public space under the First Amendment), procedure (as with video as demonstrative evidence), and decorum orders that regulate cameras in courtrooms.[36] While photographs have been used in the courtroom for more than a century, every advance in visual technology forces changes in the way images can be and are used to establish legal facts.[37]

Mass-Mediated Images

Outside the courtroom, media amplify the role of the visual for our perception of the criminal justice system, operating as another element in the complex of visuality.[38] For decades, entertainment programming has offered a preponderance of police, legal, and now first-responder fare. Effects research responding to concerns about violence in these kinds of TV shows and movies has found a weak correlation with behavior.[39] While direct effects have proven elusive, research on aggregate media exposure suggests a more generalized influence. George Gerbner used the phrase "cultivation theory" to describe this extension of Bandura's social learning theory.[40] Gerbner's team found that people who watched a lot of TV were more likely to overestimate crime rates in their cities, the so-called scary world syndrome. More recent cultivation research found a correlation between heavy TV watching and authoritarianism, and, related to this, support for then candidate Donald Trump.[41] Programs such as *Cops*, purporting to show the "reality" of policing offer the law-and-order perspective and increase sympathy for police among white males.[42] Entertainment television has long relied on the crime serials that vary according to casting but remain ideologically consistent.[43] Stuart Hall's definition of "ideology" provides a foundation for this book: "the mental frameworks—the languages, the concepts, categories, imagery of thought, and the systems of representation—which different classes and social groups deploy in order to make sense of, define, figure out and render intelligible the way society works."[44] Traditional mass media and today's digital media are all part of a visual ecosystem that constitutes such "systems of representation" and contributes to prevailing ideology.

Critical scholars have also noted the way news, which presents itself as a neutral recorder of the day's events, a "mirror" of the world, reproduces ideology.[45] For example, like entertainment shows, news programs have also focused disproportionate attention on criminal justice.[46] A natural curiosity about death, drama, and the human condition is of part of the appeal of such programs, but it is also a function of what drives the TV business: ratings, easily collected visuals, and emotional stories. The implications of this focus are myriad, but two are particularly important for understanding the role of the visual for our understanding of criminal justice. First, as Gaye Tuchman found in her classic study of journalistic practice, and numerous researchers (myself included) have found subsequently, journalists are dependent upon authorities for information and are prone to adopting the perspectives of those sources.[47] This dependence on authorities explains, at least in part, repeated findings that journalism frames activists as wild, violent deviants. Rather than focusing on issues and presenting the complaints of protesters, news tends to cover activist events as nuisances, what Chan and Lee named the "protest paradigm."[48] The second implication of interest for this book is the role of news coverage in the perpetuation of racial and ethnic stereotypes.[49] Black men are presented as criminals more often than white men, and crimes with white victims and Black suspects receive more coverage.[50] When white women go missing, they are more likely to garner major media attention than Black women.[51]

Because journalism relies so heavily on elite sources, media scholars have argued that news is less watchdog than partner in the state's ideological project.[52] News ethnographer Herbert Gans identified six specific ideological myths perpetuated by the press, including American ethnocentrism, the notion of "altruistic democracy," and "responsible capitalism," values that hardly can be considered hostile to the modern state.[53] Visual coverage exacerbates this phenomenon. Protest coverage focuses on violence to property and people, amplifying the concerns of police.[54] Politicians have learned to invoke Hollywood-style hero myths into their public persona with well-staged photo opportunities.[55]

Critics have also pointed out just how harmful this dependence is for the overall social picture. Herman and Chomsky argued that the media-government nexus created a pliant audience.[56] David Altheide and Bob Snow theorized that the relationship between journalistic practice and its product result from "media logic," which reflects both the power of mass media and explains why state institutions struggle so tenaciously for control.[57] The material conditions of visual production only exacerbate what these scholars have observed. Altheide warned that journalism's focus on crime, disaster, and other social results in a metanarrative of fear far out of proportion to reality. The facts are that, overall, the US violent crime rate has been going down for more than two decades (though homicides spiked in 2020); that the vast majority of mass shootings in the United States were perpetrated by white men, not international terrorists; that garbage collectors, truck drivers, and farmers suffer workplace fatalities at higher rates than police; and that over-the-road truck drivers have a more dangerous job than police (though many police deaths can be attributed to violence, not accidents. Also, COVID-19 was a leading cause of death for police in 2020).[58]

The nonmediated reality of the American criminal justice system presents a stark contrast to detective procedurals and TV news murder coverage. Marginalized people in the United States and elsewhere often experience a very different story in which justice is not at all blind to race, poverty, ethnicity, or gender.[59] African Americans, who make up only 13 percent of the US population, represent 28 percent of all arrests, 40 percent of the people incarcerated, and 42 percent of all the people on death row.[60] Native Americans are killed by police at higher rates than any other group, although their overall numbers are low; Black Americans comprise about 12 percent of the US population but represent 26 percent of those killed by police.[61] The number for white Americans is about 51 percent, less than their 55 percent of the population.[62] More than 2 percent of the US population is under some sort of correctional supervision.[63] Police in the United States kill someone approximately every eight hours, and though most of these killings will be determined to be lawful, this rate is higher than for any other developed democracy in the world.[64]

Theoretical Foundation: How Images Work

Images are unable to "say" much at all by themselves. While photographs do capture light waves from a moment in time and space and offer indexical value, their meaning is largely contingent. Consider how different it might be to encounter Monet's *Water Lilies* in a museum versus on a cell phone screen. Imagine viewing the painting with no cultural understanding of Monet versus having an advanced art education. When, how, and where we encounter an image changes our interpretation of it. The way it is captioned, placed in a media artifact, or transmitted makes a difference, too. A single image might inspire an individual story or work as an icon for a macro-story, while still documenting a very real moment. For example, Hariman and Lucaites argued that Dorothea Lange's *Migrant Mother* suits the overall American story of a liberal democracy—what Roland Barthes would call "myth."[65] At the time it was taken, it suited a more specific story about the plight of farmworkers during the Great Depression. The very real and unwitting woman portrayed in the image, Florence Thompson, was simultaneously part of the grounded story about reality and the larger myth.[66]

Image meaning emerges largely from the symbiosis of the image in context. When *used* by human actors to illustrate, prove a point, or persuade, photographic images can be thought of as discursive *affordances*. Psychologist James Gibson coined the term "affordance" to describe the usefulness of a being's environment.[67] His concept is useful to the constructivist paradigm for the way it accounts for human agency in defining what an object—in this case, an image—"means" in context. In Gibson's words,

> An affordance cuts across the dichotomy of subjective-objective and helps us to understand its inadequacy. The affordances of the environment are facts of the environment, not appearances. But they are not, on the other hand, facts at the level of physics concerned only with matter and energy with animals left out.[68]

Gibson's definition accounts for both photographic indexicality and the significance of context. Images reflect facts of the environment, but do not present facts with the human animal. When a person creates a mediated message or narrative, photographic images offer the affordances of the camera and its technical accuracy. Photographic images are camera-accurate records that human beings can use in discourse to advance their intentions. People can truthfully testify, persuade, inform, explain, illustrate, and yes, lie with images. Their indexicality coupled with their contingent flexibility makes photographic images particularly useful artifacts in the public sphere.

Both of these dimensions—indexicality and context—contribute to the way an image is used to frame reality. Framing is a central concept to communication studies, defined by Entman as the process by which certain facts or ideas are shown and others are excluded "*in such a way as to promote a particular problem definition, causal interpretation, moral evaluation and/ or treatment recommendation* for the item described. Typically frames diagnose, evaluate and prescribe."[69] A photographic image, however, is doubly framed. A photographer "frames" reality with the camera, and then the image is framed in discourse. These two steps do not occur in a vacuum, and they are subject to social, institutional, and political forces, as human actors use what power they have to craft visual messages according to their needs.

Constructing Visual Messages

The argument that images are discursive affordances rests on constructivist assumptions about the social world. Constructivism does not deny the realities of the physical world, but instead assumes that human beings render the world meaningful through situated sense-making.[70] Within this paradigm, this book relies heavily on the work of three scholars in crafting its argument about image construction and situated sense-making: Michel Foucault, Stuart Hall, and Walter Fisher. Each of these theorists offers insight regarding the constructed nature of the image world and the critical importance of the social, institutional, and political forces that shape those constructions.

Foucault's expansive examination of the relationships between discourse, power, and social control provide this book's philosophical backdrop.[71] His ideas are particularly useful for thinking about the epistemology of photography for his attention to the gaze as a disciplinary force.[72] Because photographic images are so often presented as and assumed to be "truthful," Foucault's ideas about truth as a discursive construction are especially important for any project that seeks to discuss the camera's version of reality.[73]

Finally, his suggestion that power is "capillary" as opposed to monolithic is well suited to the study of the myriad, mundane decisions that human actors make in the course of constructing visual messages presented in news media as "true"—and, therefore, powerful.[74]

Stuart Hall usefully bridged the concerns of Marxist theorist Louis Althusser, who argued that oppressive systems can function by way of ideology instead of brute force,[75] with Foucault's critique of dualistic notions of power.[76] Hall conceived of culture as the site where struggles over ideology occur, and the work of the Centre for Contemporary Cultural Studies, informally known as the Birmingham School, used grounded research to examine the way these struggles unfold every day, on the ground, among human actors.[77] Hall's encoding and decoding model,[78] which rejected the one-way effects conception of the audience, has not only stood the test of time for its conception of importance of media construction as well as the active audience. Hall's work is particularly relevant for thinking about today's media prosumers—who both construct and respond—in the digital sphere.

Finally, Walter Fisher's narrative paradigm, which posits that storytelling is a more accessible way than classic reason to make moral sense of the world, supports this project's analysis of images in messages about the criminal justice system.[79] Fisher identified two dimensions of narrative effectiveness: coherence and fidelity.[80] A coherent story does not stray from its internal logic—for example, magic airplanes don't suddenly appear in *Sleeping Beauty*, and characters stay true to their nature. "Fidelity" describes a story's moral, or point, which Fisher argued has five facets: values, the story's connection to those values, outcomes predicted for those who adhere to the values, the connection between the story's values and the observer's values, and the extent to which the story's values are among the most significant in human experience. These dimensions permeate news coverage of crime and punishment. Narratives about criminal justice often contend with the most essential questions of morality and mortality, which, when presented as truthful in news accounts, render them especially persuasive.

Images as Affordances for Ideology

Based on what is known about the cognitive and emotional power of images, visual messages embedded into ideological discourse can be said to amplify that power. Barthes applied the term "mythologies" to describe the way visual texts become "ideographic" and represent, simultaneously, actual objects and ideological concepts such as imperialism.[81] He used the example of a magazine cover that depicted a young Black soldier saluting, conveying the connotation of French unity and pride. A military flyover at an American football game serves the same function, at once a dramatic technological display and a message of militarism, masculinity, and violence.

So it is with the ideology reproduced in the complex of visuality presented by the relationship between contemporary media and the criminal justice system. Legal philosopher Robert Cover argued that the word of law cannot be detached from the pain it inflicts; justice is a matter of word and body.[82] Police culture itself is historically rooted in traditional white male culture, concomitant with a sense of righteous authority and superiority over women, people of color, and young people.[83] As media perpetuate the prevailing ideology, the white, male, heteronormative perspective is normalized while all other ways of looking at the world are problematically othered. This happens not because of any one decision by a reporter, judge, or police officer. It is, instead, a hegemonic system in which everyday decisions over time reproduce ways of thinking that are so commonplace they feel like "common sense." Journalists cover trials without questioning their validity. Police statements are accepted as true. Phrases like "allegedly" and "innocent until proven guilty" appear in the news but have become blandly invisible. The close relationships between reporters and authorities is similarly invisible, and representations of a fair and functional system are presented without critique.

Those marginalized by the system are further othered in media. Visual representations in the news further exacerbate inequality for people whose bodies do not fit this ideological default. Critical Race Theory is essential to understanding the link between media and state oppression.[84] Hall's classic study of Britain's panic over muggings in the 1970s demonstrated how media carry this ideological torch. In *Policing the Crisis*, Hall and his colleagues found a circularity in the discourse surrounding street crime; judges respond to reports in the press that the public is concerned, and the public draws its concerns from police statements referring to muggings in crisis terms.[85] In later work, Hall also tended to the importance of photojournalism to this ideological project, which not only serves the state but the cause of white supremacy. In his words, "Amongst other kinds of ideological labour, the media construct for us a definition of what *race* is, what meaning the imagery of race *carries,* and what the 'problem of race' is understood to be."[86]

Race is only one dimension of oppression, though, as intersectional scholars have pointed out.[87] Feminist theory articulates the way media representations define and discipline the bodies of women, trans-people, and anyone else whose very existence lies outside the white, male, heteronormative, and able ideal.[88] To study the criminal justice system is to engage with one of the most masculine institutions outside of the military; in fact, there is considerable overlap.[89] If indeed the state is "a man," with a righteous monopoly on violence, then gender is part of the visual culture that reflects prevailing ideology.[90] Because visuality is so often associated with the body and emotion, photojournalism has gendered dimensions that cannot be ignored.

Arising out of a complex interactive system of embodied social actors, every individual media story about the criminal justice system is woven into the primary narrative of American justice. Cultural critics and legal scholars alike have argued that justice is an ideological construction that won't "work" unless people believe it exists: That is, the public must have faith in the legitimacy of its legal institutions. Media images contribute to both cultivating that belief and hiding the system's failures. That's not to say it's all a show, but instead that the show can distract from the truth—justice in the United States is not equally distributed, the law is enforced unevenly, and the real human beings who participate in the system are just that: human.

A Model for Image Construction and Circulation

Photographic images and video are exceptional discursive affordances. The two levels of framing, at their moment of creation and subsequently in discourse, enable multiple actors to shape and define an image within a social system as represented in Figure 1.1, a model for recontextualization. The term "recontextualization" is used because it incorporates contexts beyond what is typically considered part of media framing, such as the larger culture, feedback from the audience, and embodied practice.

Note that the person using a camera must operate within a social system to gain access to a scene, framing the moment in terms of angle, view, and distance while also working within a social system that grants access, or

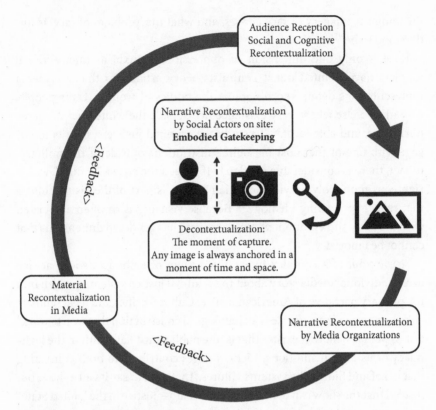

Figure 1.1 A Model for Recontextualization.
The traditional mass media model for recontextualization includes "gates" throughout the process, where social actors, often associated with media organizations, make a series of decisions regarding a particular image.

embodied gatekeeping. These social interactions control the way the image is constructed de novo, and can in turn shape the way that image is subsequently used in discourse. That is, once the scene is recorded, or "decontextualized," the image or video can then be iteratively recontextualized in a variety of discourses as it is processed and presented by a news organization, received by an audience, and used in narrative by various stakeholders. The map in Figure 1.1 does not include symbols for the economic, institutional, organizational, or ethical forces that shape those contexts—but these energies are always in play. The various social institutions that shape the meaning of a particular image act as ideological filters in the model. Note that both the de- and recontextualization processes operate within a larger ideological context and both are recursive, as human actors respond to feedback within the system.

This model is helpful for thinking about the double framing process and the way human actors work to control both the creation and use of photographic imagery. Consider the video of Eric Garner dying on the sidewalk at the hands of New York City police officers. The document-truth of the video portrays a large man on the ground struggling to cry out, "I can't breathe." This video was recontextualized in discourse on television and on the web and eventually inspired a book by journalist Matt Taibbi in 2017.[91] It was embedded into news stories and may eventually be played in court for the disciplinary trial of the officer who put Garner in a chokehold. The video is likely the very reason officer Daniel Pantaleo faced a disciplinary trial.[92] Just as significantly, the video became part of a macro-story about race and policing. Garner's last words, "I can't breathe," became part of police brutality protest, and the video morphed from document to icon.

The video of Garner's death circulated in news reports, but it was not made by a photojournalist on assignment. If not for a bystander who wanted to record police action that day, Garner most likely would have died anonymously. Digital media have democratized access to the visual public sphere, offering new opportunities for citizens and activists to document injustice and human suffering. Because a digital image is untethered by material forms of presentation, though, it can be recontextualized infinitely, for better or for worse. Figure 1.1, therefore, while useful for considering the conventional path of a news image, is overly simplistic for the digital world. Imagine that path turning repeatedly, with the moment of creation in real space and time in the center and accelerating moments of recontextualization, as in Figure 1.2. The institutional filters are off, speeding up the recontextualization cycle like a tornado. No longer a flat and understandable map, digitization converts the model into an ever-whirling spiral, with some stories more credible, honest, and useful than others.

Embodied Frames

The recontextualization model calls attention to the two levels of visual framing for photographic images: the moment of decontextualization when a human being uses a camera in real time and space, as well as the phases of recontextualization in mediated narrative. The model attends to photojournalism as an embodied social process, not merely a mechanical one. In the criminal justice realm, the process of creating a news image is a social one that invokes many bodies in addition to the one operating a camera, such as public relations specialists, security guards, other journalists, campaign

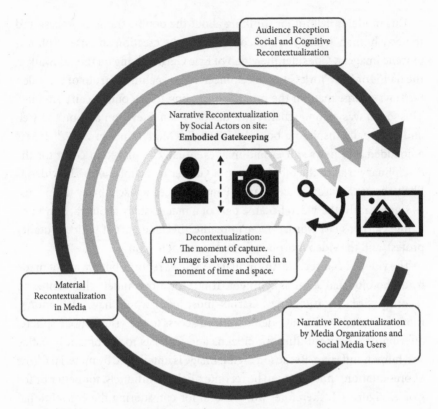

Figure 1.2 A Vortex of Endless Recontextualization.
Digitization allows for nearly infinite iterations of an image's
recontextualization. Media organizations lose control over the narrativization of
an image as soon as it is posted online. In this model, each recontextualization
inspires feedback into an endless but ever-expanding loop, much like a vortex.

managers, and of course, the subjects being photographed. Stakeholder goals
are not always in sync, and so the news images often are created within a
system of various tensions: politicians need to appear competent, judges
need the court to appear legitimate, public relations operatives want their
clients to look their best, and so on. These goals are a matter of both discourse
and document, of course, in that "appearing" competent is a matter of visual
and verbal messaging.

Controlling access to scenes in order to shape the resulting message,
"embodied gatekeeping" builds upon a foundational theory in journalism
studies.[93] Gatekeeping describes the practice of deciding which stories,
which facts, and which images are published in the news. Journalists are

not the only gatekeepers in the public sphere, however, as any social actor with power to control the flow of information is a "gatekeeper." Because of the role of the body in photojournalism, the practice of controlling those bodies—whether in terms of access, placement, or movement—allows for some images to be made and others to be occluded. Embodied gatekeeping describes the way human interaction affects the physical processes of photojournalism and its resulting visual artifacts. The importance of embodied gatekeeping becomes clearer when the power of a single image is considered. One image can influence a jury; one iconic image can rally a movement; one poignant news image can evoke public outrage. Who controls who sees what and how?

Photojournalism's physical dimension has profound significance. Photojournalists must be present on a scene to cover it, position their body in relation to the action, and manipulate equipment in real time. Even remote cameras and drones must set in place by human beings and (as Sekula would emphasize) for a discursive as well as documentary purpose. Much, if not most, visual research understandably neglects the role of the body in photographic construction. Even though scholars have pointed out the many subjective decisions that go into their creation, the output of that work tends to capture researchers' attention. Neglecting photographic practice is less of a problem in the world of art criticism or rhetoric, as the text is central to those fields. It is an unfortunate gap for the study of photojournalism, however, because its practice occurs in such a dynamic social environment. As James Carey put it, "the site where artists paint, writers write, speakers speak, filmmakers film, broadcasters broadcast is simultaneously the site of social conflict over the real."[94] Some researchers have examined the way photojournalists work in concert with word-based journalists, pointing out that journalism has traditionally favored language over image.[95] A few ethnographies have examined the everyday work of different types of photographers, such as TV-news videographers, solo video journalists, or newspaper photographers.[96] Rachel Somerstein recently used a survey and interviews to understand the grounded experiences of photographers and the way other social actors interfered with their work.[97] Ethnography has also revealed that photojournalism is a competitive practice, which does not, as one might expect, lead to creative work but, similar to other forms of journalism, instead encourages homogeneity.[98]

The historic neglect of practice in visual research is understandable for several reasons.

First, field research of professional practice is time consuming and expensive.[99] Second, images are a rich site for inquiry by themselves, whether for rhetoricians, social scientists, or historians. Third, many researchers, like journalists, favor the documentary value that flows from a camera, and have therefore focused a great deal of attention on icons: images with historic significance and cultural resonance that everyone recognizes.[100] Most of the images we encounter, however, are not at all memorable nor do they carry the aesthetic punch of an icon. Similar to Mirzoeff's notion of a complex of visuality, Poole theorized the "visual economy" to consider visuals as part of a larger, ever-moving social system.[101] Thinking in terms of a complex of visuality or visual economy shifts our attention away from individual images in favor of the larger system of image creation, distribution, and value in the public sphere. Photographic practice is irrelevant in the world of art criticism or rhetoric, for in these fields, the text is central. Photojournalism is more than its images, however; it is a practice that occurs in a dynamic social environment and for an imagined public, and the scholarly neglect of these processes perpetuates what Sturken and Cartwright called the "myth" of photographic truth.[102] The photojournalist's work is often ignored for the sake of this myth, especially in documentary contexts, because the *camera* can be offered up as a tool of objectivity.

So while the body is a neglected component of the process by which photojournalism produces and presents images, it is still, of course, merely one part of a larger social system. In the context of crime and punishment, myriad institutional practices involve stakeholders such as police officers, lawyers, judges, court administrators, activists, journalists, editors, and citizens. The "rules" of the process may be laws, codes, and regulations, or they might be informal understandings between various stakeholders. In some instances, these stakeholders may ignore the rules, as when a police officer tips off a photographer regarding the location of a prisoner transfer or a clerk leaks documents to a reporter. Economics are also part of the "rules" of this game, because most US news organizations are commercially supported and profit driven. Further, coverage of the criminal justice system reflects the larger social system's concerns with morality, safety, and fear of the other (however defined). The result is a complex of representations that are simultaneously highly abstract at the macro-level and viscerally simple at the individual level. Defendants are found guilty or not guilty. Perpetrators are seen or hidden. Victims are dead or alive.

Discursive Frames

Photography's theorists have generated numerous models for thinking about the relationship between image and context. Semiologist Charles Peirce offered a typology of visual signs, classifying them as icons (images that look like what they are supposed to represent); symbols (which represent abstract concepts without necessarily resembling them); and indexical signs, those whose representations are connected to their creation, such as footprints for feet, smoke for fire, and importantly, photographs for unique sets of light waves reflected from a moment in reality.[103] Barthes identified the mechanically recorded dimension of an image as its "denotation" and its larger context as its "connotation." Importantly, he added a third dimension, "anchorage," to describe the way images are labeled with language.[104] When he theorized the "invention of photographic meaning," Sekula argued against thinking of connotation and denotation as distinct, writing that "no such separation is possible."[105] For Sekula, even what might normally be considered the perfect recording of reality belies its rhetorical function. In his words, "A photographic discourse is a system within which the culture harnesses photographs to various representational tasks. . . . Every photographic image is a sign, above all, of someone's investment in the sending of a message."[106]

In a later essay, Sekula again attacked the notion of photography as a universal language, positioning it instead as an expression of power, specifically tied to capitalism and oppression. Tracing photography's historical connection to the Victorians' obsession with human classification and beliefs in physiognomy, Sekula argued that photography is not merely a reflection of society nor a completely neutral technique but instead extends ideology through the way it gives form to "discursively borne ideologies," such as the "family," "technology," or "history."[107] Documentary evidence enables discursive claims to truth, in a Foucauldian sense, that go far beyond the reality of the light captured by a camera Fisher's narrative paradigm offers an explanation of how these discourses, or stories, become a society's moral myths. Hall rightly noted that these myths perpetuate oppressive systems.

This is why it is so important to study the way crime and punishment are represented visually. Photography's iconicity and discourse must be addressed simultaneously, and these characteristics further operate within a larger ideological context. Simply stated: photographs are artifacts made by human beings for various purposes, and those artifacts are recontextualized in both material and discursive ways, yet always within a larger social realm. This does not negate the evidentiary potential of the photographic image—it just forces us to consider all the circumstances of its creation, narrativization, and assorted recontextualizations. Documentary producer and critic Errol Morris summed up the duality in an editorial for the *New York Times*:

> Even if photography doesn't give us truth on a silver platter, it can make it harder for us to deny reality. It puts a leash on fantasy, confabulation and self-deception. It provides constraints, borders. It circumscribes our ability to lie—to ourselves and others. Pictures provide a point around which other pieces of evidence collect.[108]

The "point" around which those pieces of evidence collect begins when an image is made, but this moment is finite and fleeting. The first step of constructing image meaning does indeed reflect the framing of what's tangible, but the second step, recontextualization, is largely a matter of discursive framing.[109]

Digitization and Counternarratives

New media pose a challenge to the existing ideological apparatus for the way they've democratized message production and distribution. Any of the five billion people with a smart phone can, to use Hall's term, encode a media message.[110] They are, to use Toffler's[111] term, "prosumers," able to both produce and consume online media. Citizen counternarratives are among the more celebrated consequences of the democratized visual public sphere. Twitter was credited with energizing the green movement in Iran in 2009, as was Facebook in Egypt's 2011 protests.[112] Early research about the internet's impact on democracy tended to be somewhat optimistic.[113] Activists, citizen journalists, and other media amateurs seized upon opportunities to access an audience and call attention to issues or perspectives neglected by the so-called mainstream media.[114] Traditional journalism, already struggling to survive devastating reductions in advertising revenue in the new digital economy, was forced to defend its claims of legitimacy against the newcomers.[115] *Visual* citizen journalism has evolved and distinguished itself as an activity distinct from freelancing, as individuals pursue previously marginalized topics.[116] Key to the credibility of citizen video and photojournalism is the authoritative role of witnessing.[117] To bear witness is historically a form of sacred testimony, which fortifies counternarratives from citizen photo- and video journalists.[118]

In this way, new media are able to extend our civic "voice," or what Nick Couldry described as "our capacity to make, and be recognized as making, narratives about our lives and the world within which we act."[119] For voice to "count" in a democracy, Couldry argued that, in addition to having a process dimension (its social, reflexive, and material activity), voice needs to be seen as having *value*. It's not enough to simply express ourselves—we need to be recognized and respected. Social activists have always known the importance of visibility, which works in concert with embodied protest; to "peaceably assemble" is as much about being seen as it is about being heard.[120] This is why, in today's visual economy, I suggest that voice is as visual as it is linguistic. Democratic participation is enhanced by one's ability to be literally seen, and to display accounts of one's life. Blending Couldry's ideas about civic voice with the proposal that photography invited liberal citizenship (what Azoulay calls a "civil contract") extends the importance of visual media for democratic goals.[121]

Of course, the mobile web has granted voice to people and ideas that are entirely undemocratic. Far from a utopian public sphere, the web has come to reflect the full spectrum of human qualities, including the very worst, with trolling, doxing, and intentionally misleading accounts posing as "news" purveyors and creating very real harm.[122] While YouTube provides access to citizen journalists and activists with sincere motives, it has become a go-to site for conspiracy theories, hoaxes, and terrorist recruitment efforts.[123] Lured by ostensibly "free" content, social media users have opened up their most personal data to corporate operatives who might as well be complete strangers.[124] Authoritarian regimes and police agencies use social media to spy on activists, and individuals are losing control over their own genetic information.[125] There are good reasons to be pessimistic about the potential for contemporary media to advance democracy.[126]

Tempting as it might be to simply live off the grid, a more promising response to the dystopian elements of today's digital public sphere would be to democratize it even further by working on ways to protect individual users from harm, enhance civic engagement, and foster ethical practice for all participants. To that end, I finally propose that one more key theoretical strand be woven in with Couldry and Azoulay, namely the capabilities approach to human rights articulated by Amartya Sen and extended by Martha Nussbaum.[127] The capabilities approach is not a media theory; Sen's work emerged from the fields of economics and philosophy, yet his ideas about human development as something more than a matter of national financial models offer a useful way for thinking about democratic voice and visibility in the digital age. Nussbaum extended Sen's theory with a focus on women's rights by specifying key "capabilities" that allow individuals to live well, including the ability to control one's health and body, to exercise one's imagination and thought (namely, to pursue education), and to have control over one's material and political environment.[128]

Multimedia access and literacy constitute a twenty-first-century capability for extending civic voice. Democratic participation today requires people to be able to access the digital sphere, critically interpret its messages, and participate in civic conversation. Creating and using images to account for our lives is part of that participation. More than bridging the so-called digital divide for technological access, having a voice today requires multimedia literacy, as defined by media literacy researcher Renée Hobbs: "a process that involves accessing, analyzing, creating, reflecting and *taking action*."[129] I italicized "taking action" because, in order to fully participate in today's digital public sphere, individuals must have capabilities beyond *interpreting* messages: they need to be able to create and disseminate their own messages using the most popular and powerful forms available, which requires both verbal and visual literacy. Contemporary accounts and tellings are often produced with a camera, as individuals attempt to literally show their concerns—particularly about criminality, police accountability, and social justice—to the rest of the world.

Because we are surrounded by images, discounting their power becomes easy. Additionally, a philosophic preference for language over corporeality that goes back to ancient Greece has normalized this neglect. Plato elevated the soul over the body—thought over experience—which has translated to centuries of favoring word over image. Thinking of the visual in terms of this binary is unfortunate. The written word has to be seen, after all; ask any typesetter about the importance of design to readability. Journalism has long neglected the importance of images and their makers, treating image as supportive documents at best, as last-minute eye candy at worst. The result is a media environment in which the powerful carefully craft visual messages while news organizations record and distribute those images without adequate appreciation for their significance.

Images capture light, and light is energy; each photograph records something that was once there, written with photon power. The man who made what is considered the world's first photograph, Joseph Niépce, called his work "heliography," or sun writing. One of the earliest critics of this new craft, Lady Elizabeth Eastlake, described it as "a power, availing itself of the eye of the sun." Like fire, the power of photography might be minute or ferocious, helpful or harmful, even in the same instance.[130] The meaning of any particular image varies across contexts, as this book describes, but we discount an image's force at our peril. When we make, alter, use, distribute, and discuss images carelessly, we are essentially playing with fire.

In sum, studying the process by which images are created and then used in discourse allows for a clearer understanding of their influence in the digital public sphere, which offers unprecedented ways for individuals to account for their lives while accentuating the need for ethical conversations about visual communication. Photographic images are rendered meaningful phenomenologically and discursively. They are created in a system that engages the body, then used mimetically in discourse. Social actors struggle over ideological representations through the encoding and decoding of messages in grounded and discursive ways. Digitization has vastly expanded the encoding capabilities of everyday citizens, allowing them to add visibility to their expression of democratic voice, yet the ethical rules for visual expression remain inchoate. Many more social actors are struggling to control visual narratives about criminality, morality, and justice, but this is a machine without brakes, and naïve notions of images as "real" impede normative conversations. For the capability of visual communication to serve democratic voice, such normative conversations are imperative.

How This Book Was Researched

This book blends more than a decade of research on images in criminal justice coverage. I draw from ethnographic observation and interviews with journalists, citizen-journalists, public relations representatives, people who've been photographed in the news, and others. I watched photographers in action inside courtrooms, outside justice centers, and on the sidewalks where they set up live shots. I went along on police accountability patrols. I struck up conversations and requested interviews and relied on the generosity of countless professionals who talked to me over the phone. Some interviews were conducted face to face and many more by phone. All were recorded and transcribed, and key elements for each case study are provided where appropriate. The book also draws from case studies involving specific images and visual moments in the news, such as the Brock Turner mug shot trend on Twitter and the Laquan McDonald shooting tape from Chicago. The images and texts chosen for analysis in these cases are detailed in their relevant chapters.

My research was conducted within the ethical guidelines of the institutional review boards at the University of Pennsylvania and the University of Texas at Austin. Ethnographic material was analyzed using the open coding system of grounded theory as prescribed by Glaser and Strauss.[131] Some interview subjects wished to be on the record, and in those cases, their names are used. Other subjects have been given pseudonyms. These distinctions are identified throughout.

In addition to the ethnographic material, this book relies on both content analysis and critical discourse analysis of visual materials, such as video trial evidence, broadcast news stories, and YouTube postings. Content analysis is primarily a quantitative method that identifies traits or categories and keeps count in order to answer questions about a text.[132] Critical discourse analysis (CDA) is a research method that examines the way power is manifest in language.[133] It "aims to investigate critically social inequality as it is expressed, signaled, constituted, legitimized and so on by language use (or in discourse)."[134] The parenthetical in Wodak and Meyer's definition is important, as it allows for CDA to be applied to multimodal discourse, that is, those texts that combine words, images, video, sound, and so on—the language, really, of the digital age. CDA can help identify the way language is used to hide harsh realities through jargon or euphemisms, establish the "position" of a speaker or reader, and, significantly for studies of news, establish assumptions about common sense.

This book uses the lenses of embodied gatekeeping, discursive recontextualization, and the visual's contribution to voice based on a series of illustrative case studies. The next four chapters focus on the criminal justice system and the way news media and state actors construct coverage in complex, embodied, and discursive practices. Chapter 2 presents the last adjudicated hanging in the United States to illustrate its discussion of the way Americans have viewed executions in the past, and the significance of what is not seen today. Chapter 3 studies the way American journalists cover perp walks for visual media and how these cultural rituals serve the interests of the criminal justice system. Chapter 4 extends the examination of the way state actors work with journalism to shape visual coverage of the judiciary with a detailed study of three major trials.

The project then shifts to examine digitization's disruption of the conventional recontextualization model and the democratization of image framing. Chapter 5 uses recent mug shot controversies to illustrate this shift in the power over framing. Chapter 6 theorizes the unique affordance of video to narrative in the public sphere now available to billions of smart-phone users worldwide. Chapter 7 focuses on the way activists use video to hold police accountable, and the unique dimensions of organized cop watching as it compares with spontaneous filming. Chapter 8 studies the way law enforcement organizations have responded to the new media environment to reframe their image, with mixed results. In Chapter 9, I study what might now best be called "Karen" videos: those clips of everyday rudeness that offer new narratives about social inequality while raising concerns about image ethics.

Finally, in Chapter 10, I summarize the ethical concerns raised throughout the book and their implications for journalists, members of the criminal justice system, and everyone else: we are all the media now, whether we like it or not. Everyone in the digital public sphere must take images more seriously if we are to find our way through the internet fog.

Here and in subsequent chapters, I acknowledge my subjective biases: as a former journalist, I am sympathetic to the everyday challenges of reporting on crime. I am also sensitive to the inequalities in the American criminal justice system based on race, class, and gender, while acknowledging that as a middle-class white woman with a PhD there are limits to my understanding. I've started many chapters with memories from my work as a TV journalist, some of which make me uneasy today. My current position allows me a longer view, one that takes larger democratic concerns into account instead of the day-to-day demands of deadline news-work. The critiques lodged in this book are offered with sincere appreciation for what life is like for journalists and the people who interact with them. I really, truly have been there. I have made my share of mistakes and I will make more in the future.

Many of the phenomena described in this book represent relatively small human actions that might not seem significant in isolation: decisions about who gets a press credential, where a courtroom camera may be placed, how to hold a smart phone while taping an arrest. None of these small actions on their own account for injustice in the criminal justice system. It is their aggregation that matters, and the overall media discourse that results from the way stakeholders operate in their own habitus. The mass media are highly dependent on the image factory in order to attract viewers, and the decisions the media make on the ground every day render a discourse that teaches us about the criminal justice system—identifying the "bad guys," honoring the good, and reproducing faith in the system. Examining these everyday small decisions and the way they contribute to a larger ideological system represents a constructivist approach, which rejects the idea that news reflects reality and assumes that media create social reality.

As with any human construction, media discourse about criminal justice is an imperfect rendering. Because power remains unequally distributed, it is easy for those involved in the construction process to claim they are representing reality fairly. For those on the margins, however, such representations are not necessarily fair or real. This is why focusing on the minutia of image production offers a dual advantage. First, this constructivist approach enables critique by revealing the ways that journalists operate in coordination with the state to cultivate faith in the criminal justice system. Constructivism can show just how technological affordances enable counternarratives. More importantly, deconstructing the process reveals *alternative* constructions. Once we know how the system works, we can imagine it working differently. Focusing on the construction of news images opens our eyes to their limitations—to the images not made, shown, or seen. Studying practice makes possible conversations about alternatives for more ethical, democratic practice.

To summarize, photographic images are rendered meaningful phenomenologically and discursively. They are created in a system that engages the body, then used mimetically in discourse. Social actors struggle over ideological representations through the encoding and decoding of messages in grounded and discursive ways. The encoding capabilities of everyday citizens are burgeoning, as digitization offers opportunities to add *visibility* to their expressions of democratic voice. At the same time, the ethical rules for visual expression are precariously inchoate. Many more social actors are struggling to control visual narratives about criminality, morality, and justice, but this is a machine without brakes, and naïve notions of images as "real" impede normative conversations. For the capability of visual communication to serve democratic voice, such normative conversations are imperative.

2

Images of Discipline

Scene one: An estimated twenty thousand people gather in Owensboro, Kentucky, to watch the hanging of a Black man—what would turn out to be the last public hanging in the United States. A local shopkeeper decides to attend, expecting to see a large, hulking criminal, but instead notes that Rainey Bethea looks like a "kid." The shopkeeper left.

Scene two: A man is strapped to a table in the middle of a room, surrounded by onlookers. Needles carrying saline, soon to deliver a lethal injection, are already inserted into his outstretched arms. From above, the man's position would suggest a crucifixion. That view is purely imaginary, as there is no view for anyone except the hand-picked witnesses allowed inside the execution chamber because all cameras and recorders are banned.

Public punishment has been part of the human story for far longer than its largely hidden form in the United States today. Colonial Americans put each other in stocks in the public square to publicly shame them for smaller infractions, and held public hangings, drowning, or burnings for the crimes of murder or witchcraft. To watch the killing of another human being may not have been a pleasant form of entertainment for everyone (though picnic baskets were often involved), but the realities of death were directly witnessed and very public.

Today, the average American is far more likely to see a suspected criminal appear to be killed in a movie or television show, in a sanitized representation that glorifies the violence while softening the fear, pain, and stench of death. Executions in the United States are essentially invisible, sanitized killings. Most members of the public will not see one and must rely on the written observations of the few journalists allowed to witness the events. Imprisonment itself is similarly invisible while the United States has the highest incarceration rate in the world. Thousands of people, a majority of them Black and Brown, are convicted, sent to remote institutions, and hidden from the public. Not surprisingly, visual representations of executions and

Seeing Justice. Mary Angela Bock, Oxford University Press. © Oxford University Press 2021.
DOI: 10.1093/oso/9780190926977.003.0002

prison life reflect long-standing patterns of economic, racial, and—less acknowledged but appreciable—gendered inequality.

This chapter examines the ways that the penal system has been represented
in the media and the controls that authorities exert to shape visual coverage,
largely through embodied gatekeeping. I draw from the 1936 coverage of the
hanging of Rainey Bethea, the last public hanging in the United States, and
archival newspaper clippings of legal hangings from the nineteenth century
(including any and all that included photos from the Harry Ransom Center,
the University of Oklahoma Libraries, the Library of Congress, the National
Archives, and others). Interviews with observers, journalists, and gatekeepers
involved with the US prison system complete the material gathered for
this analysis. This chapter does not address, with any adequate depth,
representations of extrajudicial executions—lynching incidents—because
this project contends with the judiciary's role in managing optics. Exceptional
studies of these other American horrors already exist.[1] Moreover, it's hardly
necessary to contend with illegal executions in order to find injustice in the
current, completely legal, and properly adjudicated system.

The combined corpus of historical archive and contemporary interviews
suggests that coverage of executions focuses largely on their legitimacy and
propriety, while the penal system itself receives scant attention from the day-
to-day news. In fact, outside of long-form investigations, prisons rarely receive mainstream coverage unless information regulations are breached, as
when someone leaks information or an internal surveillance tape reveals
malfeasance within an institution. Execution reportage shifts from the facts
of the case that send a person to death row onto the procedure and its successful consummation, while the ideology of authority is nourished by an absence of stories about day-to-day life in prison. Indeed, the shift from public
to hidden punishment only enhances the criminal justice system's implied
message that it alone can be trusted to punish properly.

Lethal Inequality

It would be inappropriate to discuss the way executions are covered in the
news without first addressing the massive inequities in the way the death
penalty is practiced in the United States. According to the American Civil
Liberties Union, 43 percent of the people who've been executed since 1976
were Black, a disproportionate share since Blacks constitute only about
13 percent of the US population.[2] Research suggests that Black defendants

are more likely to receive the death penalty for murder if the victim is white[3] and that the death penalty is imposed on Hispanic people at disproportionate rates.[4] The federal government, the US military, and thirty states have capital punishment provisions, though some states have not executed anyone in so long that they might well be considered to have effectively eliminated it.[5] Perhaps most importantly, scholars have repeatedly established that the death penalty has no deterrent effect.[6] Its imposition, therefore, is symbolic, not practical.

Thurgood Marshall's words from his concurrence in *Furman v. Georgia* (the 1972 case that temporarily halted executions in the United States) still ring true: "Assuming knowledge of all the facts presently available regarding capital punishment, the average citizen would, in my opinion, find it shocking to his conscience and sense of justice."[7] Of course, few citizens engage with these particular facts, and the visual information about defendants is scant.

Photographing Death

Most Americans alive today have never seen a legal execution. They're likely to have witnessed countless murders in entertainment media, perhaps with some fictional representations of legal executions thrown in. Some internet users may have seen the beheadings or other horrifying images of executions by terrorists, posted, for instance, by the Islamic State as part of a global propaganda campaign.[8] Lynchings in the United States, which occurred long into the twentieth century, often attracted hundreds of onlookers, some of whom photographed these scenes of domestic terror and collected those images like trading cards.[9] Legally adjudicated executions in the United States, however, are no longer put to the public's view.

This is not to say Americans have not seen death in the media—only that they rarely, if ever see the state *lawfully* kill anyone who's been convicted. Fishman's exhaustive content analysis of material spanning thirty years found media organizations to be surprisingly hesitant to display death, at least of American citizens.[10] As other researchers have found historically, Fishman identified a pattern of a "tribal" partitioning of images, with American deaths not shown but bodies of non-white, non-American victims far more likely to be seen in the news.[11] Taylor found a similar pattern in British journalism in 1998.[12] Fishman did not find tabloid practices in visual choices, but instead found nationalism and a strong resistance to showing bodies; the editors she interviewed talked about monitoring "tone," with the aim of keeping that tone down.

Images of death were historically more prevalent, particularly when those images served the purposes of the powerful. The crucifixion of Jesus is not normally thought of as an "execution image," but it is one of the most recognizable ones in history. Early depictions were often especially grotesque displays of his torture and suffering, a trope repeated in paintings of the sufferings of various saints. Artworks such as these enforced God's law and served as a warning to sinners. Once photography was invented, it too was put to work on behalf of authority by depicting the deaths of wrongdoers. After a failed rebellion in 1871 by the Communards in Paris, the French government displayed photos of their corpses to dissuade future dissent.[13]

Another way media represent death is through visual implication, or *imminent* death. Barbie Zelizer identified the "About to Die" image as a familiar trope, one that she labeled as using a photographic version of the subjunctive voice.[14] If a dead body shows what was, the "about to die" image shows what might have been, requiring the audience to fill in what is not seen. In this way, Zelizer pointed out that "about to die" images are not the only ambiguous and hypothetical texts in media, and the unsettled nature of images may craft "a counterenvironment to the landscape of cool appraisals by which the information environment is *presumed* to work and understanding thought to be achieved, a parallel world of news work thus may be thriving at the same time, one that makes engagement and the crafting of multiple meanings as primary as information relay and definitive understanding."[15] In Zelizer's conception, images of things that *might be* are compelling and emotionally riveting in ways that definitive images are not.

Images of definitive death in American journalism are usually presented with an extra layer of context justifying their publication. During World War II, for instance, when American media first published images of dead US soldiers, the editors of *LIFE* magazine defended the decision in part by having permission from the president and the War Department, but also because, in their words, "This is the reality that lies behind the names that come to rest at last on monuments in the leafy squares of busy American towns."[16] The faces of those soldiers could not be seen, incidentally, showing a sort of consideration not granted to Japanese soldiers during the same era.[17] The publication of Emmett Till's mutilated face in *Jet* magazine and the *Chicago Defender* came at his mother's urging, to show the world how her son had died: at the hands of two men for allegedly disrespecting a white woman in

Mississippi.[18] The two men were acquitted of Till's murder, but images of his disfigured face were, and in many ways still are, a call to conscience for white Americans.

More than fifty years later, the death of another Black teenager would make national news, but this time images of his dead body were not widely circulated. Trayvon Martin was seventeen years old when neighborhood watch volunteer George Zimmerman shot him to death in a Florida subdivision.[19] Two photos of Martin were widely circulated in the news, a portrait of him wearing a Hollister T-shirt and smiling, and another, in which he is not smiling and wears a hoodie. Similarly, two images of Zimmerman, who was later acquitted, were widely circulated: a mug shot and a portrait of him wearing a plaid shirt.[20] While they were eventually released during the trial, images of Martin's body at the crime scene were not published nearly as often. Lying on the ground, his eyes still open, legs and arms splayed on the grass, his lanky youth is apparent. These compelling crime scene photos were released during the trial itself—long after many members of the public formed opinions about both victim and perpetrator.

Early Execution Imagery

The opening passage to Foucault's *Discipline and Punish* is difficult not because the French philosopher-historian had an abstruse style (well, at least not in this instance) but because he painstakingly describes in vivid detail the way an eighteenth-century prisoner was tortured to death.[21] This opening passage serves to illustrate one of Foucault's primary arguments in that book: that over time society has shifted from physical discipline to discursive forms of social control. The very public mutilation of a prisoner is horrifying and, indeed, the sort of punishment targeted by the writers of the US Constitution. The Constitution's Eighth Amendment in the Bill of Rights forbids "cruel and unusual punishment," and in a sense codified the shift Foucault describes for white Americans.[22] Foucault's account of the shift in civic punishment offered an alternative to the "humanitarian" thesis and has inspired many scholars to examine more critically the role of discourse, culture, and social control.[23] Halttunen studied Victorian etchings of punishment from this era and found that the representations of floggings, for example, were presented as "obscene," almost pornographic, thus complicating their humanitarian function.[24] Significantly, while the role of the public witness is a common thread in this scholarship, the visual record of executions, and the role of those who create that record, is largely assumed, to the detriment of our knowledge of the way executions are understood today.

Adjudicated public hangings were not considered cruel or unusual in early America; indeed, they were accepted as the norm. Photographic documentation of hangings appeared early—during the Civil War and the westward expansion—and images during this era generally fall into one of three categories: preparation of the gallows, the roping of the prisoner, and death itself.[25] Other images do show hooded figures swaying by a rope. They are only palatable to a twenty-first-century audience for the way such historic images are removed in terms of space and time and their quality: colorless, distant, and not always crisply focused.

Photographs from the 1865 hangings of the four coconspirators in the Lincoln assassination exemplify the full triptych. Alexander Gardner and his team captured the preparations of the gallows, the condemned prior to death, and their bodies after the supports were removed, as seen in Figure 2.1.[26] One of the condemned was a woman, Mary Surratt, who had to be supported by two soldiers for fear she'd collapse before the traps were opened.[27] About three thousand people, mostly soldiers, attended the event on a day when temperatures reached into the nineties. The Gardner series also includes an image of the graves prepared for the four condemned alongside the gallows; each of them was buried only feet away from where they were executed. *Harper's Illustrated Magazine* published a set of illustrations based on the photographs, which was typical during this era prior to the invention of halftone printing.[28]

Generally, though, while public executions were exhaustively covered by newspapers in the late nineteenth and early twentieth centuries, the stories rarely included photographs. This was partly a technical matter: even after the halftone process made photographic reproduction possible, it was not routine until the 1920s, popularized by *New York's Illustrated Daily News*. That newspaper, known today as the *New York Daily News*, published one of the most famous execution photos of all time in 1928, a surreptitious image of the electrocution of Ruth Snyder.[29] Also in 1928, the *Pensacola News Journal* published photos from a firing-squad execution in Mexico, described in the accompanying story as "the stark drama of life and death played out complete before the camera's undying lens, from the man's first step toward doom, to his shudder as the bullets struck home."[30] In these exceptional instances, the images themselves were news beyond the events.

Figure 2.1 Hanging of the Lincoln Coconspirators
This photograph is part of a series by Alexander Gardner and his colleagues.
Titled "The Drop," it is possible to see the blur from the bodies swaying (1865,
Library of Congress).
Credit: Alexander Gardner
Permission: no permission necessary (Library of Congress)

Newspapers also illustrated executions indirectly, with photographs of
trees where hangings had taken place, or with images of the objects of death.
In 1888, for instance, the *San Francisco Daily Examiner* published a lengthy
story with line drawings of a syringe for lethal injection and demonstrations
of a new execution technology, electrocution.[31] For high-profile executions,
coverage often included details about the gallows and the executioner. When
John Garfield's assassin was executed, for instance, the *Bloomington Daily
Pantagraph* described the prehanging ritual: "At 9 o'clock the jail officers

had a rehearsal of the part they are to play in the execution, for the purpose chiefly of testing the appliances of the gallows. . . . The rope on the scaffold stood the test well."[32]

Mistakes: Botched Executions

Rational faith in the court system's validity rests on a swift and competent execution. The state is expected to kill someone properly—or more specifically, humanely enough to not violate the Eighth Amendment's prohibition against cruel and unusual punishment. The pattern revealed in the material collected for this study shows a concern for properly orchestrated executions and fascination with those that go wrong. The modern expectation is that the condemned person dies without extended suffering, so naturally, botched executions attract more attention in the news.[33] Sarat studied 276 such cases from 1890 to 2010 and found that botched executions disrupt the state's intent to display a form of lethality that contrasts with the crimes of the condemned. Executions are expected to be "civilized" rituals that reinforce the state's legitimacy, as opposed to the savagery of a convicted criminal. Sarat further found that botched executions have been rehabilitated by way of technological policy but have *not* historically inspired as much debate about the merits of capital punishment as one might expect.[34]

Understandably, the visual record for botched executions is thin, as they are a minority of all executions. While the archives contain occasional images of gallows preparations and hanged prisoners, documentation of executions gone awry is largely word-based. No clippings exist in a modern archive about the 1861 hanging of Paula Angel in New Mexico, but an Associated Press feature about the case nearly a hundred years later described it as botched.[35] She was actually hanged twice because she was reportedly able to put her hands around the noose in the first attempt.

The execution of Silan Lewis in 1894 is a notable exception in the visual record. Lewis was a member of the Choctaw Nation, and the last member of the tribe to be legally executed under tribal law before Oklahoma statehood.[36] The sheriff attempted to shoot Lewis in the heart, missed, and a deputy reportedly smothered Lewis to death instead. A photo of the event, Figure 2.2, ran in the Oklahoma paper years later, in 1919, as part of a romanticized account of Native American justice and bravery.[37]

Figure 2.2 The botched execution of Silan Lewis, who was shot on the wrong side of his chest and was eventually smothered to death
Credit: Library of Congress
Permission: no permission necessary (Library of Congress)

More than a century later, a concerned judge presented to the public a far more realistic vision of a botched execution, making use of an emerging technology, the internet of 1999, to call attention to the case. This was the third of a series of flawed executions that eventually led to Florida adopting lethal injection as the official way to kill inmates, but only after State Supreme Court Justice Leander Shaw posted visual evidence to the web as part of his dissent.[38] The first electrocution mishap occurred in 1990, when convicted murderer Jesse Tafero's mask caught fire from the current.[39] The same thing happened a second time in 1997, when flames shot out of the mask of Pedro Medina, who was also convicted of murder but never gave up declaring his innocence.[40] The third instance involved not flames but blood, in the case of Allen Lee Davis, who bled from the nose during his electrocution and was burned during the process.[41] When another inmate sued on Eighth Amendment grounds, the Florida Supreme Court stood by electrocution as a legitimate form of execution, but Shaw dissented and published the gruesome photos online.[42]

Shaw, who was Florida's first African American state Supreme Court justice, wrote, "Execution by electrocution, with its attendant smoke and
flames and blood and screams, is a spectacle whose time has passed."[43]
Subsequently, Florida's legislature gave inmates the option of electrocution or lethal injection.[44]

Mobs: Horror and Sympathy

Scholars point to concerns about mob violence, or rather, mob behavior
more generally, as another variable in the shift to private executions. Large
gatherings who watched executions were thought to be unruly and unpre-
dictable; the possibility that women might be in such a crowd was considered
problematic.[45] Mob violence was a very real possibility in the late 1800s and
early Progressive era in the United States, when lynchings were at their peak.
Garland pointed out that state-run executions, private and purportedly painless, constitute a cultural obverse to the very public and torturous horror-
carnivals of the Jim Crow era.[46]

In Garland's words,

> If lynching is "the very essence" of open, full-throated, retributive violence,
> as George Herbert Mead (1918, p. 584) once remarked, we might with some
> truth suggest that the modern American death penalty is its essential oppo-
> site: a lawful punishment overlaid with ambivalence, anxiety, and embar-
> rassment, a deadly punishment that strives to represent itself as "civilized,"
> nonviolent, and necessary.[47]

Garland further noted that extra-judicial executions by unruly mobs
represented a rejection of the law, a slap in the face of government, particularly the federal government, by citizens of the southern states after the
Civil War. Yet during this era, lawful hangings and lynchings were both
photographed and as noted above, lynching photos were often turned into
postcards, a grotesque form of memorabilia. In keeping with this thesis,
therefore, the state had no choice but to also ban cameras from executions.
If today's staid, medical executions, witnessed by a small, mostly white and
male group, are to be the obverse of an illegal, bloodthirsty lynch mob, photography had to be banned.

The Feminine as Oddity I

Only woodcuts commemorate the Salem Witch trials, some of the earliest instances of white women being legally executed in the colonies, and while they are the minority, women have been condemned to death in the United States ever since. In the photographic age, images of hanged women are few. The Andrew Gardner photo of the Lincoln conspirators that includes Mary Surratt is exceptional. A woodcut commemorates the botched Texas hanging in 1863 of Chipita Rodriguez, who supposedly haunts the Nueces River near San Patricio, and her femininity no doubt fueled the mystique.[48] The criminal justice system is patriarchal territory, and women's presence within it is usually presented with tabloid-style curiosity, shock, or prurience. The surreptitious image of Ruth Snyder's 1928 execution journalist was the culmination of months of illustrated tabloid coverage.[49]

As for the living, while racial disparities in the American penal system are well established, gender disparities have only recently entered public debate. Advocates have called for prisons to provide menstrual products for women, for example, and to end the practice of shackling women who give birth. Public sympathy for women in prison may well have been inspired, at least in part, by the popularity of *Orange Is the New Black* (*OITNB*), a series produced and distributed by Netflix that depicts life in a women's prison. *OITNB*'s fictional portrayal of everyday life for incarcerated women stands in stark contrast to the usual tabloidesque media treatment of female convicts.[50] The series has attracted considerable scholarly attention for its portrayals of race and sexuality and the way it has provided visibility for female prisoners.[51] Critical scholars have noticed, however, that this increased visibility often maintained stereotypes and white supremacy.[52] McHugh studied the use of face close-ups in the series' opening credits, and Schwan examined the series' filmic techniques, but for the most part the scholarship regarding *OITNB* takes for granted the show's normalizing of prison life through visuality.[53] Pop culture representations of prison life have usually focused on the male experience, with drama and violence. *OITNB* features scenes of women brushing their teeth, hiding snack food, and doing laundry, using the banal to render its characters as fully human. Even though it is fiction, it remains one of the few representations of any kind into the lives of female inmates.

The Last US Hanging

Imagine what life was like in Owensboro, the seat of Daviess County, Kentucky, in 1936. This was the depth of the Great Depression. There was no TV, only cinema for moving pictures, and that required a ticket. News came by radio and newspapers. Owensboro sits just south of the Ohio River, Kentucky's border with Indiana, less than forty miles from Evansville, Indiana. That river, however, was once the Mason-Dixon line, and Owensboro is culturally southern. Even today its residents' speech has a soft southern sound.

The Feminine as Oddity II

Strange to imagine also that in 1936 Daviess County had a female sheriff. Florence Thompson "inherited" the position from her late husband, taking charge at the request of the local judge.[54] She was in charge when Rainey Bethea, a twenty-two-year-old Black man, was convicted of raping and killing a local woman for her jewelry. After a single-day trial that included testimony of his confession, Bethea was sentenced to die by hanging for the rape.[55] (Had he been convicted of murder, Bethea would have faced death by electrocution out of sight within prison walls.) When his execution was scheduled later that summer, it set off a perfect media storm: a heinous crime, a lady sheriff, and a public hanging. No one knew at the time this would be the country's last public execution; the case caught national attention because a woman was expected to legally kill a man.

While the Depression was the primary concern of most Americans in 1936, issues of racial equality and justice were part of public discourse. Lynchings occurred throughout the 1930s and inspired a major motion picture released only months before Bethea's execution. Fritz Lang, who directed *Fury*, escaped fascism in Germany only to find new forms of injustice in the United States.[56] Spencer Tracy starred in Lang's movie about lynch mobs, as Lang tangled with MGM to feature Black actors in roles other than train porters or shoeshiners. Lang still managed to include a few scenes depicting Black life in the thirties, and even foretold the era of cop-watching for a dramatic reveal of the lynching suspects with a newsreel played in court. A monologue by Tracy's character when he dramatically ends the trial of his tormentors eerily echoes today's concerns and is worth quoting here:

I don't care anything about saving them. They're murderers. I know the law says they're not because I'm still alive. But that's not their fault. And the law doesn't know that a lot of things that were very important to me . . . silly things, maybe, like a belief in justice . . . and an idea that men were civilized . . . and a feeling of pride that this country of mine was different from all others.[57]

The *New York Times* praised *Fury* for its "mature, sober and penetrating investigation of a national blight," and quite possibly may have been in the minds of those who attended Bethea's execution, as the film had been released two months earlier.[58]

The Last Execution Photos

Little of the coverage leading up to Bethea's execution could be described as "mature" or "sober." While the first *New York Daily News* article on the case was short and straightforward, the role of Florence Thompson was headlined as "Woman Sheriff to Hang Youth Aug. 14."[59] She, apparently, was the reason this rural crime became national news, and the *Daily News* used images of her several times in advance of the execution. The portraits were head-and-shoulder shots of a matron with a pleasant expression, as if to emphasize the juxtaposition of her femininity with a man's job. On the Friday before the execution, the *New York Daily News* published a photo of Thompson (wearing a short, patterned sleeves with her hair crimped and either bobbed or pulled up) and a man identified as G. Phil Hanna, a noose expert. A grotesque pun headline, "Noose Conference," preceded the caption:

> With the zero hour for execution of Rainey Bethea, Wirefoto pictures Mrs. Florence Thompson, woman sheriff of Owensboro Ky, in conference with G. Phil Hanna, noose expert yesterday. They went over the details of the hanging which is scheduled for sunrise this morning. Hanna is to tie the knot when Bethea ascends of the gallows. Ministers last night helped Mrs. Thompson steel self to spring trap.[60]

Understandably, local coverage started with its focus on Bethea's case and trial security. Extra officers were called in for a crowded, one-day session. The *Owensboro Messenger-Inquirer* published a photo of the defendant with a cigarette in his mouth on page one the morning after he was found guilty and condemned to death. Inside, two more photos, including an overhead shot, depicted the crowd gathered for the trial.[61] The paper reported that Bethea looked frightened only once, when the crowd advanced upon officers who were helping him into a squad car for transport to the jail.[62] As with the *New York Daily News*, however, local coverage quickly shifted to the novelty of a female executioner. About a week after the trial, the *Messenger-Inquirer* ran a two-column-wide photo, seen in Figure 2.3 of Thompson above the fold, with the headline, "10,000 May See Woman Sheriff Spring Trap at Bethea Hanging."[63] While her hair is not crimped in in this photo, she again is portrayed as a dignified matron, an odd fit for a story that previewed the location of spectator space for the imminent execution.

Eventually more than twice the number of spectators descended upon Owensboro for the hanging, with a crowd estimated at twenty thousand. Entrepreneurs sold hot dogs and refreshments, and with all hotel rooms in the area booked, some travelers simply camped out.[64] The *Chicago Tribune* sent a truck with a darkroom, the *New York Daily News* flew its journalists to

Figure 2.3 Florence Thompson, Sheriff of Daviess County, Kentucky, in 1936
Credit: From the Collections of the Owensboro Museum of Science and History
Permission granted by the Owensboro Museum of Science and History

town, and the Associated Press made arrangements to airlift photos for swift publication.[65] Keith Lawrence, a reporter with the *Owensboro Messenger-Inquirer*, wrote an anniversary story about the case in 1986. He remains with the paper and recalled some of the details:

> People rode trains. They put on, the railroad put on extra cars, and stuff. Flatcars and stuff, people sat en masse on, ride up here from surrounding counties. It was a big day for the people who got to see stuff like that.[66]

Prior to the hanging, the captain of the state police threatened to smash any cameras brought to the execution, but the press corps appealed to then-governor Chandler, who overruled the order even though he later was quoted as saying, "I didn't care for 'em takin' pictures of it."[67]

Florence Thompson did not pull the trap to kill Rainey Bethea; instead she enlisted the help of an experienced hangman and a former police officer, Arthur Hash. Hash, though, was reportedly too drunk to pull the lever at the hangman's signal, and another deputy leaned into the mechanism to complete the execution.[68] For the anniversary story, Lawrence interviewed an elderly woman who in 1936 was a little girl living near the gallows:

> She and her sister snuck out of the house and didn't tell their parents, and went down there and worked their way up to the front of the crowd . . . and pretty traumatic, she said. . . . She never did tell her mother because she knew she'd be in trouble.[69]

In 1946, the day after the hanging, the *New York Daily News* published a double-page spread of the scene, which included photos of Thompson, the immense crowd, and the gallows. One of the central captions reported that the paper flew back the "fotos" by plane.[70] While the *Daily News* reported that the crowd grabbed at Bethea's hood after he was killed, there is no evidence to support it. In fact, more than one photo after the execution portrays Bethea's body hanging undisturbed in the distance, with an enormous crowd in the foreground. Local residents were incensed that their community had been maligned as bloodthirsty hooligans. A subsequent letter to the editor of Louisville's *Courier-Journal* attempted to set the record straight:

> Unfortunately, this event has been made a sensation and the articles which have been written about it throughout this country have been of such a

nature that the city of Owensboro its inhabitants and those living in surrounding counties and states have been condemned by the reading public.
I was within 5 feet of the prisoner during this entire time. There was a hush
over the entire thousands of people who had witnessed this execution
during all this period of time. The newspaper and radio comments to the
effect "Hang the Negro," "Let us have the negro," "Kill the negro," are entirely false and preposterous. I have 15 or 20,000 witnesses who will tell you
the same thing I doubt if in history you can find where so many thousands
of people stood in utter awe as the black Angel of death came forward to
claim its toll.[71]

The letter writer believed that the national press made claims about racism
and mob violence because they were disappointed that Thompson did not
perform the execution. Owensboro tour operator and writer David Wolfe II
explained that it remains a sore point for the community[72]:

The media got mad and so they drummed up a bunch of lies that they—
They came all the way from New York, like you said, some other states,
came down to watch this lady pull the trigger, and she didn't. They made
up a bunch of lies and said that Owensborians rushed the stage and tore the
body limb-to-limb and tore clothing off. That didn't happen. That' a bunch
of rubbish.

The visual record supports Wolfe's argument. None of the photos of the event
depict a crowd rushing the gallows or touching Bethea's body. Not even the
Daily News, which reported Thompson "lost her courage," and that "part of
the throng fought for shreds of the dead man's black hood," provided any
visual evidence of mob violence.[73]

An Era Ends

No one in Owensboro knew that this would be the last public execution in
the United States. But the shift to electrocutions behind prison walls was already underway. Had Bethea been convicted of murder he would not have
been hanged but executed in an electric chair outside of town.[74] For the community of Owensboro, this was the last execution of any kind. Today there
is no marker where the last public hanging in America occurred. The site

is near a Hampton Inn motel. Wolfe told me there is little enthusiasm for a marker.

> That's the thing. I'm glad you asked that. No. In my opinion there should be, but Owensboro city officials look at it as a black mark, a dark mark, on Owensboro, Kentucky. I don't see it. I see it as tourism. I can't tell you how many people go on my ghost tour and that's one of the first questions. "Can we see the site of the last public hanging?" Yes, you can. I take them there and we talk about, obviously, the history, and a couple of the ghost stories around the area.[75]

Lawrence, the local reporter, recalled another elderly witness interviewed for the anniversary story who wanted to let the past be past:

> People who were there, I think a lot of them want to forget it. It was embarrassing, have that kind of attention focused on them. I talked to one man who ran a restaurant just kind of across the street from where the hanging was. He said he walked over there, and he was expecting to see this big, burly guy. He was a little, skinny guy, looked like a kid. He said, "Oh gosh, I just couldn't stay and watch." But he said, "I saw that man in my dreams for weeks, after that." So that was in 1986, so 50 years later, he was still remembering that.[76]

Perhaps out of pity or appreciation for her circumstances, Sheriff Thompson was reelected later that year and served as sheriff until 1938.[77] She was appointed deputy by her replacement and served the department for another nine years. For all the controversy surrounding Bethea's death, his guilt seems unquestioned. He confessed five times, and a ring that belonged to him was found at the crime scene. State and local authorities made the effort to protect him from the crowds during his trial and preceding the execution.

Even after talking to residents who regretted watching the execution, Keith Lawrence, the reporter who wrote the retrospective, believes he would have been among the crowd.

> I don't know if I would have gone or not. Probably would have been working, so I'd have to have been there, but on my own. I think I probably would have, just to see what was going on. . . . I think I would have regretted seeing it. But I think I would have gone.[78]

Critics targeted not the system's legitimacy but instead, the people of Kentucky, who likely had a variety of reasons for wishing to see the execution—no doubt some racist, some prurient, but others may have simply been curious about the angel of death.

Witnessing Death

The shift from hangings to electrocutions—which were thought to be a cleaner, quicker, and therefore more humane way of killing—coincided with the move to executions behind prison walls. Today, the state kills inmates in highly controlled, closed settings with few witnesses, some of whom serve as the public's proxy. These tightly choreographed executions in the United States occur regularly in former slave states such as Texas, Florida, and Georgia, which are among the busiest contemporary death penalty jurisdictions.[79] News photography is prohibited in today's execution chambers, but a few journalists are usually granted access along with family members of the inmate and the victim. Because the process of obtaining a credential and then access to an execution is somewhat elaborate, some reporters become "regulars." Three themes emerged from interviews with execution reporters: their work is tightly regulated, unpleasant, yet democratically essential.

Choreographed Witnessing

Michael Graczyk[80] is one such regular. He has covered more than four hundred executions for Associated Press in Texas. He's accustomed to the maze of rules reporters must follow at the "walls unit" (nicknamed for the twenty-foot walls around the facility) in Huntsville, Texas. It starts with a walk from a waiting area to another building.

> In the past you were searched. The security got very, very intense after a couple of escape attempts. They really tightened down, but it has relaxed somewhat in recent years.
> There are no metal detectors, no body search for people going in, you're reminded that you can't take anything in there except a writing implement

and a pad . . . so pen and paper, essentially . . . no cameras, no recorders, no computers, no laptops, no whatever.

In Texas, Graczyk is able to at least use his own pen and paper. In Florida, the prison provides those materials:

> We'd go through security, I had to empty all our pockets. No tape recorders, no notebooks, nothing. And they would give you a pad of paper, a legal sized pad of paper, yellow, and an envelope with two pencils. ("Greg")[81]

Florida has chairs in the viewing area; Texas does not. Reporters often must crane their necks or hope they don't end up behind a tall colleague. Journalists are not allowed to use laptops or phones during an execution, and they are cut off from their newsrooms while in the prison complex:

> There have been times when I've gone to the prison for executions and stayed there for six hours and then the execution doesn't happen and then you leave. So you're just literally trapped. You cannot talk to anybody. You don't know what's going on. I think that the last one that I did, I think it actually happened at 9:00, so we were in there a good two and a half, three hours. ("Amy")

Because reporter witnesses are so restricted and cannot use phones or laptops in the prison, Greg says he would compose drafts ahead of time, describing the crime, victims, trial, and the inmate's basic biographical information.[82] Unless something unusual happens during the execution, only a few details need to be added once the inmate dies.

> We actually wrote our story before we went into the prison. And then as soon as I witnessed, I'd come back and you'd make any changes. We had a phone line, which the phone company had installed in a pasture across the road from the prison where there was a media area, and areas where protesters gathered. And so we'd come back and I, the first thing I'd do when I got back from being inside the prison was to get on the phone to the bureau in in Miami.

Both Texas and Florida have glass windows between the execution chamber and the viewing area. In Texas, Graczyk explained, witnesses are able to hear what is going on:

> There's a microphone that dangles over the inmate, who's strapped on a gurney. When you enter the room, the inmate already is prepared for execution. The needles are inserted, they're running a saline solution through the IV needles in his arm. You walk in and the inmate can see you and you can see the inmate. At one point the door is shut, a prison official tells the warden that he may proceed, and then the warden moves forward with the process.

Because news cameras are not allowed into the execution chamber, reporters who witness executions act as public representatives, providing the descriptions and putting the inmate's death into context. Visual coverage generally consists of anything that happens outside the facility, such as protests or statements from officials or family members, and file footage from the crime and the court case.

Viewing as Burden

The ritual of the closed execution is designed to add more dignity to the process, but it does not necessarily mask the reality of death. Now retired, Graczyk continues to cover executions as a freelancer. He maintains his journalistic distance while acknowledging the pathos of his specialty:

> I've told other folks this, that it has I guess reinforced for me the belief that life is very, very fragile and it can be taken very, very quickly. Both as a result of the crime that occurred in these cases, and in most cases the death has been very quick. A gunshot to the head generally ends life pretty quickly. Likewise, a lethal injection with a powerful sedative that stops your heart within a matter of seconds, that's also very, very quick.

Because he remains an active journalist, Graczyk will not discuss his personal views about the death penalty:

As far as the impact, staying there and watching, you essentially watch someone go to sleep under the current drug protocol and they just don't wake up and you leave the room. That's the cold reality of it.

Greg, still writing but retired from the news industry, was forthright about the discomfort of viewing sixty-two executions:

Yeah, that's way too many. Q: So why do you say that? So probably the average American has probably seen several hundred people die on fictional TV over time. What's different about what you went through?

Well, it's real. I mean it's not like I have nightmares or anything but it's very, it's as a reporter covering something like that, once a month or twice a month, it gets to be wearing, I guess.

Amy, who has covered fewer executions but also a long list of mass shootings, was even more terse about her on-the-job trauma:

I despise covering them. I really despise covering them. They're really among the worst things. I mean, I cover a lot of really terrible things. I mean, I'm on sabbatical right now. . . . After a lot of mass shootings and 12 executions and whatever else I've covered, I can't. I just can't. You may have gotten me at a particular moment where I'm more bleak about it than normal. I've been a reporter for a long time. My tolerance for violence and dark things is pretty low.

A TV reporter ("Gina") who witnessed an execution for the first time found herself conflicted:

You know as a human being, personally, I knew the horrible crimes that this man committed. We covered the story a lot of times, but as a human being, if I could be perfectly honest with you. It was kinda sad, I kinda caught myself getting a little emotional.

'Cause at this time Billie Wayne Coble, he's old, you know he's white-haired. . . . He looked like a cute old man and as I'm watching him die, I felt really sad, like I almost wanted to cry. Knowing that he committed a horrible crime and he murdered multiple people, but still just seeing him die

like that. It was like, it kind of became personal because now it's like I'm the
last person to see this man before he died.

While not a botched execution, the Coble case was unusual because the
condemned man's son became violent at the sight of his father's death,
throwing punches and spewing profanities at other witnesses.[83] Gordon
Coble and his own son were led out of the prison and later jailed themselves on charges of resisting arrest.[84] What's notable here is how unusual
it is for such fits of emotion to erupt during contemporary executions.
The clinical solemnity of today's procedure seems to influence most
participants. Outbursts like those from the younger Coble call to mind the
sort of uncontrolled "hooligan" mobs that private executions are intended
to quell.

Greg witnessed several botched executions in Florida, including two
electrocutions in which the inmate's heads burned:

> For years they wet the top of the head and make sure, they used a sea sponge.
> And it was getting worn out after 30 years or so. And then somebody says,
> well we'll put a new sponge at the top. Well they bought, like a Brillo pad or
> whatever. And it caught fire.
>
> Mary: Ay yi yi.
>
> And we're still there and all of a sudden there's fire coming off the top of
> this guy's head. You're wondering what the hell is going on.

Greg also witnessed instances in which lethal injection, the latest form of
killing that's supposed to be painless and humane, turned out to be neither:

> The inmate took a long time to die. With the lethal injection it's actually
> quite a bit longer than five minutes, maybe, or six minutes. And this one
> went on for like twenty something, thirty minutes.
>
> Mary: Oh.
>
> And that's when I really learned that the prison would lie to us. The
> prison said because of bad kidneys, I think is what they said, it took
> his body longer to spread the chemicals out. There was kidney disease
> or . . . well the next day, the state medical examiner released a report and
> said, the kidneys had nothing to do with it. What they'd done is push the
> needle all the way through the vein into the muscles. And that's why it took
> so long to die.

As difficult as it might be to watch a botched execution, such moments are part of the motivation for the reporters who do this kind of work. Discomfort is part of the job, but it is offset by a sense of duty to the public, the form of witnessing that Peters[85] identified as most solemn: not merely watching but *bearing* witness.

A Sense of Duty

Reporters who witness executions find the process discomfiting, yet they believe it is important that they attend. Amy put it this way:

> It's essential that we're there. A lot of people would always ask me, "Why do you cover them?" Especially because I'm personally very anti–death penalty, but I felt like it was a really important thing to cover as a reporter because what if the state puts somebody to death and no one was there to witness it?

Reporters also mentioned their duty to witness in the context of botched executions.

> Well, because I think that we need to be—we, I mean, we as a press—need to be there to monitor to see what the state is doing. The state can't just execute people in private, in secret. That kind of goes against what we stand for, I think, as a country. I could be completely wrong of course these days, but personally I think if the state is going to execute people, somebody needs to be there to at least possibly see if something's going wrong. (Amy)
>
> That's kind of the big thing for having a reporter in the room. I mean they coulda said, well, everything went as scheduled. And that's what they'd do if they could do that. (Greg)

While Graczyk believed in his role as a proxy for the public, he has doubts about the impact of execution coverage:

> I think society as a whole, I think they've become somewhat ho-hum about it. I think if the case certainly affects you directly—in other words, if it's your loved one who's being put to death, or it was your loved one who was murdered as a result of us getting to this point of the punishment—then it's

deeply, deeply personal. I think the sheer numbers of executions have made the common readers or common TV viewers or the public, they just kind of shrug at it and decide, "Well, another execution in Texas." And I think that's where it's at right now.

None of the designated witnesses I interviewed had a strong position regarding whether the public ought to be able to view video recordings of executions, or whether such a policy might make a difference to public sentiment. Here's how Amy answered:

> It might. The visuals of the actual death chamber are kind of frighteningly mundane. It's a room. It's a gurney. If you had no idea what you were looking at, you would have no indication that somebody was going to die. I know a lot of people say this, and it sounds terrible. It's almost anticlimactic because it's so calm.

So while reporters who serve as the public's proxy for executions believe it is a civic duty, they seem to also sense that the public does not truly appreciate what happens in the death chamber. They are aware of holding a special social role as designated viewers, but its "special" nature is not particularly rewarding.

Hidden and Forgotten

Executions mark the end of a sentence for very few of America's 1.4 million prisoners.[86] Most serve out their sentences hidden and forgotten. Modern high-security prisons are usually far from urban areas, which further limits visits and visibility. It may seem frustratingly obvious that the corporal demands of visual journalism inhibit coverage of an eighty-billion-dollar enterprise,[87] but this does not diminish the consequence. In the case of the prison system, embodied gatekeeping operates at the level of geography, simply because prisons are usually constructed far outside populated areas, and everyday practices by law enforcement restrict journalistic—especially photojournalistic—access. The news audience learns little about prisons, and the people inside those prisons are easily ignored. This is, of course, part of the punishment, as losing one's democratic voice and visibility renders prisoners less human. Incarceration scholar and activist Dan Berger wrote that prison reform advocates in the 1970s "named invisibility as the enemy" and worked to call attention to the injustice, racism, and violence of the modern prison system.[88]

In a strange way, therefore, the federal inmates in Brooklyn, New York, may have been lucky in 2019 when their prison lost power for a week during an extreme cold snap. The facility was in an urban center, where passersby might at least be aware of its existence. The loss of heat, however, was unreported until a journalist with the *New York Times* received an email from someone connected to one of the more than one thousand inmates who were kept in lockdown during the outage.[89] She had to confirm the story with public defenders and leaders of the correctional officers' union because the warden's office would not respond. After Annie Correal's first story was published in the *New York Times*, the warden did call and claimed that the inmate areas were "minimally impacted," contradicting every other person she'd interviewed. Protesters gathered outside to show support for loved ones inside the prison, communicating on their side with bullhorns to inmates who could only bang on their walls and windows.[90] While some video footage was leaked, apparently by way of contraband cell phones, most of the visual story was told by way of the building's exterior. In a way, it was the edifice itself that announced the story's resolution, as Correal recounted in the *Times* podcast *The Daily*: "And that's kind of a moment, because the protesters are still there. And it's late at night, and the lights come back on and you see all of the inmates flipping the switch in their cells and the jail light up, and everyone sort of cheer on the street."[91] Visual coverage of the event focused on what happened outside the facility, blended with a few shots surreptitiously collected from smartphones inside.

The private prison model, borne from "tough on crime" campaigns in the 1980s that the most news organizations interrogated poorly, prioritizes the warehousing of human beings over rehabilitation.[92] US prisoners work literally for pennies, pay high prices for access to email or telephones, and are often denied essential health services.[93] Located far outside urban centers, strategically *out of sight,* prisons deny inmates the chance to be seen or heard, as even their own families struggle to visit.[94]

Tightly controlling journalistic access to prisons has not stopped all coverage of the penal system, but the virtual ban on visual coverage means that TV news will rarely, if ever, touch the topic. When TV cameras are in prisons, it is usually by invitation in order to cover a feature story inside the facility.[95] When breaking news occurs in a prison, the story is usually told with distant exterior shots of the facility. Officials occasionally set up a media area where officials hold news conferences, but this is at the state's discretion. Access to inmates is difficult, and case law has sided with prisons, suggesting that journalists have no more rights than the general public to prison access.[96]

When the Trump administration started to put migrants seeking asylum into camps at the southern border, journalists were not able to go inside to bear witness. Reports of abuse, intolerably cold rooms, and children being covered with foil blankets were difficult to confirm without any type of third-party auditing.[97] While some legislators and journalists have been allowed to tour the facilities, the US Customs and Border Protection's Rio Grande Valley Sector made and distributed the images, keeping the visual message under tight control.[98] CNN's coverage of conditions at the border for child migrants, for instance, relied on leaked images that showed very young children sleeping with foil blankets on the ground.[99] In the summer of 2019 US representative Joaquin Castro, a Democrat from Texas, took the extraordinary step of smuggling a camera into the facility and leaked photos by way of Twitter.[100] It is hard to overstate the importance of that moment: a lawmaker defying regulations in order to show the public how the United States was treating the human beings who had crossed the border to request asylum. Castro knew that voters need to *see* as much as they need to know what their government is doing.

What we do *not* see of the criminal justice system, therefore, is just as critical as what we do see. Journalists are rarely allowed inside prisons, and nearly never are allowed inside with a camera. Shane Bauer, who took a job as a prison guard in order to expose conditions in an American private prison, carried a hidden camera inside to do so. At one point during his undercover work, he recorded video of a naked inmate being pepper-sprayed while in his cell, part of the story that would be hard to believe if conveyed by word alone:

> There's certain things in writing you can kind of get across better than with visuals, and certain things that's opposite. And that I think is a really good example of something that I could just never really get across with just words. It's just such an image, this guy in his cell naked, pacing back and forth, who's full of pepper spray. And I think that people seeing that stuff impacted them and made them feel in a way they wouldn't have otherwise.[101]

The Society of Professional Journalists advocates for improved journalistic access to prisons and encourages reporters to do what they can in spite of restrictions.[102] Amy, for instance, was able to tour death row in prison once during her career and with a colleague created an infographic because no photography was allowed. Images from an Alabama prison—again, *leaked* to the *New York Times*—drew attention to the lack of photojournalistic access in 2019.[103] The images—bloody, torturous, and horrifying—inspired columnist Shaila Dewan to ask, "Would we fix our prisons if we could see what happens inside them?" A subsequent story in *Mother Jones* (the same progressive and investigative magazine that sponsored Bauer's undercover project) dug further, with input from Pete Brook, who runs a photography class inside San Quentin.[104] Brook and his students endeavor to render their lives visible through image and argued that the impact of prison images depends on who sees them, noting that his inmate students believe visibility is beneficial. In his words, "Social change and political change can't happen in a visual vacuum." Brook took issue with Berger, who, based on his decades of research and advocacy, was more sanguine in a Twitter thread.[105] Berger argued that visibility is not a panacea, and indeed is harmful when it portrays violence, which only perpetuates stereotypes and stokes fear. Berger argued on Twitter for the long game, with increased contact and journalistic coverage that does more than hype occasional spot news, but humanizes inmates and draws attention to the larger issues of incarceration in the United States.

The American penal system shuts prisoners off from public view to extremes under the guise of protecting inmate privacy, maintaining order, and security concerns. It is hard to imagine that the slow but constant drumbeat of abuses reported in word-based journalism would continue if the public could see inside more often. The impact of prison abuse and exploitation on inmates and their families is dire, not at all rehabilitative, and therefore potentially dangerous for the public. Inmates with untreated mental health problems and no chance of rehabilitation are less likely to successfully reintegrate upon release, which puts communities at risk. Furthermore, incarcerating more than two million people a year is extremely expensive, estimated to cost one trillion dollars a year, more than the amount necessary to provide that many people a college education.[106] The mere fact that inmates are human beings and their imprisonment is ostensibly done in the name of the public interest should render this topic worthy of news coverage. Yet the way crime is covered in the news (cheaply and often), the way criminals are portrayed in entertainment and the news, the restrictions on coverage generally, and the near blackout impediments to the visual press make it easy to understand why these stories are left to long-form investigative journalists.

News organizations are beholden to the concerns of their audience, and if the audience cares about crime—but not criminals—why bother?

Conclusion

Views of executions and the prison system are occluded for the state's benefit, not the public's. As Garland put it, "If the modern execution is a suppressed spectacle it is because state officials and political elites have decided that the public's preferences ought, in this case, to be *denied*" (italics added).[107] The right to visibility would suggest that there needs to be more transparency in the prison system, with more access for citizens, advocates, and journalists. Berger's assessment on Twitter is correct: no set of photos will change public opinion. The need is not for more images per se, but in the creation of photos, the performance-embodied witnessing and the use of vision to render voice.

As for executions, they are the endpoints of a long process of dehumanization in America's prisons, and the egregious excesses of America's current incarceration system can be attributed, in part, to the fact that is it largely, *literally*, invisible. Ironically, the shift from public to closed executions only serves to undermine the myth of the death penalty's deterrence effect. If they are not to be witnessed by the general public in real time nor appear elsewhere in the visual record, the disciplinary shadow of the gallows disappears. All that is left is society's revenge.

Foucault philosophized about the shift from public to private executions to describe the way social discipline has been internalized.[108] The shift in visual culture also changes what happens at the more practical level of civic life. What we see and, more importantly, what we do *not* see of prison life and death affect the way we think about the people affected. Event-driven news extends this effect and obscures systemic inequality. Without a view of prison life and the human beings within, the public sees only the narrative of law and order, and never its ending.

3

Walks of Shame

Scene: In April 1986 the Iowa State Legislature erupted in a scandal that could make many a #metoo tweet seem tame. During a stag party for a soon-to-be-married lawmaker in a Mingo, Iowa, tavern, a stripper pulled one of the legislators to the stage and appeared to perform oral sex on him. Months later, when a grand jury was gathering evidence about the incident, I was among about two dozen journalists from print, television, and radio outlets staking out for a glimpse of the stripper at the center of the case. When she exited the courthouse alone, wearing slacks and her hair in a ponytail, she ran, and so did we. This was not a powerful person deserving the public ire; this was a young woman who, for whatever reason, chose to make money as a stripper in small-town Iowa. And I was part of the hunting party that managed to capture about ten seconds of video of her frantic, rabbitlike dash.[1]

Perp walks have long been part of media practice, but discourse about them in pop culture is relatively new. The term originated in the 1940s but became popular in the 1990s.[2] Over time the phrase spread from the occupational jargon of journalists and police to the public vernacular.[3] Today, pundits critique perp walks like fashion writers watching a runway. Lori Loughlin was criticized for smiling too broadly when she appeared in court on charges stemming from a college admissions scandal.[4] When Harvey Weinstein appeared for his preliminary court appearance in New York City in 2018, his perp walk was broadcast live, internationally. Observers weighed in on everything from his demeanor to his blue sweater to the book he carried into the building.

Perp walks can be defined as the nonconsensual or coerced recording of individuals involved with court cases, and they present a special type of disciplinary image. They are, for the most part, government-sponsored media productions, as visual journalists and the subjects of perp walks are both regulated by the state's embodied gatekeeping. This renders perp walks a type of

Seeing Justice. Mary Angela Bock, Oxford University Press. © Oxford University Press 2021.
DOI: 10.1093/oso/9780190926977.003.0003

media ritual identified by Nick Couldry, who argued that familiar mass media tropes must be considered for the way they operate in concert with the state.[5] Couldry's analysis focused on examples such as reality TV programs and talk show self-disclosures, but his argument transfers well to American perp walks, which offer a site where it is possible to learn the detailed *mechanisms* the state uses to construct its authority. Perp walk images are created from a complex of social interactions, including embodied gatekeeping and cultural rituals, before they are recontextualized into criminal justice narratives. This chapter uses ethnographic observation from key cases, celebrated and obscure, to examine the relationship between grounded practice and media narratives.

Perp walks are troublesome texts because they are often a form of de facto punishment, with journalistic complicity. The images are recontextualized as an accusation, if not a full imprimatur, of guilt. This particular media routine can easily become aggressive, as individuals become prey for photojournalists who *must* deliver an image to their newsroom or face professional embarrassment.[6] The combined economic, deadline, and professional constraints that journalists face create a high-pressured situation in which getting the shot overshadows concerns about law and fairness.

While some perp walks are tightly regulated and carefully orchestrated by police (as with the Weinstein case), others might resemble a chaotic game of cat and mouse, with the state playing a more passive role. When the Pennsylvania attorney general appeared in court on corruption charges in 2015, she brought her twin sister along to confuse photographers gathered for her perp walk in a courthouse hallway.[7] As a young TV reporter in the 1980s, I staked out the one place in the Polk County (IA) courthouse where all members of the public must pass in order to help my colleague shoot a perp walk of a defendant in a child sex abuse case. His mother covered his head with a jacket as he passed by the camera.

In the United States, police have enjoyed court endorsement for orchestrating perp walks. Other countries, such as France and England, explicitly forbid the photography of a person who has not yet faced trial. In 2011 the Dominique Strauss-Kahn case highlighted the contrast between American and European sensibilities about pretrial photography, as the one-time managing director of the International Monetary Fund was outraged to have been subjected to street photography in this way.[8] Defendants in the United States are quite often subjected to this ritual before they are found guilty, and while the Strauss-Kahn case inspired momentary introspection in the American press corps, the practice persists.[9]

Visual Habeas Corpus

The phrase "perp walk" ("perp" is short for perpetrator) is police lingo for the transport of a defendant from one place to another, often in front of news cameras. The *Encyclopedia of Law Enforcement* credits the Second Circuit Court of Appeals with one definition: the "widespread police practice in New York City (and many others) in which the suspected perpetrator of a crime, after being arrested, is walked in front of the press so that he [*sic*] can be photographed or filmed."[10] The ritual has a deep history, as similar walks of shame have been imposed upon criminals for centuries. In ancient China, transgressors wore stones around their neck. Puritans used scarlet letters, and even the Passion Play's "Walk of the Cross" can be considered a sort of perp walk.[11] Its growth as a media trope parallels the development of photojournalism in the early twentieth century. Confrontations between subjects and photographers in courthouse hallways were part of early tabloid practice.[12] The term was not in fashion, but the police transport of Lee Harvey Oswald and his death at the hands of Jack Ruby is widely considered the most well-known modern-era perp walk.[13]

Ruiz and Treadwell argued that the perp walk is an unfair tool of prosecutors and police to further public relations and publicize a case.[14] They also contend that perp walks are downright dangerous, citing the Oswald killing. Beyond issues of personal safety, though, the matters of unfair pretrial publicity and grandstanding by police and prosecutors remain the top complaints about the phenomenon.[15] In 1999 John Lauro of New York successfully sued the city in federal court after officers deliberately displayed him to news cameras by walking him around police district offices. The US District Court of the Southern District of New York ruled Lauro's civil rights had been violated.[16] But in a later case, a judge ruled that "perp walks" serve a legitimate function: essentially that of *police public relations*.[17]

Shooting video of a perp walk is routine for many US photo- and television journalists. It is largely an American phenomenon, as many other countries, even those with free-press traditions, ban media portrayals of defendants prior to trial. A classic perp walk involves a defendant in custody with a police escort. Another form of walk might involve a person who is out on bail or even a person with a connection to a court case who must appear before a judge. The common element of all walks is that they are *imposed* on a subject; they are nonconsensual portraits. Also, the term "perp" (for "perpetrator") automatically implies that this *is* the person who committed the crime; it's not a "defendant walk" or an "alleged perpetrator walk." The very name implies a guilty subject.

Visual ethics scholar Julianne Newton's typology of photographic interaction might classify such an imposition as anything from visual intrusion to "visual rape."[18] Because they are accused criminals, the plight of those subjected to perp walks does not inspire public sympathy the way a celebrity hounded by the paparazzi might. As a visual trope and photographic ritual, perp walks share some dimensions with the work of celebrity paparazzi in that perp walk rituals usually involve multiple photographers and a single subject being photographed involuntarily.[19] As McNamara and Mendelson have noted, while celebrities usually want attention, they want *beneficial* attention, so conflicts with the much-maligned paparazzi are largely matters of when and where (and conflicts might be exploited for publicity as well).[20] Celebrities want to be photographed on their terms, but the subjects of perp walks usually do not want to be photographed at all.

Most research on perp walks has centered on legal issues, such as a defendant's right to a fair trial or First Amendment questions, but journalism scholars have largely neglected the phenomenon.[21] One experimental study found that images of people wearing handcuffs or in custody caused viewers to consider the portrayed person to be guilty, threatening, or both.[22] Cavender and colleagues did not study perp walks specifically, but traced the way media coverage of crime stories constitutes what sociologist Harold Garfinkel identified as "status degradation ceremonies."[23] For the most part, researchers have not explored the phenomenon from the perspective of the people most directly involved: visual journalists and their subjects.

It is one thing to identify a news image as a site of general semiotic struggle, and another still to engage in the specific ways an image is chosen, composed, worked on, and treated according to professional norms. Only with specifics does it become possible to deconstruct the message. Conceiving of image-making in terms of both material and discursive recontextualization provides a framework for doing so. Therefore, the concept of embodied gatekeeping, as part of the recontextualization model, is especially useful for the study of perp walks. This media ritual is dependent upon two actors—a journalist and the nonconsenting subject—meeting in a state-arranged space and time.

Cases of Guilt and Exoneration

This chapter is based on case observations: interviews with visual journalists, attorneys, and people who have been subjected to perp walk photography. The cases include six instances in Philadelphia and its suburbs, and in Bellefonte, Pennsylvania. Most of the cases involved local media only, but the 2012 case attracted national attention: that of former Penn State coach Jerry Sandusky, who was eventually found guilty of child molestation. Three of the participants who'd been subjected to nonconsensual photography had been criminally charged and later exonerated, a fourth was the mother of a man who'd been charged with murder and exonerated; she herself had been photographed outside her home during his adjudication. Whenever I was able, I used my own camera to take visual notes and to attempt to emulate the practice of the photojournalists under observation. This chapter also draws from interviews with photographers who shot perp walks for national news stories, such as the Harvey Weinstein case and the Kermit Gosnell illegal abortion case in Philadelphia.

Three of the observed cases involved suspects in custody; two involved suspects on bail, including a celebrity rapper, Beanie Sigal. The Jerry Sandusky case was national in scope and interest and lured hundreds of journalists to the bucolic town of Bellefonte, Pennsylvania. Another case occurred in a suburban courthouse that allowed cameras indoors but not in the courtroom itself. One case failed to yield a perp walk when a different story broke inside the courthouse and the stakeout (for an alleged pedophile) was abandoned. Several themes emerged during a careful review of the field notes and the interview transcripts, reflecting (1) the perspectives of the photojournalists about their work and the skills it requires, (2) the emotional responses of perp walk subjects to the experience; and for both sides, (3) the ritual's dehumanizing effects.

The Photographers: Skilled and Cooperative Hunters

So great is news organizations' demand for a perp walk image that visual journalists will wait hours for one glimpse of a subject. After George Zimmerman was arrested in the Trayvon Martin case, photographers waited all night, in some cases taking turns on stakeout. One photojournalist waited sixty-six hours for a second opportunity, and because he worked alone there was no one to provide a break. He got the shot, but needed help sending the image back to his organization: "I was so tired, I had to have help getting up. I got the shot, but I couldn't get up. My legs just wouldn't do it. So, different people helped me up and helped me walk back and transmit."[24]

Just as Tuchman found that reporters will help one another with generally available facts, photographers help each other during stakeouts for perp walks.[25] They give each other advice on such things as what the subject might be wearing, whether they've arrived, or the number of possible entrances. It's also not unheard of (though it didn't happen during this project) for photographers from competing stations to split up the task, with each one covering a door and promising to trade video. While waiting for Jerry Sandusky to arrive for court, photographers stood outside for more than an hour behind sawhorses designed to control their movements. As the trial attorneys, the judge, and Jerry Sandusky's car would arrive, a technician from a national network who had a good vantage point would alert everyone with a simple, "Heads up, Hollywood!" During coverage of Beanie Sigal's trial, the photographer for the ABC affiliate pointed out the rapper to the photographer from the competing CBS affiliate while Sigal waited in a security line that was visible through a window.

Mark Makela, whose extensive coverage of the Bill Cosby trial was featured in a *New York Times* photo essay, shot one of the most iconic images from the trial, when the man who once played Dr. Huxtable was led out of the courtroom in handcuffs.

> We were not given an ideal spot to photograph from and he was—The hallway itself is, probably, the width is ten feet. So on a wide angle lens, I was as far away as I could and yes, I was on my knees. I thought that would be a cleaner view and more dramatic from that perspective. And I was fortunate, like I said, he was blocked, by and large. . . . Luckily I had a clear angle right when he came in front and it came together.

The make-or-break pressure on photographers to come back with that picture is the likely source of this cooperation. For the good of the group on location it makes more sense to help one another (and live another day) than to compete. I spoke with a couple of the photographers on stakeout at family court about not getting the shot. One said the immediate response would be, "Aww, Christ Almighty," then feeling like he was "condemned to death." He continued, "They're very condemning at our place. . . . If everybody else got it and you don't and you were here—" He doesn't finish the thought with words, but with more of a shake and a sigh. Another photographer was more sanguine: "Eh, what can they do? They can be a little mad. . . . It depends on how important it is." Sandra, a major market photographer with more than fifteen years' experience, still finds the process stressful:

> I always feel pressure. . . . You know, other people go in there cool as a cucumber, but I am so worried that I'm going to miss something and let everybody down, so I hate being the pool camera. But on the flip side of it, I love watching court proceedings, so I do get front-row seats to the greatest show on Earth.

The pressure seems as much a matter of professional pride as being externally imposed by management. Photojournalism scholar Lisa Henderson found this sort of pride in getting whatever shots are necessary during the course of her research.[26] Similarly, Robert Steele found his subjects so determined to do their job that they would meet the demands of a shoot even it meant contradicting their personal ethical beliefs.[27] I asked Sandra whether this high-pressure, hunter-prey dynamic ever felt uncomfortable:

> While I'm doing it, I don't think about the emotional part, I get rid of the emotional part. My job is to get a picture. So I get my picture. . . . There are days when I maybe don't feel so good about myself for getting the shot or whatever, and some days I feel great. But not while I'm on the job, never while I'm doing the job. Never.

A slightly different but related source of solidarity comes from the photographers' relationship with their managers—assignment editors, producers, reporters, photo managers, and news directors—and other colleagues. Reese has noted that journalists answer to a wide variety of stakeholders within and outside their newsrooms.[28] Observations from this project indicate a predictable tension between those who work in the field ("on the street") and those who stay inside the newsroom. During one perp walk stakeout, I asked the photographer, "Martin," what the defendant looked like and which courtroom was scheduled for the proceeding. "Why," he asked sarcastically, "should I know that?" His response implied not only that the supervisor didn't or wouldn't help him with the most basic information about his assignment but that this happens regularly. Such complaints were a frequent part of the everyday banter.

The demands of the task seem to bind the photojournalists and TV photographers more to one another than to their immediate supervisors in the newsroom. The photographers have more in common with one another, having shared more time, aching feet, and rainy days than with their indoor colleagues. One consistent observation for all field visits is that the first people addressed by a photographer were other photographers. They did talk to police, bailiffs, and other sources but started by taking cues from one another. Often the conversation focused on which of the three doors at Philadelphia's Criminal Justice Center (CJC) is best monitored when working alone (east door, closest to the parking garage), or about lighting, new equipment, or where the story stood. Just as often, though, the stakeout resembled a family reunion, replete with gossip and jokes that had nothing to do with the story. In Doylestown, two newspaper photographers spent quite a bit of time comparing notes on the new flash one had acquired. Here, in a circular windowed hallway, a brief conversation could be heard about the lousy lighting in the place. At the CJC, "Ted" explained the optimum time to arrive was about 8:40, before the guards inside opened up the gates at the metal detectors—that way, one could still get video of the person standing in line. A video photographer from a major city told me, "The bosses don't know this," but the photographers are "tight."

> So, if someone actually needs to get away to get a bathroom break or something like that, someone who shoots in the same format will say, "Look, if it happens and you're gone, I'll give you my shot." So, we all kind of watch out for each other. But the bosses don't know we do that, and that's the rule, nobody talks about it.

During the few seconds of a perp walk, though, the camaraderie becomes more of a friendly joust. A major-market newspaper photographer ("Stuart") described it this way:

> You just kind of work with everybody. And use a—you have two cameras, one with a wide angle lens and one with a longer telephoto lens, and you might have to use the elbow technique, as in, putting up the elbows.

Photographing a perp walk takes speed, technical skill, and confidence. I attempted several and failed each time. At the family court stakeout, photographers put their cameras on tripods in order to take advantage of focal length. "Len" knew exactly how far away he could be and still get a shot. Ted described his system for walking backward with a defendant. The trick, it seems, is to keep the lens wide and look backward most of the time, just occasionally taking a quick peek into the viewfinder. I tried this at the Bucks County courthouse and managed to get a photograph of the floor.

For Harvey Weinstein's walk, veteran wire service photographer Spencer Platt joked that he brought a small stepstool to the event, which made it a serious assignment. Because the walk occurred at a police precinct and not a courthouse, everyone was on their toes that morning:

> I think we're all kind of improvising. We're all, "How's it gonna go down? Where's the car gonna come from? Where are they gonna drop him? Is he gonna walk this way?" It's always a matter of, "Am I going to shoot this wide?" Maybe by the time the black car pulls up, you have maybe 15 seconds to shoot. And it's not enough time to—Let's say you have a 7200 on one camera, and a 16 and 35 on another camera. So, you don't have enough time to drop one camera when you get out. You always want a tight shot when he exits the door of the car. But if you're getting to that shot, if you're going to go tight, you're going to have to stick with that. You don't have enough time to drop that camera and pick up the next camera.

At Philadelphia's family court, Len listed all the gear he brings along to survive a long stakeout—not just for his camera, but for comfort in whatever weather. Another one of Len's concerns was theft. Many photographers put their camera down during a long wait, but Len said thieves have been known to provide a distraction and walk away with equipment worth tens of thousands of dollars. This worry is not unwarranted: at the Sandusky case, one photographer was robbed of a gear bag while he was shooting at the sawhorses.

The Subjects' Experience: Prey

People who are caught in a perp walk predicament often try to find ways to avoid photographers, and if they cannot, to hide their faces. As a young reporter in Des Moines, I worked with a video photographer to keep watch for a man accused of child sexual abuse. All public stairwells in the Polk County courthouse converge on the first floor, and so we divided our attention. When we spotted our target, his mother covered him with a jacket, led him out, and literally hissed at us as she passed. When Stormy Daniels appeared in court in New York City, her security staff tried to usher her out of view of the cameras, creating an accident that sent veteran wire service photographer Spencer Platt tumbling:

> They were clueless. They were trying to lead her into a sideway entrance door. They had probably never been there before. There were barricades up. So her security, they tried to pull in these barricades, and people were tripping over the barricades. And people fell on me. And in the photo the next day, I'm like in the corner in the back being stampeded upon.

Former state attorney general Kathleen Kane used an unusual strategy to avoid cameras when she arrived for a preliminary hearing on corruption charges: she had her twin act as a decoy. While photographers were shooting her twin, Ellen Granahan Goffer, Kane walked by before some of them could recover and reshoot.[29]

All four of the perp walk subjects interviewed for this study had been photographed nonconsensually. Two were men; two were women. Two were exonerated when prosecutors dropped the charges against them; one was found not guilty by a jury; a fourth was pursued by photographers because her son had been charged with a notorious murder. Two of the subjects ("Steven" and "Tom") experienced classic perp walks, in handcuffs and with police escort, after being charged with child sexual abuse.[30] "Carrie" was a suburban mom charged with child abuse. She was photographed while on bail, not with a police escort. "Kim," the fourth subject, was photographed leaving a police station after her son was arrested. Reporters and photographers soon staked out her home to shoot her comings and goings in the days following his arrest. (This is somewhat unusual in that she was not charged with the crime, but the notorious nature of this case likely inspired a "shoot whatever moves" policy for the visual media.) When the subjects' homes were surrounded, they simply refused to go outside, as Carrie explained:

> Q: Did they ever get a picture of you under those circumstances?
> In my mom's home?

Q: Leaving or coming into the—
   No, because I didn't leave.

In this situation, the woman remained under siege for several days rather than face the cameras. Kim eventually lost her job because she refused to leave her house when photographers from all the local TV stations were camped outside:

> I have to call my job because I can't go to work. I can't go to work because 3, 6, 9, 29, and 17[31] is sitting right outside my door with the antennas going up and everything, you know what I mean? My neighbors [were], like, wondering why all these news people are out here and I just didn't come outside.

The two men charged with child sexual abuse first encountered a scrum of photographers after they were charged, and for both of them, the encounter was a shock:

> I remember pulling into the parking lot of what was supposed to be, according to the attorney representing me at that time, a routine hearing in front of the district justice. And all we're going to do is go through the motions, then you and I will drive in my car to the police station, and we'll take your picture, take your fingerprints, and that'll be it. You know. And that wasn't it. We pulled into the parking lot and I thought, "Who's going to be here?" because all these television and radio vehicles and then a cadre of reporters and photographers and I just realized that, and they were not at the front door, they were at the back door. I thought "Omigosh" [sighs]. "They're here for my hearing." (Steven)

Tom's hearing was delayed by hours, something he believes was contrived in order to make sure the press was able to gather:

> They took me over there and when I got there, as they were pulling up I said "Omigod," it was Channel 3, Channel 6, Channel 10, think it was a couple other channels too were there. And, uh, then when they pulled up, of course, all these, uh, reporters came around the car and I got out and they said, "Are you guilty, Mr. —? Did you do this?" And I had enough sense 'cause I'm by myself there was no attorney there at the time. . . . I had

enough sense to say nothing. Well, actually I did mumble that "I, I didn't do anything."

While the circumstances of their perp walks were varied, the four share a common complaint, namely, the way they and their pictures were recontextualized in news stories. They saw themselves as innocent, but their pictures carried a "guilty" frame. As much as they disliked the physical perp walk situation, the overriding complaint was less about the recorded image and more about the way that image was recontextualized in discourse that portrayed them as criminals. Each one of these subjects felt that they were portrayed in a bad light, if only because the news coverage of them as "charged" or "connected to the crime" did not square with their own self-image of innocence.

> But what's happening in the picture, the way they took the picture, it was—it looks like I'm guilty because I'm looking down. But the reason I'm looking down—in fact, the policeman's looking down, too—the reason I'm looking down is because there's a curb there. Now I had my head up all the time, but they had this curb, Can I show you that picture? (Tom)[32]

Kim's situation was unusual in that she was photographed in connection with her son's case. Her anger was less over the fact that her son's face was on television but over the particular image of his face, the mug shot, which to Kim implied guilt:

> It's how they put it on TV. It's how they put it on TV. . . . When they showed pictures of him on TV, they didn't ask me for a picture of him when he was a kid, or when he went to the prom. You know what I'm saying; they didn't ask me for no pictures like that. They showed the pictures of him after he had been locked up for forty-eight hours with no sleep with questioning, drowsy, hair all over his head like, they, they take the worst. . . .

Why do the subjects perceive these news photos as so damning? After all, news photos are merely supposed to reflect reality. Photographers are trained to take pictures head-on, without any kind of angles or style that would reflect bias, but the *context* of the ritual imposes what the subjects experienced as bias:[33]

The content of the articles was as repugnant as the image. To be photographed with handcuffs was bad, to be photographed in that situation, with especially whatever the headline was 'cause that's the killer. (Steven)

They should get their facts straight before they even speak out about anything, and they need to watch the way they word things. I mean in the beginning for me it was "accused of child abuse," instead of saying "an allegation pending against her." These are things that people have seen and read that stayed in their mind which didn't help my process or—I don't think it helps any process. (Carrie)

The press undoubtedly considered its facts to be perfectly in order, but a perp walk connotes for the viewer that law enforcement has solved a case. US journalists are careful to use caveat words in copy about individuals charged with a crime, referring to them as "a suspect," or "the man police believe is the culprit." But visual primacy crowds out these caveat words when the news image shows that the police have "got their man."

From Steven:

Q: What does a does a perp walk–style image say?
   Steven: To the average person?
Q: To the average person.
   Steven: You're guilty. You're guilty. Because to the average person, it is, well, if you weren't guilty, they wouldn't do this, you know.

From Tom, on the effect of perp walks:

I don't think they tell the true picture.... In fact, it's funny I had a friend that years ago was falsely accused—he went to jail, in fact—but when I see his picture on the news and the television, he looked guilty. So it just, uh, I don't know [sigh]—eh, it just gave me that feeling that, uh, "God they're showing me in the most horrible light," like I was really, really guilty of this thing.

This may be why—even though Tom lost his job, Steven was kept away from his business, and both men had been jailed—they perceived their perp walks to be among the worst aspects of their journey through the legal system.

Part of the guilt frame is built discursively from the "arrest made" narrative, but tangible visual elements such as police uniforms and guns or handcuffs also contribute to this recontextualization. Certain gestures, such as the hanging head (as Tom addressed) or the hiding of one's face, also carry a message of guilt.

> People don't realize this, when you see cameras, you also see lights. And when they shoot, putting those cameras in your face, they're also putting those lights in your face. And most people are going like this [shielding face with hands] not because they're guilty but because they're shading their eyes from the lights, even in midday. (Tom)

All four of those interviewed say they themselves once interpreted these visual symbols to judge other people as signs of guilt. Not anymore:

> Q: When you see someone else now on television who's charged with a crime, what do you think now that maybe you didn't think before?
> I don't believe anything that I see on TV or anything that I read. And I give them the benefit of the doubt until the verdict comes in. I'm not as quick to judge as I was before. That was a big lesson I learned from this . . . very big lesson.
> Q: Before, did they, did they look guilty to you before, when you saw them?
> Sure. (Carrie)

The common analytical thread that applies to all cases, then, is this complaint: the image of the accused is not objective, and therefore the journalists are not doing their job.[34] Each subject had a different explanation for the bias, ranging from racism to incompetence to conspiracy with police. As if to echo Michel Foucault's assertion that modern justice seeks to hurt the soul, not the body, it was not the perp walk ritual itself but the recontextualization of their images in a shameful discourse that caused the most discomfort.[35] These individuals had no power over the discourse about their portrait—no way to control its creation, no way to control its meaning in news.

Without having read Tuchman's classic "Objectivity as Strategic Ritual," these interviewees spoke its language.[36] They believe they were portrayed in a news frame that marked them as guilty. They discussed this in ways that displayed not only a rather remarkable awareness of imagery, but of news routines that rely on official authorities:

It's always an inside connection. So after going in to [the police station] and then coming back out, someone from inside must've said, "That's the mother' of one of the children, she's on her way out" or something. And that's how they knew that was me. And they were coming up and shooting the camera all in my face and asking me all kinds of questions, questions that I couldn't even answer for myself, you know, because I didn't—hadn't talked to my son, you know? (Kim)

Steven (like Tuchman) understands that reporters work with police and prosecutors because they need authorities as sources, but found it to be unfair to him and other defendants:

You had the two guards, and you had this whole press corps. What our supporters would notice would be whenever [the prosecutor] would open his yap, they were taking notes, and they sat, they physically placed the press right behind the D.A. Okay? Whenever [Steven's defense attorney] would get up and speak they would be sitting there. Now, see, I couldn't see this, but the people said, you know, "That is so bizarre."

Each of these four subjects had a normative vision of journalists as truthtellers and believed their portrayals, whether visual or in print, to be *untrue*. Being forced into a photograph and then discursively framed as criminals was devastating. The "reality" that the image invoked was not the reality they experienced. The interviewees all considered this disjoint to be a journalistic failure. After all, to their mind, journalists are supposed to be objective and disseminate facts. The objections seem not to be on the news as much as what seemed to be a biased recontextualization:

Q: How about just having your picture taken? What did not feel right to you about just walking outside and letting them shoot video of you while you got in your car?

Kim: Well, I feel like this: They weren't trying to take no video of me any other time. Why when something happens, they need to come out. Like, like the news people, they don't really come out to a neighborhood of this stature—like, I live in the bottoms—you know what I mean, and most of the people down here are Black or, um, Hispanic. And, um, they don't come down and see the good people do. They just, they just feed on the negative.

Each of these subjects was exonerated and consider themselves to have been "framed" to begin with and saw themselves as inappropriately framed a second time by the journalists. The primary tension for each of these subjects is between their idea of truth and whether the journalists were presenting that truth.

Underscoring this interpretation is the way the subjects' assessment of the journalists changed as their cases changed. Tom was quite pleased with the way he was treated after the district attorney held a news conference to exonerate him.[37] Steven appreciated the work of a reporter who wrote a story after the charges were dropped. Kim held her head high when the case started to turn in her son's favor:

KIM: When I was on the TV at that point, I wasn't nervous, uh, I wasn't—I didn't have the anxiety that I had before when the news media was, uh, you know, recording me. Then I was like, you know, um . . . justice will prevail.

Carrie's attorney asked some of his own questions during the research interview:

ATTORNEY: Did you feel at the outset, at least—when you were first arrested— you were being portrayed accurately?
CARRIE: In the beginning? I don't believe I was portrayed accurately at all.
ATTORNEY: Did that change over time?
CARRIE: Yes.
ATTORNEY: When was that?
CARRIE: When I was acquitted.
ATTORNEY: Okay.

When the situation became more favorable, subjects' complaints about media presence and truthfulness attenuated. Yet before, during, and after the switch in the "facts" depicted on television, the *photographers* asserted that they were continually presenting an unbiased picture, and that their practices were unchanged. They consider themselves to be doing their job properly: collecting objective and truthful images of the situation.

A Mutually Dehumanizing Ritual

During field visits, photographers spoke little about the defendants they were assigned to shoot, except in matters of what they look like or what they wear, in order to spot them. The defendants became a form of prey. The photographers interviewed did not consider it their job to find out much about the person, only to carry that image back to the newsroom. As such, the subjects are objectified. Ethical considerations about "consent to take" or "consent to use" seem light years away. No one asked the defendants whether they consent to either.

Interestingly, though, the subjects didn't see the photographers as people either. Even when asked for photographer-versus-reporter distinctions, the subjects merged the two. Each saw the photographers as part of a journalistic mass. If asked about the cameras, they'd respond about the microphones. When asked about images, they'd respond about questions and headlines. For these subjects, the photographers were part of a group that was not doing its "proper" job, not telling the "truth." What the subjects knew of the photographers was simply that they got too close. Steven says both he and his son were hit by lenses:

> They make no effort to get out of the way and they're shouting questions, to anybody who will talk, knowing in a sense that you can't, and I don't know, hoping that you'll lose your tem—I don't know what they're hoping for.

Kim and Carrie were followed through parking lots:

> They followed me from the car to the door, into the courthouse, with microphones and cameras, and then when I left, they surrounded the car. (Carrie)

A newspaper photographer, upon being asked whether he ever thinks about a person's guilt or innocence, responded no and called the defendants (particularly those charged with violent or sexual crimes) "cockroaches." He did express pity, though, for people charged with one-time nonviolent cases, like drunk drivers.[38] I described the cases of Steve and Tom to another photographer, who said that he and his colleagues did not discuss questions of guilt or innocence while on assignment, because the job is to shoot the assignment:

> I guess I'm looking at my side and saying, listen, this is a job that, it's just some assignment, we got to cover it, a job, but then, you're right, what happens if it's the other, then the other shoe drops? And then I think you really . . . oh. (Stuart)

Spencer Platt has considered the "other shoe" and says his goal, for those accused but not convicted, is to grant the subject "dignity."

> I'll just say, it is an unfortunate aspect of the profession. It's something that we're renown for, as news photographers. . . . So, yeah, at the end of the day, what makes a great perp shot, I think, is [it's] super-informative. Something that engages the reader. Something that, if you're looking at a newspaper or a magazine, or online, you're going to stop and you're going to look at this picture, and you're going to say, "Wow, that's interesting." But it's something that doesn't take away from the humanity of the subject. And at least give them the dignity that they deserve before they are sat in front of a judge.

One of the television photographers described the way he explains it to perp walk subjects: that he's just there to take a picture, he's in a public place, and they both have the right to be on the sidewalk, and he's not saying they're guilty or not—that's up to the court. "I give them their space," he says, but then adds that he has a right to his space, too.

Ritual and Ideology

The fleeting nature of the perp walk, coupled with intense organizational demands for an image of the accused, cause photographers to cooperate rather than compete. Their movements as a team create, for those on the other side of the camera, a sense of being hunted down and exploited. For both sets of stakeholders, the process feels dehumanizing and unpleasant. Yet the demands of television, especially, for crime news and visuals to illustrate that news perpetuate this ritual that is simultaneously completely legal and ethically questionable.

Visual Journalism, Access, and Embodied Gatekeeping

The American Bar Association banned cameras in the courts in 1937 (shortly after Bruno Hauptman was tried in the Lindbergh baby murder case).[39] A 1981 Supreme Court case clarified whether a person can receive a fair trial when cameras are present, reopening many courts to camera coverage.[40] Today, while many jurisdictions in the United States allow for some in-court photography, the federal courts, many municipal and domestic courts, and seventeen states do not.[41] Visual journalists operate under a patchwork quilt of laws, regulations, and administrative forms of embodied gatekeeping. Pennsylvania allows cameras in some appellate courts but not for criminal trials. Interestingly, Pennsylvania's canon prohibiting cameras in the courts does not mention an individual's right to a fair trial, instead emphasizing the need to maintain courtroom decorum. In states like Pennsylvania, perp walks are a primary source of visual news about trials.

But even outside a courtroom, officials who control court property enforce rules about where cameras can and cannot be. In the Pennsylvania suburbs, for instance, some courts allow cameras in the hallway while the Philadelphia CJC bans all cameras indoors (although the guards will generally allow photographers inside to warm up or stay dry in the lobby if they have their camera "off the shoulder" and turned off). At family court in Philadelphia, there were even places on the sidewalk prohibiting news photographers.

Photographers were never observed breaking these rules during this study, reflecting the sort of cooperation with authority that Tuchman observed. "News," she wrote, "is a social institution: it's an 'ally of legitimated institutions' created by professionals working in organizations."[42] Breaking the rules could mean sanctions that prevent future coverage, so it is understandable why journalists would work within those rules.

The Subjects' Perspective

Not surprisingly, perp walk subjects interviewed for this project report an overall sense of disempowerment and lost faith in the criminal justice system. Photographers talked about power in terms of "just following orders" and having limited power over their assignment and how it could and should be completed. Part of the anguish seems rooted in the contrasting emotions of the moment, where for one person the perp walk is just another day's work, and for the subject, it might be one of the worst days of their life.

> My misconception was that you, uh, you view the members of the media, the fourth estate, who are there to find the facts. In reality, nothing could be further from the truth. The press are essentially extensions of the prosecution. And that's not entirely their fault, and in some respects it is. (Steven)

Tom says that after his arrest, police officers would drive by his house to watch him, and once even stopped, parked, and pointed directly at him while he watched from his living room window. The experience radicalized this suburban retiree:

> I used to trust the police. When I was a kid they'd cross you on the corners and everything like that. But now . . . there's a couple good policemen around, but I, I think most of them are all they care about is their careers. Y'know, their advancement.

In *Caldarola v. County of Westchester (2nd Cir. 2003)*, the court held that because the defendant was moved from place to place for legitimate purposes and the movements were not staged *solely* (italics added) for the media's benefit, the defendant's rights had not been violated.[43] In the court's words, such publicity serves the "serious purpose of educating the public about law-enforcement efforts," and further, "The image of the accused being led away to contend with the justice system powerfully communicated government efforts to thwart the criminal element, and it may deter others from attempting similar crimes." It seems that even judges consider perp walks to carry a guilty connotation, for if the ritual is to properly serve as a form of police public relations, the images must convey the message, "We've got our man." Steven felt as much when he was escorted in front of the press:

> With the cop behind me, with his, I think he had it, but you had to be able to see the Glock and the badge. Ah, he was living for that, you know!

Steven says he was also transported and photographed a second time so that police could put him on the internet. Tom believes his perp walk was staged so that his image might attract more (supposed) victims to come forward. Kim felt the entire system was stacked against her family:

> You're innocent 'til proven guilty, and on TV, they would, they had my son guilty. I thought it was like a back-porch lynching, like a Mississippi back-porch lynching.

The State as Media Producer

Perp walks cannot occur without the state's direct or indirect involvement. Even when police are not escorting an individual, the law brings them to a particular location where visual journalists are able to lie in wait. Rarely is law enforcement as directly involved as it was in the case of Kermit Gosnell, a doctor in Philadelphia who was convicted of killing infants who were still alive after abortion attempts. Gosnell's trial took place inside the CJC, a facility in Philadelphia with an underground parking garage that allows prisoners to be transported without ever stepping outside—or being seen. One local photographer told me that media have cut back significantly on their perp walk coverage at the CJC because it is so hard to shoot there. Yet on the day Gosnell was found guilty, something unusual happened:

> So the verdict came out. On Thirteenth and Filbert with everybody assembled, they have microphones set up for the attorneys to speak. . . . We were just walking around the courthouse thinking, all right, how are we going to do this? . . . The sheriff looked up to us and said, where are you from? And we told him and he said, okay, you got to come inside. So we went inside the garage door, we just waited near there. And then the garage door closed. There was a van and next thing you know they said they're going to bring Kermit Gosnell down the elevator to the van. . . . We just looked at each other and went, what? So that right there, the authorities gave us that opportunity. (Stuart)

Mark Makela's moment was unusual, too, for the fact that Bill Cosby was *not* flanked by deputies, giving him a better line of sight for the shot:

> For that actual, the perp walk there, he was given somewhat preferential treatment as a worldwide household name and celebrity. I mean unheard

of. What we were hoping for just selfishly from a visual standpoint is that he'd be led out with the flanks of sheriffs. If not police officers, Montgomery sheriffs. But in fact, he was ushered out with his two publicists and there was only one police officer.

I observed numerous interactions between police and the press during my field visits. At family court, the photographers simply stopped the first sheriff's van to ask about the defendant they were assigned to cover. In Bucks County, reporters and photographers talked at length to prosecutors and the chief of police, never a defense attorney. One of the print photographers was wearing a shirt from a local volunteer fire company; to an outsider, he looked like another official. An experienced prosecutor learned from journalists how to best publicize his cases:

> Well, I knew from talking to you and others, that you don't want to have to use more than one crew to cover a story. I always made certain that, when were arresting somebody or doing something that required filming by you people, that it was done at a time where you could send a crew to me, leave there and have time to go to your next location to get the shot. I never set those things up so they would be at the same time 'cause I knew that that would make you have to have two crews. I always scheduled press conferences—well, not always—as often as I could, I scheduled press conferences so that you guys would have time in the mornings to get your assignments and get your crews out to Montgomery County, where they needed to get.

The most crystallizing observation of the role of police took place in Bellefonte, where police established the literal lines of the perp walk with sawhorses and patrolled the lines to make sure photographers remained in place during the Sandusky trial, as seen in Figure 3.1. Police were present as Sandusky's attorney backed his car very closely to a sheltered tunnel adjacent to the courthouse, minimizing the number of steps the defendant would have to walk before he was hidden from view (only about twelve feet). After Sandusky was found guilty and he was in police custody, the ritual changed. From video and photos of his courthouse exit on the night he was found guilty, it was clear that police parked their squad car on the far end of the parking lot and escorted Sandusky for the longest possible walk in front of those sawhorses.

Figure 3.1 Waiting for the Defendant
Photojournalists in place to capture a perp walk of Jerry Sandusky in Bellefonte,
Pennsylvania. Note the tunnel set up at the doorway to limit the view of anyone
coming and going from the back door of the courthouse.
Credit: Mary Angela Bock

Visual Assault

An analysis of the ethnographic material collected for this project yielded
three insights about this state-supported media ritual: photographers in the
field cooperate rather than compete with one another, subjects feel hunted
and betrayed, and each side dehumanizes the other. Perp walks exemplify
the way the everyday work of a journalist often intersects with the most intensely tragic days of other people. What Sontag called the pain of others
becomes just a collection of facts to be packaged through news practices.[44]
Photojournalists consider it a part of the job and say their intrusion isn't anything "personal," without giving much consideration to their partnership
with law enforcement in the perp walk ritual.[45] That a perp walk is simply
"another day at the office" for news photographers contrasts starkly to the
anguish of their subjects. Echoing Steele's findings about the primacy of the

assignment over ethical beliefs, the photographers in this study often hid behind the idea that an image can be objective and claimed to be "just following orders."[46] Most photographers considered the impact of the process on subjects, but their assignment—to capture the moment—took priority. Subjects reported a sense of being doubly violated.

Perp walks are especially important to television news operations in jurisdictions that prohibit cameras in the court, because they often yield the only photo of an accused person. This research suggests that cameras in the courts could allow for defendants to be photographed in a more dignified style. Expanded access for cameras in the courts might provide incentive for police to end the practice of devising perp walks for the sake of public relations. A now-retired veteran TV reporter—who covered trials in Pennsylvania, where trials cannot be covered with cameras, and New Jersey, where cameras are allowed in the courtroom—observed, "it was far more civilized to have the camera in the courtroom and where you had to follow rules and regulations and it wasn't crazy and far more civilized than a perp walk, for sure."

Given that other democracies eschew perp walks before trial, it also seems reasonable to discuss the basic fairness of these visual representations in journalism. The courts have concluded that they serve a public relations purpose for law enforcement. They also provide material essential for contemporary media's insatiable demand for images. The most important question may be whether perp walks serve the needs of a democratic public, and this issue remains unexplored. During a conversation about this project with one of my former colleagues, I pushed a little harder than usual about the ethics of shooting perp walks prior to conviction. It's easier, after all, to be critical from my academic distance. "Just because it's legal doesn't mean it's right," I said. He waited an extra beat before saying, "Yes." He waited one more beat to deliver a now-uncomfortable truth.

"But look, it's complicated. I made a career out of perp walks. So did you."

4

Spectacular Trials

> *Scene:* I am surrounded by trailers with generators powering air
> conditioners in the sweltering Florida heat. Pop-up tents dot traffic
> islands in the enormous parking lot of the Seminole County court-
> house. A security moat surrounds the property. The only others out-
> side in the humidity are those delivering pizzas and sandwiches to
> the journalists huddled in their trailers. In the distance, a carnival—
> an actual carnival with high tents and rides—can be seen past the
> treetops. After years of pushing back against the phrase "media
> circus," I am forced to accept that the insult may be appropriate.

The spectacle of justice is highly uneven around the world. Different nations
and states within the United States differ on their rules for photographic
court coverage. Some states, including Florida and California, have permissive regulations for courthouse coverage and have spawned a popular genre
of news coverage. Media coverage of such events can be interpreted through
Guy Debord's notion of the spectacle and Jean Baudrillard's concept of the
simulacra, in which the representation subsumes experience.[1] Spectacular
trials are not merely big news events. They advance ideology through myth,
using symbols and familiar narratives to shape our ideas about criminality.[2]

The Court as Spectacle

News organizations are heavily regulated in practical terms in exchange
for camera access to court facilities, making them highly dependent upon
the state's largesse. Photojournalistic practices are also interpretive, but
faith in the camera's accuracy usually overshadows the public's understanding of this construction process. The work is embodied, space-specific,
highly dependent on geophysical access, and therefore all the more vul-
nerable to manipulation by authorities. As Sparrow found with political
coverage, this dependency undermines the role of news as a watchdog and

Seeing Justice. Mary Angela Bock, Oxford University Press. © Oxford University Press 2021.
DOI: 10.1093/oso/9780190926977.003.0004

instead perpetuates the reassuring narrative that justice is being done.[3] What Altheide and Snow dubbed "media logic" shapes both the way these trials are covered and, in turn, how the criminal justice system operates in order to maintain the public's faith.[4]

Regulation of the visual press, specifically, controls the narratives that are constructed about trials, especially for television and online media, though not entirely. Even journalists who work with words alone are subject to the impact of camera access. Occasionally they work in "overflow" rooms and view only what comes through a video feed. They use the same mug shots and ask questions along with other reporters during perp walks. The rhythm of the news cycle affects all journalists, whether they wield a smartphone, a video camera, or a pen.

Journalists and the judiciary have long debated the merits of camera coverage inside courtrooms. The debate is complicated by competing constitutional principles, such the right to a fair trial and the rights of a free press. Much of the existing scholarship on cameras in the courts examines the American case, but this is a global issue that continues to evolve.[5]

Whether cameras are in the courtroom or not, however, visual journalists cover trials using a variety of representational strategies. Perp walks and mug shots, already staples for coverage, become even more important. When budgets allow, organizations might also rely on sketch artists, whose drawings constitute another theoretically rich set of texts. Such artists are also regulated by embodied gatekeeping and engage in grounded practices to visually interpret the criminal justice system, sometimes working from memory because they are banned from drawing inside the courtroom itself.[6] Sketches constitute their own kind of reality in that they are interpretive. The collection of sketches presented by Williams and Russell shows the rich history and artistry behind such interpretations.[7]

In this chapter, I focus on three "spectacular" recent court cases in the United States with an eye on how work practices contributed to the construction of narratives and, in turn, ideology. These narratives are both coherent, in Fisher's typology, and offer fidelity, a "point," which at the event level report on the details of a particular crime, but at the macro level reproduce the legitimacy of the criminal justice system. Moreover, viewers do not see trials, but instead *shows about trials*, products resulting from complex social, technological, and embodied interactions between media and the state. Based on on-site observations, interviews, and court documents, I argue that visual coverage is highly choreographed in ways that occlude justice in favor of drama, that coverage rules operate in ways that reproduce the system's legitimacy, and that the technical challenges of such coverage homogenizes rather than diversifies coverage.

Spectacular Reality

How might visual media overpower reality? Debord suggested that in a hypermediated society, experience is buried by spectacle.[8] Media coverage of major events can indeed render them larger than life. But how does this work? More importantly, what do these messages say? Recall the way Barthes offered a way to think about "myth": how the relationship between media and reality advances ideology in ways that are disconnected from that reality. His often-cited example described a young Black soldier saluting on the cover of *Paris Match* and the way this image conveyed a sense of patriotism while simultaneously occluding the racist realities of French society.[9] Key to Barthes's conception of myth is the way viewers are carried away by an image and the ideology it represents, forgetting or ignoring actual experience.

Barthes's concept of mythology, which holds that familiar symbols can provide shortcuts to ideological lessons, is also helpful for studying spectacular trials. Millions of Americans experience the justice system through their mediated coverage—which is to say that millions of Americans do *not* experience the justice system, but they do consume its symbolism. For many citizens, most of what they "know" about the justice system comes from entertainment and news media—its spectacle—and very little from direct experience. The mythmaking of spectacular trials depends on the journalistic routines, which in the United States have evolved from a back-and-forth relationship between the state and the press. Because camera access usually is not always considered part of the public record, the state quite literally holds the keys to the courts' visual representation.

Visual Court Coverage

American journalists and the judiciary have long debated the merits of camera coverage inside courtrooms. The debate is complicated by competing constitutional principles, such as the right to a fair trial and the rights of a free press. Case law concerning cameras usually balances the rights of the accused with the public's right to know. This project focuses on the American system, but the issue has been a matter of international debate.[10]

Every state in the United States has a different set of rules for camera coverage. California, Arizona, and Florida stand out for their open rules about cameras, which foster the proliferation of spectacular trials. The story of courtroom camera regulation usually starts with the Lindbergh baby trial, when Bruno Hauptman was on trial for murder in Flemington, New Jersey.[11] Hundreds of journalists crowded into the courthouse, and photographers took the brunt of the blame for disrupting the court, though subsequent research suggests there was plenty of bad behavior on the part of reporters and the visual press.[12] Nevertheless, the case inspired the American Bar Association's Canon 35, which banned cameras from courtrooms across the United States for decades.[13] A 1965 Supreme Court case effectively banned cameras in courtrooms based on the belief that visual coverage could violate a defendant's right to due process.[14] Fifteen years later, cameras returned to the courtroom when the justices clarified in *Chandler v. Florida* that the *Estes* case was not an outright ban.[15]

The role of cameras in the court regained prominence in 1994 during live coverage of the O. J. Simpson murder trial in California.[16] Today, most state court systems allow cameras in courtrooms, although a look at a resource maintained by the Radio Television Digital News Association shows that the rules vary widely.[17] Some states established relatively liberal camera rules, and others, such as Iowa and Texas, give judges case-by-case power over visual coverage. Federal courts, including the U.S. Supreme Court, continue to ban camera coverage in most instances.

Photography inside courtrooms is less interpretive but not entirely objective. When cameras are allowed, they are usually pool cameras (serving multiple news organizations) set in place ahead of proceedings and immoveable. One or more cameras might be allowed for a proceeding. Photographers are expected to be as quiet as possible and dress appropriately for court. Because the cameras cannot be moved, photographers are limited to the shots they can collect. For a live feed to a pool of many news organizations, the pool is generally expected to deliver a head-and-shoulders shot of the person on the witness stand whenever they are speaking and follow the action of other speakers as circumstances dictate. Courtroom photographers are generally instructed to never capture images of a jury. Just as importantly, institutions can take steps to control their own visual image, by engaging in embodied gatekeeping with visual journalists. Because cameras are considered to be such faithful documenters of reality, the regulation of photographers is rarely seen, debated, or discussed.

Three Cases

Three cases serve to inform this inquiry: the 2012 sexual abuse trial of Jerry Sandusky, the 2013 murder trial of George Zimmerman, and the 2017 retrial of Bill Cosby for sexual assault. Sandusky, who worked as a coach for the Penn State football program for thirty years, was tried for and convicted of child sexual assault in Bellefonte, Pennsylvania. Zimmerman, a town watch volunteer at the time, was accused of killing seventeen-year-old Trayvon Martin, in a case that heightened racial tensions in the United States. He was acquitted after a trial in Sanford, Florida. Bill Cosby was a highly successful comedian and actor accused of sexual abuse. His first trial ended in a mistrial; he was convicted of one instance and sentenced to prison after a second trial in Norristown, Pennsylvania. See Table 4.1 for details on the corpus and the dates of observation.

An analysis of the observation notes, interview transcripts, and courthouse documents reveals patterns of interaction between the various social actors involved in covering a spectacular trial. In each case, court officials and journalists negotiated elaborate rules for camera access to specific views of the event. Because camera coverage was heavily choreographed, the

Table 4.1 Observations and Interviews

Event	Location	Date
Sandusky Trial	Bellefonte, Pennsylvania	June 18, 2012
Sandusky Trial	Bellefonte, Pennsylvania	June 19, 2012
Phone Interview: Court Administrator		June 1, 2013
Zimmerman Trial	Sanford, Florida	June 6, 2013
Zimmerman Trial	Sanford, Florida	June 7, 2013
Zimmerman Trial	Sanford, Florida	June 8, 2013
Zimmerman Trial	Sanford, Florida	June 9, 2013
Zimmerman Trial	Sanford, Florida	June 10, 2013
Cosby Hearing	Norristown, Pennsylvania	August 22, 2017
Phone Interview: TV Photographer A		June 7, 2017
Phone Interview: TV Photographer B		June 13, 2017

visual journalists tended to shoot the same material. Pressure to gather certain scenes and produce content on constant deadline also caused the visual journalists to illustrate stories more than creatively cover them.

Choreography

In each of the three cases, camera access was negotiated between cooperative news organizations and court officials. The Pennsylvania Association of Broadcasters and the Pennsylvania News Media Association negotiated the rules for the Sandusky and Cosby cases. A confederation of news organizations from central Florida, formed to negotiate coverage of the Casey Anthony child murder trial in 2011, reconstituted to negotiate with Seminole County court administrators regarding the Zimmerman case. The coordinator for Seminole County said that working with experienced journalists made the process a little easier: "We basically have the same group of people that were able to come pretty fresh from that experience and y'know, as one of them joked, 'Get the band back together.'"

The chief engineer from WFTV in Orlando, Dave Sirak, worked for months with court administrators and media representatives to work out technical plans for covering the Zimmerman case. Once known as the "Mayor of Caseytown" for his role in planning the logistics for the Casey Anthony trial, Sirak's priority was equal access for all media outlets.

At least six months before the start of the trial, court administration reached out to the media and invited us to submit some ideas and some logistical plans that would ease the burden on everybody, including court admin and the media. Through a series of meetings with court administration and the local media outlets, we were able to map out a plan which accounted for video distribution, seating, and daily logistics of viewing the evidence and basically providing open access to all media outlets on a very organized level.

Logistics for the Zimmerman case were elaborate. Approximately half of the parking lot at the front of the courthouse was cordoned off for large satellite and production trucks. Stations and networks cooperated to pay for power to be supplied to the encampment, and spaces were assigned long in advance. Sirak used a Bingo cage to pull numbers for the spots. As Figure 4.1

Figure 4.1 Technical Challenges
Hundreds of feet of cable were needed to transmit a video signal from the
courtroom where George Zimmerman would be tied to a distribution point a
parking lot away. Fiber optic cable was planted underground, even underwater,
and tied to the same power system as the local traffic lights.
Credit: Photo by Dave Sirak
Used with permission from Dave Sirak

shows, the transmission cable was buried where possible, but moat around
the courthouse created a thorny challenge. An engineer from one of the local
stations who was in charge of technology was able to run a fiber optic cable,
which is not conductive, right through the water. Sirak and his colleagues

were mindful of the rise of new media, including blogs and citizen journalism websites that offered alternative perspectives:

> One thing I thought was very interesting, when you look at the Casey
> Anthony trial, the Casey Anthony trial started with Cindy Anthony making
> news by making comments about Casey Anthony's comments on MySpace.
> By the time we made it to the Zimmerman trial, MySpace was gone, and
> we were now in Facebook and Twitter. So now news elements were now
> moving in an entirely different sphere.

Many stations and networks erected temporary shelters for shade when
working outdoors. The humidity was so oppressive, however, that the
journalists worked inside the air-conditioned trucks as often as possible. The
heat was tough on equipment, too; I watched Sirak demonstrate to another
technician how to keep a light on in the feed trailer while keeping the door
shut, to allow the technician, as well as the machinery, to stay cool enough to
function. In the overflow lot, where I also parked, tourists walked through
the media camp to the annoyance of those working.

Journalists followed the system's rules to obtain the video and images
needed to construct their stories, and in many ways the system worked for
them because access was equalized and there was little chance of chaos. Their
needs, however, were secondary to the court's primary purpose, according to
the court liaison:

> The only thing that I'm responsible for is trying to maintain court decorum.
> The rest of it is up to the attorneys. But the planning and organization we've
> done is to make sure that we have a well-greased machine, that they are,
> um, ready, that they know the rules, that they're going to abide by the rules,
> and you know—the technology's there to serve them. To make it easier for
> them, and in turn that they're abiding by our administrative order.

The midday heat in Florida turned the media encampment into a virtual
ghost town, visited only by the occasional food delivery. In contrast, the mild
Pennsylvania weather in Bellefonte, where Jerry Sandusky's trial took place,
allowed hundreds of people to work outdoors for hours in what could only
be described as a festival atmosphere. In Bellefonte, a journalistic cooperative also arranged for electricity from a truck-sized generator and portable
toilets set up near the courthouse. Pennsylvania does not allow cameras in

courtrooms, and Bellefonte did not allow a camera into the courthouse at all. Photographers staffed the back of the courthouse for the arrivals and departures of key actors, and a sketch artist came outside once or twice a day to put her illustrations on an easel for paying stations to record.

The single-day Cosby hearing I observed did not have a tent city, but photographers still worked within strict guidelines about where to stand, both outside and inside. The rhythm of the news day could be charted simply by watching the cluster of photographers move from a sidewalk where Cosby arrived, to the courthouse door, to a plaza adjacent to the courthouse where attorneys gave their news conferences. One TV photographer described the arrangement for recording Cosby's arrival as a sort of cattle chute:

> They lined, like a ninety-degree angle that bordered the courthouse. This 90-degree barricaded lane where Cosby would get out on one leg of the "L," let's say, out of his car. Then he would come along a long handicap ramp that came along one half of the front of the courthouse. Along that ramp, and that little corner, that ninety-degree corner, there were crowd control barricades set up.

Photographers claimed space in two key sections of the barricades. One location was particularly valuable because Cosby would have to walk directly toward their lenses before making the turn, shown in Figure 4.2. Other photographers gathered at the barricades after the turn, for Cosby's walk along the front of the courthouse. As with the Sandusky case, the court used decorum orders to establish the ground rules for camera placement. Figure 4.3 presents one such order. Here are two rules for covering the Cosby case in 2018:

> 14. A pool camera operator for video footage and a pool photographer for still photographs will be permitted in two locations inside the Montgomery County Courthouse: (1) immediately outside of Courtroom A and (2) near the Swede Street entrance to the Courthouse. All other cameras are prohibited inside the Courthouse. The pool camera operators and the pool photographers will be selected by the PAB and PNA.
>
> 15. No news media interviews whatsoever shall be conducted in Courtroom A or the immediate vicinity of Courtroom A.

The penalty for violating these and other rules is temporary or permanent loss of access, which would render photographers completely unable

Figure 4.2 Choreography
Photographers wait for the arrival of Bill Cosby to the Montgomery County
Courthouse in Norristown, Pennsylvania. Note the variety of ladders, camera
rests, and footstools used to improve their access to the scene.
Credit: Mary Angela Bock

to work. I never observed photographers willfully disobey court rules. Small
transgressions, such as stepping over a line or bending over a barrier, did
occur and were usually corrected by security officers. Even the protesters
at Zimmerman's trial were never observed disobeying the rules and stayed
within their designated corral outside. I did witness transgressions of informal rules *between* photographers, as when a still photographer got into the
shot of someone who'd already claimed space in a scrum, prompting a loud
and angry rebuke.

Unified Action

Through formal rules, informal professional norms, and the physical struc-
turing of technology in space, photographers and the images they created
were tightly regulated. This is a victory for court officials whose job is to

IN THE COURT OF COMMON PLEAS OF MONTGOMERY COUNTY, PENNSYLVANIA
CRIMINAL DIVISION

COMMONWEALTH OF PENNSYLVANIA   CP-46-CR-3932-2016

VS

WILLIAM HENRY COSBY, JR.

DECORUM ORDER GOVERNING
SENTENCING

And now this 4th day of September 2018, after consultation with the District Court Administrator, the Montgomery County Sheriff, local law enforcement and the Administrative Office of Pennsylvania Courts the following Order is entered.

The terms of this Order apply to the conduct of the Sentencing scheduled to begin at 9:00 a.m. on September 24, 2018 in Courtroom A of the Montgomery County Courthouse, Norristown, PA. A satellite courtroom for the general public and reporters will be located in Courtroom C of the Montgomery County Courthouse, Norristown, PA.

The provisions noted as "Mandatory" shall be applied by the Court and enforced accordingly by its officers and agents. The provisions noted as "Informational" are intended to provide meaningful structure and guidance to those reporters and members of the general public who will be attending the Sentencing.

Figure 4.3 A Decorum Order from the Cosby Case
No permission needed; public record

maintain courtroom decorum and the image of the criminal justice system. Such a tightly calibrated system has another consequence, however, which is the homogenization of coverage. When everyone has to point in the same direction from the same spot, everyone collects essentially the same material, which in turn is used to tell the same basic story.

In the case of Jerry Sandusky's trial, shown in Figure 4.4, the staging outside the courthouse included a podium with a mult-box (a device that allows many participants to plug in a cable to transmit sound to their own recorder) in a central spot. Anyone who wished to address the press could simply walk up to this podium to speak. Certain attorneys who were comfortable talking to reporters did so more than once, likely knowing that the press corps is always hungry for, and grateful for, soundbites. Yet the size of the reporting crowd does not necessarily mean that multiple perspectives covered the case. For the most part, coverage overlapped and repeated itself, with only slight shades of difference, as when the sports reporters focused a bit more on the trial's impact on Penn State's football program.

Figure 4.4 Unified Action
Visual journalists vie for a view of the podium set up outside the courthouse in Bellefonte, Pennsylvania. Podium placement represents a cooperative effort between legal officials and journalists to regulate camera positions.
Credit: Mary Angela Bock

An anecdote from a photographer covering the Cosby case illustrates how a spectacle event causes visual journalists to work in unison. This TV photographer, working alone, missed a chance to talk to a lawyer leaving the courthouse, but realized the lawyer would eventually have to go back in, so the photographer waited:

> As he came back, I started to roll my camera and said, "Oh, you were saying before about how Mr. Cosby's doing. How is he?" He stopped and he started talking. He talked and he talked. I threw out a question and he talked. . . . Basically, suddenly the media swarm. He stepped closer and I was able to ask a couple questions. I thought, "Well, this is great." Eventually he said, "Okay. Thank you, folks," and he walked back in.

This paradox of multiple news outlets all telling essentially the same story is understandable because the event was so heavily preprogrammed. In such situations it is difficult if not impossible to put a creative mark or unique angle on the story. Instead of an ideological buffet with multiple perspectives, the viewer is left to choose between presenters and program graphic styles.

After a typical Florida afternoon storm that sent everyone into their trailers outside the Zimmerman courthouse, several correspondents and photographers gathered to socialize in the cooler air. I was not welcomed nor was I really shunned from the cluster of journalists gathered to talk about the day's events. I was, after all, an outsider—and a somewhat suspicious one at that because I carried a notebook and watched the people who prefer to do the watching. Finally I butted in and asked the big man on campus, a network correspondent, why everyone was doing the same story. His response was that "it doesn't matter" because people make their choice of what to watch based on the "stars" they prefer. Stars like him, it seems, are not worried about scooping the competition, for their following is based on personality.

Production for Its Own Sake

Media, as Altheide has explained, have their own logic that dictates which stories they choose to cover and how.[18] Because it is tied to the clock and must deliver content in real time, over time, broadcast news logic is both peculiar and unrelenting. Research notes from the third day of jury selection for the Zimmerman trial provide a description:

> It is 5:30 in the morning and the parking lot is humming with spotlights. Young reporters (no one appears to be over forty) are preparing to do live shots with the courthouse behind them. Some perform multiple "hits" during their morning shows, to report that essentially nothing has happened since the night before. It is oppressively humid, and the journalists retreat back into their air-conditioned trailers as often as they can. The researcher jokes with one TV reporter, a young man who appears to be in his twenties, about what the story will be today—the "media circus" story, the "impact on a small town" story, or the "how does jury selection work" story—or has he already finished all three of these? The young man laughs and shrugs knowingly. He knows he will have to have a package that day, but there is nothing to report. Meanwhile, the live shots around us continue, and the lights stay on, while about half a dozen reporters deliver live reports about—nothing.

Figure 4.5 Production of the Spectacle
A technician sets up staging for coverage in the parking lot of the Seminole
County Courthouse in Sanford, Florida. Stages are necessary to frame a reporter
and the courthouse without any other visual intrusions.
Credit: Mary Angela Bock

By "nothing," I mean that the trial had not yet started. The case was still
in the pretrial and jury selection phase. There was little to say, yet as seen in
Figure 4.5, the trucks were here, the stages were built, stations were investing
thousands of dollars daily to be on location—and there was time to fill. A television executive who was running a Florida newsroom at the time estimated
it cost him two thousand dollars per day for his out-of-town station to cover
the Zimmerman trial:

> It was the overtime, it was the meals, and it was the hotel expenses of sending
> someone to cover it. So, for an out-of-market station, within Florida a lot
> of people went, the cost really involved just probably one- or two-person
> crews. But for any station in Florida, that's, I'll say, significant cost. Not a
> major cost, but significant cost.

The number of live trucks, equipment, and people in Sanford represented millions of dollars in newsroom expenditures, as did the media camps outside the Sandusky and Cosby courtrooms. Once a newsroom has invested that much money on a story, content must be created, even if that content is essentially empty. Reporters outside wait for anyone connected to the case to stop outside and grant interviews, or more colloquially, "give them a soundbite." Visual journalists start shooting "whatever moves" out of boredom. The person who does give a soundbite outside a courthouse during long days of procedural calm can influence, if not control, the day's narrative. During the Zimmerman case, one photographer told me he'd been assigned for the full trial, which would run more than a month. He complained that there'll be "no creativity"—nothing but talking heads and scrum interviews.

This is not to say that visual journalists work mindlessly. Perhaps because of their training or perhaps because they are often face to face with the people they cover, the photographers observed and interviewed for this project tend to sympathize with the human condition. When asked about working in the hot sun during a long day outside a courthouse, this TV photographer became philosophical:

> We're documenting real life. With all of the tragedies and the scenarios that we see every day, we're taking pictures of people. We're documenting other people's experiences. If our experience exceeds what's going on that we're supposed to be documenting, then we're doing something wrong.

For that reason, he explained, he avoids conflict with other photographers in the scrum and takes measures to be comfortable enough on assignment to not let heat, hunger, or exhaustion interfere with his work. The Zimmerman case was spectacular in part because Florida has permissive camera-in-the-court rules. The former Florida executive said when cameras are not permitted, it changes the way newsrooms budget their resources: "I was working in the North during the Martha Stewart trials," he explained, "and there were not cameras in the court. And we did not put as much into it."

He noted that a major trial will be covered no matter what, of course, as borne out by the extraordinary media crowds at the Cosby and Sandusky cases. But in markets where cameras are allowed in the court, news organizations are more likely cover smaller cases or less critical moments:

The camera in the court plays more of a role in lesser trials. Trials that aren't as big of a name. I mean, some stations have a tendency, they go through a lot of criminal hearings. Arraignments, sometimes they'll even go to a hearing that has to do with, say, a motion that's been entered. Not very exciting, maybe not even that informative in terms of the case. But they're, "Oh, what if something happens? You don't wanna miss it, so we'll send a camera so we can just plug in."

The relative ease of shooting a story is a major factor in coverage decisions for visual journalism. TV news certainly covers stories without compelling visuals or an easily illustrated narrative, but given the constraints of resources and the limits of time, space, and the body, it is easy to see why crime and traffic accidents are so prevalent in broadcast news—and why some trials become spectacular when others do not.

Embodied Gatekeeping and the Spectacular

In the aggregate, what seem like small choices in practice create significant patterns. Decisions about where to place a mult-box, what supplies to bring to the field, or whether to stay low or stand on a ladder outside the courthouse defined the work of visual journalists covering spectacular trials. These daily choices, which affect the images that are created, and then the images that are chosen, supply the energy for the reproduction of ideology. A pool feed is not ideology—but the relationships it represents between court handlers, the justice system, and journalists foster a shared discourse about how a trial is supposed to appear. Standing outside for two hours to obtain ten seconds of a defendant walking by is not ideological, but the belief that this task is necessary fosters a shared sense of how the court system works. Taken together, the practices of visual coverage and logistics of embodied gatekeeping produce a metanarrative (or *myth* to use Barthes's nomenclature) that legitimates the criminal justice system while occluding its problems.

Visual Practice

Visual journalists cannot cover events without being on location. Gaining access requires that they interact with gatekeepers—in this case, court administrators. The various regulations and informal norms that control this process, what's been called "embodied gatekeeping," affect the nature of the resulting image. Gatekeepers have forever worked to protect the visual images of politicians for the sake of their individual authority, but embodied gatekeeping, in the realm of court coverage, shapes our ideas about the larger legal system. While this process is in play for any kind of visual news— whether politics, commerce, or feature stories—it is of critical importance for the public's view of justice, because this process shapes our very ideas about morality.

The grounded decisions of photographers covering these cases represent a cooperative endeavor with the state. Rules were negotiated and then followed in order to make sure journalists could collect visual story elements while the court maintained its decorum and, presumably, the defendants could receive a fair trial. The many individual decisions involved in these cooperative endeavors constitute a complex choreography, yet everyone knows what to do. Trials are always productions of a sort, but here the productions went meta.

Images in Narrative

Media present two levels of narrative when they cover trials. First, the news stories report the facts of the day, such as who took the witness stand, what was said in court, or what happened at the procedural level. In many ways, covering a court case is much like covering a sporting event, as there are two teams, rules to follow, and an eventual winner. Visual journalists who engage in this day-to-day coverage must collect specific materials for the daily stories. In the courtroom, visual journalists, whether they are shooting stills or video, must remain completely alert as long as court is in session, in order to make sure they record all testimony and turn their camera (when allowed) for significant reaction shots. The pressure to not miss any moment requires visual journalists to study the players in advance. The pressure is keenly felt, much as during a perp walk.

Significant moments in court are often fleeting and largely unremarkable visually. Trial writing becomes formulaic: the prosecution says one thing, the defense another, and a judge plays referee. Outside the courthouse, family members might provide emotional soundbites and attorneys might offer legal analysis. The images tend to consist of one talking head after another, until or unless an exhibit might be included. If cameras are not allowed in court, visual journalists will work with sketch artists (who usually charge each station or outlet for the use of their work) to shoot the sketches during court breaks. To break up the talking-head monotony, photographers work to capture participants in symbolic ways, wearing handcuffs, for instance, or carrying books. This collection of visual symbols becomes part of a trial's metanarrative, which reassures the public that the American judicial system is functioning and fair. Viewers see the "bad guys" led away in custody as Justicia stands tall in a churchlike building designed to cultivate faith in its authority. These images become part of a story about what is right, fair, and good, in keeping with Fisher's narrative paradigm.[19]

Court officials are invested in ensuring that the news audience maintains faith in the system, and image control is central to this objective. The system for covering spectacular trials exemplifies the ideological state apparatus that Althusser describes, with media and the government working in concert.[20] This is not to say that journalists are dupes, court administrators are tyrants, or the audience is ignorant. Instead, I argue that practical, everyday practices have unintended consequences for the public's understanding of how the system works, because in concert these practices advance the state's interests. The problem is that the news organizations rarely explain the constructed nature of visual coverage..

For the justice system to operate, a majority of citizens must have faith in its basic fairness, and so it must always appear in ways that are consistent with prevailing ideology. Consequently, the state endeavors to control the visual representation of criminal justice in order to establish its authority. Because of the way journalists worked closely with court officials in each case studied here, the court's legitimacy was never an issue; the focus instead was on the particular contest at hand and whether each defendant would win or lose.

Economics are part of the rules of this game, because most US news organizations are commercially supported and profit-driven. Add to this system the role of morality, our most basic beliefs about right and wrong, our desire for safety, and our fear of the other (however defined), and the result is a system that is simultaneously highly complex in the macro and viscerally simple at the individual level. Defendants are found guilty or not guilty. Perpetrators are seen or hidden. Victims are dead or alive. This ideological story is advanced by authorities who wish to maintain the public's faith in the law. Black people, nonbinary people, and LatinX people in the United States experience the law very differently, but their perspective is not centered in mass media narratives.

Homogenization and Myth

Finally, the consistency of coverage reinforces its ideological message. The incredible technological and economic investment necessary for news organizations to cover a spectacular trial mean that a broadcast schedule must be filled, even when there is little to say. The labyrinth of decorum orders, truck parking maps, and camera staging causes visual journalists to work in similar, not creatively unique ways. Rather than cover a story visually, they supply illustrations for formulaic stories. Their victories tend to be in the details, not in scoops or exceptional approaches to news.

This overturns the journalistic ideal of a marketplace of ideas, wherein the audience can pick, choose, and judge policy for themselves. Spectacular trial coverage gives them few choices beyond which stars they wish to see deliver the same headlines. Alternative views are presented only within certain guidelines, as narrative "also-rans," much like the corralled protesters outside the courthouse where Zimmerman was tried. David Sirak, the engineer who managed media for that case, was appropriately proud that small bloggers and alternative presses were able to tap into the same signal as other media and produce counternarratives. Mainstream coverage of each of the cases, though, were event-driven, with the macro issues of social inequality at the root of each case (abuse, racism, sexism) eclipsed by details of the legal proceedings.

Spectacular Trials as Routine

Covering a trial is not all that different than covering a football game. Visual journalists don't know who'll win the game, but they know how it's played and that certain key moments must be recorded. As explained in Chapter 1, because images are recontextualized into preconceived news stories, the work is largely a matter of routinized illustration. Visual journalists don't cover trials so much as they collect symbols: Bill Cosby being led away in handcuffs, Jerry Sandusky being escorted into a patrol car, George Zimmerman shaking hands with the defense team. Spectacular trial coverage is possible for the very reason that it is predictable and that all participants share a sense that what is supposed to happen will happen.

Coverage of spectacular trials is predetermined by ideology, as court administrators and visual journalists interact in embodied gatekeeping, regulating photographers' bodies in ways that manage the court's image. These practices in turn cause visual journalists to work together, rather than compete. Coverage rarely, if ever, reveals the cooperative mechanisms between journalists and the state to produce these *shows about trials*—cultivating, instead, camera naivete. Spectacular trial coverage puts Barthes in conversation with Jean Baudrillard and Guy Debord, as the resulting media stories *subsume* reality and themselves become shows.[21] The result is myth-making in action: a system of visual practice that supplies illustrations for a metanarrative that validates the justice system.

Each of these cases was itself unique. Zimmerman was tried for murder and acquitted. Sandusky was found guilty of sexually abusing children. The observations at the Cosby hearing took place prior to his eventual retrial, conviction, and sentencing. The little things noted in this chapter have larger implications for our understanding of the connection between practice, narrative, and ideology. None of the individual actions alone constitute ideology. Their aggregation is what matters, and the overall media discourse that results from interactions between court officers and journalists. Mass media are highly dependent on the image factory in order to attract viewers, and the decisions they make on the ground every day render a discourse that teaches us about the criminal justice system: identifying the "bad guys," honoring the good, and reproducing faith in the system. As with any human construction, however, this discourse is just one, incomplete rendering of the world, but one that is so highly prevalent, so often repeated in media, that it has dominated the public agenda—until now. New media—highly fragmented, technologically nimble, and more accessible—are producing counternarratives that cast doubt on the system's promise of justice for all. Everyday people now have the ability to use their smartphones to expose injustice and challenge the dominant discourse, although as the chapters ahead describe, these efforts demonstrate the limits of visual evidence as dramatically as its strengths.

5

What Picture Would They Use?

Scene: "Please don't use his mug shot." That was a plea from the public defender who was handling the case of Scott Demarco Newman, one of several men accused in connection with a horrifying shotgun murder of a local attorney in Des Moines, Iowa. It was 1985, and the first major trial I covered as a TV reporter. (This was long before the hashtag "whatphotowilltheyuse.") The attorney, now a law professor at Drake University, knew that potential jurors who saw Newman's mug shot would presume him to be guilty. Robert Rigg gave me access to his client's school portrait, which we incorporated into coverage.

Each photo shows the same young man. In the first, he is smiling, wearing a tie, his hair short and neat. In another, he's also wearing business clothes, though he is not smiling, and his eyes are focused out of frame. In the third—taken the night Brock Turner was arrested—his hair is mussed, he stares straight ahead with glassy eyes, and he is wearing a hoodie. Reporters tangled with two different police agencies for the release of this image and finally received it four days *after* Turner was sentenced to six months in prison. The short sentence—delivered because in Judge Aaron Persky's words, "A prison sentence would have a severe impact on [Turner]"—so angered activists that Persky was recalled and lost his seat.[1] Anger over the sentencing boiled over on social media, and as the case went viral, critics noticed that Turner's mug shot had not appeared in mainstream coverage.

The Turner case illustrates the significance of mug shots in discourses of criminality, and the way digital media can and have changed how images are recontextualized in the public sphere. This chapter examines the discourse surrounding Turner's mug shot and another highly publicized case involving the former governor of Texas, Rick Perry, as well as other controversial mug shot moments. These simple, unflattering headshots are modernity's scarlet letter, taking on significance far beyond the law

Seeing Justice. Mary Angela Bock, Oxford University Press. © Oxford University Press 2021.
DOI: 10.1093/oso/9780190926977.003.0005

enforcement catalog. Police mug shots are simultaneously the products of state power and illustrations of the way context subsumes depiction, as even the most aesthetically pleasing mug shot is discursively unflattering. Social media intensifies and accelerates the recontextualization of mug shots in narratives once monopolized by journalism. Digitization enables new recontextualizations by everyday social media users, outside the control of traditional media and the criminal justice system. Long a cheap staple of crime news coverage, the permanence of the digital archive has prompted some journalists to reconsider how and when mug shots ought to be published.

Mug Shots as Criminal Branding

Mug shots have been part of policing almost since the invention of the camera. The most famous early example of state use of photography comes from the barricades of Paris in 1871, when police used images to find and execute the communards.[2] Subsequent images of their bodies in coffins served as warnings to other would-be rebels. German police started collecting photos of criminals as early as the 1870s.[3] In 1891, French police administrator Alphonse Bertillon started the first scientific police lab and systematized the use of photos in the form of mug shots as they are known today.[4] Critical scholars have pointed out the way this photographic cataloguing of human beings constitutes a form of state power, control, and domination.[5]

Sekula elegantly argued that mug shots cannot be understood outside of their categorizing function, for without a classification system, the images are meaningless. Ellenbogen noted that Bertillon was initially overwhelmed by the challenge he first encountered: thousands of images of previously arrested criminals and no way to match them to suspects in new cases.[6] Bertillon was not the first to see the value of photography, but he was instrumental in harnessing it with a replicable system for organizing images and rendering them useful by attaching the photos to cards with a carefully selected set of physical measurements.[7] Mug shots and their visual brethren, wanted posters, have been studied not only for their policing functions but their aesthetics and commodification.[8] Using contemporary cases, this chapter builds on this rich body of work by examining the role of human practice in the way mug shots are contextualized, recontextualized, and occasionally subverted in today's digital discourse.

Human Classification

Photography was a tremendous gift to the Victorians' propensity to categorize humanity and advance their colonial sensibilities.[9] Bertillon was not alone in his impulse to employ the camera as a tool for science. Belief in the camera's indexical perfection meant that mug shots could be used as evidence of the deviance of others.[10] Lashmar described the overlap of criminal documentation and eugenics research that used photography as "proof" of the inferiority of Blacks, Native Americans, disabled people, and others.[11] Physiognomy and phrenology were considered scientific approaches that justified long-standing beliefs in a connection between appearance and character.[12] Photography's indexicality lent scientific authority to the classification of human beings for judicial, medical, and white supremacist ideology, because after all, a hierarchy of humanity built upon "science" could be morally justified.

This human cataloguing is also an aesthetic equalizer, rendering a sort of sameness to subjects. This aesthetic uniformity may be part of the cultural fascination with mug shots of celebrities, for in their case, the equalizing is a matter of pulling them down.[13] In the American frontier and days of prohibition, wanted posters and mug shots elevated certain criminals to legendary status.[14] In an evolutionary sense, the expressions of those depicted in mug shots might also hold fascination for viewers seeking cues in the faces of these debased others charged with crimes.[15]

While it is valuable to consider the myriad ways mug shots serve as disciplinary texts, it is essential to not lose sight that they are, essentially—like perp walks—a form of state violence. These specialized images are created by force and distributed for the purpose of reifying the law. Mug shots represent a form of embodied gatekeeping imposed on human beings in custody, whose bodies are subjected to criminal branding. Journalism's reliance on mug shots as free, easily obtained material for crime coverage deputizes them in service of the criminal justice system. Yet because photographs are considered harmless and accurate visual facts, a mug shot's technological assault is rarely acknowledged.

Mug Shots in the Digital Age

The relationship between mug shots and journalism started before photography, when newspapers would publish illustrations of escaped slaves.[16] Head shots distributed by law enforcement have been a routine component of crime coverage for more than a century, but only recently have discussions about the ethics of their use gone beyond the community of photo editors and visual scholars. *Time* magazine's use of a darkened image of O. J. Simpson in 1994 inspired public conversation about the ethics of photo illustration and the depiction of race in mass media, and the case remains part of the photo ethics canon.[17] The ethics of mug shot publication inspired a larger public conversation in 2012 after George Zimmerman killed Trayvon Martin. Memes online compared the fresh-faced school photo of Martin with his tough-guy selfies alongside Zimmerman's mug shot and his professional portrait. The online debate foreshadowed the Turner case for the way the images were repeatedly recontextualized at dizzying speeds, freed from the shackles of analog publishing and institutional editorial control.

The ease with which mug shots can be shared has spawned a small industry with websites such as mugshots.com, bustedmugshots.com and tabloid newspapers such as *Cellmates* or *Just Busted*.[18] Some sites are predatory, making money not from advertising but by charging individuals high fees to take down their mug shots.[19] Mug shot websites also raise concerns about privacy, public records, and the way the camera "captures" subjects beyond their embodied arrest.[20] Traditional newspapers regularly include mug shots in crime coverage, and some even publish them in online galleries.[21] Small wonder, then, that mug shots, like perp walks, are seen as their own punishment: a mark of shame for anyone arrested, no matter the circumstances of their case or the merits of the accusation.

Controlling Recontextualization

Even though prosumers may have a more powerful visual voice than ever, the state retains ultimate control of the display and recording of citizen bodies. An arrest means we are recorded, and while having our portrait taken is not physically invasive, it is narratively so. As soon as a person's image is made— decontextualized from its moment of conception—it can be recontextualized in narratives of crime, victimhood, adventure, or even, in the case of Jeremy Meeks (a particularly attractive man arrested for gun possession in 2014), supermodel stardom.[22] One way to understand this dynamic is to examine an exceptional case, in which the mug shot moment *subverts* the criminal narrative. It took a tremendously powerful person to do it: former Texas governor Rick Perry.

Rick Perry's Mug Shot Moment

In 2014 a dispute between then-governor Rick Perry and a local Texas district attorney boiled over into a criminal case. Perry's decision to pull funding from the state integrity unit, headed by Travis County Democrat Rosemary Lehmberg, sparked the first indictment against a sitting governor in Texas in nearly a century. Perry justified his action by the fact that Lehmberg had been convicted of driving while drunk and served time in jail for that offense. After Perry vetoed funding for the public integrity unit, a Travis County grand jury indicted Governor Perry for abusing official powers and coercing a public official.[23]

The political theater that ensued was everything the public expects from Texas, as Perry proclaimed not only his innocence but that he would do the same thing again. But Perry and his supporters and advisers raised the bar even higher for this sort of court drama with sophisticated control of the visual narrative. One week after the indictment, the governor entered the Travis County Courthouse to be booked on the charges and presented a performance that turned the usual crime story upside down.

Perry was indicted and booked in the course of eight days in August 2014. This case study involves a guided tour of the Travis County Courthouse booking area, interviews with journalists covering the event, and examples of newspaper and television coverage. Interviews were collected using a snowball sampling method and were conducted with institutional review board oversight. Television stories were collected from what was available online. Newspaper coverage (including online videos) was collected according to the time frame starting when Perry was indicted until the weekend after his booking, which ran from August 15 to August 24, 2014. The analysis included all online and print stories (in PDF form) from the *Dallas Morning News* (the state's largest paper) and the *Austin American Statesman* (the major newspaper for the city where the event occurred), and all online stories from the

Houston Chronicle, the second-largest paper in terms of circulation in Texas, for total of 345 items.

Coverage of the Perry indictment fits the usual tropes for political crime stories, with soundbites and quotes from the special prosecutor and Perry's defense team. Headlines focused on the news value of "unusualness" and the fact that a sitting governor had been charged with a crime for the first time since the turn of the previous century. Preliminary accounts were largely word stories focused on the indictment and its analysis. In contrast, the booking event presented a visual and audio banquet generously provided by Governor Perry and his aides.

The Indictment

The indictment of a sitting politician is big news—but often not a very visual event, and this indictment was handed up late on a Friday afternoon. Governor Perry did not respond directly that day, though representatives issued statements. Visual coverage centered upon the prosecutor Michael McCrum, who spoke to reporters in an impromptu session in the courthouse hallway, and TV reporters held printed copies of the indictment during their standups and live reports. Word-based coverage highlighted the historic nature of the event, details of the criminal accusation (including the fact that he faced prison), and the fact that he would be forced to have his mug shot taken. Print media used a traditional visual cue—the large, bold, front-page headline—to alert readers that this was a big story, metaphorically and upon the page.

The next day, Governor Perry met with reporters in his state capitol briefing room. Presumably having had a chance overnight to meet with his defense attorney, Perry issued a prepared statement and took a few questions during a session that lasted less than ten minutes. Photo coverage from the event included the well-dressed governor at a podium in front of the state seal. He referenced the video many Texans had already seen of Rosemary Lehmberg in custody while drunk, haggard, and belligerent, saying, "I think Americans and Texans who have seen this agree with me" about wanting her out of office. Some photos were published with a side view that included the scrum gathered in the room. Video coverage of the governor's statement was posted to multiple online story pages.

The governor's actions reflected his usual practice. One photojournalist with experience in the Texas statehouse explained that Perry's news appearances are typically tightly controlled:

> The only time we have access to Perry is when he makes a public appearance. You know that's usually a press conference or something at a podium. He may take a few questions on those remarks and then after that he is gone.

The following Monday, Perry's legal team took the stage at a news conference to announce an aggressive defense in terms of law and imagery. The leader of the team, Houston attorney Tony Buzbee, used a commanding voice and style to denounce the charges as a political attack. He and the other attorneys referred to the Lehmberg video three times, with the implication that the tape was evidence of Lehmberg's overall professional incompetence. Newspaper articles did point out in subsequent stories that Perry had not censured two other *Republican* prosecutors in Texas who'd been charged with drunk driving. The visual scenes of Lehmberg's night in a jail cell became her own crime, in a sense, beyond the DUI for which she'd already pleaded guilty and served time.

In the days between the indictment and the booking event, another visual was discussed extensively before it even existed: Perry's mug shot. Much in the way Buzbee used Lehmberg's video as a crime of its own, the governor's political opponents spoke of the *hypothetical* mug shot as evidence of a crime, even though Perry had not—and still has not, as of this writing—been convicted of anything. In straight news stories, journalists mentioned that the governor would be required to be booked and have his mug shot taken. A *Dallas Morning News* story quoted a former prosecutor cementing the theme of punishment before conviction, labeling the booking and mug shot events as "indignities associated with the process that [Perry] is going to have to endure."[24]

In blogs and commentary, journalistic discourse about the upcoming mug shot tended to be humorous, with puns about the governor going to "get mugged." A print feature, expanded in its online version with photos of the consultants, went so far as to give Perry advice on how to dress and smile for the photo. Experts weighed in on whether he should wear his glasses (part of his more serious second-round presidential campaign look) and how he should smile.[25] More than one columnist in Texas recalled the way former congressional leader Tom DeLay wore a tie and smiled for his mug shot, making it almost indistinguishable from a professional portrait.

One other story is worth noting here, a video report from a journalist who works for both the *Austin American Statesman* and one of the local television stations, KVUE. During the weekend after his indictment, Perry appeared for a live interview on the FOX network to denounce the charges, an appearance that received both straight and opinion newspaper coverage. Reporter Tony Plohetski somehow ascertained Perry's location for that live interview and managed to approach the governor in the public areas of an office building in order to conduct an impromptu interview in the elevator. Before he could even get a question out during this very limited opportunity, the governor smiled and asked, "How do I look?" Plohetski breathlessly responded, "You look good," and tried to ask a question, but before he could, the governor quipped, almost flirtatiously, "Oh, come on, you can give me better than that!" Plohetski managed to ask a couple of questions about the indictment, all the while following the governor down in the elevator, through the halls, and into his car, before security literally slams the car door shut between the governor and the microphone. Plohetski managed to say to the closed door, "Thank you very much."

Booking Day

While a governor's office normally issues news releases about daily activities, a defendant rarely issues a news release in advance of what is going to be a variation on the perp walk, but that's exactly what Perry's office did—and in plenty of time for media to gather at the Travis County Courthouse. One can report for booking with the Travis County Sheriff's Department after hours at the courthouse simply by knocking at the door and requesting to turn oneself in. Doing so in the dead of night is one option for a person who wants to avoid a public display. But in keeping with his aggressive public defense, Governor Perry did just the opposite, showing up during the day, organizing supporters to a rally, and sending a news release to announce his plans, upending the usual media ritual of a perp walk and, as shall be seen, the mug shot itself.

The event was organized for late on a Friday afternoon, allowing for live television coverage. With the help of Facebook to call supporters to the courthouse, Perry arrived not only for his booking but for a political rally and a speech complete with his own podium set up outside the court-house door. Hundreds of people were there, including dozens of reporters, photographers, and video journalists. The reporter for KVUE described the scene as a "media circus . . . the first time in one hundred years a sit-ting governor of Texas [has been] indicted on criminal charges." In research interviews, photojournalists also used the word "circus" in their description. A few anti-Perry demonstrators were in the crowd, notably one carrying a sign that read, "Nice mug shot criminal."

One newspaper photojournalist compared this event with every other major story he covered in Austin throughout the eleven years he spent in the area, "I couldn't recall ever seeing that many out-of-town photojournalists." Another defined the crowd as "a wall of photographers." A photojournalist for a weekly local said the scrum was comparable to those he'd seen for pres-idential campaigns. A TV reporter explained that the governor's decision to publicize the event was exactly opposite of what a typical criminal de-fendant does:

> Most people typically, when they're going into a courtroom, are ei-ther trying to avoid the cameras or letting their attorneys handle all the speaking. It's not usually as organized, so that was a little bit different for sure. I don't think I've covered anything where the defendant in a case has stood at a lectern and given a prepared speech.

Perry's declaration—"I'm here today because I believe in the rule of law. I'm here today because I did the right thing. I'm going to enter this courthouse today with my head held high, knowing that the actions I took were not only lawful and legal but right"—was featured multiple times in video coverage on TV and online, as was the background sound of supporters chanting, "Perry! Perry! Perry!"

The spokesman for the sheriff's office offered to escort the governor past security into the building, but the governor declined the offer. One inter-viewee heard Perry jovially tell the Travis County deputies, "I'm all yours," as he entered the courthouse. Video of his walk through the courthouse shows officers helping him move through the crowd of journalists, who yielded him space to stride through. Perry's stroll into the courthouse, facilitated and protected by uniformed officers, was also more like a celebrity greeting fans at a rope line. In his speech, he said he planned to walk in with his head held high. He did so, and the paper of record for Travis County used those very words to open its front-page story. One veteran photojournalist on the scene confirmed that the procedure was unusual and not a

> booking mug taken just like everybody else. . . . Because he is the governor and because he has an army of attorneys, they all shepherd him in and go through the process and get him, you know, in and out in that controlled fashion.

Perry can be seen smiling during the walk, acknowledging the crowd around him and the journalists giving him space. He never paused near the smaller scrum of photojournalists gathered in the lobby area outside the glass-walled booking room, controlling the space with his wall of lawyers and handlers, who tried to block cameras' views. One photojournalist described the dynamics of the situation as a "kind of cat-and-mouse game," and a colleague agreed that there was no mistaking the intent of the men standing along the window: "It was really obvious that they were intention-ally standing, I mean, they saw all of those cameras. They were intentionally standing in front of it, I think."

The spatial control that Perry and his team established pushed visual journalists to think outside the box in terms of the tools they used to cap-ture images. Journalists had to improvise on the spot and came up with a relatively unorthodox method to capture the scene when it became clear that their view of the mug shot moment might be obstructed:

> Like I said, it was kind of a frenzy. We're all trying to figure out "where should we put our GoPros?"[26] This and that. Someone from the inside came out and said you cannot attach anything to the window.
>
> We're like, "Oh, Okay," we're all scratching our heads. I just decided, okay, well, I'll just put it right down here at the—It has like a little shelf to that window, so it was wide enough for the GoPros to sit on that shelf.

In the end, the image that was widely used turned out to be a screengrab from one of those miniature video cameras, rolling automatically. One of the newspaper photojournalists said, "Despite having three photographers and two videographers, the image that made our front page was that from a GoPro camera." Even that was a matter of chance: if not for one member of the governor's entourage shifting his weight for mere seconds, the *Statesman* might not have had a photo of the "taking of" moment, when Perry literally has his back against a wall.

> That was actually . . . in retrospect, the value of running it as video. It was really just, now I can remember I was scrolling through—it was thirty frames a second. There was just really one frame that showed it.

Forced by circumstance to take a pose, the governor also chose how to perform for the camera. Because he wore a suit and tie and skipped his glasses, the Perry mug shot appears much like a professional portrait (see Figure 5.1). His expression is remarkable: a touch of a smile bordering on a smirk—not so extreme that he could be accused of disrespecting the court, but absolutely a nonverbal slap at the charge. Indeed, Perry displayed an almost flirtatious expression, rather than one of shame, anger, or resentment. The wry smile is one reflective of someone who just heard a joke—the joke, of course, being Perry's assessment of the charges against him.

A longtime Austin photographer said it's not clear whether the nonchalance was real or feigned, but the result made for good politics:

Figure 5.1 The Official Mug Shot of Texas Governor James Richard Perry
Credit: Travis County Sheriff's Department
Permission: public record/no permission necessary

He wasn't fazed at all, not at all. . . . I mean, I think that was part of it; he put on a good face for this, you know? I mean, he still insists he's innocent, right, so he was there like, "Hey, I've done nothing wrong. This is a joke" . . . He was smiling like this is a joke. That was his attitude. I think he believes it, too. I mean, I don't know. He was a good politician that way, a good actor, so it could be hard to tell.

Travis County mug shots are usually not released to the press for two weeks, but even here, the Perry booking was unusual. The sheriff's deputy in charge of public relations said that sometimes he'll speed things up; in his words, "I'll go through the hassle and get it" to help reporters. This was one of those cases, and since the governor's attorneys did not object to immediate release, the mug shot could be distributed to news organizations via email almost immediately.

Following his obligation inside, the governor returned to his podium outside to address the crowd again, then briskly left the courthouse plaza and all the TV reporters tethered to their live shots during the early evening newscasts. To underscore his nonchalance, Perry made one more visual move by Tweeting a smiling group portrait with his legal team outside an Austin ice cream stand. This image, along with the mug shot, appeared online and in TV coverage that evening, but the dominant visual of the day came from the rally: Perry looking magisterial at the podium, surrounded by a crowd of supporters. The primary oppositional interview came from the executive director of the Texas Democratic Party, Will Hailer, who included this remark while speaking to reporters: "Kids are going to go back to school next week and they're going to learn that their governor got a mug shot and was indicted the week before." The governor's pronouncements were the primary soundbites, and the sounds of supportive cheers were played repeatedly on TV and online. The paper version of the story, of course, did not appear until the next day.

Follow-Up

On the front page of the next day's *Austin American Statesman*, the lead sentence of the top story echoed the governor's words from the day before: "His head held high amid cheers," and included the GoPro shot (very large) as well as the mug shot itself (significantly smaller). The mug shot was a central concern for reporters before, during, and after the booking event, talked about ninety-two times, though it only appeared thirty-eight times. It was speculated about and used as a metaphor for shame before and after it existed, but coverage after the booking, when talking about this specific mug shot, was often laudatory. Online coverage used the mug shot more often, and two news outlets, the *Statesman* and the *Houston Chronicle*, posted a photo gallery of memes that users had created with the mug shot. Memes included an image of Perry wearing a cowboy hat, Groucho Marx nose-and-moustache glasses, and a side-by-side with Lehmberg's mug shot and the headline, "Rick Perry Wins."

That was the consensus from political comment writers, too, with headlines using phrases like "the mug shot heard 'round the world" and that the governor "knows how to say cheese." Online coverage included a link from the *Statesman* site to a *Wall Street Journal* video in which the presenter declares, "Believe it or not this is an actual mug shot," and noting his perfect hair and confident grin. One local columnist was a bit more derisive, calling Perry "Governor Good Hair," and another writer wryly pointed out that Perry would have to wear a buzz cut in prison. Print and online coverage also mentioned work by an artist with Republican sympathies, SABO, who created a mock wanted poster with Perry's image headlined by "Wanted for President 2016" and in a smaller font, "If looking good's a crime then I'm guilty baby." Photojournalists who covered Perry often were not surprised by his poise. "He tries to make friends with the journalists, even including the photographers," explained one. Another noted that Perry has "personable ability interacting with the public."

The glowing follow-up coverage contrasted sharply with the coverage leading up to the booking shot, which implied that the mug shot would be its own sort of punishment. This explains why the photo appeared only once in each of the printed versions of the *Statesman* and the *Dallas Morning News*. Even though the photo was flattering, the event was not. "It was only used because it was a newsworthy image that day," explained a photo editor, adding that no matter who is depicted, he avoids publishing images just to make a "cheap shot."

Interestingly, none of the coverage before, during, or after the event explicitly reminded the audience that a booking photo is not evidence of guilt. A TV reporter who covered the story said he hoped everyone knew this already:

I would hope that most people realize that it is simply a charge at that point. They have not been considered guilty, but I think the mug shot is the visual representation of that charge and of that first step in the criminal justice process.

By Thursday, the visual story had shifted to New Hampshire and Perry's campaigning there. The *Statesman* ran a photo of him speaking to supporters and using his iPhone to photograph a pig roast. Still, the mug shot got a mention from one New Hampshire voter—who said it didn't matter.

As might be expected, subsequent coverage included little commentary on the role of journalists in political theater. Also, Perry's performance was well reviewed, it was still covered as though it happened spontaneously. Yet key moments of the unfolding story were anything but spontaneous. Perry controlled camera access during the weekend before his booking; he was able to control when and how everyone gathered for a rally outside the courthouse, and he left journalists tethered to their live shots while he went for ice cream and tweeted about it. Each of these actions suggests a sophisticated awareness of how visual journalists operate. The photo editor remarked,

> Everything is so scripted now. . . . You have to be cognizant of that and careful of what you shoot. . . . Don't let them control the message and don't let them try to fake you out, although it's not just them. Everybody—once there's a camera present, the game changes. There's no such thing as an invisible camera, and you, yourself, if somebody was doing a story on you, you're aware of it.

A photojournalist who was there resisted using the word "manipulation" but acknowledged that the power to control a situation in time and space affects the resulting image:

> I mean, I don't really feel manipulated, but yeah, you have to work around things like podiums, wires, tripods—so that's not really manipulation, that's just the scene.
>
> Q: That's just time and space.
>
> Yeah, but it's manipulative in that, yeah, he decides when and where and what to say.

What about the public's awareness of the rules of engagement? A multimedia journalist succinctly said, "We work in it and we know it, but I don't think the public gets it at all."

A few stories and images revealed that process to the viewer. In a post to her newspaper's photo blog, a multimedia journalist reported on the challenges of working that day, the size of the scrum, and how good planning—and the GoPro—saved the day. A photo by one of her colleagues at the Saturday news conference revealed the extent of the scrum inside the governor's briefing room. And a columnist described being there when the governor walked in and winked at him in a way that brings home how strong the pull can be when a powerful person simply acknowledges you. But the "best" photos of the day did not include other cameras and other journalists, because a "good" shot is a clean one, and journalists are supposed stay out of the story. The governor set the stage, wrote the script, played his part well, and got good reviews for his performance—but almost no credit for his directing abilities.

Swimmer, Student, Rapist

Perry's mug shot started on the more conventional path of recontextualization presented in Chapter 1 (Figure 1.1), with considerable mediation on the part of traditional journalistic institutions. In contrast, the representations of Brock Turner are better illustrated by the more dynamic tornado model (Figure 1.2), as they were recontextualized thousands of times in shaming narratives. How did Turner's case, out of more than three hundred thousand rape or sexual assault cases that year, take on such notoriety?[27] Ironically, *delays* in the release of Turner's mug shot may be part of the reason he became a visual icon for rape culture. Turner's case represents a perfect storm of symbolism and online activism.

A Young Man with a Future

The Brock Turner case, after all, is not all that different from many other instances of campus sexual assault. Sadly, the crime for which he was convicted was not remarkable, as a person is sexually assaulted in the United States every ninety-two seconds or so, and women in college are three times as likely to experience "sexual assault through physical force, violence, or incapacitation."[28] Turner was charged after two other students witnessed him on top of the victim in January 2015. The *Fountain Hopper*, a Stanford University student news blog, first broke the story, which remained largely of local interest when Turner was tried and convicted in March 2016.[29] But the story went national and inspired outrage in June 2016 when, in spite of a prosecutor's recommendation for six years and an impassioned impact statement from the victim, Judge Aaron Persky sentenced Turner to six months in prison and ordered him to register as a sex offender for life.[30] The light sentence so enraged local activists that they embarked on an eventually successful effort to recall Judge Persky.[31] Turner served three months. Later, when he had to register as a sex offender, his mother blocked the cameras in a classic perp walk moment.[32]

Campus sexual assault was high on the public agenda at the time: the documentary *Hunting Ground* had been released in 2015, and Columbia student Emma Sulkowitz was still carrying a mattress to protest her university's response to sexual assault allegations.[33] Turner's trial also attracted national attention because of his athletic prominence: Turner was considered an Olympic hopeful, and he was labeled a "Stanford Swimmer" in some headlines. Mentions of his swimming prowess—and the use by news organizations of his swimming team headshot—was another target for criticism by feminists, who saw it as an example of patriarchal sympathy for assailants. The response from his family, including a letter that described the assault as a "few minutes of bad judgment," added heat to the fire, and the victim's decision to publicly release her impact statement sparked the eventual explosion.[34]

Finally, critics considered the fact that a mug shot was missing from coverage as another sign of white male privilege. Because police had not released his mug shot, news organizations circulated Turner's swim team portrait. His swimmer's portrait presents a smiling, fresh-faced young man who appears to have not a care in the world. The *Washington Post* characterized him as "baby-faced."[35] While normally this is exactly the sort of image a defense attorney would *want* journalists to use, it eventually inspired a backlash against both Turner and the way journalists covered his case.

Where's the Mug Shot?

Two days after Turner's June 2, 2016, sentencing, @smaheraja, a Chicago woman who works in the tech industry, tweeted back to the journalists at *New York Magazine*,

> @NYMag why did you post Brock Allen Turner's yearbook photo and not his mug shot in Dayna Evans' article?

On the phone with me years later, she explained why she took that action:

> I guess it just hit home, you know, that these guys just kind of don't live within the bounds of normalcy, or morality. They get to do what they want and then they're seen as people who have so much life ahead of them. So I think it was the story. And then combined with the idea of trying to take hold of and be more mindful that kind of made me tweet that.

Calls for the mug shot spread through Twitter over the next forty-eight hours. Another woman took on the *San Francisco Chronicle*, even posting a photo from the printed page, as seen in Figure 5.2, to suggest that publishing a photo of Turner swimming exemplified rape culture.

Figure 5.2 Tweeting against Rape Culture
Permission: publicly available Tweet

Social media critics blamed Turner's dual privilege of race and gender as they clamored to see him branded as a criminal. "How come every article I've seen about Brock Turner shows his swimming head shot, not his mug shot?" asked @thejaceyedpeas on June 6, 2016, adding in parentheses, "You know why." Another user put it this way:

> kv @slvrliningril 5 June 2016 Convicted rapist Brock Turner's mug shot? Oh that's right. He's an All-American boy-next-door athlete. His Stanford YB photo will suffice.

It's not that journalists were not trying to obtain the image; they were "howling" for it, in the words of one reporter. California multimedia journalist Diana Pritchard haggled with both the Stanford University Police Department and the Santa Clara County Sheriff's Department.

> I woke up in the morning, checking social media, saw a bunch of outrage, and my initial reaction to things are, "Well, why? Why is this an outrage and why is this happening?" I couldn't find an answer as to if anyone had asked for the mug shot before.[36]

The county sent her to the Stanford University police, who told her they didn't consider the mug shot a public record. She sent a copy of the public records law to the Santa Clara County (CA) Sheriff's Office, and the jail intake shot was released within a day. The Santa Clara County Sheriff's Office booking photo from the night of the crime, Figure 5.3, was released shortly thereafter.[37] Things happened quickly after that, and Rob Beschizza from Boing Boing says it was really a matter of "dumb luck" that he was able to publish the mug shot first on June 6:

> We got some of the social media benefits and general media benefits to being first to do something that people were very hungry to see, which you see the photo of him, obviously worse for the wear with bloodshot eyes. One of the things was, it looks like a white hoodie that he's wearing, but it's actually something they give you when they've taken your clothes off, because you're a rape suspect.

Recall the model for recontextualization in the digital age, and how the speed of sharing can resemble a tornado (see Figure 1.2). It's an apt metaphor for

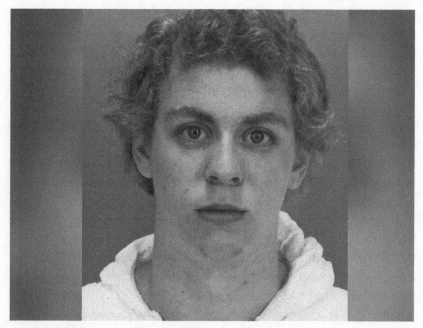

Figure 5.3 Brock Turner's Booking Photo
Credit: Santa Clara Sheriff's Office
Permission: public record/no permission necessary

what happened in Turner's case; his mug shot was uploaded to the internet, and anyone could and did share it—more than ten thousand times. Hundreds of them retweeted this sentiment:

> **Brock Turner's parents don't want his mug shot publicized, so I'm gonna help them out with that.**

Many posts and memes conflated the wishes of Turner's family with police and an amorphous "media" for their ire. Some of the criticism is a bit unfair, considering that journalists posted Turner's mug shot as soon as they had it. Plenty of other examples of inequality exist, however, as detailed by a Canadian public broadcasting journalist, who compared Turner's swim team headshot with the tearful, messy mug shot of a woman who'd recently been arrested for leaving her child in the car during a job interview.[38] O'Neil also included screenshots from the 2015 case of an Iowa news site that covered rape cases by star athletes, using yearbook photos for the white athletes and mug shots for the Black ones.

In 2017 Callie Marie Rennison and Mary Dodge, both full professors at the University of Colorado–Denver, used Turner's white hoodie–looking mug shot in their criminology textbook next to the definition of rape.[39] Subsequently, Rennison wrote an online essay explaining her decision to include the mug shot and in a passage discussed the way definitions of rape and sexual assault have shifted over time. "To see this memorialized in an academic textbook," she wrote, "even if Turner had eluded a just punishment— felt to many people like a step in the right direction."[40] Sage Publications later released a statement acknowledging that California's statute does not use the word "rape," and that Turner was convicted of felony sexual assault. Subsequent editions of the book will reflect an edit.[41]

A woman who goes by @Sarah, who said she grew up around young men like Turner, underscored the importance of seeing Turner in a criminal frame. "When I just read the details of how the rape happened, it was so vile," she explained, "and so I think he should absolutely be represented as a person who did a vile thing, and nothing more or less."

When Turner's case is compared with Perry's, the roles of embodied gate-keeping and media logic become clear. In both cases, powerful forces controlled the creation and release of these mug shots, and in both cases, news practices perpetuated hegemonic discourse until, in Turner's case, public demand for a criminalizing image reached a fever pitch. Turner had virtually no control over the way he would be photographed for his mug shot the night he was arrested; his body was subject to the state's will. Perry similarly had to capitulate to the state's habeas corpus rules, but because he was able to exercise power over time, place, and his own embodied performance, the news audience saw not a penitent, but a cool, confident cavalier controlling his fate. When he had to appear in public for what's historically a walk of shame, Perry threw a party. Turner continues to duck cameras every time he is required to appear for a court event.[42]

#whatpicturewouldtheyuse

In 2014 the hashtag #whatpicturewouldtheyuse spread across social media as Twitter users, many of them Black Twitter users, discussed the way media can incriminate simply by choosing one portrait over another. Several images of Michael Brown, whose death at the hands of Ferguson, Missouri, police sparked unrest in 2014, competed for attention, each with its own implication on his character: a graduation photo complete with his mortarboard, a candid with him wearing "Beats" headphones, and a still frame from a convenience store video that showed Brown apparently assaulting a store owner.

While the #whatpicturewouldtheyuse hashtag inspired a spirited discussion online about mug shots and context, not everyone was paying attention. That same year, TV news coverage of a trial in Austin used a mug shot for the man accused of killing a police officer and a portrait of the officer with the American flag behind him.[43] A similar case occurred in Cincinnati in 2015, when news organizations used a mug shot to depict Sam DuBose after he was shot and killed by a campus police officer—who was depicted with his professional portrait.[44] In 2017, video of teenagers mocking Jamel Dunn, who was Black, as he drowned in a Cocoa, Florida, pond shocked news audiences.[45] *Time* magazine's website published the story with a mug shot of Dunn, though in this case he was not a criminal but a victim.[46] Subsequent coverage used a casual snapshot of him from a GoFundMe page, so it is likely that news organizations used the publicly available mug shot for the sake of immediate convenience. Nevertheless, especially for Black Americans who wonder "what picture will they use," the image represented another layer of insult.

Prior to the Brown discussion, social media users debated which pictures fairly represented George Zimmerman and the teenager he killed, Trayvon Martin. Zimmerman is wearing a track suit and not smiling in the mug shot taken the night of his arrest. A second image shows some cuts and blood on the back of his head. For his professional, LinkedIn-worthy image, Zimmerman is smiling and wearing a suit and tie. There is no mug shot of Trayvon Martin. The seventeen-year-old did not have a criminal record.[47] He did, however, take selfies in a hoodie and posed to look like a tough guy. This image was frequently held up on social media next a youthful, smiling school photo of Martin, by critics who were offended by efforts to portray Martin as an innocent child.

Which of any of these images is true? Which is a fact? Which is fair? The problem for journalists, who trade in facts, is that any photograph that has not been manipulated is only a type of fact. It represents the light waves that beamed through an optical system onto a digital sensor in a particular place and time. A photo's indexicality is its fact—but this fact is not a photograph's *meaning*. As Sekula has asserted, "Every photographic image is a sign, above all, *of someone's investment in the sending of a message*" (italics added).[48]

Journalists may strive for objectivity, and the indexical fact of a photo is objective. But because a photograph's meaning relies on layers of context, a photo cannot be interpreted objectively. So all photographs of Zimmerman, Brown, Martin, Perry, and Turner are indexical facts, while at the same time *none* have an objective meaning. The moment the photo is created in the context of a mug shot, that photo is a subjective representation, one that brands the person as criminal—even when they are victims of a crime, as in the Dunn drowning case, or untried, as with Perry.

Digital Wildfires

The wild card in the #whatpicturewouldtheyuse hashtag is the pronoun "they." Because mug shots are considered public records in many jurisdictions, they've been a reliable source of imagery for crime and court coverage. But journalists no longer control the contextualization of images, which means, as the Turner case illustrates, anyone can publish and share a mug shot, even in ways that confuse the facts. Indeed, online arguments about what picture they would use are empowered by the easy transport of digital images. One of the upsides of social media is the way everyday users are able to craft counternarratives and challenge media practices.

On the other hand, the freewheeling nature of social media means that the discussion is not always going to be fair, ethical, or beneficial to the public sphere. The Turner case exemplifies both sides of this coin, as critics advanced the discussion of how mug shots are and ought to be used in media, while also occasionally mixing fact with conjecture and confusion. These images are not likely to ever disappear, either. Online images may spread like wildfire, but they don't burn to ashes. Instead, they remain online forever in all manner of recontextualizations: fair, unfair, accurate, and not.

Consider one more case: sad, strange, prurient, and widely shared—the story of the former superintendent of the Kenilworth Public Schools in New Jersey, Thomas Tramaglini. After human feces was found "almost daily" on Holmdel High School's athletic fields, Tramaglini was caught on surveillance video and charged with lewdness, littering, and public defecation.[49] A distance runner who suffered from "runner's diarrhea," Tramaglini was dubbed the "super pooper" in the tabloids. Tramaglini lost his job and pleaded guilty to one charge of public defecation; the other charges were dropped.[50] He subsequently sued the Holmdel, New Jersey, police, claiming he was improperly arrested and photographed; that he was cited, not charged with a criminal act; and that the image was improperly leaked to journalists.[51] Most people won't know his name, but they will remember his case. Most likely, thanks to visual primacy, they will also remember his face, and "super pooper" will come up any time someone searches for his name.

Brock Turner is a convicted rapist, and now he is one of the most famous convicted rapists in the world, due to the sharing and resharing of his mug shot on social media. While he is hardly a sympathetic character, it is worth asking whether it is fair that he literally became (for a time) the dictionary illustration for a rapist, not because he is not guilty but because he is only one of such a very large crowd.[52] The efforts of his family, lawyers, and other supporters to shield him from public scrutiny backfired in spectacular fashion. This time the victim refused to be quiet, and the online community responded by showing the rest of the world her attacker's mug shot. Like a colonial malefactor put in stocks in the town square, Turner was publicly shamed on Twitter, one passerby at a time.

Which Picture Should Be Used?

Bertillon was not interested in photography for its aesthetic dimension; in fact, he sought to minimize a portrait's potential to capture an individual's personality.[53] The system he designed was intended to quickly locate images in a database and to cross-check the identities of individuals with criminal records and the living, breathing human beings arrested each day. Yet mug shots are hardly "neutral," because they are part of a criminal archive; once they are taken, they are recontextualized as *portraits of criminals*. Now that these branded portraits can travel the internet permanently, some journalists have started to question their use in galleries or other police blotter–style postings. Moreover, news organizations crave images, and obtaining a picture of some kind, any kind, is essential, especially for online and TV news. In the analog age, this meant looking for yearbook photos, calling a grieving family, or visiting the police station to record a print from the archives. Today, an image can be posted online instantly and shared thousands more times as quickly with the tap of "retweet" retweet."

Consequently, some news leaders are starting to ask not "What picture will we use," but what picture *should* they use? One editor told the *Columbia Journalism Review*, a trade publication for journalists, "You're really preying

on human suffering there, and I don't think that's what we should do."[54]
In 2019 the news department at Florida's WTXL TV station announced it
would no longer publish mug shot galleries online, though it would continue
to use relevant mug shots for certain stories.[55] Matt Brown, the station's general manager, issued a statement explaining the new policy as it evolved
after an internal discussion about ethics, news values, and community service. In his words,

> The conclusion we arrived at is this: The booking reports only offer a small
> slice of a story, and we should no longer publish them because:
>   - We are not providing further context.
>   - We are not updating the stories when the facts evolve.
>   - We are pandering to lurid curiosity—that same desire that triggers
> rubbernecking at crash scenes.
>   - We are not showing compassion for those who are affected by news
> coverage.[56]

WTXL's decision came in the wake of a similar move by a trio of newspapers
in the McClatchy group. A group editor decided that those papers would no
longer post mug shot galleries, even though they received a lot of traffic. The
editor directed his newsrooms to focus less on low-level, nonviolent crime
and more on the kind of enterprise stories that affect a community:

> Basically, I wanted to go in two different directions, more of two different
> things. One, more enterprise reporting, accountability journalism, high-
> impact journalism. That obviously takes time, and there is a limited amount
> of it a small staff can do. But I also want them to juggle and add more service
> journalism, more news people can use.[57]

The decision in the McClatchy group was also based on the way mug shots
live forever on the internet. An editor for one midsize city daily said he took
many calls from people who had trouble getting jobs after their image, was
posted in the online gallery. The new policy is only for galleries, though, not
general news coverage.

> We would still cover a perp walk. Just to be clear, because I've had some
> people call me out on Twitter. We did not say that we would never run a

mug shot. If someone is arrested, we run a story, we still run the mug shot in the paper, and we still run it online. What I said we wouldn't do is just what I indicated earlier, which was stories that generally are not important enough for us to write a story. We weren't just going to do the gallery of mug shots that we had been doing in the past.

Missing from these early conversations was the way people of color have been especially harmed by the use of mug shots. News organizations have displayed mug shots of Black people even when they are victims, as in the case of Sam DuBose, who was shot by a University of Cincinnati police officer.[58] It is long past time for news organizations to take seriously the symbolic impact of mug shots and take greater care in their recontextualization into criminal justice narratives.

"Please don't use his mug shot"—the plea from the defense attorney convinced me as a young reporter of image context. Before a person is found guilty, it makes sense for journalists to avoid criminally branding a person. After a person is found guilty, as with the Turner case, publishing a mug shot seems fair—even though images live indefinitely in digital media in ways that printed photos do not. Because of the victim's refusal to remain silent and the political climate in which he was convicted, Turner will spend the rest of his life as an embodied symbol of rape culture.

Perry's deft subversion of what was supposed to be a humiliating moment is an exceptional case that proves the rule for the way mug shots operate culturally. There was no question in this instance about what picture they will use, and so the governor used his interpersonal, political, legal, and financial power to neutralize the event. Perry had another advantage for controlling his visual narrative that day and beyond, for news organizations had plenty of other images of him. As the large-daily editor noted, there is no need to use that mug shot outside of that day's news of the case. But what of the everyday citizen?

The young Black man accused of murder in Des Moines so many years ago had none of that; he only had a public defender pleading for visual mercy. Few people who are arrested have even that much. Once the image is made, whether the defendant is drunk, scared, disheveled, or dapper, it is a matter of public record, which means it can be recontextualized in an infinite number of ways—usually negative, unless you are a classically handsome, sitting governor.

6

What's So Special about Video?

Scene: Most of what you can see are moving arms. Arms waving up, then around. The top of a child's head is in frame, then moving pavement, feet, more pavement, and motion. Only very briefly do we see a basketball in frame—our clue that a police officer is playing with some neighborhood children.

There was a time in the history of TV news when carrying a video camera gave a person the aura of a shaman, the effect was so magical. A TV camera's presence changed the way people behaved—frightening some, sending others for cover, and inciting many to clown around (which is why TV journalists still occasionally call cameras an "asshole magnet"). During this era, cameras were about thirty pounds, and they needed a tape deck that weighed another twenty or thirty pounds. They were awkward and enormous, and the lights they needed at night announced their presence like a luminal loudspeaker. I knew the technology was shrinking over time, but I never imagined the day when someone could put a video camera in their pocket.

Recording a video is no longer the magic it once was, but there is still power in the act, especially in the legal realm. The slang phrase "Pics or it didn't happen" assumes that everyone can and will record events around them. This has changed news practices as journalists, much like police before them, will automatically ask sources whether video of an event exists. Yet just as the recording and sharing of everyday video reached epic levels on social media, a new threat to the camera's authority has emerged: "deep fakes," altered videos that deceive while appearing realistic. Deep fake technology was introduced to the wider public by filmmaker Jordan Peele in 2018.[1] Peele used his own voice, impersonating former Barack Obama, in a fabricated video that makes it appear as though the former president said such things as, "President Trump is a total and complete dipshit."[2]

Digital media experts are already working on technologies to ferret out deep fakes.[3] Similar digital forensics are already in use for detecting still image manipulation.[4] Political observers worry that deep fake videos could

Seeing Justice. Mary Angela Bock, Oxford University Press. © Oxford University Press 2021.
DOI: 10.1093/oso/9780190926977.003.0006

intensify the effects of deceptive postings online, the sort of genuinely "fake news" that serves propagandists and manipulates elections.[5] Without downplaying concerns about deep fakes, as they play to everything that is cognitively powerful about the visual after all, it is important to remember that still photographs have been manipulated for nearly as long as photography has existed, and that confirmation bias—the human propensity to trust messages that align with our preexisting beliefs—may actually be a more formidable adversary to democratic discourse online.[6]

This chapter shifts away from studying the way media construct visual messages in cooperation with authorities for a more theoretical discussion of video's discursive affordance; its epistemological value as testimony; and how, even in this era of deep fakes, video might still serve the interests of justice. Central to this chapter is a case study of a criminal court case in which video was essential to the testimony. The case illustrates the way photography operates as an affordance of a system of discourse and social interaction in pursuit of the facts, and how while the technological veracity of any photographic or video image matters, it is not *all* that matters. The human processes of creating, showing, and explaining with video, as well as the institutional structures in place that control such practices, all contribute to its documentary value. For instance, and this proves even more critical in subsequent chapters, video may record a scene perfectly, but the visual output remains useless if social structures prevent it from being seen. Who controls the camera? Who controls how the video is recontextualized and narrativized? Video draws more power from the human beings who wield it than technological affordances.

Visual Evidence in the Courts

The goal of citizen witnessing is to produce evidence—whether informally, to show what it is like to, as the hashtag says, "exist while Black" in the United States, or in an official capacity, as forensic proof in a court of law. Photographs and film have a long and complicated history as evidence in the US courts. The legal community quickly embraced images; they became accepted as evidence within twenty years of photography's invention and were common by the 1870s.[7] As legal historical Jennifer Mnookin put it, "Photography was recognized, almost from the time of its invention, as a potentially powerful juridical tool—perhaps even a dangerously powerful tool."[8] Mnookin further explained that while the index and construction debate started as soon as photographs were introduced as evidence, judges quickly seized upon the "illustration" as an analogy for photographs and their interpretation.[9]

Eventually, photographs came to be considered as evidence as long as they were attached to witness testimony.[10] Today, the rules for admitting a photo as evidence generally require that a witness (1) is familiar with the scene (or object), (2) be able to explain why they are familiar with the scene, (3) recognizes the scene in the photograph, and (4) attests that the photo is a "fair" or "accurate" depiction of the scene at the time in question.[11] The rules that emerged regarding image testimony, therefore, favor the traditional logocentrism of legal practice; more plainly: in court, images are servants to words.

More specifically, images used in a courtroom are servants to a very particular arrangement of words: narrative. Chapter 1 presented the essentials of Walter Fisher's narrative paradigm, which posits that humans are persuaded by stories that have coherence (they have to make sense) and fidelity (they feel morally "true").[12] In this sense, narratives convey arguments about what is good and right through what is more commonly called the "moral of the story." Many fields outside of rhetoric and literature have adopted Fisher's paradigm, including two that are pertinent to this study: journalism and law. Journalism scholars have used the narrative paradigm to explain how and why certain kinds of news stories appear repeatedly, and how they advance ideology.[13]

In an adversarial trial system, attorneys must blend the facts they have in common into the world of human frailty, motive, and emotion in order to present competing stories of what happened. Legal scholars have drawn from the narrative paradigm to show how competing versions of events—that is, narratives built from a set of facts—operate in a courtroom and compete for juror acceptance.[14] In *A Theory of the Trial*, for instance, Burns invoked the spirit of Fisher's characteristics of coherence and fidelity when he wrote, "It is through narrative that we remember, and the internal characteristics of a given narrative contribute significantly to its concrete plausibility."[15] Bennett studied dozens of court cases and used experimental methods to investigate what makes a courtroom story believable, finding a connection between structural ambiguity and juror skepticism.[16] That is, a story that "hangs together" without gaps (Fisher's coherence) strikes an audience as more truthful than one with holes in it, regardless of the details of legal facticity. Rideout's legal analysis breaks coherence into two parts, consistency and completeness, and connects the notion of fidelity to the normative elements of judicial persuasion.[17] He proposed an additional narrative dimension relevant to this study of courtroom video, "correspondence," representing the way a story's elements connect to the world outside of it, evoking the semiotic notion of indexicality.[18]

Motion pictures posed a new challenge for the courts. Judges were challenged by film in the early twentieth century on competing fronts.[19] On one side, the legal community considered movies to be culturally inferior entertainment inappropriate for court, and at the same time, jurists feared that the indexical strength of a film could overpower other types of evidence.[20] Rules for evidentiary film developed during the 1920s, and by mid-century the rules were similar to those for photos, in that they had to be authenticated and incorporated into witness testimony.[21] Today the courts contend with more than film, as attorneys use PowerPoint files, animated reenactments, and other types of audiovisual presentations to persuade juries.[22]

While the evidentiary rules are somewhat similar, video and still images operate very differently in narrative. Video combines camera images, audio, and its own embedded narrative: a timeline. This timeline can provide an additional tool for digital investigation as well as a natural narrative. Film has always had an implied timeline, of course, but raw video has one that is distinct and embedded into the recorded signal. Moreover, film was never as easily available as video is today. How might these new digital "texts" help prosecutors and defense attorneys craft competing narratives for the sake of a jury? How might video impart credibility to testimony from individuals on the witness stand? More succinctly, what role does video play in judicial narratives?

Testifying *about* and *with* Video

The case at the center of this chapter involved four clips of video submitted as evidence in a misdemeanor trial. The analysis describes the way video was talked *about*, testified *with*, and through an uninterrupted timeline, occasionally *spoke for itself* as it depicted a sequence of events. That is, when placed in temporal context, video (like film) constitutes a unique form of demonstrative evidence. Temporal context is the key: consider the way defense attorneys pulled individual scenes from the Rodney King beating video out of temporal context, resulting in acquittal for the officers involved.[23]

The analysis advances the application of the narrative paradigm in the legal setting and the affordance of video in metanarratives of justice; the ways video is incorporated into competing case narrative constructions; and the way its timeline structure establishes narrative coherence. Echoing Foucault's argument that "truth" is negotiated, this chapter demonstrates that video cannot, by itself, convey the moral of its own story.[24] Fidelity, the "point" of the story, remains the discursive job of human actors in the justice system.

As smartphone video on the web proliferates, it is useful to understand its narrative requirements, limits, and potential. This case exemplified the way multiple angles and storytelling can be harnessed by state authorities and interrogated by the less powerful. The right of everyday citizens to film the activities of police and government authorities, therefore, is essential to establishing a balance of power. Video's contribution to narrative means that its production is likely to be a matter of considerable concern and controversy for years to come.

The Scene

The case at the center of this study involves an Austin, Texas, man, Antonio Buehler, who was arrested after an altercation with a police officer on January 1, 2012. Buehler, a West Point and Stanford graduate and Iraq War veteran, was on his way home from celebrating New Year's Eve with a friend when they stopped to fuel their vehicle at a convenience store and witnessed a drunk driving investigation in progress. A woman who was originally not under arrest (Norma Pizana) was pulled from her car by officers and started crying out to bystanders to "film this." Buehler did so, taking stills with his camera because he couldn't get the video function to work. He also shouted at police when he saw what he considered to be overly aggressive tactics being used against the woman. One of the officers confronted Buehler and eventually arrested him for public intoxication, assault (for allegedly spitting on the officer), interference, and refusing to obey a lawful order.

Buehler's case made headlines in Austin after it was learned that a bystander had filmed the incident from across the street—which seemed to support Buehler's version of the event. In the months that followed, Buehler would start the Peaceful Streets Project, a police accountability activist organization that (among other activities) regularly patrolled city streets and filmed police activity. Eventually all charges except the misdemeanor of failing to obey a lawful order were dropped, and Buehler opted to go to trial on that charge—alleging that the only reason he was charged in the first place was that he had been photographing police activity on the night in question.

The Clips

Four pieces of video would be used in the trial: the bystander's clip of the incident, two so-called dashcam clips from the police department, and tape from a rooftop surveillance camera at the convenience store. The bystander's clip was incorporated into news stories by television and newspaper journalists before the trial; the police dashcam clips and the 7-Eleven surveillance video were not available to the public until the trial.

The right to film police action has become a contentious issue in the United States in recent years as smartphone proliferation has made it easier to record events and share clips online. The next chapter is devoted to the way police accountability groups have harnessed the power of video. Dozens of websites are devoted to so-called cop-watching, and a number of groups in the United States now regularly patrol high-incidence areas in order to monitor police activity.[25] Buehler, the man at the center of this case, started the Peaceful Streets Project because bystander video made a difference in his criminal defense and Buehler contended that he was targeted for using his camera during the incident.

This case study is based on participant observation in the courtroom augmented by interviews with participants, the trial's audio transcript, news stories about the case, and other documents. Table 6.1 lists the videos and their key elements. The trial was held in October 2014 in the municipal court facilities adjacent to the Austin Police Department. A member of the

Table 6.1 Videos Offered into Evidence

Clip	What Is Seen	What is heard:
Dashcam from Officer Oborski	Hill's arrest	Buehler and officers arguing
Dashcam from Officer 2	Pizana in backseat	Buehler and officers arguing
7-Eleven Surveillance video	Parking lot	No audio
Bystander Smartphone	Altercation	Buehler shouting

research team was in the courtroom for every hour of the four-day trial. We took notes by hand, discussed our observations, retyped key portions of the notebooks, and reviewed the notes to look for themes related to narrative, video, cameras, credibility, and authority.

A Misdemeanor Jury Trial

Police tested Buehler's blood alcohol content in the field, but the test rendered a zero repeatedly, and he was not formally charged with public intoxication. He was taken into custody on other charges, including two felonies: "interference with a police officer" and "resisting arrest," both of which were nullified by a grand jury. The charge that remained, "failure to obey a lawful order," is a Class C misdemeanor in Texas, which puts it in the same category as city ordinance and (nonparking) traffic violations. He was accused of refusing to put his arms behind his back when instructed by an officer during the events of January 1, 2013. Buehler faced a maximum fine of five hundred dollars; no jail time was at stake. Under Texas law he had the right to, and opted for, a jury trial as a matter of principle.

The power of cameras was acknowledged even before the trial started, as those arriving were greeted with a sign on the courtroom door prohibiting photography and video and audio recording. Before calling court to order, the judge warned members of the gallery that recording of any kind, audio or photographic, would not be allowed (though after requests from spectators and journalists, this prohibition was suspended during breaks). Throughout the case, photographs and video were referenced, displayed, created, and shared by participants. As expected, these participants talked about video as they crafted stories for the jury, and it served a documentary function for witnesses when they testified. Significantly, it also occasionally spoke for itself.

Talking about Video

Even before the jury was empaneled, video evidence was part of the courtroom process, and, indeed, delayed the proceedings. The presiding judge, Mitchell Solomon, called court into session at 8:37 a.m., and videos were offered into evidence three minutes later. Soon a courthouse employee arrived to set up a video playback system and immediately encountered technical problems because the prosecutor's computer wouldn't play a DVD. Defense attorney Millie Thompson and Buehler vacated the defense table temporarily so that software updates could be completed on their computer to allow video evidence to be played and projected, and one of the clips was briefly played as a test. Attorneys and the judge worked out a system by which the court clerk would have physical control of a switch that allowed the projector to be controlled by either the defense or prosecution tables.

The significance of the specific video clips in this case was first talked about in open court during jury selection. Defense attorney Thompson spoke to potential jurors about their role as fact-finders and asked what they would consider to be convincing evidence. The first answer, blurted out almost immediately by two potential jurors, was "video." After some prompting from the prosecutor, other members of the jury pool added "witnesses" and "testimony" to the list of evidentiary forms. As jury selection proceeded, Thompson made a pointed reference to the semiotics of a police uniform, asking how jurors might assess a speaker's truthfulness and whether officers, by virtue of their profession, are automatically more credible. At least one member of the jury pool admitted to giving more weight to the testimony of police officers and attributed that belief to "watching too much television."

It took about two hours to choose and swear in six jurors for the misdemeanor panel, and opening arguments proceeded. Almost immediately, video was discussed once again in the hypothetical, as prosecutor Matt McCabe told jurors that he would offer three videos as evidence: two dashcam recordings and the 7-Eleven surveillance video. McCabe told jurors the videos were "pretty boring" but "get good when Mr. Buehler shows up." McCabe's opening statement emphasized that the officers would be testifying, and that video was only part of what they'd use to learn about the case, saying, "I want to give a full context. I want to be able to see what led up to this situation, for today. To give you as an opportunity to focus on what really happened." At the same time, McCabe told the jury, the question of case was merely whether Buehler failed to comply with a lawful order or not, and he reminded them that this was a misdemeanor with no jail time and potentially only a dollar fine at stake.

Testifying with Video

Jurors watched the first video only minutes after the first witnesses took the stand on day one. Officer Patrick Oborski was armed and in uniform. He looked directly at the jurors when he told them that Buehler was verbally abusive and spat on him. Prosecutors then asked Oborski whether his car is equipped with a VCR (yes) and whether police are able to alter video once it's recorded (no).

Playing back the video entailed procedures that involved the entire courtroom. The lights were dimmed, and the jurors were directed to watch a large (approximately six-feet-wide) screen on the opposite wall. The judge, lawyers, staff, and gallery onlookers joined this ritualistic shared viewing, during which McCabe and Oborski occasionally spoke to explain what was transpiring on the tape. This clip included an unclear audio track. Buehler cannot be seen; the altercation occurs off camera and can only be discerned by the low-quality sound. What *is* visible on the black-and-white tape is the gas station, the time code, and, for several minutes, the back of the woman who was under investigation for drunk driving as she waited to begin her field sobriety test. She can be seen standing, apparently unsure whether to proceed, while audio of the altercation ensues.

The prosecutor backed up the tape several times during this scene in a way that interrupted the audio stream. Oborski's testimony about the video was delivered in a very flat, almost neutral manner, using simple declarative statements with little emotion or elaboration. This contrasted dramatically with his voice in the audio. Although it was often difficult to understand exact words due to the distortion caused by Oborski's proximity to the microphone and his raised voice, the aural evidence depicted an officer who was agitated, loud, and seemingly confrontational.

The prosecution played the second video after Oborski's testimony. This fourteen-minute clip from the 7-Eleven surveillance camera is completely silent. This camera was positioned to provide security surveillance of the store's parking lot and gas pumps, and the foreground shows parking spaces and foot traffic in and out of the store. The gas pumps and sidewalk are in the background at the top of the frame. The truck Buehler was driving and the traffic stop are partially obscured by the gas pumps and a beam holding up the awning over the pumps. The police vehicles and traffic stop are farther in the background. Unlike the previous dashcam clip, this video depicted the event in a discernible sequence: Buehler and his companion entered the 7-Eleven parking lot as the traffic stop was in progress, and they completed pumping gas and reentered their vehicle as if to leave and then exited the vehicle shortly thereafter. The prosecutor solicited little testimony from Oborski during the playback of this video. The absence of audio in this playback contributed to a quiet in the courtroom that was in sharp contrast to the noise of the first one.

The third video was played after lunch that day during the testimony of Officer Robert Snider, who was holding onto Norma Pizana, the woman who cried for onlookers to "film this" during the incident. Snider's dashboard camera was initially facing the traffic stop but was turned toward the backseat of his car after he took Pizana into custody for disobeying his order to stop using her cell phone. Snider testified that this was done because suspects sometimes "injure themselves" while in custody. Snider, also in uniform, testified that he felt threatened by Buehler and thought that Buehler had been summoned by the young woman to violently interfere. As in the other dashcam video, the altercation with Buehler cannot be seen, only roughly and incompletely heard.

The fourth video was not introduced until the very end of the day, during defense testimony; that video was recorded on an iPhone by John Blackbird. Blackbird was a private citizen walking along the opposite side of the street who observed the confrontation and started filming because, like Buehler, he was alarmed by the way the officers were treating Pizana. As he put it, "The way they pulled her out of the car, the way they twisted her, it just didn't seem like anybody should treat a human being like that." During Blackbird's testimony, Thompson replayed the video in slow motion, which clarified the way Buehler was thrown to the ground while distorting his shouts of, "What are you doing? Why are you doing this?" Blackbird testified that he thought the officer was the aggressor in this incident, and that he was threatened with arrest as well after loudly asking them whether they were proud of their actions.

Throughout the afternoon's events in court, uniformed members of the police force visited the gallery and sat in the back. Some of the officers wore the symbols of higher rank as they watched their colleagues testify. This sort of silent display is common in court settings where matters of police work are involved. In fact, during a different case in Austin, the chief of police prohibited his force from attending court in uniform during the murder trial of a man who fatally shot an officer, on grounds that the jury might be unnecessarily influenced by such a display of blue unity.

Other gallery watchers sitting behind the prosecutor's table (implying support for that side) were frequent visitors wearing formal suits who occasionally interacted with McCabe and were likely members of the prosecutor's office. But other than one of Antonio Buehler's supporters who wore a Peaceful Streets T-shirt, spectators sitting behind the defense table had no uniform to identify their sympathies. Members of the press were easy to spot; some wore cameras (out of their hands in order to demonstrate that they were not using them). Other journalists had laptops open for notetaking, and most sat close to the back on the prosecutor's side, near the researchers, a position with a comfortable view of the screen when videos were played.

Video Speaking for Itself

In accordance with typical court procedure, the video clips were consistently used as *documents* in support of witness testimony. Yet video cannot be experienced in the same way as a still photograph, which, while classified as document evidence, might also be experienced as "object" evidence, pulled out of envelopes, handled, and passed from juror to juror. In this case, some photographs, such as the ones Buehler took of Officers Snider and Oborski, were shared with the jury as prints and shown on the screen. The difference in materiality changes the way the video or images are incorporated into the narratives being constructed. With printed images, a juror might spend a few extra seconds examining some aspect of the photo before passing it along; another might give it a cursory look. In this case, jurors were also observed turning the still images to different angles to vary their point of view, an option that is not so easily available with projection on a screen. Video's technological, phenomenological, and semiotic characteristics lent each clip a certain voice of its own.

In contrast, the videos in this case were experienced in real time, simultaneously, and could not be touched by the jury. Video cannot be ritually handed to jurors, a symbol that they are trusted with evidence. Merely setting up the room for the video playback took considerable time before the trial even started. Interestingly, the dashcam and 7-Eleven videos were exhibits for both sides but were played back from a DVD copy held by the defense; its validity and accuracy were not questioned as it left the defense laptop and moved to the screen. The validity of each clip was never at issue in this case; each clip was entered into evidence as a raw clip.

The videos enhanced and supported the performative aspects of witness testimony beyond the words they uttered. For example, during his testimony Antonio Buehler used a whiteboard and his own body in order to demonstrate to the jury what happened on the night of his arrest. He mapped out the gas station on the whiteboard and was allowed to leave the witness box to stand and pantomime how he moved in response to Snider's movements. But even with the hand-drawn maps and physical demonstrations, it was hard to envision—based on discourse alone—the placement of the various parts of the scene: the truck Buehler drove, the police cars, the car involved in the DUI, the gas pumps, the street, and the store. The videos subjectively placed jurors into the scene and established the narrative setting with sight, sound, and kinesthetic details (motion, distance, point of view) not possible with words voiced by a witness on the stand. The bystander video had the most embodied presence, because it was obviously handheld and moved with Blackbird's hand (and breathing). This video also framed the event itself in a wide shot, unlike the dashcam and surveillance videos, which were perfectly and mechanically still and never moved in accordance with the event, to an extent that is almost frustrating to anyone who really wanted to understand what happened that night.

Finally, of course, the videos contained basic visual information—both as expected, but with details and symbols that, again, were not necessarily communicated by testimony or lawyer statements. The sight of a 7-Eleven parking lot on New Year's Eve, for instance, is something many of us have experienced, but until we watch it together, it's only a hypothetical parking lot. The sound of an officer saying, "You spit on me," and the way the tone, inflection, and volume of that statement were recorded by video compared with the way the officer repeated it in court gave the jurors an independent marker of what happened, beyond the testimonies of Buehler and Oborski. The presence of multiple points of view in video form allowed one to either contradict or amplify what was present in the others. The audio evidence of Buehler allegedly spitting occurred off camera in the dashcam version and was not supported by the visual evidence from the 7-Eleven or from across the street.

Any of these semiotic markers, whether the forensic-looking time code that dominates the frame from the dashcam video or the shakiness of Blackbird's smartphone clip that captured silhouettes of Buehler and Oborski, constituted statements of fact *independent* of courtroom discourse. Thompson called attention to the fact that Oborski's silhouette advances on Buehler's and does not appear to flinch, jerk back, or put a hand to its face, contradicting Oborski's sworn testimony that he'd been spat upon in the face. That the jurors could witness this on their own, from the vantage point of an eyewitness, might well have been the factor that led to Buehler's acquittal.

Narratives Layered and Competitive

Video shapes judicial narratives in specialized ways. Much of what this case reveals reflects the findings of previous research on legal persuasion.[26] The Western trial model is generally described as a system in which two sides compete in narrative construction, and adjudication results from the "winning" story.[27] This case bears out that assertion, but also points to the existence of other narrative structures. In addition to the two competing narratives about what happened the night Buehler was arrested, the videos established their own coherent timeline. What the videos could not do is establish the story's fidelity.

Throughout the case, spectators were presented with an additional, overarching narrative: that justice was being served. This metanarrative was not articulated verbally; it was performed. Law is rooted in language, but justice is experienced. It is visual, body-centric, and rooted in ritual—from the space in which it is decided and the décor within, the clothing worn by its actors, and the multiple controls over what is seen by whom and when.[28] Before the jury was even selected, onlookers and jurors were subjected to a visual display of power and the authority of the court. One of Buehler's supporters tested this power on the first day of the trial, by not standing when the court clerk called out, "All rise," at the start of the session.

Antonio Buehler's clothing, short haircut, and posture alluded to his standing as a military veteran and business professional, contrasted with the long hair he wore the night he was arrested. Other visual and performative cues included the police officers' uniforms and weaponry, Judge Solomon's colorful shirts under his robe (a lavender shirt on day two marked him, whether intentionally or not, as unconventional), benches that resemble church pews, wooden paneling, and a high desk that puts the judge above the room. Performances such as the choreography of attorneys before the jurors and the way that supporters from each side entered the room and sat behind a divider that separates the public from what is essentially a stage support the ritualized performance. Indeed, because onlookers are expected to be silent and subject to the rule of the word (law and testimony), these displays are all the more important.

Video both supports and challenges a courtroom's visual rhetoric. While the four evidentiary clips were only part of the performance of justice in this case, they challenged the court's power because of their indexical relationship with reality. They were used to support and contradict verbal testimony. Even though no single clip settled the fact, their visual, aural, kinesthetic and temporal information presented a narrative timeline that defied discursive contextualization. Multiple videos from different perspectives were incorporated into competing narrative constructions, preserving the court's authority and the metanarrative that justice was being done.

Recontextualizing Video

One essential characteristic of this case is that not only were videos used as evidence but the citizens' *creation* of videos and photos was also at issue. Buehler became involved that night by shouting at police and pulling out his camera. Officers confronted him and Blackbird for allegedly getting "involved." More than once, Thompson asked questions of witnesses regarding the First Amendment right of a citizen to film police working in public.

The truthfulness of raw video was never questioned in court. Instead, much of the prosecution's effort appeared to be trying to construct a narrative that diminished the power of the video evidence while helping jurors to empathize with the officers in order to explain their decisions and actions. The prosecutor and prosecution witnesses consistently worked to explain why officers needed to control the situation and why they might want to defend themselves from bystanders in order to justify the conduct the jurors could observe.

Another way the attorneys minimized video's indexicality was by pointing out the constructed nature of video, such as the framing, angle, and microphone placement. The fact that there were four videos from multiple angles further emphasizes video as a construction of reality.[29] In this way, much of what we observed in the way video was talked *about* worked to reify the law, containing and controlling video's message.[30] By talking about video as a technology and of cameras as something that might cause concern for police, the power of the clips' content could be mitigated.

Video as Affordance

The most famous early instance of a police accountability video—Rodney King's beating in 1991—also offers the textbook case on how to undermine such evidence.[31] Prosecutors simply rolled the tape, expecting its documentation of fifty-six baton strikes and six kicks to make their case, ceding control of the narrative to technology. But the officers were acquitted after defense attorneys showed the jury the same video in pieces, reediting and altering the beating's timeline.[32] The case study in this chapter shows how much has changed since a single video could make a case in 1991. *Four* tapes from different angles and sources were shown to a jury more accustomed to multimedia a generation after riots in Los Angeles called attention to the fallibility of police officers.

But the narrative lesson of the King case prevailed in our case study: video's voice can be answered with discursive strategies. When the videos were played in court, witnesses were asked to explain what was happening in real time; at some moments, they even were invited to point to the screen to highlight particular actions. The police officers, for instance, relied on their dashcam videos to explain DUI arrest protocols, attempting to persuade jurors why they would feel threatened by someone pulling an object out of their pocket.

The dashcam videos from this case were incomplete, since they were focused on the drunk driving investigation and not the confrontation with Buehler. The audio was hard to hear and interpret, and the action of interest was usually out of frame. Snider's squad car camera, for instance, was focused on an apparently inebriated Norma Pizano in the backseat while jurors were expected to focus on the audio from Snider and Buehler, who could not be seen. That audio may have proven to be critical in this instance, however, in the way the profanity and shouting by officers on tape contrasted with their calm accounts in the witness box. In this way, video undermined the credibility advantage police have traditionally had in court by virtue of their position, uniform, and even their familiarity with court regulations and personnel. Video that contrasts with this performance might be just as much of a problem as one that represents different facts.

While the clips were occasionally played without comment and the truthfulness of raw tape was not an issue, one side or another always mentioned the video as part of the narrative constructions. In this way the clips also were folded into the metanarrative performance of justice. The court maintained authority over projection and contextualization of the evidence, allowing the jurors to assess for themselves what they saw. Yet even though it was controlled and incorporated into narrative constructions, the video challenged police testimony, largely because of the way the events depicted by the clips unfolded in real time.

Video's Own Narrative Timeline

On first blush, one might be tempted to think of video evidence as an extension of photographic evidence. Photographs have been presented as evidence and used for forensic purposes almost since the invention of the camera.[33] The essential difference is that photographs contain no inherent story; they are objects, artifacts, frozen moments in time that without context and interpretation are meaningless. As a number of visual scholars have explained, a single image is ambiguous and requires context in the form of language to be understood or rendered persuasive.[34] The indexical relationship of an image to reality can enable truth-telling and memory but can also be miscast and seductively deceiving.[35] In court, because photographs are material, they can be used as props to support the testimony of an individual—handled, examined, and then explained.

But video cannot be handled; it must be played and experienced temporally. Raw, unedited video represents a timeline, with technological, phenomenological, and semiological characteristics that constitute a narrative structure that speaks for itself. More than once during this case, the judge, the accused, the jury, court staff, attorneys, and spectators all shared in viewing a video's projection simultaneously. Because it must be viewed using some sort of device, video exists in its own moment in the courtroom. More than its audio and images (which can be frozen and even printed), video communicates a timeline when it is played back. This timeline is its own evidence and cannot be discursively contextualized the way a single image can.

The phenomenology of the timeline in an unedited, raw clip is what allows video to speak for itself, providing, in a sense, a hard line that the trial's two competing narrative constructions cannot bend. Philosopher Paul Ricoeur, whose work influenced Fisher's, argued that the power of narrative is rooted in its metaphorical connection to human temporal experience.[36] Unedited, raw video mimics this experience in time. That is, we move through the world in a temporal sequence, and this embodied experience lends power to narrative's persuasion.

When tied to the timeline, the visual and aural information is especially rich. It can add insight that is not communicated verbally and answer questions the jurors didn't know they had. For instance, the 7-Eleven video showed other bystanders in the parking lot and the way they reacted, or didn't, to what was going on near the gas pumps. The dashcam videos have a forensic style: the camera tends to not move, it has the time code, and it is plain and static, much like the security camera footage. Blackbird's video is connected with his body; it moves according to the action in the frame and, as a smartphone lens, is more familiar to the average viewer than the wide-angle flatness of the police cruiser. Distant, out of focus, and somewhat shaky, it still portrayed the backlit shadows of two men. Played back in real time, this unanticipated video from someone who thought to record what he was witnessing better matched Buehler's testimony that he was unnecessarily shoved and pushed to the ground, and at no time showed an officer recoil or wipe spit from his face.

Video Coherence and Fidelity

As they constructed their competing narratives, each side talked about and testified *with* video strategically. The defense sought to explain the video while the prosecution needed to explain it away. At the same time, video's hard-edged timeline spoke for itself, providing structural coherence and completeness for those narratives. Inconsistencies between the police officers' polite answers and harsh audio and their explanations about feeling threatened when the video shows them throw a grown man to the ground most likely influenced the jurors' decision in this specific case.

In connecting its characteristics to narrative theory, video seems to fulfill the elements of coherence as proposed by Fisher and expanded by Rideout.[37] Unedited, raw video presents events in sequence—a plot. There is at least one actor—the videographer—and a video might also depict other characters who speak and act. Video establishes a setting and places the viewer within that setting. The technology phenomenologically and semiologically contains the structure of a story. What is missing is the very point of the story, which in this case, as with other court cases that have relied on the camera's output, was decided by the jury.

The persuasive power of a narrative, as Fisher explained, is in how well it rings "true" for its audience, and whether actors within a story use "good reasons" for their actions. Legal scholars have connected this idea to courtroom narrative, noting that the moral component of Fisher's "fidelity" is largely a matter of how well the story matches the jurors' (as representatives of the community) normative ideas about right and wrong. Here, video is not particularly useful in playback. The hard edge of its timeline makes no normative statement. Fidelity is established instead through the creation and use of video by human actors; it is the performance of justice.

The videos in this case were all created as part of human activity, but only one was created directly and with human hands: the one Blackbird shot with his iPhone. Peters's typology of witnessing is helpful for thinking about how the creation of video in the conduct of witnessing is an embodied activity with moral dimensions.[38] To document an event in order to bear witness on behalf of others, putting one's body on the line in the course of that action, is at the heart of the sanctity of witnessing. Such an act empowers others and lends voice to another's concerns as well as the concerns of a video's creator.[39] Blackbird's decision to film the scene, like Buehler's decision to use his camera, was affirmed by the jury. In this way, the act of creating a video, itself a performance, was incorporated into the court's overarching narrative: justice was done.

Video's role in this case has important implications for public policy. Several federal court cases have affirmed the right to film police in action, but it continues to be the subject of debate in everyday encounters.[40] Police departments are investing in body cameras, but this video presents a highly subjective perspective and sometimes difficult to interpret.[41] In this case study, while no single clip settled the facts, the spontaneous wide shot from across the street, filmed by a bystander motivated by concern, likely made the greatest difference.

Spontaneous, citizen-generated videos constitute embodied witnessing on behalf of others, gives voice to their experience, and supports individuals as they account for their actions. Buehler's decision to get involved got him arrested, and Blackbird was nearly arrested as well. But based on the way video constitutes narrative coherence and its creation shapes fidelity, it seems better to consider the documenting of police activity as a form of public service that deserves social support and legal protection. While federal courts at the district level have confirmed that right, but the Supreme Court has yet to take it up.[42] Even with citizens' constitutional protections, however, officers using the "apologize later" strategy continue to grab phones, shine lights into cameras, and otherwise try to interfere with filming.

Controlling Video Narrative

The trial at the center of our case study was hardly the first to introduce video as evidence, nor was it the first case to contend with citizen rights to film police. It illustrates the way officers attempted to use embodied gatekeeping in order to control their narrative from the scene. Unique to this case, however, is the number of videos, their sources, and the fact that the right to film police was one of its underlying themes. In 2019, the Pew Research Center estimated that more than five billion people worldwide had smartphones, and mobile devices are overtaking desktop computers for internet access.[43] As smartphones continue to proliferate along with badge-cams, dashcams, and other forms of surveillance, many more trials will likely incorporate multiple pieces of video as evidence.

This case study allowed us to explore the way video served and challenged the performance of justice: video was *talked about*, was *testified with*, and through an inviolable timeline, occasionally *spoke for itself*. These findings advance the usefulness of the narrative paradigm in the legal setting for the ways that video plays a role in the meta-narrative of justice, the ways it is incorporated into competing case narrative constructions, and the way its timeline structure establishes narrative coherence. Video cannot, by itself, convey the moral of its own story, and fidelity remains the discursive job of human actors in the justice system.

Finally, this case illustrates key characteristics of video that distinguish it from other forms of evidence, whether in court or everyday life. As smartphone video on the web proliferates, it is useful to understand its narrative requirements, limits, and potential. State authorities can harness multiple angles and storytelling, which the less powerful can then interrogate. The right of everyday citizens to film the activities of police and government authorities, therefore, is essential to establishing a balance of power, especially in light of the extraordinary growth in police use of body cameras. No single stakeholder in the media-citizen–law enforcement environment should have sole access to the video timeline's power. E. G. "Gerry" Morris, as past president of the National Association of Criminal Defense Lawyers (NACDL), argued this is the reason policies are needed to ensure that law enforcement's tapes are available to all parties. "In any given case, that may mean, well, I lose, because there's my client doing exactly what the police said he or she was doing. In the overall scheme of things, that's the way the system is supposed to work."[44]

While a video's untouched timeline does offer its own, uniquely powerful form of documentation, the process of narrativization can undermine its evidentiary strength. Today what may be "special" about contemporary video is the way it has become prosaic. Once specialized territory, the power to produce and distribute video is literally in the hands of billions of everyday people. Filmic triangulation, as used in the investigation of the John Kennedy assassination, is so commonplace that it is taught in workshops as integral to cop-watching practice.

Using Video Effectively and Ethically

Recall Sekula's assertion that a photograph's meaning is always a matter of discourse and context, which does not erase its documentary value, but changes it.[45] Consider a case that occurred a year after Buehler's trial: the shooting by police of Terrance Crutcher.[46] As with Buehler, there were multiple camera angles, one from a helicopter above and another from a police dashcam. As with Rodney King, the case seemed obvious to those outside of the law enforcement community. A man who has his hands up next to his car is shot and killed by police during a traffic stop. Surely this was police overreach, right? And yet—the actual moment of the 2016 shooting in Tulsa, Oklahoma, cannot be seen, neither in video from a too-distant traffic helicopter overhead nor the dashcam blocked by the bodies of officers on the scene. Officer Betty Shelby later testified that Terrence Crutcher was reaching into his car and she was taught to shoot before a suspect can grab a gun. Less than a year after Crutcher died on the highway, Officer Shelby was acquitted.[47]

For video to have solid evidentiary value, it must either be unedited or its editing must be transparently explained. Recent technological developments, which make it harder to detect editing, pose a significant challenge to video's authority. In 2015 an outside viewer noticed anomalies in the dashcam video released by police in the Sandra Bland arrest.[48] Bland died in jail days later in a reported suicide, after she was arrested and thrown to the ground during a traffic stop.[49] Online observers noticed that the dashcam video had missing pieces; the department claimed it was an innocent digital glitch. With deep fake technology, however, the likelihood that someone at home might be able to detect video manipulation shrinks. Unless forensic experts are able to keep up with the mischief makers, video may soon lose the qualities that render it a special form of evidence.

Each technological advance requires new procedures and presents new epistemological challenges. Feigenson and Spiesel suggested three ethical principles as guides for visual territory, two of which reflect general legal ethics—namely, any image introduced in court is an accurate depiction of what it is purported to be, and attorneys openly explain the relationship between the image and the reality it is purported to document.[50] This echoes what I have argued in the journalistic context, in that attorneys need to understand and be able to explain the process by which images are made. Third and finally, Feigenson and Spiesel argued that the legal community has the obligation to become more visually literate, and to be able to critique, interpret, and defend the use of images they introduce to the court.[51] As the final chapters of this book emphasize, visual literacy is essential for everyone to navigate today's digital public sphere, and not only for the sake of watching and interpreting. Democratic participation today demands that each of us can critically watch *and* that we have the capability to produce and share our own visual materials competently and ethically, if for no other reason than to provide counternarratives to those in power.

7

Filming Police

Scene: It is a comfortable spring evening in Berkeley, California. A woman in a worker's brim cap approaches an encampment of homeless people. She has quiet conversations with several men before turning her attention to a pair of police officers nearby who are picking up items left in the park. Andrea Pritchett, one of the founders of the US cop-watching movement, believes those items belong to a homeless person, but is unable, during a businesslike conversation with the officers, to convince them to leave the bucket and other items behind. A university student stands nearby, videotaping Pritchett as she makes the rounds in People's Park. Almost nothing happens; there are no confrontations, no arguments, no fights—it's a typical cop-watching shift.

It lasts for eight minutes, forty-six seconds. The recording of George Floyd gasping for breath under police officer Derek Chauvin's knee and Floyd's plaintive cry to his mother inspired protests around the world that lasted through the summer of 2020 and beyond. Some municipalities considered changing their police budgets; political campaigns focused on the more violent riots, and many white Americans made social media pledges to do better. Even the NFL issued a statement in support of Black lives. It might seem that the Floyd video proved the value of photographic once and for all. Yet just as the protests for Black lives were underway, detractors started doubting the veracity of the Floyd video, and the "law and order" narrative returned to political campaigns. Corporations crafted public service announcements with inspiring music about diversity and inclusion, while the cases continued to mount: a bystander was recording video when Jacob Blake in Kenosha, Wisconsin, was shot seven times in the back, leaving him paralyzed.[1] In Rochester, New York, protests erupted after video was released showing police putting a spit hood on a man having a psychotic episode who later suffocated to death.[2] Around the United States, sports teams took a knee or sat out games, but Colin Kaepernick is still not playing football.

Seeing Justice. Mary Angela Bock, Oxford University Press. © Oxford University Press 2021.
DOI: 10.1093/oso/9780190926977.003.0007

None of this would likely be happening without videos being posted online. While the video's value as evidence is subject to recontextualizations in court, news, and social media, the impact of photographic reality remains. This power has fueled the grown of a practice known as cop-watching in both organized and spontaneous forms.

Cop-watching is nothing new. It predated the smartphone by decades, when the Black Panthers started armed patrols to monitor police activity.[3] One of the oldest groups devoted specifically to police accountability, Berkeley Copwatch, was founded in 1990, when Andrea Pritchett and two other women started a group devoted to protecting homeless people from police harassment—months before a bystander used an analog videotape recorder to document Rodney King's arrest in Los Angeles.[4] Pritchett remains on patrol with Berkeley Copwatch, still concerned with the way police treat the homeless as well as other populations who disproportionately bear the brunt of police abuse: the mentally ill, people of color, and trans people.

The primary function of nonviolent, organized cop-watching is the voice it gives to citizens via visibility. At its best, it enables marginalized people to be seen and heard and works to prevent violence—but cop-watching can also be used as a label for activities that are antagonistic and purposely confrontational, as when gun-rights activists film one another openly carrying weapons in public spaces. Contemporary cop-watching draws power from the documentary tradition of film and stills and might in some cases be said to elicit social epiphany, as with *LIFE* magazine's photos from the civil rights movement in the 1960s.[5] Like other forms of citizen witnessing, police accountability activism illustrates the way visual literacy has become an essential democratic capability. It is an antidote to state-sponsored surveillance.

Cop-watching has been theorized in terms of Foucauldian bio-power, highlighting the disciplinary role of surveillance.[6] The work of the police accountability movement is not entirely about visual evidence, however, so it is necessary to borrow from other parts of Foucault's philosophical toolkit—namely his idea of power as fractured, variable, multidirectional, and of course, constructed through discourse.[7] That is, theories of surveillance can only go so far in interpreting the work of the people who make a regular practice of monitoring police activity in their communities. Everything that is special about video—the way it *is talked about, testified with,* and *presents its own narrative* by way of the electronic timeline (as discussed in Chapter 6)— empowers social activism.

While cop-watching predated the smartphone, mobile video has put its power in the hands of billions. Its evidentiary value, offers striking evidence to counter police claims about events.[8] Yet video alone does not make the difference. Cop-watching's second leg of power relies on its contextualization in narrative. Video from the Rodney King beating is held up as the quintessential example of the power of narrative, as lawyers for the police indicted for assault stopped and started the tape in court and changed the narrative so effectively that all five officers were acquitted.[9] The riots that ensued reflect how subjective the narrative process is. The testimonial link between video as document and video as narrative constitutes the third leg of cop-watching's discursive power, that of embodied witnessing.[10]

While the texts of cop-watching are what have inspired new conversations about police procedure in the United States, these texts cannot be entirely understood outside their embodied production. Cop-watching requires, protects, and records bodies in action. It cannot be theorized without a feminist dismantling of the body-text binary for the way it combines word and image, embodiment and discourse.[11] Critical Race Theory augments the feminist perspective for its interrogation of bio-power, violence, and ideology.[12] This chapter therefore describes three dimensions of cop-watching's power: evidence, story, and practice. The analysis draws from material collected from 2013 to 2017 in several US cities: direct observation of cop-watchers in action, interviews with cop-watchers and police officers, and cop-watching videos. The latter constitute their own distinct genre, but as with other forms of photographic messages, much of what they mean relies on their recontextualization in narrative.

Cop-watching video should not be conflated with body-cam video, even though both types of visual evidence contribute to police accountability discourse. Cities across the United States are embracing badge-cam video systems but are still working through regulations about how such video can and ought to be released to the public and used as evidence. The convergence of digital media, in which all media forms are seen on the same sort of screen, "flattens" reception, which means the public may not differentiate between video sourcing. Yet the difference is extremely important—and serves to highlight the thesis of this book. Police departments use badge cams as an investigative tool and the public's right to access video is often murky. As Christopher Schneider pointed out, police still tend to "own" the narrative.[13] Only citizen video presents a literal version of public oversight.

Video Testimony and Human Rights

Video cameras in the hands of everyday citizens provide a check on the embodied gatekeeping normally imposed by the state. Activists worldwide are employing video to advance their cause, using material created by nonprofessionals.[14] The affordance value of photographic recordings to the cause of human rights is not new, of course. Images from the Holocaust were published immediately after the war to force Germans to face their crimes and have been used ever since to commemorate its horrors.[15] Historical research has examined the way film was and notably was *not* used in the Nuremberg trials for Nazi war crimes and other human rights investigations.[16]

What is new is the ease with which video can be produced. There are far more digital cameras on Earth than people. An estimated five billion people around the world own smartphones, but other types of cameras, including drones, robotic cameras, and surveillance cameras, are proliferating so quickly that one marketing company estimates there'll soon be forty-five billion of them.[17] A video camera, recorder, and editing system that once cost tens of thousands of dollars is now standard issue for smartphones. Easily and cheaply produced video has made it possible for nongovernmental organizations and other human rights groups to bypass news media and create their own documentary evidence.[18] These organizations provide the institutional infrastructure that renders video useful, for as Yvette Alberdingk Thijm, the executive director of Witness.org, explained, their organization is essential if video is to make a difference. "A lot of people think that the moment you film something, then justice will happen," she said, "but what we've seen is that that doesn't necessarily happen."[19] Producing video evidence is only the start; it must be narrativized, contextualized, explained, and distributed.

Andén-Papadopolous used the phrase "citizen camera witnessing" to describe the embodied way nonjournalists work to document the world around them.[20] Her attention to the role of the body in such witnessing, and the risk it poses, echoes the work of John Durham Peters and other scholars who have pointed to the historic authority of direct eyewitnessing.[21] Allan's theorization of citizen journalism emphasizes witnessing in order to distinguish its authority away from the objectivity norm in conventional journalism.[22] Such direct witnessing, with the help of photographic documentation, has had an impact on twenty-first-century social movements, such as those addressing the war in Syria,[23] sexual violence in Egypt,[24] and unrest in Iran.[25] In the United States, citizen witnessing efforts have focused on police accountability,[26] animal abuse,[27] and the rights of the disabled.[28] Spontaneous video witnessing has also captured scenes of racist and ethnocentric behavior, a trend covered in Chapter 9. Not all image-based human rights investigations involve citizens or activists taping events. Forensic architecture, for example, is an investigative technique that uses images from whatever sources are available, including drones and satellites, and then layering or combining them into texts that answer questions about—to consider one application—the location of secret prisons or the location where an alleged war crime too place.[29]

Many news organizations have systems in place for vetting video, as do the courts, and so deep fakes are most dangerous on social media, where propagandists take advantage of unsuspecting users.[30] Video shot by nonprofessionals, however—sometimes known as "viewer video," "citizen video" or "user-generated media"—is not treated consistently across the journalistic field.[31] Claire Wardle used the term "eyewitness media" to describe all forms of contributed material. Sandra Ristovska proposed "eyewitness video" to specify *moving* images in order to better theorize what is special about this form of evidence.[32] Finally, while video can provide human rights activists with tremendous documentary authority, it works just as well for their opposition. Surveillance goes both ways—so when people use their cell phones for freedom, the state monitors back and keeps tabs on activists.[33] Police use social media for investigations and constantly develop new technologies for solving crimes, tracking criminals, or infiltrating protests.[34] Indeed, law enforcement institutions adopted the camera for surveillance and criminal identification faster than news organizations embraced photography.[35] Cop-watching merely turns the camera around to surveil the powerful.

Cop-Watchers: Who They Are, What They Do

Eyewitness media and video have proven to be invaluable for human rights activists around the world working to undermine oppressive regimes. In the United States, such activism has focused on monitoring law enforcement for the way it has historically meted out unequal justice for marginalized groups. For some of the individuals observed and interviewed for this project, police accountability activism was a response to negative encounters with law enforcement. Others became involved as part of overlapping political concerns, such as civil rights for people of color, the LGBTQ

community, disabled people, or from a completely different angle, the rights
of gun owners. Cop-watchers represent a wide range of political viewpoints,
ages, genders, and races. They share a common motive (holding police accountable), method (shooting and uploading video), and mode of representation (social media).

One Night on Patrol

This typical cop-watch patrol for the southern city organization under study
("Group-1") started at 9 p.m. with a meeting at a coffeehouse. The researcher
is one of six people who will patrol. Five are male, including a teenage
boy who happens to have the most professional camera in the group. One
other person, a woman, is expected to meet up with the group downtown.
The leader, "Charles," uses his cell phone to text latecomers before carefully going over the rules of the evening, a step he likely took because the
researcher was tagging along. Rules for Group-1 include no weapons, no alcohol or substance use while cop-watching, and no interfering with police
activity. This last edict, of course, is a matter of considerable debate between
US cop-watching groups and police officers, as "interference" is a slippery
legal concept that can and often has been used as a charge against those who
film police. Volunteers work in pairs or trios and communicate by cell phone.
Charles also told volunteers to avoid verbally abusing officers, though he and
other volunteers were later observed yelling at officers and questioning their
actions throughout the night.

Those with cars drive, giving rides to the others from the coffeehouse to a
strip mall closer to the city's center to park for free and walk several blocks to
the nightclub district. Charles drives an old, repainted police squad car because "it bugs [the police]" and pulls his camera equipment out of the trunk.
On this night of observation, the nightclub district is particularly crowded
because the weather is pleasant. The city blocks vehicle traffic on the week-
ends so that crowds can mingle in the street.

Upon arrival, volunteers walk the strip looking for officers and record
video simply of officer locations, faces, and badges. "Sean" explains that they
do this so that the group knows who's working that night; it makes it easier
to report on their activity later. Sean—a white, male, one-time Occupy activist with facial piercings and black leather collar—asserts that the officers

in this city are "racist." He believes that his group's regular patrols have had a preventative effect. He also tells a story of being pushed and prodded by officers on horseback; the mounted patrol is a particular thorn in the side of the members.

The group walks back and forth on the strip in this way for about four hours, waiting for the bars to close and watching for arrests and altercations. When police appear to be arresting someone on the sidewalk, three volunteers surround the scene to tape it from multiple angles. The youngest member of the group is trying to live-stream from his professional-grade video camera but is running low on battery power. Police surround the incident as well, so that three officers ring the event, and the cop-watching volunteers form a ring around them. Onlookers pause to watch as the man, who appears to be drunk, is arrested and led away. As the night comes to a close, the group walks back to their cars. When two mounted police officers made their way back to the police stables, Sean shouts to them several times, with statements such as, "You're the real criminals," and "You're a horrible person!" The officers do not respond.

Subsequent observations of the nightclub district patrols found that the number of volunteers diminished over time, and as some volunteers left the group (burnout was blamed in two cases), others joined in. A bystander's scream about gunfire one night scattered the group, and only when it was clear that a gun had not been fired did everyone come out from the various bricked doorways and alleys to regroup with their partners. One of them, an Afghanistan war veteran, "John," took a protective tone and stance as he asked whether the (much older) researcher was okay. On another night, volunteers encountered an apparently underage boy, severely intoxicated, face down on the pavement. The researcher asked whether they should get help, and the volunteers roused him to ask whether he needed help. He was able to stand and talk and walk away, so the group proceeded with patrol.

None of the patrols observed yielded video of overt violence, though Group-1 posted clips that labeled police behavior as overly aggressive or rude, or outside protocol. No videos from the observation nights were picked up by local news media. During the observations, it did seem clear that police in this city knew what Group-1 did and were aware of the cameras. Officer responses varied from ignoring the group to shining flashlights directly into camera lenses to disrupt recordings.

Who Are These People?

Organized cop-watchers represent a small subset of people who are concerned about or protest against police violence, and this ethnographic study represents only a small subset of the group. Nevertheless, the in-depth interviews reveal a wide range of political views: the far, libertarian right and the far, progressive left. Among the interviewees in this study were several veterans, numerous gun rights activists (two of whom could be described as open-carry agitators), a former professional journalist, a nurse, students, software technicians, and the former Occupy protester. Women are active in the accountability movement and were present with men during the patrols I observed. Ages ranged from teen to post-retirement age, and most of the cop-watchers who participated in this study were white, though participation in the larger project of police accountability in the United States is racially diverse.[36] An analysis of the interviews yielded some common themes regarding motives, practices, and representations. For instance, the libertarian-leaning subjects were white, male, and more likely to be concerned about constitutional principles as much as police violence. Everyone, however, reported that they either witnessed or experienced a negative encounter with police that inspired their activism.

Motives

Spending time walking the nightclub district for hours at a stretch well into the night while occasionally risking arrest does not strike most people as a good time—unless they're paid for it. Nearly every one of the cop-watchers interviewed for this project say they were inspired by either directly experiencing injustice and learning the power of the camera, or by witnessing injustice. They have, in a sense, "heard" messages from other segments in society that have complained about police harassment and abuse.

> I saw [Charles's] video . . . and I knew immediately that I did not agree with what the police did. . . . I knew that I didn't agree with it and that something could be done. (John)

"Don" joined the same group and was similarly inspired by the story of its founder being arrested while filming a drunk-driving arrest:

> That was, I guess, just one of those enough-is-enough moments. I started paying attention then. When he and some of the others actually started forming [Group-1], I was all for it but I didn't think it would get off the ground. I didn't think it would work. I went to the first summit in 2012 and on the way home I filmed a DWI stop with a bad cell phone camera that I had at the time. I haven't stopped since then.

Many cop-watchers have had a negative experience with police and have turned their anger into activism. "Clint" is one. Now retired, he recalls being harassed in his youth by his hometown police. Clint no longer goes out to his city's nightclub district to directly observe police, but he's posted hundreds of videos in an effort to hold his local civilian oversight board accountable:

> Well, I'm trying to show—by going into these meetings where citizens are coming forward and saying, "Hey, you're not following these laws and you're not doing what you said you—is on the books, and you're not following your own policies and procedures, and you're not doing this and you're not doing that"—to show that it's like, I don't want to get vulgar here, but it's like they've put icing on a piece of crap, all right. . . . I'm trying to show people that the truth is something else. The truth is really something else, and that's the big picture.

Cop-watching seems to draw from an overall antiauthoritarian impulse, whether anarchist or libertarian, that generally distrusts institutions and fuels an impulse to individually monitor government activity. "Leonard" started out as a Tea Party leader but now says many of his views are more sympathetic with America's traditional left:

> I started to pay more attention, I suppose, and I started to see police harassing kids in the subway. . . . That prompted me to create Know Your Rights cards and start handing them out to kids on the subway, basically admonishing them or encouraging them not to even speak to police. That's

really how I got involved, and it just kind of evolved from there, in terms of video and more of an activist, journalist thing.

Another subject, "Nick," called himself a right-wing "volunteerist" and put it this way:

> A great many of them want to claim they're libertarian when they're in- volved in this because they realize that you follow all the planks of either of the two given government approved platforms and you're an idiot, es- sentially. There's a lot of anarchists-communists, as well as anarchists- capitalists, that are involved in police accountability.

The more politically oriented cop-watchers tended to find inspiration in neoliberal or libertarian ideas about the balance of power, which crossed over into their gun rights activism. This latter strand is ambiva- lent about whether race is a factor in what they consider to be a pattern of police abuse. Nick demurred when asked about the unrest in Ferguson, Missouri, after an unarmed Black man was killed, but Charles, Sean, and other members of Group-1 believe that minorities in the United States have long been bullied by police and were observed participating in pro- test marches on behalf of African Americans alleging systemic police brutality.

Clint was inspired by the police shooting of an unarmed homeless man in his community, yet no longer goes out on patrol in favor of monitoring the local citizen oversight board. So far he's uploaded more than three hundred videos to his YouTube channel.

> There was a sit-in at the mayor's office. I can't even remember when that was. It was last year, and [an officer] made claims that a tenured . . . well, now-tenured . . . University of New Mexico professor committed battery on him during this sit-in in the mayor's office. My video and video of a few other folks proved that to be wrong.

The interviewees, it seems, have seen and "heard" the voices of those who have long complained about police harassment—who, until now, did not have the means to prove their claims. Unlike the unplanned witness who uses a cell phone to spontaneously record a scene, organized cop-watchers blend activism, journalism, and technical skills to create a specialized discourse that was impossible before the digital age.

The Practice

Organized cop-watchers walk a beat much as police officers do, covering ground where conflicts are common, such as nightclub districts or impoverished neighborhoods, usually at night, as seen in Figure 7.1. Cop-watchers might start by documenting the presence and names of the officers on location. If they start filming an incident, they draw upon practices borrowed from documentary filmmaking in order to use the camera to make objective claims about reality. Project participants displayed considerable sophistication about filming techniques in order to claim the authority of camera "truth." "Bruce" explained that he invokes the power of the "wide" shot even while on location—explaining to those who balk at being filmed

Figure 7.1 Witnessing With a Camera
A cop-watcher monitors police activity from a distance.
Credit: Mary Angela Bock

that he's including everyone in the shot so that everyone's actions can be seen, and all can be held accountable. Study participants generally agreed that smartphones fueled their movement:

> This government is supposed to be transparent. That's what this whole country is built on, supposedly. The cameras add another dimension of the transparency, where for years, cops have always been able to create their own truths when they are making arrests. . . . They get the benefit of the doubt because you're supposed to believe cops. The camera adds a dimension where it shows what really happened, not just what the cop says happened. ("Roberto")

The importance of using the camera to pull in the whole scene is a repeated theme. The Berkeley Copwatch online handbook stresses a need to remain uninvolved observers. At a national workshop on cop-watching, one session leader explained how to triangulate visual coverage, encouraging volunteers to spread out and record police activity from different angles in what might be considered a visual "strategic ritual" for the sake of objectivity. "Larry" explains why it's important to travel in groups—for protection *and* multiple angles:

> You travel in groups and you make sure generally you have more than one camera. When it's possible sometimes we try to have it so that we have somebody not with the group but close by that can film from a distance.

Nick explained it in more combative terms:

> We try to arrange it so that whoever it is most likely to be in direct contact with the police officer, which is usually me because I know the law better than most of the guys, then whoever that person is, is covered by multiple angles, so they can't claim any BS they may try to claim on us. We do try to arrange ourselves where we have good coverage all around, we have multiple angles, and that whoever's most likely to be contacted dealing with an armed violent thug, [a police officer] is more likely to be covered by multiple angles whenever we can.

Camera angles, triangulation, and the need to patrol to "be there" on a regular basis are embodied components that add credibility to the work of cop-watching. Harnessing the moral power of the human witness with the technological power of the camera imbues the narratives with the cultural authority normally associated with journalism. When asked whether they considered themselves to be journalists, most subjects equivocated, though they were aware of the parallels:

> I guess in a way—you know you're observing a situation you're assessing it, its credibility and, uh, the importance to society and you're passing it along the same. Yeah, I guess it's something I've never really thought about, though, but it makes sense. (John)

Roberto is a former freelancer, and members of his site are listed as reporters. The answer to "Is what you do journalism?" tended to shift according to the subjects' perception of mainstream media. Nick, for instance, sees the modern journalist as part of an entertainment complex, and his work as a purer form of government monitoring:

> That's what inspired me and motivated me to get out there and be part of the First Amendment movement, to take reporting back and take media back. I don't consider myself a news journalist, but I do exercise rights of the press.

The subjects who spoke to me as part of this project talk about gear much the way professional photographers do, and many of them have invested in semipro or even professional-grade technology:

> I'm more of a grab-and-go, kind of on the run, so I use a shotgun mic mostly, but I do have all the audio gear. Then, you know, a laptop computer these days, it comes with some pretty rudimentary editing software that I use. I'd like to learn how to use some more sophisticated editing software, but I don't know if it's really worth the time and trouble. (Clint)
>
> Both [my partner] and I use Canon DSLRs. Both of us have purchased telephoto lenses because now our perimeters keep getting moved back farther and farther to prevent us from filming. We use long lenses and cell phones, too. We've been trying to live-stream whenever we can. ("Anthony")

To ensure that the video is recorded, cop-watching groups have turned to live-streaming apps that automatically save their clips in case police seize their cameras. The American Civil Liberties Union has even created an app that makes it easy for individuals to record and automatically upload video to the organization for safekeeping and possible legal advocacy.

Proper camera technique is only part of effective cop-watching. The dissemination of narratives is essential.

Representations

Videos posted by Group-1 after observation nights did not mimic the dramatic sorts of scenes as captured during the deaths of Eric Garner or Walter Scott. Most of them portray people moving in the darkness. It's hard to tell in some ways who officers are and who citizens are; there are many rude conversations, some videos with pushing and shoving, and one in which an officer simply walks through an apartment complex politely (almost solicitously) asking residents whether they'd seen anyone on the property fighting.

The websites, Twitter feeds, and Facebook pages for cop-watchers offer videos that reflect broad categories of group practices. The first, discussed above, includes videos of interactions between police and the public made during cop-watch patrols. Another broad category (for this is not a content analysis but a description with an eye on practice) might be labeled as "car conversations," in which cop-watchers or sympathizers film themselves from within a car during a police stop, with conversations that are sometimes pleasant, other times contentious, even violent, as some officers are depicted grabbing cameras or knocking them to the ground. Cop-watcher sites also post videos of their protests and meetings. Finally, another category represents what some organizers call "First Amendment Checks," which record the responses of security officers at public locations either trying to kick photographers off the property, telling them (incorrectly) that they don't have the right to be using a camera, or again, occasionally violently grabbing at or destroying a camera. The videos are largely self-serving for the cop-watching groups and sometimes captioned with highly inflammatory headlines—even when, to an outsider, the incident is hard to interpret or seems innocuous.

Study participants say they post these videos not only as occasional illustrations of police abuse, but as a way of maintaining the larger surveillance effort, sharing advice and information, and keeping their connection to the cop-watching community. In this way, the network and social media seem just as critical to the process as the images. The posting, sharing, and reposting of videos help to connect the various groups and maintain community—a function beyond the documentary messages for the larger public. Maintaining their websites also allows groups to work around mainstream media:

> The internet is the real key, being able to share this with somebody. You needed the five-o'clock news back in the day to get a story out. Now anybody can be the reporter or the journalist and with no swing or bias in any way. It's, like, turn the camera on, here we are, my actions, your actions, and you bring everybody to that scenario. (Bruce)
>
> Yeah, video's a really powerful tool, and social media is great for spreading that video. They're like a one-two punch. (Leonard)

As with their use of the camera, subjects report that they try to stay current with the latest online technologies. Adding to their arsenal of websites and apps is a set of tools designed to let them protect what they film, even when an officer confiscates a camera. Live-streaming apps like Meerkat and U-Stream send video to the cloud to ensure that any evidence collected remains under the photographers' control.

The Officers' Perspective

Law enforcement is a culture of control: controlling situations, people, and messages. Cop-watching represents a threat to all three, and interviews with police representatives suggest a grudging acceptance of police accountability activism. Many departments already have policies in place that uphold federal court rulings establishing a general right for citizens to film police. A police information officer from Philadelphia says the department occasionally sends out reminders:

> I think it's something that our department has seen for quite some time. We're used to it in a sense, but we do reiterate that with our officers via the policy, making them aware and reminding them that it's the right of the public to film you unless they're causing some type of danger or something to you.

Another city's public information officer (PIO) put it similarly:

Anybody can take pictures. That's a First Amendment right. In a public setting, you can take pictures. There are certain—so if you're taking pictures
and you're not in our crime scene, then clearly you have the right to do
that. There isn't—where we set our policies and procedures on more is the
part of whether or not somebody is hindering our ability to conduct our
investigation.

Officers may not be able to control the message, but they expect to control
the scene. The police chief of a suburban department with extensive experience in a major city issued a written order reminding his officers that people
have the right to record them as long as, again, they do not interfere with
an investigation. The chief also emphasized that video helps police with
investigations, and in fact may be more beneficial than not.

There's no doubt that we are under a microscope like we have never been
before. I've been doing this for fifty-two years, and the last several years
with the technology of the cameras, the iPhones, I think it's good that it
holds police accountable. It's also good for the police doing investigations,
because I can't tell you how many crimes we've solved. . . . There's probably not a day goes by that we don't download, extract, forensically examine
some type of cell phone for some type of criminal activity. Just on the cell
phones. The cameras, I mean when we go to a crime scene: robbery, rape,
murder, shooting, stabbing, the first thing we look for is cameras, because
everybody's got a camera.

Nevertheless, video for the sake of accountability seemed an annoyance for
some officers, even when they quoted official police. For instance, a public
information officer from Berkeley explained that the department respects
the rights of citizens to film, but that members of Cop-watch operated differently than the average onlooker:

Generally members of the public are filming usually from a greater distance.
Cop-watch has a tendency to really get closer than anybody else generally
will, which oftentimes makes officers uncomfortable from an officer safety
perspective. They're trying to pay attention to a person who is standing very
close to where they're trying to conduct an investigation, as well as monitor
the movements of the person that they have detained.

Q: From a policy standpoint, are there any policies about how close people can get?

We have a general order that governs the community's right to watch. That's what the general order's called, the "Right to Watch." It doesn't give any specific number of feet. It says that you may watch from a safe distance, and that officers are encouraged not to tell people to move back, but if it becomes a matter of officer safety, and they feel like that person's efforts are obstructing an investigation, they may ask them to move back.

How close is "too close"? Police officers are the ones who make that decision, and the subjective nature of the call is often where friction develops:

Let's say in the downtown area, there's a drunk that just got into a fight with somebody or there's a drunk that just beat up his girlfriend or whatever. We're actively trying to arrest him and there's a fight, and people are getting up too close or whatever. We have the ability and the authority by state law and by the Constitution to tell people to back away. We can't tell them to stop recording, and we don't, we can't tell them to put their cameras away. We can make sure that they're ten to fifteen feet away and not two to three feet away. Does that make sense? We have every right to do that to keep ourselves safe. (western city PIO)

None of the officers interviewed thought cameras were inconsequential:

I think it changes the perspective of a lot of people involved, not just police officers, but I think you change the perspective from both sides of the table. It's going to change the behavior of individuals that encounter police or engage police or interact with police. I certainly think it changes the behavior of police officers in terms of, if anything, making them be mindful about their level of professionalism. (Philadelphia PIO)

Perhaps because video has played such a prominent role in discourse about policing in the past decade, the officers interviewed for this project and those observed in other contexts display of remarkable visual literacy. As more citizens post videos that show what appears to be misconduct, officers are quick to call out the limits of such evidence and recontextualize it into a more sympathetic narrative.[37] The Berkeley PIO's assessment is typical:

Often what we see in the news is a patchwork of clips, and you don't necessarily get the full picture of what transpired. You see the five to ten seconds
of the fight itself, which is always ugly, which is always going to shape public
opinion, because any use of force is ugly, versus the time leading up to it and
the time afterwards.

This public information officer, for instance, would like the public to understand the limits of badge cams:

We live and we react in a three-dimensional world. Cameras are done on
a two-dimensional plane, and the scope of the camera's lens doesn't catch
everything that the human eye sees. This isn't a Hollywood video shoot
where the lighting is perfect and you have seven different camera angles
and you know exactly where the bad guy is gonna be standing when he pulls
his gun. You have a camera on a human being that is moving and making
movements, and the lighting may not be good, and so as good as the technology is, you're not gonna see everything on the camera.

The answer, according to a public information officer in a city known for its
liberalism, is to cultivate a strong relationship with the community:

If a message is sent, whether it be by the media or by a group that puts out
a video and it's out of context, . . . or they put their statement on a video,
sometimes it can be misinterpreted. I think it's very important for every department to have a very good public information office that can work with
the department and the chiefs to actually craft their own message to push
out to the media.

The police perspective on cop-watching is not surprising, given the nature
of visual evidence and the law enforcement culture. Video is useful when it
can solve crimes but has its limits, and those limits come up when police
are under critique. Attacking the evidentiary value of a cop-watching video
requires visual literacy to deconstruct its production and recontextualization
in narrative. While officers generally concede the truth value of camera evidence, most of them spoke of cop-watching—and cop-watchers—as something they were required to endure, not embrace. It may be the mark of
success that a movement designed to be a nuisance to power is felt that way.

Voice, Embodiment, Witnessing

Together, the motivations, practices, and representations of the cop-watchers in this study can be conceived of as loudspeakers, giving voice to what they perceive to be a large social problem while relying on visual evidence for authority. Dissatisfied with mainstream coverage and what they perceive as an overly cozy relationship between journalists and police, they endeavor to be their own watchdogs of government. Using the evidentiary power of the camera, they engage in embodied practices designed to record police interactions. Their stories are carried via social media to connect with other cop-watchers while presenting what they consider to be evidence of police misbehavior.

Confrontation versus Observation

The purposive nature of the cop-watchers' rituals constitutes a form of embodied narrative practice. They go out at night expecting to see injustice, bullying, and rudeness, and they employ practical strategies to capture it when they can, harnessing new media to broadcast what they find. Their work contrasts with that of the accidental citizen journalists who happen upon beatings and shootings, for they do not necessarily encounter such incidents during their routines. Instead, cop-watchers see their work as much a matter of prevention and Foucauldian monitoring. Sean says he has seen a difference in police procedures in the nightclub district since Group-1 started its patrols. Charles is dedicated to helping others in the same way he was helped by a bystander whose video convinced a jury to acquit. Steve put it this way:

> If it turns out to be something, then you're a combination of a protector of sorts, because you're there, hopefully, convincing the officer not to do what they would normally do. Not to violently harm someone and/ or not to infringe upon their rights in any way that they wouldn't care to be on film doing. Hopefully you can protect them to some extent. If not, then you've got a video and hopefully you can show that officer, that department, to the world. People, hopefully, will eventually wake up.

A college student who worked with Andrea Pritchett in Berkeley also considers cop-watching as preventative:

> We don't set out to go find police, like, acting unlawfully or something like that. We go to make sure that they are acting in accordance with the law to protect our community members, because they are at risk. Because the act of cop-watching itself and going out and making the police feel the presence, that we are there, it kind of obligates them . . . to be law-abiding police, not abuse their power and abuse their rights that they know that somebody's watching them.

A nurse who keeps watch over officers in her city's gay club district is motivated to protect her child:

> I have a transgender teen and I worry and worry and worry. I'm like, you better not ever go to jail. It's really the most frightening part to me, as a parent of the transgender child, of what would happen to him if he ever got in trouble with the police. It terrifies me, every day of my life I think about that. (Noreen)

While these subjects expressed a desire to protect, other cop-watchers are motivated by a desire to stand up to power. The Second Amendment activists, for instance, will run checks at public buildings to see how law enforcement will respond to their cameras and guns. Charles follows the principles of nonviolence when he patrols but is comfortable verbally assailing officers whom he considers to be malefactors. In fact, the group changed its rule to merely *discourage* cursing instead of prohibiting it, because, Charles explained, sometimes it seems appropriate.

> When I curse at cops, it's after they've infringed upon someone's civil liberties, or they're just acting extremely aggressive in their behavior, where basically, my caveat is, well, if they break the law, if they trample on civil liberties, they break their own policies, then, at that point, I'm not going to hold people back from cursing. . . . The only reason that you, that—the only reason why we're even listening to you is you're the gun in the room, y'know. You can use violent force against us, you can kill us, and so that's the

only reason that we're even acknowledging you. Um, but we don't respect you, in the manner that you're behaving.

Andrea Pritchett, the woman who co-founded Berkeley Copwatch, one of the oldest and longest-operating groups in the U.S., is concerned about confrontational cop-watching:

> There's a lot of groups around that call themselves Cop-watch. Our criteria is basically, if you're involved in direct observation of the police and you're committed to nonviolence and noninterfering, then we would classify that as a cop-watching activity. Some groups of people feel like they want to be able to intervene in moments of injustice or perceived injustice, and it's not what we do. It's not what we train people to do.

The propensity to be confrontational seems largely, though not entirely, a function of gender, with men more likely to be comfortable with confrontation—to emphasize: *not entirely*. A female member of the group observed during the night on patrol had a reputation for being the most confrontational, and in another city, a male cop-watcher told me he has a self-imposed rule against yelling at police. Pritchett believes nonviolence is essential to long-term effectiveness:

> It reminds me of the civil rights movement, and how they were training people to deal with racist aggression at the lunch counters, and so forth. How do you teach somebody to just sit there and take it? And it's because they had a real understanding of the strategy that they were using. People wouldn't sit there and get beat up at a lunch counter if they didn't think that it was part of a bigger strategy that was ultimately going to work. And so again, cop-watchers who feel like the whole struggle happens on the street corner, I think, conduct themselves differently from people who see the Cop-watch moment as part of a bigger strategy.

Gender differences may be a result of socialization, as women are taught to avoid confrontation and feminine activism has historically often used nonviolent witnessing as a tactic. Because police violence is so deeply rooted in the institution's toxic masculinity, however, it is impossible to avoid the police accountability movement's gendered dimension.

More Than Video

Cop-watching's effectiveness lies at the intersection of embodiment and the text. Citizens who watch, patrol, and witness provide the counternarratives, and video affords the authority. Voice and visibility—that is, the active participation in showing the reality of one's life—are linked in discourses that challenge authority. Andrea Pritchett considers the camera just part of her activist tool kit:

> To me, Cop Watch is more than video, it's about accountability. . . . We started Cop Watch without video. It was about the relationships. It was about stopping police misconduct through the act of witnessing. . . . The ability to cop-watch is improved when we have relationships with the people that we're observing—people who let us into their community or understand that we will make the footage available to them and that we're not just an adjunct of the police or something like that.

Consequently, cop-watching groups engage in other forms of activism, such as know-your-rights workshops or picketing.

> We also do protests pretty regularly. Those are mainly based on when something's happened. . . when there's a high-profile police brutality incident we do protests around that. We do have monthly know–your-rights seminars that are done by a local lawyer. (Larry)

Cop-watchers also monitor city meetings and filings for public records, taking on the role of subjective citizen journalist. In fact, Clint believes police accountability activists are doing the work that legacy media ought to:

> I think, bottom line, that's the problem with the established media in the United States today, is that they draw the line, because they know if they go over that line, they will be cut off, and that's unfortunate. As far as I'm concerned, it's been disastrous to the news business.

Noreen, who cop-watches in the same city as Clint, also considers the camera one part of the long-range effort.

We've organized many, many different demonstrations. I don't like to call myself a protester, I'm a community activist. We've organized some really good events. The main thing is, I want the city administration to know we're not going anywhere. They keep talking about let's move forward, let's move forward. My position is you can't move forward until we get these killers off our police force. We've got to get them off the force. It's not just a handful of bad apples, it's an entire culture.

By purposefully engaging in cop-watching, by using their bodies to witness and to engage in activism, this activism gives voice to the complaints of others, not only their own. At their best, cop-watchers might be considered altruistic (and at their worst, as shrill agitators). Couldry's reminders of the normative nature of voice—of listening, respecting, responding—resonate through these interviews.[38] To be able to account for one's life visually is fast becoming an essential right, or a capability, in the terminology of Sen and Nussbaum.[39] As an embodied narrative practice, cop-watching gives voice to social concerns heretofore unheard. At the start of a protest march against police brutality, one of the speakers held up her cell phone and declared, "We have the technology to stop this!" But the technology is nothing without counternarratives and embodied action.

In fact, the videos of cop-watchers are often deadly dull, for the very reason that their organized witnessing acts as a preventative. Incidental or bystander smartphone recordings have had a more dramatic impact on discussions about police accountability in the United States. In these cases, the camera's documentary power is central. For instance, after Walter Scott was shot and killed in 2015 during a traffic stop in South Carolina, the police officer involved was charged with murder.[40] Other recordings, such as the Eric Garner case in 2014 in New York City, have echoed Rodney King's—with a dramatic impact on public debate but still no sanctions against police.[41] In these and similar cases, the power of the camera and the role of surveillance prove to be uneven and complicated by other social, legal, and epistemological factors.

Video, therefore—even video of policing incidents—has limited value outside of discourse. Regina Lawrence has argued that "the status of most use-of-force incidents as either appropriate or excessive depends greatly upon who is asked to define those events. . . . Videotaped accounts are often as murky and inconclusive as the verbal accounts offered by eyewitnesses."[42] What many viewers considered "obvious" brutality in the King video was picked apart during the jury trial that exonerated the officers, a scenario that was also repeated with the more recent Garner case. If the success of cop-watching were measured only according to sanctions against police officers, it would be a remarkable failure.

The embodied, organized rituals of cop-watching—walking a patrol, staying up late into the night to drive a route through a low-income neighborhood, remaining in place when an officer charges forward—are practices that do not show up on a videotape, nor do they incorporate the technology normally considered part of contemporary surveillance. This form of activism reflects commitment to giving voice to those who've been marginalized, ignored, or outright silenced.

More than half of all midsize to large police departments in the United States have adopted body-cam programs.[43] President Barack Obama encouraged their adoption in 2014 after the Ferguson riots, and the technology has largely been seen as an important component of police accountability.[44] The cameras are relatively inexpensive, but video storage and management are very expensive, and so some cities are already dropping the programs as their true cost becomes clearer and as departments wrangle with citizens over when and how video should be released.[45] While data from one city indicate that badge cams reduce citizen complaints,[46] badge cams cannot displace the work of police accountability activists. The equipment can be turned off if a rogue officer intends to break the law, and if police control the video, then it might not be released at all. As cop-watchers themselves have observed, video alone has limited authority to define reality; oversight power lies not in the camera but in its possibility. The fact that citizens can and do record police activity is what is influencing public discourse.

8

Police and Image Maintenance

Scene: The story had to be written and edited quickly, as this was back in the days of three-quarter-inch tape and analog editing. I was covering the funeral of a police officer and had produced what's called an "insert" for my noon live shot. The visuals were dramatic, with straight lines of uniformed officers in perfect formation, dress pants, white gloves, shined black shoes. Service from the music supported the narrative, and the piece ended with a solo trumpet playing "Taps." When I returned to the newsroom, the anchor said the piece was "one of the best" we'd ever aired. It was simultaneously a moving tribute to a fallen officer and a piece of police propaganda.

During the Black Lives Matter protests inspired by George Floyd's death in 2020, police officers in several cities symbolically took a knee with protesters to demonstrate solidarity and respect for the cause.[1] One of those demonstrations occurred in Buffalo, New York, on June 3, 2020.[2] The next day, one of the Buffalo officers who took a knee appeared to be (based on facial features and his name tag) part of a phalanx in riot gear that shoved an elderly man so hard his skull was fractured.[3] One activist tweeted the next day, "This is why you don't kneel with cops."[4] The original gesture seemingly offered in solidarity in just twenty-four hours turned into what appeared to be a cynical ploy.

Police in democratic societies cannot function without the public's trust. Without trust, it is feared, no one will bear witness, citizens will ignore the law, and chaos will prevail. Law enforcement organizations have long recognized that they must have public support if they are to function and are, in the words of Chermak and Weiss, "unfortunately consumed by this battle."[5] Public relations efforts are engaged in this fight, and while visual messaging has also historically been part of the strategy, it is increasingly important in this digital age.

As seen throughout this book, police have historically used images for criminal investigation. Today, however, as visual production has become democratized, law enforcement agencies are able to reach out directly to

Seeing Justice. Mary Angela Bock, Oxford University Press. © Oxford University Press 2021.
DOI: 10.1093/oso/9780190926977.003.0008

the public with sophisticated visual messaging while ramping up rhetorical responses to visuals not under their control. Chapter 7 studied the way citizen cop-watching groups have taken on the role of surveilling police for the sake of accountability. This chapter attends to the way law enforcement's relationship with reporters is changing through a degradation of the credential system, how departments are reaching out directly to the public with their own visual messaging, and how officers endeavor to control narratives when they can't control the visuals. Faced with unprecedented calls for greater accountability, law enforcement officers are using a variety of discursive and material techniques to maintain authority.

Evidence, Authority, and Control

The nature of police work cultivates paternalism. Exerting patriarchal authority is what police do—male or female, Black or white; it becomes who they *are*, even though it is antithetical to the liberal democratic ethos. Police officers expect their authority as embodied representatives of the law to be respected and unquestioned. At the extreme, this belief may give some officers the sense that they *are* the law, not its representatives. The law enforcement community often responds with considerable resentment when its authority is questioned, even when its leaders speak publicly of accountability and transparency. This autocratic characteristic is rooted in the earliest days of policing, when men who protected royal lands in fifteenth-century England drew their power from the royal hierarchy.[6] This sense of righteous authority and its associated practice of practical violence traveled into Colonial America.[7]

Police authority historically mirrored a man's domestic authority, a hierarchy that placed masculinity, whiteness, heteronormativity, and (historically) Christianity[8] above women, children, and others. The moral dimension to the job imbues police culture with a binary black-and-white way of thinking that is associated with toxic masculinity.[9] Even today, the violent, autocratic dimensions of patriarchy permeate police culture in their departments and at home.[10] Police families experience domestic violence four times as often as average American families, a statistic blamed in part on patriarchal attitudes and the closed "thin blue line" culture of law enforcement.[11]

White supremacy is another trait common to police culture; indeed, many US police agencies started as slave-hunting groups and even today officers are occasionally found to be members of the Ku Klux Klan.[12] The Plain View Project, which examined the social media accounts of current and former officers in cities including Philadelphia and St. Louis, found hundreds of racist, violent, misogynistic, and Islamophobic posts—so many and so shocking that some departments immediately started internal investigations.[13]

These cultural markers, coupled with the unique stresses of policing, reinforce blue-line culture, in which many officers consider themselves uniquely apart from the civilians they are sworn to protect, a sort of deep-seated siege mentality.[14] While many law enforcement agencies are responding to pressure from the community to diversify their ranks and engage more closely with civilians, blue-line culture remains a force of its own, often not even under the control of formal leadership. Stress, trauma, and constant interaction with criminals fuel this estrangement, which then seeks balm from righteousness. An essay by former New York Police Department officer Graham Campbell describes the emotional price of everyday police work:

> There have been many studies on the effects of poverty on communities, and rightfully so—the toll on their safety and health is vast and consequential. Less examined is what happens to officers who work 40 hours a week in [surrounded by?] abject poverty. I'm not saying it's the same. We officers have homes to go to in places that look much different. But you can't tell me that there's not some effect on us. We're not robots. And every time I'm working—dealing with the terrible things happening to unfortunate people—and someone yells, "Hands up, don't shoot," it hardens me a little more. I back into my corner with my brothers and sisters in blue, people who understand me.[15]

Add to this the hypermasculine taboos against asking for help, showing emotion, or even deescalating a confrontation, and it's no wonder that today's pressure on police to become more accountable to civilians seems primed for a backlash. Until recently, police have been able to influence the creation, narrativization, and presentation of their visual story. For decades they made and archived the mug shots, printed the wanted posters, and decided what went into the blotter each night. Their authority was largely unquestioned by the mainstream; only "troublemakers" and minorities had problems with the law. Journalists have historically relied on police reports as primary sources, often quoting them verbatim. Law enforcement had the advantage of institutional authority as well as usually being first to narrativize an event. Digital media have eroded these advantages, as activists post videos of police work and communities put pressure on agencies for transparency.

Powerful institutions don't give up easily, and so police agencies have countered with their own measures for regaining control. First and foremost, they work to control the release and dissemination of images, particularly any image that might undermine their legitimacy. Second, they're working to create their own visual record in terms of evidence, with surveillance video and badge, body, and dashcams. In keeping with long-standing practices of using the camera as an investigatory tool, police departments today are also using visual messages to bypass news organizations with public relations projects. Finally, police efforts to recontextualize visual media into legitimizing narratives are becoming increasingly sophisticated.

Police Public Relations

Police work is largely a matter of public relations, as officers cannot be everywhere all the time. Citizens must have faith in the system, which is why Christopher Wilson argued, "The police have always been knowledge workers of a kind."[16] To that end, they have used whatever symbolic means available to tell their story, whether with badges and uniforms, elaborate funeral rituals, or today's controversial "thin-blue-line" version of the American flag. Mug shots, wanted posters, and perp walks are also part of law enforcement's visual tool box, which goes beyond the use of images for crime-fighting itself, as with surveillance cameras and image-evidence.

In the mass media age, public relations efforts also meant that police organizations worked closely with journalists, with their two institutions forming a sort of tense symbiosis that generates the prevailing ideology. Police feed newsrooms stories and tip photographers to perp walks in exchange for long-term goodwill. Because crime is one of the most essential forms of local news, journalists have traditionally been highly dependent on police to the point that ethnographers believe reporters can succumb to a variant of the Stockholm Syndrome, adopting an ideological perspective that favors their patrons.[17] Finally, while power is usually negotiated in these relationships, sources—in this case, the police—usually hold the trump card in the form of information or geophysical access.[18] The ability to open and close the gates to information grants institutions the power to influence, if not set, the news agenda. Yet even though journalists rely on police for information, they still do play a watchdog role on behalf of the community at large and might not accept law enforcement's interpretation of events, especially now that more citizens are able to produce their own visual documentation—much to the aggravation of marginalized communities that have long complained that their accounts have been discounted in favor of police reports.

Police public information officers (PIOs) are likely to disagree that they hold the gatekeeping power in this relationship. Police officers often feel misunderstood by the public, journalists and academics.[19] The thin blue line cultivates a siege mentality, aggravated by the authoritarian nature of police work, in which only those inside really understand the job's challenges. In a seminal study based on observations of police encounters with the public, Albert Reiss noted, "The most common complaint officers in our studies voice about citizens is their failure to show respect for authority.[20] Perhaps the main reason police officers generally seek deference toward their authority is that it assures order and control in the situations they are expected to handle. Moreover, it is their major mean of control apart from the use of force or the threat of coercion (e.g., threats to arrest)." I quote Reiss here because this statement so perfectly summarizes the perspective of law enforcement to this day, suggesting that only two things are possible in any encounter: civilian obedience or the use of force. Cultivating authority is the essence of law enforcement's ideological project, and visual messaging is effective to that end.

As with any institution, it pays for police agencies to cultivate good relationships with the journalists who cover them. Traditionally, credentials served to manage a department's relationships with news reporters, but now that digital media allow for so many more people to participate as citizen journalists or activists, far fewer departments today issue credentials.[21] Very large cities, however, such as Chicago and New York, continue to issue press credentials. Acquiring a credential, or badge, gives reporters "insider" status and cultivates the sort of informal connections that promote sympathy for officers and the work they do. As such, credentials offer a way for agencies to exert formal and informal control over coverage, including the practice of embodied gatekeeping to control journalists' bodies and their geophysical access to news conferences, events, or crime scenes.

Because crime news is a staple of journalism, especially TV and visual journalism, physical and information access is extremely important for most news organizations. Crime news is popular in part because it is easily covered compared with more complex or abstract "issue" stories[22] and for its emotional draw (which at its worst is sensationalism). Access is the "capital," as Pierre Bourdieu would describe it,[23] under negotiation between police and the press.

Access is a powerful drug—one reason political elites learned to use it to curry favor with the visual press.[24] Heavy film and video cameras contributed to the rise of what Boorstin dubbed the "pseudo event,"[25] an activity whose primary purpose is to attract media attention, which at its worst might be considered a form of collusion in which journalists put more effort into producing a "show" than covering the news.[26] Today, cameras are much smaller while the number of people producing media is much larger. Managing the press is more complicated, and many agencies are responding by not managing the press at all, but working around journalists, especially journalists who are considered to be unsympathetic.

Shutting out reporters or news agencies that produce unflattering stories is commonplace. In Georgia, investigative reporter Brendan Keefe, who reported on several discipline problems at the Roswell Police Department, was barred from covering a police award ceremony held in the municipal building—public property.[27] My station was subjected to a brief blackout by the Des Moines police in the 1980s in response to an unflattering story. In Chicago, the Fraternal Order of Police Lodge Seven suggested that the *Chicago Tribune* has "worked as a kind of ally to the special prosecutor for the Laquan McDonald case. This is nothing new for the Tribune." The lodge's Facebook post concludes, "The wholly biased coverage of this case and so many others by Tribune reporters like Jason Meisner, Dan Hinkel, and Megan Crepeau is the key reason the FOP Board unanimously voted earlier this year to cease all cooperation with the Tribune."[28] Note that the post uses the names of the reporters as a way to single out those the FOB considered to be bad actors.

While police unions use social media to mobilize members, the democratization of multimedia production on social media has also opened up new opportunities for the police departments themselves. By producing their own media messages, departments can bypass journalists for the purposes of public relations. Facebook, Instagram, and Twitter have become important tools for police agencies in cultivating positive relationships with the public, and images are a key part of that effort. One very effective use of social media comes during emergencies, as with Amber Alerts for missing children or warnings about flooded roads: or nonviolent, apolitical situations that highlight law enforcement's protective ethos. Police social media, though, can also go far beyond conducting official business to constructing positive optics online.

Bypassing Journalists

Traditionally police departments have had to rely on local news organizations to cover good news or feature stories, but that is no longer necessary. While departments might still conduct weight-loss contests with the fire department or host ball games with children through a Police Athletic League, social media allow departments to take these stories directly to the public. Many departments have found considerable value in good-news badge-cam video, posting to social media clips of officers rescuing animals or playing basketball with neighborhood children.[29] The democratization of production has also given departments the tools to entertain, and in a sense create their own feature stories. The Philadelphia Police Department, for example, injects humor into its everyday Twitter feed as a way of cultivating a more human connection. A Philadelphia public information officer in 2016 said,

> I think at this point now—I mean, social media is something that—it allows you to see a different side of policing, but it also keeps you, allows you to stay informed in terms of—when I say "informed" I mean from the side of as police officers—we stay informed by looking at social media and seeing what people are discussing, what people are talking about, things that are at the moment, in terms of that are out there at a particular moment in time, the things that are hot topics and all those things. We get to see that, but I also think it gives us the opportunity of keeping people informed. . . . That's the good part of social media.[30]

Most departments now have Facebook and Twitter accounts to communicate with the public officially, and many agencies, professional organizations, and even police chiefs have accounts. Houston police chief Art Acevedo, for instance, was an early adopter during his time as chief in Austin, remarking on specific cases, public safety, and even politics. Research on the way police use Twitter is only beginning, but one early study found that while Toronto police used the network regularly, officers had wide discretion in the way they interacted with the public and largely ignored any Tweets that questioned their work.[31]

When prosecutor Kim Foxx dropped charges against entertainer Jussie Smollett, who'd been accused of staging a hate crime and filing a false police report in Chicago, the Fraternal Order of Police Lodge 7 used Facebook to publicize a demonstration against her.[32] Supporters of law enforcement similarly use social media to promote positive messages about policing. A mixed-methods analysis of the Facebook page Blue Matters (the national counterpart to a New York page called Blue Lives Matter) found that posts to the page reflected police culture in word and image.[33] All the dimensions of blue-line authoritarianism were reflected in the comments, videos, memes, posts, and images uploaded to the page. Police supporters also used the page to sell merchandise such as the blue-line flag, jewelry, and T-shirts.

Singing and Dancing

Fun challenges for the sake of publicity are a long-standing staple for police public relations. In many cities, police and fire departments have challenged one another for various "battles of the badge," such as in boxing tournaments, weight-loss competitions, even blood donation contests. These efforts required the cooperation of local media to cover them as feature stories—which often did for the sake of maintaining a good source relationship with the departments.

Because video equipment is now cheaper and easier to use, many more people, including police department staff, have relatively sophisticated production skills. Today's challenges are often depicted in high-quality music videos, with special effects, drone shots, and story lines. In 2016, dozens of departments were inspired by an online trend of NBA players posting videos while dancing to a 1996 song, "My Boo," by Ghost Town DJs. The so-called Running Man challenge bounced from department to department as police challenged one another to create similar dance videos.[34]

In 2018 music video mania struck again, with several hundred police and sheriffs' departments around the country challenging one another to the "Lip Sync Challenge." The trend made national news, and USA Today created a bracket so that viewers could vote for their favorites. The genre is replete with self-effacing humor and insight into police culture. Marin County's video features a dancing skeleton in the medical examiner's office.[35] Some scenes in the Lip Sync Challenge videos feature donut jokes, and more than a few videos reference friendly rivalry with firefighters. Some departments posted behind-the-scenes and interview videos *about* their lip sync videos. Mobile, Alabama, shot as a courtesy by a photography from a local TV station, featured an African American officer dressed and dancing as Michael Jackson on the city's streets.[36] Corporal Joshua Jones's behind-the-scenes interview summarized the purpose of these efforts for many departments: "We just hope that the world can see that police are human. Just like everyone else. And all we want to do is have fun, and protect and serve, and give our all to the people that we protect and serve."[37]

For instance, the most popular video in the sample, from the Norfolk, Virginia, Police Department, apparently used only one continuous shot, moving gracefully through nine different locations of the department. The camera appears to move from scene to scene seamlessly as Officer Christopher Taveras lip-synced and danced with his colleagues down hallways, through various offices, and finally into a parking lot for a crowded finale. The video used one song, the dance hit "Uptown Funk" by Mark Ronson featuring Bruno Mars. Officer Taveras, who became somewhat of a local celebrity because of the video, appears to be of mixed race, as is Mars.[38] The video was so popular it was shown on the *NBC Nightly News*, which featured video of Taveras posing with members of the public who wanted selfies with him.[39]

Seattle's entry to the Lip Sync Challenge of 2018 was similarly sophisticated, with scenes across the city that mimicked the original music video it borrowed from Macklemore and Ryan Lewis' "Downtown." The police department paid homage to a favorite son with dance moves straight from the original, a crowded street scene that seems to have included members of the public, even a trophy mooseead like the one Macklemore used. A local dance team contributed to the production, but the officers themselves proved to be exceptional as they lip-synced with the fast-paced rap. This video also included the sample's only instance of a reverse lip-sync crossover, for one of the officers who lip-synced while sitting on another officer's shoulders is Black (Macklemore is white). The result is an exultant video that presents the Seattle Police Department as fun, hip, and diverse.

For the sake of systematic study, I conducted a visual content analysis of a sample of these videos. Using the search term "2018 Police Lip Sync

Table 8.1 Production Values

Department	Length	Shots	Ave. Shot	Songs	Locations	Public?
Norfolk, VA	4:41	1	281.0	1	9	N
Cleveland, TN	2:30	37	4.1	1	4	N
Apple Valley, MN	3:49	22	10.4	1	11	Y
Flower Mound, TX	3:53	54	4.3	1	15	N
Warwick, CT	7:04	86	4.9	6	8	N
Skokie, IL	5:00	23	13.0	13	12	N
Granite Falls, NC	5:20	36	8.9	7	10	N
Kings County, CA	9:51	93	6.4	2	10	N
Seattle, WA	5:27	104	3.1	1	18	Y
Virginia Tech, VA	4:58	71	4.2	3	6	N
Averages	5:15	52.7	34.0	14:24	10.3	
Adjusted Averages		*58.4	*6.6	**2.5		

*average without Norfolk, VA; ** average without Skokie, IL

Challenge" on YouTube, I examined the top-ten 2018 listings according to YouTube's viewing stats, skipping over videos from fire departments and two that had actually been produced in 2016. I watched each video at least three times and coded them according to their demographics, song choices, editing pace, and inclusion of police symbolism (badges, guns, sirens, etc.). I logged each video (listing what is seen and heard on a vertical timeline) to note what was said and what was shown in each scene. I paid attention to the songs used in the videos, whether animals appeared (particularly police dogs), and whether members of the public took part in the production. Table 8.1 lists the videos and their production values.

Because marginalized communities are so often in conflict with the larger institutions of policing, I also examined the videos with an eye on race and gender for any scene with ten or fewer performers. I took particular interest in demographic crossover, that is, instances of a gender or race mismatch between the person lip-syncing and the original musical artist, that is, a male officer lip-syncing to a female artist or a white officer lip-syncing to a song from a Black artist. Table 8.2 presents the race and gender for the performers and crossover instances. While logging the tapes I also paid attention to the activities, story lines, and symbols incorporated into the videos, such as squad cars, flashing lights, or uniforms.

Table 8.2 Appearances by Race and Gender

Department	Officer/Staff Race and Gender				Crossover?
	WM	WF	Non-white Male	Non-white Female	
Norfolk, VA	8	3 (1 staff)	5	4 (2 staff)	None
Cleveland, TN	4	0	2	0	Gender, plus a stereotype match
Apple Valley, MN	22	10 (5 staff)	0	0	None
Flower Mound, TX	13 (1 staff)	7 (5 staff)	1	0	Gender and race
Warwick, CT	13 (2 staff)	5 (2 staff)	1	1	4 Race
Skokie, IL	25	5 (3 staff)	1	2 (1 staff)	6 Race
Granite Falls, NC	9	3	0	0	2 Race
Kings County, CA	4	1 staff	5	6	2 Race
Seattle, WA	18	6	4	5	*Reverse Race*
Virginia Tech, VA	12 (2 staff)	2	0	1	2 Gender
Totals	128	42	19	19	
Percent of N = 208	61.5%	20.2%	9.1%	9.1%	

Quantitative Findings

The music videos in this sample ranged from two and a half minutes to just over seven minutes, for an average of five minutes, fifteen seconds. The Norfolk, Virginia, video is extraordinary for its use of the steady cam and no apparent edits. The entire video appears to be one shot, which requires a great deal of practice for those performing and the steady-cam operator. For this reason, it was also useful to take Norfolk out of the average for the average number of shots in a video and resulting shot length. The average shot for the other nine videos was only 6.6 seconds long, which reflects high production values. These musical productions are not kids' play, but professionally conceived, carefully crafted artifacts.

Who performed for these videos? Most of the performing police are white men, 61.5 percent. About a fifth of those who appeared were white women, 20.2 percent. Non-white men (Asian, Black, Hispanic, or undetermined) appeared at the same rate as non-white women, 9.1 percent of the time. These numbers are out of sync with the population at large; there are far more people of color in the United States than appear proportionally in these videos, but because this is a small sample based on popularity, it cannot be used to make a statistical point about the demographics beyond the observation that the performers are mostly white male police officers.

Dominant Narratives

Looking at the videos at face value, or what Stuart Hall called the "dominant" reading, these videos are, as the Mobile, Alabama, officer explained, intended to show police officers as real people who can have a little fun.[40] The Norfolk video features a handsome officer who appears to be Hispanic leading other officers through an energetic dance around the station. When the horn section blows in "Uptown Funk," officers raise small traffic cones like trumpets. Officers in Flower Mound, Texas, dance to Meghan Trainor's "Me Too," in locations throughout the police station, including in front of a wall-size mural of a badge. Six male officers from Cleveland, Tennessee, depict a story of going to a mansion's pool, dancing, and then swimming while in uniform, all while channeling "Havana" by Camila Cabello, who is female The Kings County (CA) Sheriff's Department tells the story of officers arresting a man for dancing badly to Drake's "Kiki, Do You Love Me?" The prisoner is comically sent to a strip search, dressed in a chain gang–style prison outfit, and then he leads the whole department in a rollicking dance to LMFAO's "Party Rock."

Police from Skokie, Illinois, mixed thirteen songs into their music video, which starts at a public park with police arresting a perpetrator, played by an officer, for vandalism. The youthful officer lip-syncs to Will Smith's "Prince of Bel Aire," then other officers take over with Queen's "We Will Rock You," the "Macarena," and an officer who appears to be Asian leads a crowd through the hallway dancing to PSY's "Gangnam Style." Skokie's video ends as the chief playfully gestures to himself as Vanilla Ice raps "Yo, V-I-P" in "Ice, Ice Baby." The chief leads the way out of the station to a parking-lot scene where the entire cast dances to the Village People's "YMCA."

The group-dance closing shot might almost be considered part of the genre. While the video from Cleveland, Tennessee, featured only six officers, they all end up in the pool. Kings County's video ends with a big crowd scene, as do Skokie's and Norfolk's. Virginia Tech shot crowd scenes in a stadium, while officers from Warwick, Connecticut, used a jet and an airport as a backdrop.

The videos take advantage of sophisticated camera and editing techniques. Seattle's "Downtown" uses a special shuddering effect in some of its crowd scene edits. Other departments used drones for overhead crowd shots. (A 2016 video from Dakota County in Minnesota, which set the stage for these lip-sync videos, even used Go-Pro video from a skydiver.) The sound quality is consistently good, though in most cases the editors are merely using "borrowed" (i.e. copyright-protected) music.

Those acquainted with police culture might enjoy some inside jokes conveyed in the videos. Seattle and Virginia Tech included officers eating donuts.[41] Videos from Seattle and Granite Falls, North Carolina, make good-natured jibes at firefighters, part of a long-standing civic rivalry. Several videos open with and make a strong point from the start that they are answering a challenge, which in masculine culture cannot be ignored.

Negotiated Readings

A negotiated reading, in Hall's taxonomy, examines a text from a particular reader's chosen perspective. Here I choose to examine the videos according to their representations of race, gender, and police culture, because these are among the problematic dimensions for law enforcement today. A negotiated reading of this small sample suggests that while the videos did indeed show officers having fun with the music, they were often culturally tone-deaf, hawking a highly white, patriarchal, even oppressive version of fun.

In addition to the basic demographic count from the videos, Table 8.2 also lists the number of times a video includes what I've dubbed a "crossover," in which an officer lip-syncs a song sung by someone of another race or gender. The white officers from Cleveland, Tennessee, who lip-synced to "Havana," for instance, would be counted as a gender crossover. For anyone who is not acquainted with the group that sings the "banana" song, Apple Valley's video might *seem* like a crossover, but the Tokens, the group behind "The Lion Sings," was composed of white men. The white male officers from Warwick, Connecticut, lip-syncing to Flo Rida's "My House" would be counted as a racial crossover. Usually the crossovers involved white men or women lip-syncing to music from non-white performers, a form of cultural appropriation that might not be so awkward if not for the racial disparities in police violence. Non-white viewers might not see the lighthearted fun in lip-syncing to Black music from an institution that kills Black people six times more often than white citizens.

Other awkward moments in the videos included Warwick's use of "Under Pressure" by David Bowie, in a scene when officers are visiting inmates in the city jail, and the Flower Mound, Texas, female officer vamping with dominatrix boots in the department's gym. When the Skokie officers act out to the Village People's "Macho Man" in their gym, the group's blatant gay camp seems an odd fit. Anyone who knows the history of chain gangs in the United States might cringe to see a non-white man wearing a striped jumpsuit while dancing with the Kings County deputies, people who "arrested" him on the video-fiction's pretense of "dancing badly."

While it may seem unsporting to critique officers having fun with "Uptown Funk" or NSYNC's "Bye Bye Bye," these awkward moments undermine the positive intentions of such videos and reflect a lack of social awareness. Perhaps the most cringeworthy scene from the sample comes during the gender-crossing "Havana" video from Cleveland, Tennessee. Camila Cabello's version of the song includes a rap bridge from Young Thug. Who lip-syncs to the bridge in the video? The only Black officer in the group. The imagined audience for these videos seems not to be the marginalized people most in need of messages about law enforcement's humanity but instead other officers who live and work in blue culture.

Oppositional Readings

Hall described textual interpretations that reject and reverse the intended message as "oppositional readings." In the case of the 2018 Lip Sync Challenge, critics might take a cynical perspective and ask whether police ought to be involved in such public relations efforts at all. Several of the videos did try to preempt such criticism in the credits with a message such as, "No tax dollars were used to produce this video," but the critique might be about more than the money. From the production values, many of these videos clearly required considerable time, energy, and effort.

The trend caught attention from the national media in the summer of 2018, however. *USA Today* tallied the videos' popularity and kept a score sheet. Many of the videos were featured on local television broadcasts (and often produced with a local station's assistance), as well as the *NBC Nightly News*. If the goal of the videos was to generate positive press at a time when departmental morale was low, then the 2018 Lip Sync Challenge was a win for law enforcement, at least in the case of the dominant reading. A negotiated reading uncovers some blind spots on the part of producers, who seemingly overlook the dynamics of race and gender at the root of public distrust. An oppositional reading suggests an even more cynical perspective in which the lip sync challenge is yet one more strategy police might use to distract the public from the racist, misogynist, and violent dimensions of the criminal justice system.

Answering Citizen Videos

Law enforcement really needed a public relations win because of the number of negative videos that had gone viral prior to 2018. Clips of abusive police encounters made national news repeatedly: NFL player Desmond Marrow being choked on the sidewalk, the fatal shooting of Walter Scott after a traffic stop in South Carolina, the violent arrest of Sandra Bland, and the fatal shooting of Stephan Clark in his own backyard.[42] These events were often exacerbated by findings that officers had downplayed or twisted the facts in their reports, and perhaps more disturbing, most officers had suffered little consequence beyond bad publicity.

In the face of negative videos, police have developed a discursive tool kit for explaining away the video, one that is surprisingly effective. Law enforcement's discourse *about* video has become quite sophisticated for its use of film production language. Authorities' use of social media can augment this discourse by allowing officers to seek support directly from the public, bypassing journalists and controlling their own narrative. *Control* is the operative term, and it is the reason officers often interfere with police accountability activists on the street, in spite of directives reminding police that cop-watching is generally protected under the First Amendment.

There are, of course, myriad concerns involving privacy and criminal procedure with regard to the release of video from prisons, courtrooms, and crime scenes. At the same time, there can be no democratic accountability if law enforcement operates out of sight. Left unchecked, power tends to protect itself, and the state's ideological project demands control of the creation, distribution, and contextualization of visual media.

First Strategy: Block the View

When video is unflattering, authorities use whatever means are available to hide it from public view. Police accountability activist Antonio Buehler had to wait until his trial to see video that police had obtained from a convenience store camera—video that exonerated Buehler. An inside source for Shane Bauer's exposé of the private prison system told him that unflattering recordings from surveillance cameras were frequently destroyed.[43] In the case of Laquan McDonald, the Chicago police held on to the tape for more than a year, in part on the justification that McDonald's family did not wish for it to be released, even after the family had won a multimillion-dollar settlement from the city.[44] The McDonald video was only released after journalist Brandon Smith sued based on freedom of information laws.[45] Other reporters in the room used Twitter to ask questions on his behalf when he was barred from the city's news conference for lacking a press badge. In Texas, the couple who wanted to know what happened to their son fought two years for the release of a tape that showed him dying after being tased repeatedly, including a jolt to the testicles, while he was suffering from a bad LSD trip.[46]

Dashcams and badge cams often do not record the most important scenes, for both legitimate and suspicious reasons. There was no audio from the dashcam video of the McDonald case. Lance Becvar, the sergeant in charge of downloading video and audio from squad cars the night McDonald was killed, said that the microphones were not attached to the dashcam and were instead in the glove box with their batteries removed or turned upside down.[47] Under questioning from defense attorneys for Jason Van Dyke, the officer accused in the shooting, Becvar said the Chicago Police Department often had problems with video equipment and that he had no evidence that anyone deliberately tampered with the system that night.[48]

Police and prosecutors also try to withhold video from the public even after it has been played in open court. Attorneys for two officers tried for excessive force in Austin were depicted on badge-cam video using a taser on a man who was kneeling on the ground with his hands up. The pair was acquitted and successfully quashed the video from being released to the press, even though it was part of the trial's public record.[49] In Delaware, prison personnel were videotaped while standing, watching, and doing nothing while Tyrone Daniels died. The tape was played in court, but the officials fought its release ostensibly to protect the identity of the dead man: "According to counsel, the video does not provide information that furthers insight to the workings of government and depicts a dying patient victim whose identity we cannot protect from subsequent dissemination," explained a spokesman.[50] After journalists filed open-records requests, prison officials did release the video under order from the state attorney general's office.[51] The nurse in charge had already been sanctioned, but the video brought home the reality of Daniels's death to his family. "That facility just allowed our son to lay there and die," Daniels's father told reporters. "Why didn't help come? He needed help."[52] The argument that video cannot be released in order to protect the identity of an inmate does not stand up to logic: the names of people arrested for crimes are a matter of public record, as are their mug shots, prior to trial when they are presumed innocent. As explained in Chapter 3, even perp walks have been sanctioned by the courts for their public relations value to law enforcement.[53] For authorities to claim that hiding a tape is for the protection of a defendant would be laughable if these cases did not involve death at the hands of the state. To maintain that the public is somehow not capable of interpreting such videos is both disingenuous and disrespectful.

Efforts to hide or destroy visual evidence don't always succeed, though, and when the evidence is released, authorities are left only with discursive strategies. The Laquan McDonald case from Chicago serves as a useful illustration of three strategies that authorities use to explain away a video showing police misconduct. Each of these strategies has roots in the acquittal of the Los Angeles police officers accused in the Rodney King beating and represents key nodes in the recontextualization model described in Chapter 1. Three strategies can be seen in law enforcement language *about* video: the first might be called police "film criticism" for the way it focuses on media construction. The second strategy might be nicknamed "cop-splaining" for the way it focuses on police procedure. Employing language in this manner is a well-known strategy to scholars who use critical discourse analysis to investigate the way people in power draw upon euphemism, jargon, or doublespeak.[54] Finally, when all else fails, police discourse resorts to authoritarian appeals. These patriarchal justifications claim that they must protect us and imply that the police must be our disciplinarians. When officers use this strategy—the primary strategy of police unions—the effect of criticizing law enforcement is to undermine its protective capabilities.

Controlling the Narrative

One of the most important strategies for discounting a negative video is to provide the narrative first, which has the discursive advantage of "naming" the event. Getting ahead of the story is a standard public relations technique, and the Chicago Police Union has used this technique to its benefit, making sure media have an officers' version of events before anyone else has had a chance to comment, such as a union representative whose job it is to get a scene immediately in order to address reporters.[55] Crafting a narrative this way can influence the headlines even when video is released later that contradicts the police version of events.

If police can't be first, there is still an opportunity to renarrativize the recording once it's released, because police have the advantage of traditional authority and media influence, though this may not be as strong as it once was. Renarrativization takes advantage of the fact that while raw, unedited, and unmanipulated video has evidentiary value, it only presents what was recorded. Especially in the case of bystander video, this means that the precipitating events will not be on tape, because witnesses won't hit "record" until they are aware that something is happening. Since any clip can never tell the whole story, officers hoping to explain away negative news are quick to exploit this weakness. The critique is so ingrained in the law enforcement community that during a citizen workshop, an officer was able to get the group to respond in unison that video "doesn't show the whole story!" A related critique, made more relevant by badge-cams, is that a camera can only document what was in front of it and that one angle cannot possibly show everything that was happening. One PIO referenced video from his department of a police officer playing basketball with children as an example of a body camera's subjectivity. Throughout the tape, it's possible to see people moving and hear shouting and ball bouncing, but the ball is hardly seen at all:

> It kind of goes to the fact that we live and we react in a three-dimensional world. Cameras are done on a two-dimensional plane and the scope of the camera's lens doesn't catch everything that the human eye sees. . . . This isn't a Hollywood video shoot where the lighting is perfect and you have seven different camera angles and you know exactly where the bad guy is gonna be standing when he pulls his gun.

A badge-cam's subjective, wide-angle lens moves with an officer's body and can only record what's in front of it. Even this is a distortion of what an officer sees. A large-city PIO explained that his department had to learn not only what cameras to buy but how they should be worn. "Do you wear it on your shoulder, do you wear it on your lapel? Do you wear it in the place of a button? Where do you wear this thing?" Other considerations—besides when and how the public might be able to view any badge-cam video—include when to turn it on and off, how long video should be stored, and how videos should be redacted to protect the privacy of innocents.

The discourse of film critique, rooted in theories of media construction, is old hat to media producers and scholars, and it is valuable. Yet it is a bit of a twist for law enforcement, and somewhat ironic considering the degree to which images have historically been used to combat crime. Officers are often quick to acknowledge that badge-cam video cuts both ways and can exonerate officers as much as disparage them. One of the earliest and most-cited studies—from Rialto, California—found that citizen complaints against police went down after officers started wearing badge-cams.[56] This may not be because officers changed their behavior. One theory suggests that complaints went down in part because citizens would withdraw their complaints after viewing video of *their own behavior*.

Discourse about the constructed nature of video was among the defense strategies at the Jason Van Dyke trial in Chicago. For example, defense attorneys reminded jurors that video is a two-dimensional rendering of reality, as the *Chicago Tribune* reported:

> On cross-examination of the FBI analyst, Van Dyke's lawyer, Daniel Herbert, noted that videos may not completely and accurately capture what actually happened, particularly a relatively low-quality video like the dashcam footage.
> "It's difficult to judge proper depths on a video, correct?" he asked Paul Rettig.
> "That's because it's two-dimensional . . . so distances are distorted, correct?"
> "They can be," Rettig replied.[57]

Van Dyke's partner went so far as to reenact his movements from the night McDonald was killed, though his demonstration contradicted the video's timeline. Again, it is worth quoting the *Tribune*'s coverage at length, because it so perfectly describes the strategy of film criticism:[58]

Toward the end of his testimony at Jason Van Dyke's murder trial Tuesday, indicted former Chicago police Officer Joseph Walsh stepped off the witness stand and walked in front of the jury box.

He then performed his version of events leading up to Laquan McDonald's shooting. Playing the role of the 17-year-old victim, Walsh swung an imaginary knife behind his back and then up to about shoulder height. The teen, he told the Cook County jury, then turned his head toward the officers, looking at them with "a stare and a focus beyond us."

Walsh's message was clear: The infamous video did not accurately depict what happened that night.

But as the *Tribune* reported, what Van Dyke's partner claimed in court did not match the video evidence:

> The dramatic re-enactment, done at the defense team's behest, didn't match the police dashboard camera video that has made national headlines and sparked citywide protests. While depicting McDonald's actions, Walsh also took much longer than the six seconds it took Van Dyke to open fire after exiting his vehicle.

Another witness, an FBI video expert, manipulated the video in order to try to make a point. He used a slow-motion version of the dashcam videos and tried to connect images of puffs of smoke to bullet directions; this testimony was stricken from the record by the judge, who said, "He has no background in what the smoke means."[59] The defense tried again the next day, playing the video at quarter speed, changing the reality that was experienced in real time. This extreme slowdown manipulation of the video is straight out of the Rodney King trial playbook. Slow-motion video can help uncover additional information, but it can also confuse the issue at hand—in this case, whether Jason Van Dyke had lawful reason to shoot and kill McDonald or not. During the trial, the lack of sound on the tape (which may have been the result of police sabotage), a key element of video's epistemological authority, was missing, which also makes it possible to undermine the evidence.

> Video was also used in slo [*sic*] motion to determine where the bullets hit based on debris from the pavement—but without audio, it was hard to interpret. Van Dyke's partner apparently flinched, too, indicating that he wasn't expecting gunfire.[60]

The dashcam video from the McDonald case is unclear about whether the teen was walking toward or away from officers, and so on this point the defense was able to undermine the video's evidentiary value. But the discrepancies between what *could* be seen on the video and what officers initially reported and then testified to in court cast doubt on the police version of events. An expert on the use of force who testified during the trial concluded that Van Dyke's decision was "unsound."[61]

Procedural Explanations

"Awful but lawful" is police-culture jargon that sums up the second strategy for explaining unflattering video, in which procedural explanations are used as justifications.

This was the strategy successfully employed in the trial of officers involved in the Rodney King beating, and it often employs euphemisms such as "subdue," "neutralize," or "control" in relation to situations rather than human beings. A public information officer from the Southwest sought sympathy for his colleagues while explaining his department's video policy:

> We don't expect our officers to be confronted with a life-or-death situation and turn their cameras on before they defend themselves. That wasn't written in the policy, so we had an officer that was ambushed in his police car, for example, and he defended himself and he shot and then there was no video. Well why didn't he turn his video on? Well, because his first responsibility is to protect himself, not video recording and protecting himself.

Procedural language elides questions about whether the suspect was hurt or whether the alleged crime was worth such a confrontation. Moreover, by replacing words like "suspect" or "person" with "threat," an individual is no longer human, which further distances police work from the lived experience of citizens. In the Laquan McDonald case, for instance, the teenager who was fatally wounded was recorded in police reports as the offender, even though eventually the officer was charged with murder and four officers were fired after a panel determined that they'd exaggerated the threat McDonald posed in order to justify the shooting.[62]

The training justification strategy played a significant role in Van Dyke's trial. For example, Officer Dora Fontaine, who never saw McDonald threaten the officers with his knife, contended during cross-examination before the grand jury in 2015 that McDonald was still a threat even while he was lying on the ground. "Still has a weapon. As long as he has a weapon, yes," was her answer, an assessment she continued to maintain during trial testimony.[63] Nicholas Pappas, a former firearms instructor who trained Van Dyke, was also called to the stand, and he testified that officers are trained to look out for knives because they can pierce a bulletproof vest and a person with a knife can move more than twenty feet in less than two seconds.[64] Another defense witness reenacted such a scene for jurors by bounding toward an attorney with a toy knife, to demonstrate how fast an attacker can move.[65] When Officer Van Dyke testified on his own behalf, he referred to his training to explain why he continued to fire even after McDonald was on the ground. The *Tribune* quoted the exchange with his defense attorney:

> "I ejected the magazine from the gun and started to reload the weapon as I was trained," he told the jury.
> He stopped reloading when his partner told him it wasn't necessary.
> "He said, 'Jason, I got this,'" Van Dyke said.
> Van Dyke said he watched his partner, Joseph Walsh, kick the knife out of McDonald's hand. Once that threat was eliminated, he called for help, he told the jury.[66]

Van Dyke was eventually found guilty of second-degree murder and sixteen counts of aggravated battery, one for each shot. He was acquitted of official misconduct charges and was sentenced to what observers called a relatively lenient eighty-one months in prison.[67] Months after the sentencing, the lead prosecutor and defense attorney Dan Herbert met for a public discussion of the case, where, once again, the defense relied on police training to explain Van Dyke's decisions, as quoted in the *Chicago Sun Times*: "[Van Dyke] was not an individual that was acting out of malice, he was not acting that different, at all different, from how he was trained," Herbert said.[68] During the discussion, Herbert suggested that Van Dyke was not "charming" enough, a comment that is interesting for the way it draws from the discourse of patriarchal logic by implying that the jury needed an emotional appeal could not see the cold facts.

Authoritarian Appeals

Finally, when it is impossible to deny what is shown on video, police officers often resort to what might be colloquially named the "good guy" defense or the "righteous cause." This strategy is based on law enforcement's authoritarian role and need for autonomy in making judgment calls. Rather than speak to the incident in question, law enforcement officers stake claim to the virtuous position of a crime-fighter willing to combat evil. New York City police commissioner William Bratton charged that what he called the "YouTube effect" would make officers less aggressive about fighting crime.[69] Similarly, in comments to journalists in 2016, FBI director James Comey suggested that "viral video" causes officers to be less aggressive, resulting in more danger on the streets. "There's a perception that police are less likely to do the marginal additional policing that suppresses crime," he told reporters, "the getting out of your car at two in the morning and saying to a group of guys, 'Hey, what are you doing here?'" [70] Conservative media have been quick to declare that there's a "war on cops" in the United States, which contradicts the evidence.[71] The war, it seems, is really one of words, in which some journalists and members of the public no longer automatically believe everything that officers say. Declaring, without evidence, that there is a "war on cops" uses a metaphor that divides officers from the public, evoking the siege mentality noted by those who've studied police culture.[72] Such rhetoric reflects the zero-sum perspective of toxic masculinity: if Black lives matter, surely that must mean that Blue lives do not.

This ethos, and the appeal to moral authority, has extended into police public relations. Many departments now run workshops for public outreach, to lead civilians through brief classes about police procedure. One popular component of these classes involves citizens role playing or using a virtual reality video game that reenacts use-of-force decisions. The director of one such workshop explained, "We give them a chance to make the decisions and they realize how hard it is to make a decision in that unusual situation."[73] Civilians are taught the militaristic phrase "neutralizing the threat," which applies to all sorts of actions—hitting suspects, using headlocks, wielding batons and throwing people to the ground—framed as justified moral authority.

Bad publicity about officers killing unarmed civilians during traffic stops—such as Philando Castille in 2016[74] and Paul Witherspoon in 2019[75]—have inspired educational campaigns for drivers on how to behave when pulled over by an officer. The state of Texas, for instance, now *requires* all high school students to watch a video about how to behave during a traffic stop (and not, though this is unsaid, get shot.)[76] The sixteen-minute video, introduced by a Black legislator (State Senator Royce West), features white teenagers clearly violating the speed limit and officers who are unfailingly polite—not at all the type of traffic stop that prompted public concern in the first place.[77]

Traffic stops are particularly scary for police, and the training videos about them are terrifying,[78] even though statistical research shows that such stops are not particularly dangerous.[79] Even though the odds are far in their favor, there is always the chance of being ambushed and killed by a criminal who doesn't want to be caught at a traffic stop. Police training videos emphasize the unknown, and law enforcement then uses this fear as a justification for killing drivers at traffic stops. As much as it makes sense for authorities to exhort drivers to remain calm and keep their hands visible, it also adds to their responsibility for their own safety. The victim-blaming, "don't make me hurt you" theme of this sort of campaign is eerily close to the outlook that of a domestic abuser.

The terror runs both ways. Sandra Bland died in a prison cell in 2015 after she'd been arrested on traffic charges in Waller County, Texas.[80] Her death was ruled a suicide. Video from the police dashcam recorded a confrontation between Bland and State Trooper Brian Encinia after she was pulled over for failing to signal and had the temerity to refuse to put out her cigarette, which was fully within her right. The officer can be heard threatening to use the taser on her, then throwing her to the ground outside her car, barely in view of the dashcam. Encinia was charged with perjury for claiming that he was in danger during the stop, but those charges were dropped after he was fired and signed an agreement to never work in law enforcement again.[81] Activists continue to question the official version of how she died, casting doubt on the official report that she'd hung herself with a plastic bag. A few weeks before the fourth anniversary of her death, her own video of the encounter was released on YouTube, showing Encinia threatening her with the taser and demanding that she put down her phone while she argued for her right to record the encounter.[82]

In the wake of Bland's death, state lawmakers in Texas fought to improve prison procedures for people who might be mentally ill but lost on a proposal that would forbid "pretext" traffic stops. Law enforcement lobbyists pushed hard against that proposal on grounds that it would erode their ability to make judgment calls—a form of righteous authority—in the field. Chris Jones, the training coordinator for the Combined Law Enforcement Associations of Texas, used the moral justification strategy when he testified, "There have been times that I have arrested folks on traffic violations because I knew, the hair stood up on the back of my head, the kid in the back seat wasn't right."[83]

Returning to Chicago, the McDonald–Van Dyke case illustrates this last component in the video debunking tool kit. After Van Dyke was convicted, the president of the state Fraternal Order of Police, Chris Southwood, invoked the righteous-case defense and attacked those calling for police reform in Chicago:

> This sham trial and shameful verdict is a message to every law enforcement officer in America that it's not the perpetrator in front of you that you need to worry about, it's the political operatives stabbing you in the back. What cop would still want to be proactive fighting crime after this disgusting charade, and are law-abiding citizens ready to pay the price?[84]

Note the markers of hegemonically masculine rhetoric: the zero-sum frame, use of the adjectives like "disgusting" and "shameful," and warning the public that reform will put everyone at risk. Chicago's FOP Lodge newsletter is filled with columns using similar angry binarism. Van Dyke's attorney, Daniel Herbert, wrote an editorial that was published after the officer's sentencing. "Today, armed criminals who have attempted to kill innocent people are permitted to storm through neighborhoods and ignore lawful commands by police," he wrote. "Enforcement is dead. Police are expected to monitor the situation and hope the criminal gets tired and gives up before harming someone." Herbert suggested that no one in the media or political sphere was paying attention to the specifics of Illinois law regarding police use of force, even though it was cited extensively during Van Dyke's trial. The editorial continued with the sort of bellicosity designed to deflect attention away from the teenager bleeding out on the pavement: "In response to the critics' public lynching of police officers, I hope for someone to point to this law and acknowledge the justification set forth therein to mitigate the situation."[85] This is the rhetoric of an angry father. No one dare question the decision-making process of police without incurring his wrath, as officers do not enforce the law, but instead they become the very law citizens should respect.

The Value of the Master Shot

No one wants to be videotaped every minute they are on the job. I would not want to be recorded on my bad teaching days, or when I sit and scratch my head while I write, or as I (so frequently) say something stupid at a faculty meeting. Yet I, and most Americans, do not have the legal right to kill people as police do.[86] For this reason, police officers need to be recorded, period, and not only by their own systems. For a balance of visual power, citizens must have the right, and exercise that right, to record public police behavior every chance they get.

"I will light you up," shouted the officer who arrested Sandra Bland. Her own video of the incident, not shared with the public until nearly four years after her death, overshadows police public relations efforts. The tape renders her experience visible from the grave; it gives voice to her futile determination to be treated with dignity. No lip sync video can undo the terror that comes with viewing that video, from her subjective perspective out her car's driver-side door. The same authoritarian anger was captured on cop-watching video in May 2019, when a Decatur, Alabama, officer answered, in response to a suspect asking for his name and badge number, "Fuck you is my name."[87]

These incidents might seem unbelievable, particularly to white Americans, without the evidence offered by citizen video. The culture is so imbued with media messages sympathetic to police, in news and entertainment, that such moments would be unthinkable without documentation. Most white Americans have only encountered the kind of officer who appears in the Texas instructional "Creating Safe Interactions between Citizens and Law Enforcement" video. Black and Brown Americans, who have long complained of police abuse and racism in everyday life are less likely to need such tapes to believe. The racial divide for police encounters is only starting to truly be understood by the general public, and only because individuals are now able to *visually* account for their lives.

The power to visually account for one's life must be available to everyone. Officers are understandably not always required to turn their camera on when their life is in danger, often the very instances where video evidence would be useful. Law enforcement agencies control the use and distribution of video; it is not always immediately available to the public, and regulations very across jurisdictions. Finally, badge-cam video shows reality from the perspective of the police officer, literally, which can help explain a response but does not always reveal a scene's larger context—the very sort of context that public oversight needs. Limited experimental research on how potential jurors interpret video based on camera angle and subjectivity shows just how hard it is to interpret body-cam video.[88]

In filmmaking, the "master shot" is the scene that shows the audience all the action: all the relevant actors and their activities. In contrast with body-cam video that provides the embodied perspective of a single subject in the video, a master shot provides more comprehensive scene. Cop-watching videos, when shot from a distance great enough to take in the full scene, can serve as master shots. Badge-cam video is not. Badge-cam video is a subjective perspective that only shows what an officer can see. Moreover, such video is controlled by the very people who are accountable to the public. More bluntly, any video *controlled* by the state will be used primarily to reproduce state power, and law enforcement institutions continue to fight for control of visual evidence and their narratives, using the strategies of hiding, renarrativizing, justifying, and demanding moral authority. Public relations efforts to remind the audience that officers are human can only succeed when departments are truly accountable. For this reason, cop-watching videos remain critical to police oversight. They are the best antidote to blue culture excess.

9

Everyday Racism and Rudeness

Scene: A group of male high school students wearing red "Make America Great Again" hats jeers at a young woman passing by and yell, "It's not rape if you enjoy it." They are gathered near the Lincoln Memorial, not far from an Indigenous People's Day demonstration. A Native American man with a drum approaches the students and is blocked by one of the teens, who stands with him eye to eye and smirks.

Scene: A group of male high school students who had attended the Right to Life March waited for their bus near the Lincoln Memorial. A group called the "Black Israelites" shouts insults at the boys, who respond with boisterous school spirit cheers. While they chant, an elder from the Indigenous People's March approaches them while playing a drum and chanting. One of the boys stands and watches the elder, unsure how to respond.

Scene: A group of male high school students in Washington, DC, for the Right to Life March encounters protesters from the Indigenous People's March and an antagonistic fringe group called the Black Israelites. All three groups chant in their own way until the boys leave to board their bus.

Descriptions of the meeting between Nicholas Sandmann and Nathan Phillips on the steps of the Lincoln memorial 2019 included these interpretations and others in the days that followed the first Tweet about that moment, highlighting the polysemic nature of visual evidence and the way values are communicated through narrative. So far, this book has studied the visual representations of the criminal justice system. This project would be incomplete, however, if it did not pay attention to the way digitization has expanded our visual ecology to include a glimpse at informal, everyday justice in the larger *social* system, with a genre dedicated to exposing rude, intolerant, or racist behavior. Insurance portfolio manager Amy Cooper became perhaps the most famous face of this genre when she threatened to call police in a

Seeing Justice. Mary Angela Bock, Oxford University Press. © Oxford University Press 2021.
DOI: 10.1093/oso/9780190926977.003.0009

Central Park bird reserve because a Black man (Christian Cooper, no relation), dared to tell her that her dog was not allowed there.[1] She can be seen in his recording saying that she would tell police a Black man was threatening her life. Cooper was later charged with filing a false report.[2] In 2018 a string of such videos caught the national spotlight, and clever tags like "Barbecue Becky" and "Permit Patty" fueled their virality and captured the public's attention. By 2020 a single name was used to describe women who behaved this way: "Karen."[3] These hashtagged incidents have inspired considerable discourse about what it's like to live as a person of color in the United States while also raising questions about fairness, privacy, and overreach.

Videos that document white misbehavior tie together some of the theoretical threads of this book: the role of the visual in the cultivation of democratic voice, digitization's untethered and frenetic recontextualization of images, and the continued indifference to the unique nature of visual meaning. Here again, video offers a unique discursive affordance: by documenting everyday racism, people of color are able to account for their lives in ways that words alone cannot. Once any video is on the web, however, it can be recontextualized in new narratives infinitely, often in ways that undermine the original message or even harm the public interest when used as propaganda.[4] Continued carelessness with images, by laypersons and media professionals alike, stokes confusion and has the potential to change lives—and not always for the better.

This chapter is based on a multimodal analysis of bad-behavior videos that garnered national news coverage in 2018 and 2019. The full list can be found at Table 9.1. The videos were chosen because they'd been covered in national media and analyzed according to a set of basic filmic conventions, such as shot length, camera movement, and photographer engagement, as well as nonverbal dimensions, such as the depictions of violence, emotions, and affect (emotional intensity). I logged each of the tapes, taking note of what was said and what was seen. I counted certain attributes of the videos, such as whether police appeared in the videos, whether anyone became violent, and the race (if known) of the person who made the video (Table 9.2). Most of the analysis that follows is qualitative, however, and combines basic filmic analysis with critical concepts such as racial formation and feminist and narrative theories. This chapter ends with a video that departs from the genre in that it does not depict a person calling police or otherwise verbally and publicly berating a person of color, but was nevertheless presented in national media as a moment of bigotry.

Table 9.1 Shaming Videos

Subject	Length	URL
Barbecue Becky	24:52	https://www.youtube.com/watch?v=MLwiFozt-x4
Permit Patty	0:15	https://www.youtube.com/watch?v=y0OQEeudpZk&feature=youtu.be
Taco Truck Tirade	0:48	https://www.youtube.com/watch?time_continue=48&v=Zs7npv6q_Ng
Pool Guard	4:08	https://www.youtube.com/watch?v=_DJkirCONUo
Apartment Blocker	4:11	https://www.youtube.com/watch?v=faI8kacPGbQ
Cornerstore Caroline	4:15	https://www.youtube.com/watch?v=_GyoP4QIZPk
Golfcart Gail	10:51	**https://www.youtube.com/watch?v=UzURhUWPu68** (the African Diaspora YouTube Channel posted this, the longest version)
Deli Attorney "'ICE'"	0:40	https://www.facebook.com/eddiesuazo16/videos/1637928712991933/?t=3
Coupon Carl	1:35	https://www.facebook.com/camillahudson31765/videos/10215005357398777/
Starbucks Meeting	0:45	https://twitter.com/missydepino/status/984539713016094721?lang=en
Craft Store Rant	10:41	**https://www.youtube.com/watch?v=hT5KrRGfJBI**

Everyday Bigotry and #ExistingWhileBlack

Most of the visual material for this book has depicted full-bodied action: cop-watching videos, wide-angle badge-cam imagery, or lip-sync videos filled with dancing performances. Videos of mundane racism and rudeness are more intimate. The subject's body is usually presented from the waist or knees up, and faces are more central. Everyday encounters are nearly always shot vertically, in accordance with what feels natural to a smartphone user. Sound is essential to interpreting these videos, as the actions depicted are often merely a matter of a person talking on a phone. The voice of an unseen person, usually the person recording, is often the key element for making sense of the video. Of course, the video's captioning and uploading to social media are also recontextualization cues for these visual testimonials.

Table 9.2 Shaming Video Details

Subject	Photographer	Target?	Police?	News coverage?	Came forward?
Barbecue Becky	W	N	Y	Y	No
Permit Patty	B	Y	N	Y	Y
Taco Truck Tirade	H	Y	N	Y	Y
Pool Guy	B	Y	Y	Y	Through attorney
Apartment Lady	B	Y	Yes but not seen	Y	Y
Cornerstone Caroline	B	N	N	Y	Y
Golfcart Gail	W	N	Y	Y	No
Deli Attorney "ICE"	–	–	N	Y	Statement
Coupon Carl	B	Y	Called but not seen	Y	N
Starbucks Meeting	W	N	Y	Y	N
Craft-Store Lady (Chicago)	W	N	N	Y	Y

Viewing these videos with deliberation underscores the psychology of film.[5] Unlike news stories, which present events verbally and visually in an observational style, these participatory encounter videos foreground facial expressions and nonverbal cues. Much like a badge-cam video, which subjectively reveals an officer's encounter, these recordings of quotidian rudeness bring the viewer face to face with negative emotions, often *intensely* negative emotions. Research on mirror neurons suggest that we feel empathy when we "read" the faces and actions of others.[6] When we watch someone dance, smoke, or grasp a cup of tea, our mirror neurons are also at work, reminding our own bodies of what each action is like.[7] Humans are incredibly good at reading faces, too, and much of the information we glean in conversation is nonverbal.[8] These clips of everyday rudeness and bigotry add, to an extraordinary degree, the power of nonverbal cues to video's already rich empiricism.

Like cop-watching videos, these bystander videos present evidence for counternarratives. The counternarratives are not new: people of color in the United States have long attested to being treated differently in public, of being singled out for "technical infractions," or of being followed around by store clerks. Social media—Twitter, in particular—have offered marginalized groups the means to coalesce around issues without relying on traditional media.[9] Black Twitter, for instance, uses hashtags such as #BlackLivesMatter and #SayHerName to connect users who are interested in social justice, to share stories and anecdotes, and to bypass newsrooms that have historically ignored Black members of their audience.[10] A leading expert on Black Twitter, Meredith Clark, argued that it is a "meta-network" that uses "collective action to solidify and affirm a social identity through digitally based conversation."[11] Similarly, Tarana Burke's use of the hashtag #metoo (even before Twitter existed) united thousands of women of all races and ethnicities through their common experience with sexual harassment.[12] These metanetworks, to use Clark's term, allow for users who feel ignored, marginalized, and covered in demeaning ways by mainstream media to provide one another with social support as they share information. At the same time, news media harvest stories from Black, feminist, and other hashtag assemblies, which both energizes such activism and exploits it.[13]

Add to these networks the power of visibility to account for one's life using visual communication—to *show*, not merely tell—and counternarratives rise to significance outside their social media nodes. It is one thing to find support online through hashtag conversation, still another to show the world documented examples of rudeness and racism. The clips examined here all caught mainstream media attention after millions of people watched and shared them online. This analysis identified three attributes that distinguish the genre: stressful phenomenology, audio primacy, and significance to the larger media audience. The situations they depict would likely *not* be news without the preliminary narratives of bigoted behavior rendered by social media metanetworks. They also would likely not be news without the evidence video provides. If not for the power of visual communication, these incidents would be brushed off as everyday arguments. Instead, these instances of everyday social conflict are rarified and, for better or worse, *magnified.*

Stressful Phenomenology

Unlike the more distant action shots of cop-watching, everyday racism videos generally put the viewer into the role of participant rather than observer. Watching them is extremely stressful, especially for the conflict averse, because they capture interpersonal conflict in its most heated moments. For instance, when onlookers try to tell a woman nicknamed "Cornerstone

Caroline" (Theresa Klein) to just go home after calling police because she believed a Black boy in the store put his hands on her behind, she walks into their personal space and even waves a finger in the face of the person filming. The "Barbecue Becky" video goes on for more than twenty-four minutes and includes conversation between Jennifer Schulte, who called police, and the woman taping her, Michelle Snider, an Oakland social justice activist with her own YouTube channel. Schulte refused to return a business card of one of the men barbecuing at the lake, which Snider had showed her by way of explaining that the man worked with a fire department and knew what he was doing. Schulte refused to return the card, and the incident escalated.

When Jennifer Boyle, a Chicago woman upset about her treatment by employees at a craft store, briskly approaches the woman recording Boyle's tirade, the viewer is placed into the receiving end of her rage:

> I don't know what YOU think your videoing, lady. I don't know what you think you're videoing. I was just discriminated against by two Black women. Yes I was, and you being a white woman, you [*she is now at conversational distance, pointing her finger at the photographer*], literally thinking that that's okay. You, standing there with your baby thinking that's okay.

Interestingly, in about half of these cases (as shown in Table 9.2), the person who chooses to film the scene is white and enters the conflict as a way of correcting another white person's bad behavior. This was the case in Chicago, after Boyle's tirade. The woman who filmed the incident, Jessie Grady, started a GoFundMe campaign online for the store manager and raised more than thirty thousand dollars.[14] Snider, the woman who followed Schulte around Oakland for nearly half an hour, posted an additional video to explain her actions, saying that she just wanted the business card back.[15] "Barbecue Becky" was evaluated by police on the scene for mental health issues but they determined she did not pose a harm to herself or others.[16] Simply watching the entire video provokes anxiety, as Schulte continues to walk while talking with police and Michelle Snider follows her around the park, through a convenience store, and finally to a parking lot where police arrive. The interaction is emotional and strange, with each woman stubbornly holding to her course of action. At one point the police dispatcher suggested that Schulte end the standoff. "What's the panic over a barbecue? I don't understand," the dispatcher asked, as quoted by *Newsweek*. "So why are you in an argument with these people? Can you walk away?"[17]

In other videos, the person targeted by the white person recorded is the one using the smartphone. Camila Hudson recorded her own confrontation with managers at a Chicago CVS after they questioned the authenticity of a coupon:

> Once he was on the phone with the police, I didn't even catch the beginning of that, because I was just kind of, you know, in the moment, deal with it in real time. But once I was standing there . . . is when I really looked at my phone. And realized, "I should be documenting this," hit the record and held the phone so that I knew that I was videotaping everything that was happening.[18]

Listening to Hudson in the video, it is clear that she is angry but under control. In her interview with me, she said was disappointed to eventually be told, by police, to leave the store, but CVS reviewed the clip she posted to her Facebook page and its own store surveillance video, and the company subsequently fired both managers and apologized.[19] Interestingly, commenters online used the same critiques police use to undermine video evidence introduced in Chapter 8—that she didn't record what *led up to* the confrontation. But as she explained, that would mean she'd have to essentially wear a body cam and keep it rolling all the time:

> I really wish I had recorded the whole thing. It would be a rather long video, 10 minutes or so, from when I reached the register and how this all played out. . . . And again, who walks around videotaping what they're doing, from the time I get out of my car to the time I enter a store? That would be really strange to me. Why would I do that on an average day, under average circumstances?[20]

The everyday rudeness video genre is itself strange, a documentary form unique to the experience of minority Americans. These clips capture social conflict in the moment, usually from the perspective of a participant, and while they are not violent, they are discomfiting. As visual evidence, though, they are very limited. Such videos can be used to identify a person deemed racist using social media, often with the invitation, "Okay, Twitter, do your thing." Yet as with most visual documentation, much of the information is linguistic, from the audio and contextualizing narratives.

Audio and Narrative Evidence

Sometimes everyday rudeness videos depict a person who is clearly upset, with an angry expression and aggressive body language. More often, however, they depict a person in conversation, sometimes heated, sometimes not. Unlike cop-watching videos, which might document physical actions of government actors, these videos are almost entirely about conflicts between citizens. They affirm longstanding claims by marginalized people that they are routinely over-scrutinized in everyday life.

As always, being *first* to contextualize a video makes a difference. In these instances, it is the public discourse equivalent to throwing down the gauntlet. Jessie Grady posted her video of Jennifer Boyle melting down in the Chicago craft store with the label "Racist White Woman Trump Rant in Chicago Store." Melissa DePino called attention to the way Black people are subjected to "technicalities" when white people are not when she tweeted her Philadelphia Starbucks video to Twitter on April 12, 2018. Note that she also hailed Starbucks' corporate account on Twitter:

> @Starbucks The police were called because these men hadn't ordered anything. They were waiting for a friend to show up, who did as they were taken out in handcuffs for doing nothing. All the other white ppl are wondering why it's never happened to us when we do the same thing.

The power of language to contextualize and render meaning to the image is well illustrated by the way #ExistingWhileBlack videos have traveled through public discourse. Videos are almost always uploaded as a social media post, with an accompanying tweet, caption, or label. YouTube videos have file names and occasionally appear with additional text. Even when traditional media cover the incidents and repost the videos, they might echo the original label, as ABC News did by captioning the pool guard video as, "Video shows white man racially profiling black woman, son at pool," an accusation made by the woman who posted the video, Jasmine Edwards, *denied* by Adam Bloom, and *impossible* to discern visually.[21] Context makes Edwards's case: she had a key card for the pool, the police demonstrated to Bloom that it worked, and their case was closed.

D'Arreion Nuriyah Toles was the first to narrate his own experience coming home after work, posting on Facebook the video from the encounter with his neighbor. He encouraged his friends to share the video, and it eventually received five million views:

To Be A Black man in America, & Come home,

Women tries to stop me from coming into my building because she feels insecure,

Downtown St. Louis luxury loft, because she don't feel that I belong, never really thought this would happen to me, but it did!

Then 30 mins later police knock on my door, because she called! I was shocked this is America in 2018!

Please share share

NewsRadio 1120 KMOX

Fox2Now

Real Stl News[22]

Being first with the narrative is powerful because opposing views are immediately placed in a defensive position, either to deny an accusation or redefine what happened. Even though the video does show Hilary Brooke Mueller (who also uses the name Hilary Thornton)[23] blocking the door and Toles pushing his way through, the visual documentation is not enough to comprehend the situation. As with the other videos, the audio tells the story, as Toles refuses to dignify Hilary Brooke Mueller's request to see his key fob, suspecting that his race was the only reason she suspected he didn't "belong" in the building. She called police to his door even *after* she watched him use his key to enter his own apartment on the fourth floor. Hearing him calmly tell her good night as he enters his apartment, leaving her with, "Don't ever do that again. You look pretty stupid on the video. Have a nice night, and my name's Mr. Toles. Thank you," captures the essence of the #ExistingWhileBlack complaint: that Black people in America are held to a different standard in everyday life and they are expected to respond calmly, even reassuringly, in the face of insulting behavior.

Technically Right and Socially Wrong

Jennifer Schulte ("Barbecue Becky") was actually right about the law, as there *was* a regulation against burning charcoal in that part of the park, a fact not mentioned in most news accounts of the incident.[24] There was also a trespassing law in place that allowed police to arrest two men who refused to purchase coffee at the Philadelphia Starbucks, prompting the police chief there to declare that his officers did "nothing wrong."[25] Selling water on the street without a permit, which prompted the "Permit Patty" confrontation between Erin Austin and Alison Ettel, is also illegal in San Francisco, as it is in most cities.[26] When interviewed by local television, the woman who tried to prevent D'Arreion Nuriyah Toles from entering his own apartment building said she was simply following an edict from her landlord to "never allow access to any individual you do not know," said Hilary Brooke Mueller, "I do not think that I did anything wrong. . . . I upheld the ask of me to its fullest extent."[27] But just as Philadelphia chief Richard Ross acknowledged in a subsequent apology to the two men arrested in Starbucks, the technicalities of the law can be unevenly applied—the injustice at the root of these counternarratives. Table 9.3 lists the outcomes that could be ascertained for the videos in this study.

Technically, nearly everyone has broken a law at some point, whether going over the speed limit, jaywalking, or not licensing a dog. The difference is that Black, Brown, trans, and other marginalized people face consequences for such infractions far more often than white people do. This may be one of the biggest blind spots for white Americans, who do not understand what the fuss is about because they've never experienced police action for these kinds of crimes.[28] Because officers are granted autonomy in the judgment of such infractions, they may be subject to unconscious bias, or they might be part

Table 9.3 Shaming Video Participants and Consequences

Subject	Photographer	Subject	Consequence
Barbecue Becky	Michelle Snider	Jennifer Schulte	Forever a meme
Permit Patty	Erin Austin	Alison Ettel	Lost business
Taco Truck Tirade	Claudia Lopez	"Valarie"	None known
Pool Incident	Jasmine Edwards	Adam Bloom	Resigned pool board and fired
Apartment Lady	D'Arreion Toles	Hillary Brook Mueller (Thornton)	Fired
Cornerstone Caroline	Jason Littlejohn	Theresa Klein	Appeared on local TV news
Golfcart Gail	Maria Morales-Walther Ginger Williams	Unidentified	Threats, harassment
Deli Attorney "ICE"	Emily Serrano	Aaron Schlossberg	Practices law
Coupon Carl	Camila Hudson	Morry Matson	Fired, ended local political campaign
Starbucks Meeting	Melissa DePino	Rashon Nelson and Donte Robinson	"Parted"
Craft-Store Rant	Jessie Grady	Jennifer Boyle	Appeared on local TV news

of an increased police presence in a troubled neighborhood. Enforcement bias has been blamed for the sort of policing that let to riot-level anger in Ferguson, Missouri, where for years police targeted Black neighborhoods for traffic and jaywalking citations to boost police revenue.[29]

Many white people, moreover, do not realize the full impact a 911 call can have on the life of a Black person. For white people, a police encounter is often merely an inconvenience, but for Black people, it can be life or death.[30] Erin Austin, who posted the "Permit Patty" video of Alison Ettel, directly cited this disparity as justification for shaming her neighbor.[31] Jason Littlejohn wanted Theresa Klein, the woman he recorded and nicknamed "Cornerstore Caroline," to be prosecuted for a nuisance call to 911, and he told a local news reporter that he started recording the video out of concern for the child, saying the situation "broke my heart. The second I saw that little boy crying, it broke my heart."[32] Melissa DePino, the Center City resident who uploaded video from the Starbucks arrest, told *Philadelphia Magazine*,

> People ignore this kind of stuff. They don't believe that it happens. People are saying that there *must* be more to this story. There is not. This would never happen to someone who looks like me. People don't believe black people when they say this stuff happens. It does. They want to know the extenuating circumstances. There are none.[33]

After her video caught national attention and prompted Starbucks to close its stores for a full day of racial bias education, DePino and another woman who was in the store at the time, Michelle Saahene, created a nonprofit: From Privilege to Progress.[34] A concerned viewer saw the story of "Permit Patty" and donated a trip to Disneyland to the girl who was selling water.[35] After the Starbucks arrest created a national furor, the Philadelphia Police Department changed its procedures for trespassing cases, and both the city and Starbucks reached financial settlements with the men.[36] Kenzie Smith, one of the men who was using charcoal in a grill on Lake Merritt when Jennifer Schulte happened by, was nominated for the Parks and Recreation Commission but took things even further and decided to run for Oakland City Council instead.[37]

The white people caught up in the incidents fared poorly. Alison Ettel ("Permit Patty") lost her business, even after going on national television to explain that she was just trying to get some peace and quiet on her street during a busy day working from home.[38] Hilary Brooke Mueller, who tried to block her neighbor from entering their apartment building, also went on TV to give her version of events, but she lost her job anyway.[39] Pool guard Adam Bloom was fired, as were the two CVS employees who called police over the argument about a coupon.[40] Posting the phrase "Come on, Twitter, do your thing" has serious consequences—so serious that it begs the question as to whether the punishment fits the crime. Christian Cooper, who filmed Amy Cooper as she threatened to file a false report against him, thought that by losing her job and achieving internet infamy she'd suffered enough without being criminally charged.[41]

Should the consequence for *apparent* but not adjudicated discrimination be professional devastation? The question arrives too late, as the court of public opinion—at least its Twitter faction—has already spoken. Furthermore, for Black citizens who've watched George Floyd suffocate under an officer's knee, or Sandra Bland pulled from her car for refusing to put out her cigarette, or Philando Castile shot to death for telling police he has a licensed firearm in his vehicle, getting fired may seem tame. What's less clear is whether this is the most effective way to change *society*. Racists who believe people of color are naturally inferior will focus on the technicalities of the law and condemn the firings of people who try to enforce the rules. The value of everyday rudeness videos lies in the fact that, without them, the average white person might not believe what it's like to be Black in America: facing the possibility of arrest for the sort of infractions white people commit every day without admonishment.

Visuality as Voice

The capability that everyday people have to use visual communication in the exercise of their democratic voice is changing society. No longer can complaints about everyday racism be easily dismissed as exaggeration or hypersensitivity. Nicole Fleetwood has described the way Blackness has been performed and visualized in traditional media, with narratives and representations controlled by the dominant group.[42] She extended Stuart Hall's argument that the visualization of Blackness is one of the most harmful ways to perpetuate stereotypes.[43] By posting videos of everyday rudeness and bigotry, marginalized people are able to visualize their experience *themselves*, amplifying their concerns and lending power to their democratic voice.

Even if it is undermined by competing narratives, video forces a conversation. In spite of the harassment she's received online and "in real life," Camila

Hudson, who recorded the CVS manager calling police, said she would do it again:

> It becomes irrefutable. What happened in that video is irrefutable. What happened before, what led to it, what happened after it—you can ask all of those questions. But, I definitely maintain, there's nothing I could have done, short of, I think, assaulting someone, or stealing, or outright criminal behavior that would make it make sense to call the police, or both to call the police, because they both did. . . .
>
> For whatever issues there are, questions that remain, I still think it's a very helpful tool on all fronts to document what's happening in the lives of people.[44]

Because it combines visuals, audio, and a timeline, video's extraordinary evidence has changed the way Americans are talking about race, policing, and justice. The summer of 2018 was marked by conversations on social media and in journalism about police policy, racism, and social injustice, abstract topics that have concerned marginalized people forever, but that came to the fore because individuals used their smartphones to record *tangible* examples.

The powers attributed to video *beyond* documentation, however, can be dangerous. That is, the phenomenological, emotional, and holistic attributes of the visual can seduce viewers into thinking they know more than they do—or, at least, more than can be proven. Much of this book has presented the evidentiary value of video for documentation, but that value is limited. So the clip video of Nicholas Sandmann face to face with Nathan Phillips at the Lincoln Memorial in early 2019 constitutes one final case study, for the very reason that it says so much about what Americans *feel* about social justice while illustrating the limits of what they *know* about any particular instance of it (Figure 9.1).

Testosterone on the Stairs

The encounter between Nicholas Sandmann and the Native American elder Nathan Phillips in 2019 was remarkable for many reasons. What started out as a social media post that criticized Sandmann and his classmates as disrespectful inspired a now-familiar shaming ritual online,

Figure 9.1 Nicholas Sandmann and Nathan Phillips on the Steps of the Lincoln Memorial, January 18, 2019
Screen grab from the WashingtonPost.com, January 19, 2019

which was then picked up as a story in national news outlets, which then became a story about news practices and today remains a political Rorschach test. This was not a criminal case, but one focused on civility and morality and the epistemology of video. Part of Sandmann's libel lawsuit against the *Washington Post* was dismissed in the summer of 2019, another part was settled for an undisclosed amount in 2020, and as of this writing other cases remained in litigation.[45] Sandmann became a media darling for the Right and delivered a speech during the Republican National Convention that year, condemning cancel culture.[46] His case exemplifies the churning vortex of today's visual economy in that the video was shared millions of times, each time offering users a chance to weigh in with their own judgment. The debate played out in the court of public opinion and eventually reminded everyone, including journalists, of the ambiguity of visual media.

The story of the Lincoln Memorial video is remarkable for the media mea culpas that followed the initial stories. Many other shaming videos remain unquestioned online, with some of their subjects turned into memes. Online videos of everyday social infractions document all manner of xenophobic, racist, and misogynistic behavior. Yet the social media pile-ons that ensue run the risk of turning racists into sympathetic figures. Within days of the incident, Nathan Sandmann's family hired a public relations firm, and he told his story in a highly controlled, well-lit interview with NBC's *Today Show*.[47] More videos came out—and using the timeline, analysts were able to better dissect the event. See Table 9.4 for the clips I was able to analyze. This case has much in common with the other shaming videos in that it judges colloquial rudeness at a level normally reserved for criminality. The online outrage machine always operates in high gear.

Documenting versus Covering Events

The Lincoln Memorial videos, even more so than the everyday rudeness videos discussed earlier, illustrate a key difference in the way professional visual journalists and citizen witnesses shoot video. These differences reflect the ways video serves as a discursive affordance. Professionals learn early to shoot with a narrative purpose.[48] While it's important to catch all relevant action, especially in a dynamic situation, a visual journalist is not likely to hit Record and shoot a scene nonstop for hours. Editing from an extended recording is arduous, and so unless an event is being covered live, or the event is so dynamic that every minute must be captured, a professional shooter is most likely to shoot relevant action and editing sequences (wide shots, medium shots, close-ups, over-the-shoulder shots, and so on).[49] Citizen witnesses and activists, however, are not necessarily planning to edit their tape for a summarizing narrative. They often attend events for the very purpose of documenting every minute of it for archival or evidentiary purposes.

Videos posted from the Lincoln Memorial were created by citizen witnesses who let their cameras roll. Viewers move with their moves, as the videographers climb the stairs, pan from speaker to speaker, and move through the crowd. The shots pause to take in a specific action, as when Sandmann faced off with Phillips, but then turn to other parts of the scene, such as when another person participating in the Indigenous People's March argued profanely with one of the boys from Covington Catholic High School.[50] Unlike typical news coverage, which normally would try to use a "master" or "establishing" shot to help the viewer discern the overall scene, the citizen witness videos from the Lincoln Memorial incident are largely point-of-view shots from *within* the incident. The *Duncan* video does take

Table 9.4 Lincoln Memorial Confrontation

Subject	Length	Notes
Original posted to Twitter	3:44	**Indigenous Peoples March, Washington, DC** With comment: "Is this how we make America great again?"
Original		Kaya Taitano https://www.youtube.com/watch?v=sIG5ZB0fw1k
View 2	9:15	John Duncan
Duncan		**Who really started this Indigenous People taunt Cov Cath boys aK1uWzTtkT8** Added note: "Reuploaded since it's been memory holed." https://www.youtube.com/watch?v=npX801xLSFY
View 3	1:46:00	**Shar Yaqataz Banyamyan facebook video** Caption This video was saved shortly before being deleted from facebook. It may have possibly been the first backup so the world could see the entire circumstances that lead to a media frenzy over a tiny clip. I hope it helped the kids to be exonerated from the crazy accusations. Here is the tweet where I posted it as it was processing. https://twitter.com/reinforcedtv/stat . . . FYI: To debunk some rumors—due to the new youtube rules this video has not had a single ad played on it. The channel just got 1k subs as of 230pm pacific time Jan 22 and could take a month for youtube to say yes or no. However, it would have been nice because it has about 139638.8 hours of viewing time. that is equivalent to 15 years 339 days. :) The channel was monetized years ago but lost it when the rules changed. was asked to add this. not asking for anything. *updated bitcoin—38CSNfyviakW6P4cMmeszS9swnazswHRBp
Black Israelites		Shar Yaqataz Banyamyan facebook video / Hebrew Israelites https://www.youtube.com/watch?v=t3EC1_gcr34&feature=youtu.be
View 4		**Nick Sandmann: The Truth in 15 Minutes, with comment:** "2 weeks ago, the mainstream media, politicians, church officials, commentators, & celebrities rushed to judgment to wrongfully condemn, threaten, disparage & vilify Nick Sandmann based solely on a few seconds of an out-of-context video clip. It only takes 15 minutes to learn the truth. Here it is."
Attorney	13:58	Attorney L. Lin Wood https://www.youtube.com/watch?v=lSkpPaiUF8s&t=2s

the viewer up the stairs occasionally, to look over the scene from a higher angle, but none of the videos available for analysis present an eye-level wide shot. In the original video posted to Twitter (*Original*), the viewer is at Nathan Phillip's shoulder for the visual meeting with Sandmann. Literally as well as metaphorically, a viewer sees what happened from Phillips's point of view. The *Duncan* video more frequently shows the scene from the boys' perspective on the steps. The *Black Israelite* video shows the scene from the perspective of their organization, shot in vertical mode from a phone.

News organizations were not in control at the story's inception, but instead renarrativized these clips into stories as each new perspective emerged. As with the other cases covered thus far, the "opening" narrative recontextualization became the standard against which subsequent discourse compares. Because journalists were not present to cover this using their usual procedures their stories instead relied on testimonies from various witnesses as they came forward, as well as their own visual analysis of videos produced by others—*not* from direct witnessing.

Dominance Displays

The Lincoln Memorial videos call attention to one of humanity's most innate forms of communication: facial expression. Much of the criticism of Sandmann centered on his expression as Phillips played his drum, and whether the teen was smirking. When Sandmann appeared on NBC's *Today Show* to explain his actions that day, he said that he was not smirking, but smiling at Phillips, saying, "I see it as a smile, saying that this is the best you're going to get out of me. You won't get any further reaction of aggression. And I'm willing to stand here as long as you want to hit this drum in my face."[51]

Even though most of what we learn from one another in conversation is conveyed nonverbally, research on the way nonverbal communication operates in media is relatively sparse.[52] Grabe and Bucy led the way with extensive content analyses of the facial expressions of politicians.[53] They organized their analyses according to two basic labels, hedonic (friendly/happy) and agonic expressions, which combine two classic nonverbal communication categories: fear and aggression.[54] Grabe and Bucy found that the visual "packaging" of candidates made a difference in voter support.[55] Experimental research by Laustsen and Petersen found that ideology plays a role in viewer preference for a particular type of face, based on physiognomy and expression.[56] Conservative viewers preferred leaders with "dominant" faces, with a direct gaze, no open smile, and significantly, *masculine* features.

A close analysis of the videos that show Sandmann's face suggests that he is not, technically, smiling, as his zygomatic muscles do not seem to be activated (known more colloquially as eye crinkles) and his lips do not part.[57] He is also not sneering, showing his teeth, or pushing his eyebrows together in what would be considered a display of anger or hostility.[58] His closed mouth, direct eye gaze, and chin position more closely resemble something more subtle, what Witkower and colleagues have identified as a "prestige" stance.[59] Consider also that Sandmann was standing on a step, at least one step higher than Phillips. In a public relations video, his attorney's office suggests that this higher step means that Sandmann appears taller than his actual teenage frame, but at the same time, the nonverbal stance he takes is that of a man who holds rank and intends to continue holding it.[60] Much as the white people in the everyday rudeness videos who justified their actions based on their right to stand up for themselves, Sandmann stood by his right to hold his position during his interview with the *Today Show*: "As far as standing there, I had every right to do so. My position is that I was not disrespectful to Mr. Phillips. I respect him. I'd like to talk to him," he said. "I mean, in hindsight, I wish we could've walked away and avoided the whole thing. But I can't say that I'm sorry for listening to him and standing there."[61] Seen this way, yielding to Phillips on the steps would mean yielding his own rights to exist in that space, not merely letting an older person move through.

Sandmann's classmates performed far more dynamic nonverbal displays of true dominance: shouting, jeering, jumping up and down, and—quite literally—banging their chests. They took up space with their bodies and with their voices, with school cheers and tomahawk chops, a gesture widely considered to be bigoted and offensive by Native Americans and their supporters.[62] When the three videos are triangulated for analysis, the scene's confusion stands out. The Black Israelites yelled offensive insults to the unsupervised teenage boys, many of whom had likely never encountered this kind of street protest. It's possible that some of the young men had not really paid attention to the differences between the demonstrations, only that some men were yelling at them and a strange old man started walking toward them with a drum. Faced with unknown social forces, the adolescent males responded with their own testosterone-fueled tribalism.

Visual Lessons

The incident might never have made national news had Sandmann's face-off with Phillips not been posted to Twitter with the caption, "This MAGA loser gleefully bothering a Native American protester at the Indigenous Peoples March," by an anonymous user whose account was subsequently suspended by Twitter.[63] The case illustrates what happens when images move without institutional filters of the traditional recontextualization model (see Figures 1.1 and 1.2). The image is churned through a process of repeated recontextualization, as each social media user is able to append a label of their own or simply send it along with its original caption. In this case, the video was seen more than 2.5 million times, raising it to the level that captures news attention for "going viral."[64] The *Washington Post* went first, with a video posted to its website using a caption less acrimonious than the tweet, but nevertheless echoing the original poster's take: "Teens mock Native American elder on the Mall," as shown in Figure 9.2.[65]

The next line uses Nathan Phillips's name. Neither Nicholas Sandmann's name nor his point of view is included. Some outlets included quotes from the woman who shot the original video and posted it to YouTube.[66] Other national media followed suit, using Phillips's quote, "It was getting ugly," or using the word "taunted" in captions.[67]

As more videos were posted, journalists dialed it back, with headlines such as the *New York Times'* "Fuller Picture Emerges."[68] Mea culpas mounted as journalists suddenly discovered that visual media must be interpreted in context, and that no single camera's perspective is a full perspective.[69] Sandmann became a hero for antimedia conservatism and won a settlement from the *Washington Post*. He went on to speak out against "cancel culture" at the virtual Republican National Convention in 2020. "I would not be canceled," he declared.[70]

Video

Teens mock Native American elder on the Mall

A group of high school teens surrounded and jeered at Native American elder Nathan Phillips on the steps of the Lincoln Memorial on Jan. 18.

National · Jan 19, 2019

Figure 9.2 The original headline from the website, WashingtonPost.com, January 19, 2019, read "Teens mock Native American elder on the Mall."
Source: Screen grab from the WashingtonPost.com.

It is impossible to know whether any of the news organizations made significant changes to the way they work with visual information. Even with all the backpedaling during the week after the story first surfaced, the "let's be more thoughtful" columns included images from the event with vague captions that rarely explained who shot what, under what circumstances, and for what purpose. It's not at all clear from the postmortem discourse whether trained photo editors or visual journalists were involved with any of the decisions to cover the original story—people who might have asked questions about just what the video shows and does not show in an era when everyone can and does post video, but not everyone ascribes to the ethics of visual journalism.

The Lincoln Memorial videos and the stories they inspired show both the power of images and their discursive limits. Viewers can be forgiven for their visceral responses to Sandmann's expression: we are wired to read faces. As forcefully as we might feel that expression, however, whether "smug," "entitled," or merely confused, it was just one moment in a complicated situation. Multiple videos, once released, presented a richer understanding of the clash of perspectives on the steps of the Lincoln Memorial that day. Social media users offered it up as evidence that they were harassed by the boys from Covington High School, in the same way that many citizen journalists offer up video as evidence of power misused. This time, though, there were no authorities to seek for official comment, no police report, no court affidavit. Journalists had to rely only on direct witnesses to untangle the story, and while they eventually presented a nuanced, contextualized narrative, it seems that they may have confused what they knew with their eyes and what they knew could be proven.

Throughout this book I have argued for the evidentiary power of video, but this case shows what happens when we forget its limits. Journalism and law are fields based on the power of language, and the beauty of law in a democratic society is that authority is to be drawn from words, not brute strength. In a libel court, this would mean our phenomenological impression of a teenage know-it-all is worthless. All that would matter are the words— the testimony from Sandmann, Phillips, and other witnesses—coupled with the language of the various captions, stories, and narratives written about the video. The complaint against the journalists in this case rests on the way word and image are bifurcated in court, even though in the lives we lead the two operate symbiotically, every day, all day.

Taking Visuals Seriously

In 1993 one of the most important figures in cultural studies praised a set of conference papers presented at the International Communication Association for the way they took journalism seriously.[71] Barbie Zelizer, who took this maxim to heart and helped establish a journal devoted to journalism research, titled a book that surveyed the field with Carey's turn of a phrase.[72] Today, journalism studies is a recognized academic pursuit, albeit with a polyglot of methodologies and theoretical approaches, but one that supports several journals and attracts PhDs. Thanks to work from research hubs such as the Center for Media Engagement at the University of Texas at Austin, the Agora Journalism Center at the University of Oregon, the Nieman Center at Harvard, and the Tow Center for Digital Journalism at Columbia University, the study of journalism is making strides toward relevance among professional journalists, a group that is notoriously resistant to academic advice.

Visual communication's academic trajectory in many ways has evolved in parallel with journalism studies. Art history and criticism have existed from the very onset of the humanities, but the study of visual communication, particularly within media, emerged in the late twentieth century. Sol Worth, Larry Gross, David Perlmutter, and Michael Griffin are among the researchers who shaped its inception. Gross, established an early (but now dormant) journal, *Studies in Visual Communication*, in 1974.[73] The International Communication Association established an interest group devoted to visual communication in 1993.[74] Today all major communication research organizations have a similar division.

For a variety of reasons, visual scholarship in communication remains simultaneously celebrated and marginalized. No one seriously suggests that visual communication is not important, as evidence of its cognitive power continues to mount. Yet as a research focus, visual studies remain in the shadows of political, health, and digital communication research even though images are ubiquitous in these fields. This may be part of the theoretical quandary, of course, as studies of political ads, health care warnings, and social media cannot entirely decontextualize the visual. Moreover, it is extremely difficult to study images automatically; they cannot be reduced to text strings for big data algorithms. Even automated picture sorting systems are prone to the very sorts of prejudices and stereotypes of the humans who program them.[75] Visual communication is often given the lip service treatment of ethics: "Yes, it's important, but it will have to wait."

Unfortunately, the digital public sphere is not waiting. Images are uploaded, shared, clicked on, recontextualized, used, and abused at tornadic speed. The arrival of deep fake video has unmoored the last vestiges of camera truth, casting doubt on any and all visual evidence on the web. The tragic consequence is that the triumph of doubt undermines the use of visual evidence to advance human rights. Without the kind of media literacy that enables coherent interpretation and verification, visual propaganda will subsume all efforts toward sincere testimony.

It's long past time to take images seriously. Just like communication scholars, journalists will protest that they already do, and they'll point to all the workshops, the pivot to video, and the inclusion of images with every blog post as proof that images are important. But the Lincoln Memorial video incident shows that media producers continue to forget the emotional, visceral power of images over words and disregard the power and increased ethical demands of the visual in today's visual economy. It is time for a serious conversation about how images ought to be used, shared, and talked about in the digital realm. We can no longer afford to carelessly play with visuality's fire.

10

Playing (Safely) with Fire

Commandment #9: Thou shalt not bear false witness against thy neighbor.

Scene: I am packing my car in the grocery store parking lot when two squad cars arrive and a woman is brought outdoors for an arrest. I stop to film the scene, and a man in a pickup truck stops to admonish me. He accuses me of trying to exploit the scene for the sake of a YouTube hit, and I explain that I'm just trying to document the scene for everyone's safety. He leaves in a huff. The arrest ends without incident, I put my phone away, and a few days later, I delete the footage. I'm saddened by the confrontation and wonder how much more flak I'd have received if I were a teenager, or a Black man, or a native Spanish-speaker, instead of an aging white, English-speaking soccer mom.

This book opened with an anecdote about my inspiration to study visual representations of criminal justice. Why was it so important that my team and I record that shot of Alan Iverson leaving court that day? The aggregate of the cases for this project offer an explanation: media and the court officials worked in concert to perform an ideological ritual. The routinized demands of TV news for this particular visual trope are connected to individual stories about disparate court cases while serving a larger cultural narrative about the system's authority. It was not enough to use a photo of Iverson playing basketball in the stories about his domestic violence case; the norms of the larger culture reflected in news practices required that he be represented through a criminalizing lens. The label, *criminal,* was as important as the shadowy image of Iverson through the SUV's tinted windows. Disparities in the way Black men are prosecuted and the inconsistencies of domestic violence prosecutions had no place in the story that day, which rested squarely on the details of his court appearance and, for the

Seeing Justice. Mary Angela Bock, Oxford University Press. © Oxford University Press 2021.
DOI: 10.1093/oso/9780190926977.003.0010

sake of my day's work, the fact that he was "caught" under the criminal-izing gaze.

As promised, this was not a book about images. Instead, it examined the processes by which visual messages are made, and by whom, for a particular purpose. Throughout this volume I have argued that social actors struggle over the construction of visual messages in embodied and discursive ways. Digitization has vastly expanded the encoding capabilities of everyday citizens, allowing them to add visibility to their expression of democratic voice, even as the ethical rules for visual expression are inchoate. Using a series of case studies, examining the construction and recontextualization of images of and about justice, this project sought to illustrate and ex-tend theoretical understanding of the way the criminal justice system is represented, and how those representations support the system's authority. Starting with Foucault's foundational concepts of capillary power and truth as a discursive construct, Fisher's narrative paradigm, and Hall's concep-tion of culture as the site of ideological struggles, this project has described in detail the way everyday human practices construct individual stories about criminal justice, which in turn reproduce what Barthes would call its myth.

The case studies in this volume—whether how executions are and are not covered, the way social media users recontextualize mug shots in new narratives, or the way activists are able to use video's indexicality as testimo-nial affordance—invite three theoretical discussions. First: visual journalism's physicality increases its reliance on those in power, making it easy for officials in the criminal justice system to shape its own image. Second: the impor-tance of image indexicality (even while it is subject to narrative negation) as a discursive affordance in the public sphere. The third discussion deals with the visual nature of the digital public sphere, and the way participation in this visual public sphere must be considered as an essential human capability, if not a human right. Visual messaging is emotionally powerful and memo-rable; it subsumes language, and it is often naively interpreted, even when individuals are reminded of their constructed nature. Thus it is essential to examine the way visual messages are created. This research offers insight into the constructions of the "complexes of visuality" concerning criminal justice, for only by studying the way communication is constructed does it become possible to imagine alternatives.

Embodied Gatekeeping

Visuals are doubly framed, first by way of embodied practice, and then through discursive recontextualization, as Figure 1.1 illustrates. The first part of the book focused on the grounded practices of visual journalists covering criminal justice, and the way visual journalism's physicality increases its reliance on those in power. Describing the way executions and the penal system are covered, the ritual of the perp walk, and the televising of spectacular trials illustrated the role of the body in framing criminal justice, and the way legal institutions exercise embodied gatekeeping in ways that are designed to cultivate faith in the system.

Finally, while many news organizations have developed systems for imparting transparency about their processes, most of these measures are word-based, such as curated comment sections or explanations of how a story is reported.[1] The byzantine rules for visual coverage of celebrated trials do much to protect the dignity of the court, but the fact that these rules are so rarely part of news accounts only cultivates naive beliefs about camera "reality." At the George Zimmerman trial, the engineer who oversaw the incredible technological achievement in the courthouse parking lot argued that the arrangement offered equitable access for alternative news organizations and citizen journalists. Yet a walk through the lot during the newscast hours, when reporter after reporter took to their temporary stage to deliver the day's story, revealed remarkable sameness in the reports they delivered based on what happened in court, and essentially nothing about their role as journalists in this elaborate production.

Similarly, perp walks are presented as spontaneous moments that happen to capture the arrival of a particular subject. Written news accounts occasionally mention that reporters acted on a "tip" from law enforcement, and more often attribute information to "unnamed sources." In a dataset that spans more than ten years of interviews and discourse analysis, not one story has ever mentioned the role police made in helping to orchestrate a perp walk. Surely one such account exists,[2] but the contrast remains: these images are presented as "real," occurring without human interference. Naïve realism is also reproduced when news organizations use and reuse mug shots without adequate concern for their criminal context. To use an old mug shot when a subject is a crime *victim* is surely the epitome of conceiving of the image as nothing more than an easily obtained likeness. It skirts the reality of a mug shot's inherent violence and offers news organizations a cheap way to collect an image without having to do the metaphorical and physical legwork of pro-curing a more neutral portrait.

The role of embodied gatekeeping in representing criminal justice is also a matter of omission. One of the stories that TV news virtually ignored in the 1990s was the privatization of America's prison system. Given the roadblocks imposed by prison authorities for coverage—the embodied gatekeeping that prevents camera access to prisons—it is easy to understand why news organizations would cover more street crime instead. Furthermore, while cameras are usually banned from executions on the official premise that the condemned die with dignity, such privacy clearly serves the state's interest as well. News organizations need to consider more deeply their role in holding the state accountable for its treatment of all prisoners and exert pressure on authorities for increased access to institutions. Security and inmate privacy can and must be balanced with other rights. Without public access to know and *to see* prison conditions, putting a check on the state's power is impossible.

Embodied gatekeeping, therefore, offers a way of thinking about visual newsgathering and the role played by actors who control physical access to events. The way such actors in the criminal justice system use embodied gatekeeping to cultivate the system's authority is rarely accounted for in news and undermines journalism's watchdog role. By controlling the way a mo-ment in time and space is framed photographically, or by impeding access to the extent that an image is never even made, authorities have considerable control over the narratives that follow.

Indexicality as Affordance

The second form of construction of photographic meaning, illustrated by the larger arc of Figure 1.1 is the use of an image in narrative. The struggle for meaning in this step is a matter of recontextualizing an image in discourse and attempting to control that narrative, and these struggles are taking un-precedented form in today's digital public sphere. Photographic images serve as a powerful discursive affordance, but that power can be tempered by the way images are used in narrative. Digitization enables faster, more frequent, almost infinite possibilities for recontextualization, as illustrated by the "tor-nado" in Figure 1.2.

The role of the mug shot in digital culture, as described in Chapter 5, illustrates this discursive struggle and the way social media accelerate the role of an image as discursive affordance. Social media users, unhappy with the way the news had visually portrayed Brock Turner, clamored for his mug shot in order to recontextualize him as a criminal. The facts of his case had not changed; there was no "update" to the story, but users expressed a desire to circulate the criminalizing portrait. News organizations, criminal justice officials, and everyday users negotiate the recontextualization of the image in discourse, affording the Twitterverse an opportunity to punish a man they believed had escaped the consequences he deserved.

Video's epistemological trio of moving images, audio, and a timeline offers its own form of indexical discursive affordance. As the case study in Chapter 6 described, video cannot stand for itself in court but must accompany other testimony. It can serve to explain or illustrate the order of action and is especially useful for refuting testimony that does *not* match what the video depicts. While its timeline affords a natural "narrative," the narrative that matters most is the discursive one crafted in court that offers coherence and fidelity—the moral "point" of the story. Even cop-watching, while inspired by camera indexicality, relies on more than imagery for its effectiveness. Police accountability activists use their cameras in combination with other tactics, such as volunteer training, organizing, and advocating for substantive change.

Law enforcement officers, under fire from the public because of videos that undermine their authority, have developed a number of discursive techniques for reclaiming their status. When they cannot control the originated framing of an image through embodied gatekeeping, officials negotiate its recontextualization by controlling the narrative, explaining procedures, or appealing to the public's respect for authority. Many police departments are also crafting their own visual messaging, with social media accounts that highlight good deeds caught on badge cams or elaborate musical lip sync videos. As Chapter 8 described, however, such videos tend to reify the white, militaristic, hypermasculine culture under attack by police accountability activists.

Finally, the digital media sphere offers video as an indexical discursive affordance to support complaints about everyday racism and rudeness. Recordings of "Karens" as they make calls to police over barbecue grills or water stands, or because they've been told their dog should be on a leash, substantiate long-standing complaints about racism in everyday life. Without video evidence, would most white Americans believe that a clerk might call police about a coupon? Or that a craft-store customer might throw a tantrum over a perceived slight about a bag? Or that woman might follow her fellow apartment dweller all the way to his apartment, *while he is holding his key*, concerned that he does not live there. White people who have never been subjected to such degrading moments might never believe accounts of such incidents without the affordance of video's indexicality.

The phenomenological information in such videos is compelling—the tones of voice, expressions, and body language. Watching them is stressful. That same kind of information might well be the reason so many news organizations ran with a narrative that painted young Nick Sandmann as smirking and insolent; the stations were responding instinctively but not thinking through what could and could not be proven about the subjects' state of mind for anyone involved in the incidents at Lincoln Memorial. The Sandmann incident, as well as the more extreme consequences of cancel culture, highlight the danger of video as it rapidly circulates through a public sphere that has yet to contend carefully with the particular ways visual meaning operates. Images are emotionally powerful and more memorable, and will overshadow words when in competition, but the institutions of journalism, criminal justice, and social media have yet to contend with the ethics these differences demand. It is long past time to attend to the unique ethical problems that visual communication presents in the digital age.

Visibility and Voice

The third leg of this book's overall argument is that digitization has vastly expanded the encoding capabilities of everyday citizens, allowing them to add visibility to their expression of democratic voice. This is not a utopian celebration of social media echoing the early twenty-first-century celebrations of democratized digital media and its potential for citizen sousveillance and participation.[3] More recently, scholars have tempered their optimism in the wake of increased state surveillance and social media spying by authorities against citizen organizing.[4] The research for this book supports a more specific claim: that visibility today is concomitant with democratic voice and that visual communication skills should be considered an essential human capability as conceived by Sen and Nussbaum.[5] Literacy is already considered an essential capability, an affordance that enhances the life of a citizen. Today, visual literacy must be considered part of that capability in order to advance and protect the right of citizens to account for their lives visually as well as verbally.

Habermas argued that citizens must have a voice that is heard, considered, and valued in the democratic public sphere.[6] Couldry defined this form of voice as "our capacity to make, and be recognized as making, narratives about our lives and the world within which we act."[7] Civil rights activists have long strategically used visibility as voice in order to garner public support. Marches and protests are often constructed as street spectacle.[8] Martin Luther King Jr. and his allies were strategic in their relationships with photojournalists from *LIFE* magazine and other outlets that published images of Black oppression—a move believed to have made a significant, positive impact on white support for the movement.[9] Today, individual citizens are able to account for their lives visually; indeed, visual evidence has afforded many individuals the chance to be heard for the first time.

Police accountability activists who use their cameras to hold the state accountable and document their surroundings offer the most obvious example of citizens using visibility as voice. Individuals who post videos of everyday rudeness and racism are also accounting for their lives with a camera. Inmates who smuggled out video of their prison conditions would not have been believed without visual evidence. Even Chapter 5's social media users who shared Brock Turner's mug shot with the "rapist" label were using their visual capabilities to critique rape culture. In each of these cases, visibility was essential to the exercise of democratic voice.

The power to film and to show, or "sousveillance," presents a counterbalance to the power of the state and its corporate superstructure. Mann and Ferenbok used the word "veillance" to describe the way power is exercised by views from above and below.[10] In the United States, several federal appeals courts have upheld the right of everyday individuals to shoot video of public activity in public places, based on the First Amendment.[11] The Supreme Court has not yet ruled on the subject, and related issues are unsettled. For instance, while an individual may have the right to film, do they also have the right to upload to the web video of another person in distress? What about the right to film in nonpublic places when there is a public interest, as with the smuggled prison phone?

Given the exceptional rate (approximately three per day) at which police kill citizens in the United States,[12] it might be argued that citizens have an obligation to use their cameras for the sake of democratic discourse. Consider the potential for accountability efforts if *everyone*—including white people, middle-aged people, women—peacefully filmed police when they conduct arrests? Recording from the sidelines without interference provides an essential counternarrative for all citizens. It's too easy to think of cop-watching as the province of activists, but as long as they are the only ones questioning authority, they will remain marginalized. As more citizens respectfully participate, cop-watching can become a normal part of citizen oversight.

Because the digital public sphere is a visual economy, and because photographic images present the discursive affordance of indexicality, using a camera is no longer just for hobbyists and artists; it is, in the end, a human right. Access to visual technology, in terms of materiality, skills, and knowledge, rises to the level of an essential capability.[13] Federal appeals courts in the United States have affirmed the right of citizens to peacefully film police as they perform their public duties, but there is much more to being able to participate in the visual economy than cop-watching. By documenting environmental crimes, animal abuse, even their own sexual abuse, individuals have been able to harness the visual to be heard, considered, and respected.

No right is absolute, of course, and the right to visibility comes with complications. Citizens not only require access to technology but also audiovisual skills, ethical literacy, and policies that protect other rights, such as privacy and safety. There is more to advancing this capability than narrowing the digital divide by giving everyone Wi-Fi and a smartphone. Cameras can be used to intimidate and humiliate others unfairly, and accelerated recontextualization online means that even when images are responsibly made and posted, they can instantly be turned into weapons of social destruction. To advance digital visibility as an essential human capability, therefore, means extending visual literacy, balancing individual and social interests, and developing legal and ethical norms specific to visual communication.

Digital Visual Ethics

Much of the ethical work on visuality has wrestled with our responsibilities as viewers. Susan Sontag wrote eloquently about this problematic mix of the aesthetic with the tragic, concluding that ocular pleasure subsumes the evidentiary value of documentary photography.[14] A corpse might be photographed in a beautiful way, painful scenes might become objects of fascination. Sontag argued that this conversion of human pain into an aesthetic object weakened photography's power to compel social action.[15] Ariella Azoulay pushed back against Sontag's pessimism and argued that focusing on aesthetics distracts from the medium's contribution to civil discourse, in particular for the way images of suffering can offer "emergency claims" for global citizens.[16] Lilie Chouliaraki extended Azoulay's argument, noting that when images are (re) contextualized in the news, journalistic narration can guide the viewer toward a human(e) response.[17] Digitization demands more than an ethic for viewing images. Now that citizens are able to participate in the visual public sphere as creators and storytellers, a new ethical conversation is in order, as technological capabilities have far outpaced the development of social media norms.

This book ends, therefore, with a call for increased visual literacy in the public sphere.

The ethical systems currently in place focus on actors in the traditional media sphere, such as journalists and their sources, and rarely attend to the special dimensions of visual information. Yet everyone is a journalist today, whether they think of it that way or not, yet there is scant discussion of ethics for the typical social media user. In the criminal justice realm, it is essential that legal authorities, media practitioners, *and* today's prosumers start thinking more carefully about the way images are made, used, and rendered meaningful—and how they *ought* to be made and used. Visual media literacy would benefit the audience in other realms, such as political campaigns and consumer culture, but this project has focused on the way powerful institutions control our view of criminal justice and the way new stakeholders are disrupting the larger system. The audience needs to know how their view is shaped by the state, how images are recontextualized in media, and how digitization helps and hinders emancipatory and democratic objectives.

Media literacy is a contested term, and even visual scholars argue over definitions of *visual* literacy.[18] Thinking of it as an extension of art literacy does not solve our problem, though it might enhance users' enjoyment of visual artifacts. Is it a matter of understanding visual conventions? Most media literacy campaigns marginalize visuals and focus on teaching the audience how to critically analyze messages, not how to ethically craft their own messages. The amateur videos posted to the web using purposeful camera angles, special effects, and sophisticated editing suggest that today's prosumers are well versed in visual conventions. The sort of visual literacy needed today is related to a strand of media literacy proposed by Renee Hobbs, which teaches critical thinking but with an *increased emphasis* on the ethics of using visuals in communication.[19] Such a curriculum would help stakeholders to understand how to judge the credibility of messages and how to share information online responsibly.

All stakeholders in the system, whether law enforcement, citizens, or journalists, would benefit from such a curriculum. For too long, journalism has neglected the unique nature of visual meaning. The problem has roots in the generally logocentric ignorance of news leaders about the construction of images, which leads to naïve beliefs in camera veracity. Moreover, while visual journalists in the field may appreciate the framing work they do and the embodied nature of their craft, they participate in routines that can blind them to their complicity in crafting messages that serve the criminal justice system and not necessarily the people it is ostensibly serves. Of course, routines are an essential part of an occupation and the news could not be produced without them. Yet the pressures on today's media in terms of time and money mean that routines become the tail wagging the dog, *especially* in the case of the visual press, which is so highly dependent upon authorities as part of the embodied gatekeeping process. It becomes too easy to color by numbers instead of questioning the basic processes of the justice system or the state's narrative. When visual journalists collect symbols to illustrate preconceived narratives about justice—whether in the form of a perp walk, a mug shot, or trial footage—those journalists contribute to the state's larger ideological project, legitimating the criminal justice system.

Citizen video evidence has not only laid bare false claims from police about incidents of abuse, but the failings of journalists to cover marginalized communities. The riots in Ferguson, Missouri, in 2014 provided a stark reminder that the lessons of the Kerner Commission, which warned journalists to pay attention to marginalized neighborhoods, had been forgotten.[20] Oppression in Ferguson had simmered for years, with uneven law enforcement that drained African American neighborhoods financially. In spite of these conditions enduring for so long, journalists did not report on them in depth until *after* the Ferguson riots. Responding to community concerns requires truly diverse newsrooms, which is not just a matter of hiring a few minority reporters and going on with business as usual.[21] Journalists who are part of token newsroom diversity efforts quickly find themselves unhappy with their job, as they are asked to represent their demographic repeatedly while also writing from a race-free perspective.[22] A diverse newsroom is only the first step toward truly serving the entire community and the different kinds of people who live within it. The late journalism diversity advocate Dori Maynard rightly argued that covering a community in all its diversity is a matter of accuracy.[23] When news organizations only visit Black neighborhoods to cover crime, or Hispanic neighborhoods only for Cinco de Mayo, they are attending to the reality of their full audience. Here again, journalism's failures to adequately consider the special nature of visual representation are highlighted, as marginalized communities are so often visually depicted in negative ways.

Journalism training, therefore, must attend more carefully to visual ethics and the way images are rendered meaningful. The Sandmann case as detailed in Chapter 9, which has cost the *Washington Post* and CNN money and credibility, exemplifies what can happen when image meaning is taken for granted. Professional picture editors are wise to the implications of their work, but like many other newsroom specialists, they are a diminishing breed. Digital journalists are expected to research, write, and copyedit—*and* shoot images, edit video, and choose stock photos for their stories. Standards are essential for choosing stock, writing captions, and creating images. There are wide disparities in media for image treatment. Some organizations employ professional photographers and photo editors, while others use stock images and the most poorly resourced expect producers to create all their own visual content.[24] Anyone publishing images must consider the way images operate in the minds of the audience and show at least as much care in photo choice as in crafting a sentence. Journalism schools must incorporate image ethics into their classes for all students, not just those specializing in photojournalism.

This book's description of the way police agencies respond to accountability videos, attempt to control coverage of their agencies, and (as Chapter 8 details) create their own positive visual messages is evidence that the law enforcement community is acutely aware of image power. For the sake of public accountability, therefore, departments need to develop clear and coherent policies for interacting with cop-watchers and for the recording and distribution of their own visual evidence. In 2014, in the wake of Eric Garner's death at the hands of New York City police, commanders issued a reminder to officers that citizens have the right to film them working, as long, of course, as those citizens are not interfering.[25] Other departments have issued memoranda to that effect, reminding officers that filming police is a right protected under the First Amendment. Police professional organizations would do well to develop a reminder for widespread distribution. Still, as recently as 2019, an officer in Arizona confronted a twelve-year-old aspiring journalist, telling her "it's against the law in Arizona" to put his face on the internet.[26] It's not, of course, and the deputy was later disciplined. Quite likely, though, this would not have happened if the girl had not had the presence of mind to tape the episode. Officers should consistently face discipline if they lie or otherwise try to convince a citizen to stop filming.

The much-lauded badge-cam and dashcam videos produced by police will not bring reforms unless there are clear, transparent, and *enforced* regulations about the video collected. A special task force of the National Association of Criminal Defense Lawyers issued a report in 2017 with recommendations that include the following: clear and strictly enforced policies must establish when body cameras will be recording so that the decision of when to record is not left to the discretion of individual police officers; police officers must be precluded from viewing body camera video before preparing their initial reports; and independent, nonpolice agencies must be created to retain and control access to body camera footage.[27]

Many other efforts are underway to mitigate racial disparities in policing that are not related to mediated images. Implicit bias training is promising, but research on its long-term effects is unfinished.[28] Evidence-based crime prevention scholars work to collect better data on use-of-force incidents, but until now this has not been accounted for at the national level, and the best numbers available have been collected by journalists or through crowdsourcing efforts such as the "mappingpoliceviolence" online collaboration, the *Guardian's* "The Counted" (for 2015 and 2016), or the *Washington Post's* "Fatal Force" project.[29] As this book has described, even though citizen videos of police abuse are hotly contested, they provided the spark for a national conversation about law enforcement accountability.

Police are not the only members of the law enforcement community who must consider image power. Attorneys and judges must also think about the role of visuals beyond policies for "cameras in the court." Experimental research has found that potential jurors make negative judgments about people in handcuffs or prison clothing, so courts need to take greater care to protect a defendant's pretrial rights. Chapter 3's findings suggest that the time is overdue for a serious conversation about whether the state should be in the perp walk business. At this writing, no legal or informal guidelines are in place to ensure that defendants are dressed appropriately for court. E. G. "Gerry" Morris, a past president of the National Association of Criminal Defense Lawyers, agrees that having images of clients in prison garb is problematic, but solutions won't come easy: "A lot of the times a judge just won't order it," he explained. "It takes a lot more time for the jail personnel to make sure that the person is properly dressed out in street clothes and to receive the street clothes in and check them to make sure there's not any contraband or anything else that's inappropriate in them and so they don't do that."[30] In the short term, one solution is for attorneys to provide portraits of their clients so that news organizations have an option beyond the mug shot. The evidence suggests that in spite of constitutional protections for criminal defendants, today's visual messaging from the court system works largely in the state's favor.

The research for this book makes a strong case for increased visual-media literacy for journalists, law enforcement, and the public alike, and the need is urgent. The development of deep fake technology undermines video's potential to provide documentary evidence. Deep fakes simply build upon the layering technique for still images to put someone else's face onto an actual recording, or even make an entirely fictional face. The form became well known in an early instance when director Jordan Peele created the deep fake in which Barack Obama appeared to call Donald Trump a "dipshit."[31] During the 2020 presidential campaign, Donald Trump retweeted fake videos of Joe Biden appearing to disparage police.[32] People have lied with photography since the earliest days of the craft, but today it is easier than ever to deceive, by manipulating an image or by simply labeling it deceptively. These duplicitous practices are particularly nefarious because of the power images have over our emotions and memory. "Deep fake" or not, however, the role of discursive recontextualization over image meaning, and the speed with which digital images travel, are causes for concern.[33]

Digital media have complicated the issue exponentially because everyday users are able to produce messages that look and sound like those once made by professionals. A generation ago, amateur media production literally *looked* amateurish. Underground zines were printed by smudgy copiers, and home video was shaky with low-resolution. Even the earliest days of the internet offered clues to hoax-ridden websites, with questionable design choices that matched their messaging.[34] Today even the most bizarre ideas are presented with the same well-designed visual messaging as the most traditional news site. People who were raised in an era when information on the (television) screen was federally regulated must be excused for their bewilderment over a media sphere in which anyone can—and does—easily and convincingly lie with images.[35] A Texas graduate student interviewed thirty men and women attending the 2017 Flat Earth International Conference and found that *every* interviewee adopted Flat Earth beliefs "predominantly after watching Flat Earth videos on YouTube."[36]

An ecology of media literacy would also require an ethical foundation so that individuals could express their own voice and have their own concerns recognized, but do so within a truly democratic framework of mutuality, honesty, and tolerance. Today's digital public sphere is somewhat like the lawless American frontier, as users struggle to establish appropriate rules for engagement. Media ethics from the analog age simply are not up to the task, because for better and for worse, *everyone* is a media producer in the digital public sphere. This is a considerable challenge, though, considering that news organizations often treat images carelessly when compared with linguistic information.[37] In this age of hypervisuality, cop-watching, badge cams, and Twitter-shaming, however, it is a conversation worth pursuing.

Democratic society cannot function if citizens do not consider the interests of others, yet it is hard to consider the needs of others if they are rendered invisible, whether by state practices, journalistic norms, or educational, economic, and social poverty. Recognition is essential for voice in civil society, but beyond the visual, democratic responsibility requires engagement with civic life. This means seeking good information and then, for the sake of fairness, demanding that institutions truly serve the public's best interest. Such engagement also means supporting ethical journalism and then paying attention to whether police and criminal justice agencies are operating in everyone's interest. Factual information in a democracy is like water to the body politic, and digitization has made it all too easy to pollute the supply.

The simplest step is to pay for ethical journalism. Fact-checking, research, and solid reporting require money. Online media are overflowing with editorials, opinion pieces, and essays, but fact-based reporting is harder to come by. Local news outlets have been crushed by a loss of classified and display advertising. Many media organizations have struggled to figure a way to make online news profitable. To support good journalism, look for publications that publish corrections, ascribe to ethical guidelines, and deliver evidence-based reporting.

Yet online, strangers offer up memes, articles, and pithy quotations every day, and users are quick to take it in and pass it on. Some of the material might be credible and trustworthy, but because humans are susceptible to confirmation bias we tend to accept messages that match our beliefs.[38] Add to this image superiority and the seductive way that images "feel" real even when they're not, and the result is, and has been, disastrous for factual discourse online. Several media literacy groups have created guides for assessing online information (see Appendix for suggestions), and some universities are considering requiring media literacy classes for all students. Such efforts are laudable and necessary in today's digitized environment but may overemphasize education for the young. Older people, who spent decades watching TV in a regulated media environment that required fairness and had no room for liars and mischief, are much more likely than the young to be fooled by online hoaxes.[39] In other words, the Americans most likely to vote are also the most likely to be misled, and to mislead others, online. As such, media literacy efforts must be aimed not only at those in school, but spread through senior centers, community groups, and even churches. Cartoonist Walt Kelly's Pogo declared, "We have met the enemy, and he is us," for an Earth Day poster in 1970, depicting the little character surrounded by human-generated garbage.[40] There is plenty of trash to clean up in today's media ecosphere, too. Each of us today is responsible for what we toss into the visual economy, and we are the ones who can address the misuse of imagery.

To See Justice Done

This book has described the way social actors employ visuals in the narratives about right and wrong, and how having power over the visual is concomitant with power over the story. Journalists weave stories of individual cases, yet over time, their metastory, the ideological story, is one of state authority. Whether in the photographs of deputies inspecting the gallows, police department mug shots, or perp walks of wanted suspects, the visual messages are clear: there are good people and bad people, and the state can be trusted to sort them out. I have argued that members of the criminal justice system manage their visual image in order to cultivate faith in that system using embodied gatekeeping and other techniques. News professionals often (though not always consciously) play a supportive role in this ideological stagecraft. The result is a system that often occludes injustice, especially injustice rooted in social inequality such as race, class, and gender. At the same time, as we have seen, new media tools have engendered possibilities for counternarratives. Everyone is able to participate in the visual public sphere, a power that comes with great responsibility.

Using the model of de- and recontextualization, which emphasizes the very real relationship a photographic image has to a moment in time and space and the way meaning is subsequently assigned by social actors, these cases illustrate the way visual media construct and support this message of state authority. Through the practices of embodied gatekeeping, the state has considerable control over the way images are constructed, distributed, and contextualized in narrative. Journalists are often implicated in this ideological project for a variety of reasons; they rely on law enforcement more than everyday citizens for essential information; their daily work is episodic and neglects larger social contexts; and they, like most actors in the system, are invested in believing that the system is fair, just, and moral.

For many Americans, however, the system is not fair, just, or moral. The potential for citizen oversight through cop-watching and other mediated witnessing is tempered by long-standing stereotypes and faith in the judicial system. To doubt police in the United States is tantamount to sacrilege, a defiance of civic religion as seen by the furor over former NFL quarterback Colin Kaepernick's peaceful protest of police brutality by taking a knee during the national anthem.[41] Even when visual evidence shows what seems to be unnecessary violence, many viewers seem slow to doubt police accounts of events.

The rule of law is the rule of language: precise, definitive, and rational. Yet much of what we know about the world—indeed, today, one might argue that *most* of what we know about the world—arrives by way of visual media. Because our brains process images differently, it is essential that we take visual media seriously if we are to untangle our ideas about criminality, justice, democracy, and our fellow citizens. Fairness requires careful policy making and debate about the creation and distribution of images so that they can be democratically contextualized. Images cannot be treated like words: they present a very different type of information, they operate in our brains differently, and their construction is more reliant upon embodied practice. The "bain d'images" is flooding the public sphere, and we are falling behind in crafting ethical and democratic ways to use them in civic discourse.

Full citizenship in the digital age is constituted in voice *and* visibility. With this book I've attempted a fair critique of the institutions that construct those images, and I hope my self-critique has been evident throughout. Visual media cannot address the flaws of America's criminal justice system, as images are neither the problem nor the solution, but merely tools we can use to build something better. Justice is an experience, not a photograph, and it cannot be achieved until everyone is acknowledged, heard, and respectfully seen.

Resources

The *Associated Press* explains on its standards and practices page how it checks contributed images: https://www.ap.org/about/our-story/standards-and-practices.

Berkeley Copwatch has set the standard for many police accountability organizations in the United States: https://www.berkeleycopwatch.org/.

The *Knight Center for Journalism and the Americas* provides online news writing and production courses, many for free: https://knightcenter.utexas.edu/.

The *Maynard Institute* works to improve the coverage of minority communities while supporting journalists of color: https://www.mije.org/.

The *Media Literacy Council* has many helpful resources here: https://www.betterinternet.sg/.

Media Literacy Now is a national organization advocating media literacy education policy: https://medialiteracynow.org/.

The *National Press Photographers Association's* code of ethics is available online: https://nppa.org/code-ethics, as is the code of ethics for the *Society of Professional Journalists*: http://www.spj.org/ethicscode.asp.

The *Online News Association* has formulated a code of ethics for social media newsgathering: https://journalists.org/tools/social-newsgathering/.

The *Poynter Institute* has resources on ethics and journalism practice: https://www.poynter.org/.

The *Radio Television Digital News Association* (RTDNA) maintains a state-by-state guide for camera in the court rules: https://www.rtdna.org/content/cameras_in_court.

The *Solutions Journalism Network* supports journalism that seeks answers to problems: https://www.solutionsjournalism.org/.

Notes

Chapter 1

1. Nicholas Mirzoeff, *Right to Look: A Counterhistory of Visuality* (Durham, NC: Duke University Press, 2011), http://site.ebrary.com/lib/alltitles/docDetail. action?docID=10509975.
2. Nielsen Company, "The Nielsen Total Audience Report Q1 2018," July 31, 2018, http:// www.nielsen.com/us/en/insights/news/2018/time-flies-us-adults-now-spend-nearly-half-a-day-interacting-with-media.
3. Anne Marie Seward Barry, *Visual Intelligence: Perception, Image and Manipulation in Visual Communication* (Albany: State University of New York Press, 1997); Rick Williams and Julianne Newton, *Visual Communication: Integrating Media, Art and Science* (New York: Erlbaum, 2007).
4. Robert Hariman and John Louis Lucaites, *No Caption Needed: Iconic Photographs, Public Culture, and Liberal Democracy* (Chicago: University of Chicago Press, 2007); Tamar Katriel and Thomas Farrell, "Scrapbooks as Cultural Texts: An American Art of Memory," *Text and Performance Quarterly* 11, no. 1 (1991): 1–17, https://doi.org/ 10.1080/10462939109365990.
5. Hans-Jürgen Bucher and Peter Schumacher, "The Relevance of Attention for Selecting News Content: An Eye-Tracking Study on Attention Patterns in the Reception of Print and Online Media," *Communications* 31, no. 3 (2006): 347–68, https://doi.org/ 10.1515/COMMUN.2006.022.
6. Joseph N. Cappella and Kathleen Hall Jamieson, "Broadcast Adwatch Effects: A Field Experiment," *Communication Research* 21, no. 3 (1994): 342–65; Rhonda Gibson and Dolf Zillmann, "Reading between the Photographs: The Influence of Incidental— Pictorial Information on Issue Perception," *Journalism & Mass Communication Quarterly* 77, no. 2 (2000): 355–66.
7. Allison Joan Lazard, "Photo Manipulation: The Influence of Implicit Visual Arguments on Dual Processing" (PhD dissertation, University of Texas, 2015), https:// repositories.lib.utexas.edu/handle/2152/30317; Sophie J. Nightingale, Kimberley A. Wade, and Derrick G. Watson, "Can People Identify Original and Manipulated Photos of Real-World Scenes?," *Cognitive Research: Principles and Implications* 2, no. 1 (July 18, 2017): 30, https://doi.org/10.1186/s41235-017-0067-2.
8. Allison J. Lazard et al., "Visual Assertions: Effects of Photo Manipulation and Dual Processing for Food Advertisements," *Visual Communication Quarterly* 25, no. 1 (January 2, 2018): 16–30, https://doi.org/10.1080/15551393.2017.1417047.
9. Cappella and Jamieson, "Broadcast Adwatch Effects."
10. Mirzoeff, *Right to Look.*

11. Paul Frosh, "Selfies | The Gestural Image: The Selfie, Photography Theory, and Kinesthetic Sociability," *International Journal of Communication* 9, no. 22 (2015), https://ijoc.org/index.php/ijoc/article/viewFile/3146/1388; Paul Messaris, *Visual Literacy: Image, Mind & Reality* (Boulder, CO: Westview Press, 1994).

12. Astrid Gynnild, "The Robot Eye Witness," *Digital Journalism* 2, no. 3 (July 3, 2014): 334–43, https://doi.org/10.1080/21670811.2014.883184.

13. Charles A. Nelson, "The Development of Face Recognition Reflects an Experience-Expectant and Activity-Dependent Process," in *The Development of Face Processing in Infancy and Early Childhood: Current Perspectives* (Hauppauge, NY: Nova Science Publishers, 2003), 79–97.

14. Mark Changizi, *The Vision Revolution* (Dallas, TX: BenBella Books, 2009).

15. Paul Ekman and Wallace V. Friesen, *Unmasking the Face: A Guide to Recognizing Emotions from Facial Clues* (Los Altos, CA: Malor Books, 2003); Mark L. Knapp, Judith A. Hall, and Terrence G. Horgan, *Nonverbal Communication in Human Interaction* (Boston: Cengage Learning, 2013).

16. Stuart Hall, "The Spectacle of 'the Other,'" in *Representation: Cultural Representations, and Signifying Practices*, ed. Stuart Hall, Jessica Evans, and Sean Nixon (Thousand Oaks, CA: Sage, 1997), 225–79; Paul Martin Lester and Susan Dente Ross, *Images That Injure: Pictorial Stereotypes in the Media*, ed. Paul Martin Lester and Susan Dente Ross, vol. 2 (Westport, CT: Praeger, 2003).

17. J. M. Kilner and R. N. Lemon, "What We Know Currently about Mirror Neurons," *Current Biology* 23, no. 23 (December 2013): R1057–62, https://doi.org/10.1016/j.cub.2013.10.051.

18. Niccolo Machiavelli, *The Prince*, trans. N. H. Thompson (New York: Cosimo Classics, 2008), 46.

19. Kiku Adatto, *Picture Perfect: Life in the Age of the Photo Op* (Princeton, NJ: Princeton University Press, 2008); Josh King, *Off Script: An Advance Man's Guide to White House Stagecraft, Campaign Spectacle, and Political Suicide* (New York: St. Martin's Publishing Group, 2016).

20. Lazard et al., "Visual Assertions"; Cappella and Jamieson, "Broadcast Adwatch Effects."

21. Murray Edelman, *Constructing the Political Spectacle* (Chicago: University of Chicago Press, 1988).

22. Judith Resnik, Dennis Curtis, and Allison Tait, "Constructing Courts: Architecture, the Ideology of Judging, and the Public Sphere," in *Law, Culture, and Visual Studies*, ed. Anne Wagner and Richard K. Sherwin (Dordrecht: Springer Netherlands, 2014), 515–45, https://doi.org/10.1007/978-90-481-9322-6_23.

23. Linda Mulcahy, "Architects of Justice: The Politics of Courtroom Design," *Social & Legal Studies* 16, no. 3 (September 1, 2007): 383–403, https://doi.org/10.1177/0964663907079765.

24. Cathleen Burnett, "Justice: Myth and Symbol," *Legal Studies Forum*, no. 1 (1987): 79–94.

25. Max Weber posited this definition in his 1919 lecture, then essay, "Politics as Vocation." In Max Weber, *Max Weber's Complete Writings on Academic and Political*

Vocations, ed. John Dreijmanis, trans. Gordon C. Wells (New York: Algora Publishing, 2008), 127.

26. Michel Foucault, *The Spectacle of the Scaffold* (London: Penguin, 2008).

27. Peter K. Manning, *Police Work: The Social Organization of Policing* (Cambridge, MA: MIT Press, 1977); David D. Perlmutter, *Policing the Media: Street Cops and Public Perceptions of Law Enforcement* (Thousand Oaks, CA: Sage, 2000); Christopher P. Wilson, *Cop Knowledge: Police Power and Cultural Narrative in Twentieth-Century America* (Chicago: University of Chicago Press, 2000); Rob C. Mawby, *Policing Images: Policing, Communication and Legitimacy* (Cullompton, Devon, UK: Willan Pub, 2002).

28. David Lyon, *Surveillance Studies: An Overview* (Cambridge, UK: Polity, 2007); Torin Monahan, *Surveillance and Security: Technological Politics and Power in Everyday Life* (New York: Taylor & Francis, 2006); Sigmund Freud, *The Complete Psychological Works of Sigmund Freud*, ed. James Strachey (New York: W. W. Norton & Company, 1976).

29. Steve Mann, Jason Nolan, and Barry Wellman, "Sousveillance: Inventing and Using Wearable Computing Devices for Data Collection in Surveillance Environments," *Surveillance & Society* 1, no. 3 (2003): 331–55, https://doi.org/10.24908/ss.v1i3.3344; Esther Prins, "Participatory Photography: A Tool for Empowerment or Surveillance?—Esther Prins, 2010," *Action Research* 8, no. 4 (2010): 426–43.

30. Roy Coleman, "Images from a Neoliberal City: The State, Surveillance and Social Control," *Critical Criminology* 12, no. 1 (January 1, 2004): 38, https://doi.org/10.1023/B:CRIT.0000024443.08828.d8.

31. Peter Hamilton and Roger Hargreaves, *The Beautiful and the Damned: The Creation of Identity in Nineteenth-Century Photography* (Aldershot, UK: Lund Humphries, in association with the National Portrait Gallery, 2001).

32. Rachel Hall, *Wanted: The Outlaw in American Visual Culture*, Cultural Frames, Framing Culture (Charlottesville: University of Virginia Press, 2009).

33. John Tagg, "Evidence, Truth and Order: A Means of Surveillance," in *Visual Culture: The Reader*, ed. Stuart Hall and Jessica Evans (Thousand Oaks, CA: Sage, 1999), 244–73; Allan Sekula, "The Body and the Archive," *October* 39 (1986): 3–64.

34. Josh Ellenbogen, *Reasoned and Unreasoned Images: The Photography of Bertillon, Galton, and Marey* (University Park: Pennsylvania State University Press, 2012); Tagg, "Evidence, Truth and Order: A Means of Surveillance." Chapter 5 deals with mug shots in greater depth, and Chapter 9 examines the police discourse about images.

35. Neal Feigenson and Christina Spiesel, *Law on Display: The Digital Transformation of Legal Persuasion and Judgment* (New York: New York University Press, 2011).

36. W. Lance Bennett, *Reconstructing Reality in the Courtroom: Justice and Judgment in American Culture*, Crime, Law, and Deviance Series (New Brunswick, NJ: Rutgers University Press, 1981); Sandra F. Chance, "Considering Cameras in the Courtroom," *Journal of Broadcasting & Electronic Media* 39, no. 4 (1995): 555–61; Steven A. Lautt, "Sunlight Is Still the Best Disinfectant: The Case for a First Amendment Right to Record the Police Note," *Washburn Law Journal* 51 (2012): 349–82; Louis-Georges

Schwartz, *Mechanical Witness: A History of Motion Picture Evidence in U.S. Courts* (Oxford: Oxford University Press, 2009).

37. Feigenson and Spiesel, *Law on Display*; Schwartz, *Mechanical Witness*; Eyal Weizman, *Forensic Architecture: Violence at the Threshold of Detectability* (Cambridge, MA: MIT Press, 2017).

38. Mirzoeff, *Right to Look*.

39. Haejung Paik, "The Effects of Television Violence on Antisocial Behavior: A Meta-Analysis," *Communication Research* 21, no. 4 (1994): 516–47.

40. George Gerbner et al., "Growing Up with Television: The Cultivation Perspective," in *Media Effects: Advances in Theory and Research*, ed. J. Bryant and D. Zillmann, LEA's Communication Series (Hillsdale, NJ: Lawrence Erlbaum Associates, 1994), 17–41.

41. Michael Morgan and James Shanahan, "Television and the Cultivation of Authoritarianism: A Return Visit from an Unexpected Friend," *Journal of Communication* 67, no. 3 (June 1, 2017): 424–44, https://doi.org/10.1111/jcom.12297.

42. Aaron Doyle, *Arresting Images: Crime and Policing in Front of the Television Camera* (Toronto: University of Toronto Press, 2003); Sarah Eschholz et al., "Race and Attitudes toward the Police: Assessing the Effects of Watching 'Reality' Police Programs," *Journal of Criminal Justice* 30, no. 4 (July 1, 2002): 327–41, https://doi.org/10.1016/S0047-2352(02)00133-2.

43. Ray Surette, *Media, Crime and Criminal Justice* (Pacific Grove, CA: Brooks/Cole, 1992).

44. David Morley, Kuan-Hsing Chen, and Stuart Hall, "The Problem of Ideology: Marxism without Guarantees," in *Stuart Hall: Critical Dialogues in Cultural Studies*, ed. Kuan-Hsing Chen and David Morley (Florence: Routledge, 1996), 25–26, https://doi.org/10.4324/9780203993262.

45. Stuart Hall et al., *Culture, Media, Language: Working Papers in Cultural Studies, 1972–79* (London: Routledge, 2005),), http://ebookcentral.proquest.com/lib/utxa/detail.action?docID=179321; Stuart Hall, "Encoding/Decoding," in *Culture, Media, Language: Working Papers in Cultural Studies, 1972–79*, ed. Stuart Hall et al. (London: Routledge, 2005), 117–27; Stuart Hall, ed., *Policing the Crisis: Mugging, the State, and Law and Order*, Critical Social Studies (London: Macmillan, 1978); Herbert Gans, *Deciding What's News: A Study of CBS Evening News, NBC Nightly News, Newsweek and Time, 25th Anniversary Edition* (New York: Pantheon Books, 1979); Gaye Tuchman, *Making News: A Study in the Construction of Reality* (London: Free Press, 1978); Todd Gitlin, *The Whole World Is Watching: Mass Media in the Making and Unmaking of the New Left* (Berkeley: University of California Press, 1980).

46. Phyllis Kaniss, *Making Local News* (Chicago: University of Chicago Press, 1991); Danilo Yanich, "Location, Location, Location: Urban and Suburban Crime on Local TV News," *Journal of Urban Affairs* 23, no. 3–4 (2001): 221–41.

47. Tuchman, *Making News*.

Tuchman's argument has been applied in other journalistic contexts, such as video journalism: Mary Angela Bock, *Video Journalism: Beyond the One-Man Band* (New York: Peter Lang, 2012); and political coverage: Bartholomew H. Sparrow, *Uncertain Guardians: The News Media as a Political Institution*

(Baltimore, MD: Johns Hopkins University Press, 1999). Rodelo and Muñiz were able to show how government frames of events appeared in news: Frida V. Rodelo and Carlos Muñiz, "Government Frames and Their Influence on News Framing: An Analysis of Cross-Lagged Correlations in the Mexican Context," *Global Media and Communication*, December 19, 2018, 1742766518818862, https://doi.org/10.1177/1742766518818862.

48. J. M. Chan and C. C. Lee, "The Journalistic Paradigm on Civil Protests: A Case Study of Hong Kong," in *The News Media in National and International Conflict*, ed. A. Arno and W. Dissanayake (London: Westview Press, 1984), 183–202; Gitlin, *The Whole World Is Watching*.

49. Damon T. Di Cicco, "The Public Nuisance Paradigm: Changes in Mass Media Coverage of Political Protest since the 1960s," *Journalism & Mass Communication Quarterly* 87, no. 1 (March 1, 2010): 135–53, https://doi.org/10.1177/107769901008700108.

50. Eileen E. S. Bjornstrom et al., "Race and Ethnic Representations of Lawbreakers and Victims in Crime News: A National Study of Television Coverage," *Social Problems* 57, no. 2 (2010): 269–93, https://doi.org/10.1525/sp.2010.57.2.269; Travis L. Dixon and Daniel Linz, "Television News, Prejudicial Pretrial Publicity, and the Depiction of Race," *Journal of Broadcasting & Electronic Media* 46, no. 1 (2002): 112–36, https://doi.org/10.1207/s15506878jobem4601_7; Dana Mastro et al., "The Influence of Exposure to Depictions of Race and Crime in TV News on Viewer's Social Judgments," *Journal of Broadcasting & Electronic Media* 53, no. 4 (November 23, 2009): 615–35, https://doi.org/10.1080/08838150903310534.

51. Pamela Davies, Peter Francis, and Chris Greer, *Victims, Crime, and Society* (Los Angeles, CA: SAGE, 2007); Michelle N. Jeanis and Ráchael A. Powers, "Newsworthiness of Missing Persons Cases: An Analysis of Selection Bias, Disparities in Coverage, and the Narrative Framework of News Reports," *Deviant Behavior* 38, no. 6 (June 2017): 668–83, https://doi.org/10.1080/01639625.2016.1197618.

52. See Gitlin, *The Whole World Is Watching*; Perlmutter, *Policing the Media*; Sparrow, *Uncertain Guardians*; Tuchman, *Making News*.

53. Gans, *Deciding What's News*.

54. Chan and Lee, "The Journalistic Paradigm on Civil Protests."

55. Adatto, *Picture Perfect*.

56. Edward S. Herman and Noam Chomsky, *Manufacturing Consent: The Political Economy of Mass Media*, 2nd ed. (New York: Pantheon, 2002).

57. David L. Altheide and Robert P. Snow, *Media Logic*, Sage Library of Social Research (Beverly Hills, CA: Sage, 1979); David L. Altheide and Robert P. Snow, *Media Worlds in the Postjournalism Era* (New York: De Gruyter, 1991).

58. Regarding crime rates, see John Gramlich, "Five Facts about Crime in the U.S.," Pew Research Center, January 3, 2019, http://www.pewresearch.org/fact-tank/2019/01/03/5-facts-about-crime-in-the-u-s/. Jeff Asher and Ben Horwitz, "It's Been 'Such a Weird Year.' That's Also Reflected in Crime Statistics," *New York Times*, July 6, 2020, sec. The Upshot, https://www.nytimes.com/2020/07/06/upshot/murders-rising-crime-coronavirus.html. Information on mass shootings is available here: Mark Follman, Gavin Aronson, and Deanna Pan, "A Guide to Mass Shootings in America,"

Mother Jones, January 24, 2019, https://www.motherjones.com/politics/2012/07/mass-shootings-map/. Information on police fatalities is tracked by the National Law Enforcement Officers Memorial Fund: Preliminary 2017 Law Enforcement Officer Fatalities Report, NLEOMF.org, https://nleomf.org/officer-safety/nhtsa-officer-safety-initiatives/quarterly-law-enforcement-fatality-reports (accessed January 31, 2019). See also US Bureau of Labor Statistics, *National Census of Fatal Occupational Injuries in 2017*, No. USDL-18-1978.

59. Matt Taibbi, *I Can't Breathe: A Killing on Bay Street* (New York: Spiegel & Grau, 2017); Kristian Williams, *Our Enemies in Blue: Police and Power in America* (Chico, CA: AK Press, 2015).

60. "Facts about the Death Penalty," Death Penalty Information Center, May 3, 2019, www.deathpenaltyinfo.org.

61. Franklin E. Zimring, *When Police Kill* (Cambridge, MA: Harvard University Press, 2017).

62. Zimring.

63. Danielle Kaeble and Mary Cowhig, "Correctional Populations in the United States, 2016," US Department of Justice, April 2018.

64. Jamiles Lartey, "By the Numbers: US Police Kill More in Days Than Other Countries Do in Years," *The Guardian*, June 9, 2015, sec. US news, http://www.theguardian.com/us-news/2015/jun/09/the-counted-police-killings-us-vs-other-countries.

65. Hariman and Lucaites, *No Caption Needed*; Roland Barthes, *Mythologies* (New York: Hill and Wang, 1972).

66. Hariman and Lucaites, *No Caption Needed*.

67. James J. Gibson, "The Theory of Affordances," in *The Ecological Approach to Visual Perception* (Boston: Houghton Mifflin, 1979), 119–35.

68. Gibson, 70.

69. Robert M. Entman, "Framing: Toward Clarification of a Fractured Paradigm," *Journal of Communication* 43, no. 4 (1993): 52 (italics in the original).

70. Peter Berger and Thomas Luckmann, *The Social Construction of Reality: A Treatise in the Sociology of Knowledge* (New York: Random House, 1967); Klaus Krippendorff, "A Constructivist Critique of Semiotics," in *On Communicating: Otherness, Meaning and Information*, ed. Fernando Bermejo (New York: Routledge, 2009), 173–90.

71. Michel Foucault, "Truth and Power," in *Power/Knowledge: Selected Interviews and Other Writings, 1972–1977* (New York: Pantheon Books, 1980); Michel Foucault and Paul Rabinow, *The Foucault Reader* (New York: Pantheon Books, 1984); Michel Foucault, *Discipline and Punish: The Birth of the Prison*, Vintage Books ed. (New York: Vintage Books, 1979); Foucault, "Truth and Power"; Michel Foucault, *The Order of Things: An Archaeology of the Human Sciences* (London: Psychology Press, 2002); Michel Foucault, *The History of Sexuality*, Vol. 1: *An Introduction*, Reissue ed. (New York: Vintage, 1990).

72. Foucault, *Discipline and Punish*.

73. Foucault, "Truth and Power." In an interview, Foucault explained that "'Truth' is to be understood as a system of ordered procedures for the production, regulation, distribution, circulation, and operations of statements. Truth is linked in a circular relation

with systems of power which produce and sustain it, and to effects of power which it induces and which extend it" ("Truth and Power," 155).

74. Foucault, *Discipline and Punish*.

75. Louis Althusser, "Ideology & Ideological State Apparatuses," in *Cultural Theory and Popular Culture: A Reader*, ed. John Storey, 2nd ed. (Harlow, UK: Pearson/Prentice Hall, 1998), 153–64.

76. Morley, Chen, and Hall, "The Problem of Ideology: Marxism without Guarantees"; Hall et al., *Culture, Media, Language*; Foucault, "Truth and Power"; Foucault and Rabinow, *The Foucault Reader*.

77. Hall et al., *Culture, Media, Language*. Note: Much of this book's research attempts to use this grounded approach to connect everyday practice to ideological constructs.

78. Hall, "Encoding/Decoding."

79. Walter R. Fisher, "The Narrative Paradigm: An Elaboration," *Communication Monographs* 52, no. 4 (December 1985): 347–67; Walter R. Fisher, "Narration as a Human Communication Paradigm: The Case of Public Moral Argument," *Communication Monographs* 51, no. 1 (March 1984): 1–22.

80. S. Elizabeth Bird and Robert W. Dardenne, "Myth, Chronicle, and Story: Exploring the Narrative Qualities of News," in *Social Meanings of News*, ed. Dan Berkowitz (Thousand Oaks, CA: Sage, 1988), 333–50; Ruth Knepel, "The Return of Myth: Icons, Mythology, and the Universal Narrative of 9/11," in *Terror in Global Narrative: Representations of 9/11 in the Age of Late-Late Capitalism*, ed. George Fragopoulos and Liliana M. Naydan (Cham: Springer International, 2016), 139–56, https://doi.org/10.1007/978-3-319-40654-1_8.

81. Barthes, *Mythologies*.

82. Robert M. Cover, "Violence and the Word," *Yale Law Journal* 95, no. 8 (1986): 1601–29, https://doi.org/10.2307/796468.

83. Markus Dubber, *The Police Power: Patriarchy and the Foundations of American Government* (New York: Columbia University Press, 2005); Anastasia Prokos and Irene Padavic, "'There Oughtta Be a Law against Bitches': Masculinity Lessons in Police Academy Training," *Gender, Work & Organization* 9, no. 4 (2002): 439–59, https://doi.org/10.1111/1468-0432.00168; Williams, *Our Enemies in Blue*.

84. Derrick Bell, *Faces at the Bottom of the Well: The Permanence of Racism* (New York: BasicBooks, 1992); Patricia J. Williams, *The Alchemy of Race and Rights* (Cambridge, MA: Harvard University Press, 1991); Kimberlé Crenshaw, ed., *Critical Race Theory: The Key Writings That Formed the Movement* (New York: New Press, 1995); Mari J. Matsuda, ed., *Words That Wound: Critical Race Theory, Assaultive Speech, and the First Amendment*, New Perspectives on Law, Culture, and Society (Boulder, CO: Westview Press, 1993).

85. Hall, *Policing the Crisis*.

86. Stuart Hall, "Racist Ideologies and the Media," in *Media Studies: A Reader*, ed. Paul Marris, Sue Thornham, and Caroline Bassett (New York: New York University Press, 2000), 273.

87. Kimberle W. Crenshaw, "From Private Violence to Mass Incarceration: Thinking Intersectionally about Women, Race, and Social Control Symposium: Overpoliced

and Underprotected: Women, Race, and Criminalization: I. Establishing the Framework," *UCLA Law Review* 59, no. 6 (2012): 1418–73.

88. Margaret A. McLaren, *Feminism, Foucault, and Embodied Subjectivity*, SUNY Series in Contemporary Continental Philosophy (Albany: State University of New York Press, 2002); Jana Sawicki, *Disciplining Foucault: Feminism, Power, and the Body* (New York: Routledge, 1991).

89. Peter B. Kraska, *Militarizing the American Criminal Justice System: The Changing Roles of the Armed Forces and the Police* (Boston: Northeastern University Press, 2001).

90. Wendy Brown, "Finding the Man in the State," *Feminist Studies* 18, no. 1 (1992): 7–34, https://doi.org/10.2307/3178212.

91. Taibbi, *I Can't Breathe.*

92. Note: Pantaleo also faced the possibility of federal charges, but the government declined to prosecute.

    Katie Benner, "Eric Garner's Death Will Not Lead to Federal Charges for N.Y.P.D. Officer," *New York Times*, July 16, 2019, sec. New York, https://www.nytimes.com/2019/07/16/nyregion/eric-garner-case-death-daniel-pantaleo.html; Azi Paybarah, "N.Y. Today: Officer Who Choked Eric Garner Faces Police Charges," *New York Times*, December 7, 2018, sec. New York, https://www.nytimes.com/2018/12/07/nyregion/newyorktoday/new-york-news-eric-garner-pantaleo-wu-tang.html.

93. Pamela Shoemaker and Timothy Vos, *Gatekeeping Theory* (New York: Routledge, 2009); D. M. White, "The Gatekeeper," *Journalism Quarterly* 27, no. 4 (1950): 383–90.

94. James W. Carey, *Communication as Culture: Essays on Media and Society* (Boston: Unwin Hyman, 1989), 87.

95. Wilson Lowrey, "Word People vs. Picture People: Normative Differences and Strategies for Control over Work among Newsroom Subgroups," *Mass Communication and Society* 5, no. 4 (2002): 411–32; Barbie Zelizer, "Journalism's 'Last Stand': Wirephoto and the Discourse of Resistance," *Journal of Communication* 45, no. 2 (1995): 78–92.

96. For example: D. M. Lindekugel, *Shooters: TV News Photographers and Their Work* (Westport, CT: Praeger, 1994); Bock, *Video Journalism*; Barbara Rosenblum, "Photographers and Their Photographs: An Empirical Study in the Sociology of Aesthetics" (doctoral dissertation, Northwestern University, 1973).

97. Rachel Somerstein, "News Photographers and Interference: Iconophobia, Iconoclasm, and Extramedia Influences on the Ground," *Visual Communication Quarterly* 24, no. 2 (April 3, 2017): 115–27, https://doi.org/10.1080/15551393.2017.1309296.

98. For an examination of the way news coverage *in general* homogenizes rather than diversifies, see Pablo J. Boczkowski, *News at Work: Imitation in an Age of Information Abundance* (Chicago: University of Chicago Press, 2010). Greenwood and Smith noted the phenomenon in feature photography: Keith Greenwood and C. Zoe Smith, "Conventionalization in Feature Photography," *Journalism Practice* 3, no. 2 (April 1, 2009): 140–61, https://doi.org/10.1080/17512780802681173.

99. This is improving. See, for example: Kyser Lough, "A Gate in the Wall of Sound," *Journalism Practice* 13, no. 2 (February 7, 2019): 247–62, https://doi.org/10.1080/17512786.2018.1423629; T. J. Thomson, "In Front of the Lens: The Expectations,

Experiences, and Reactions of Visual Journalism's Subjects," *Journalism & Communication Monographs* 21, no. 1 (March 1, 2019): 4–65, https://doi.org/10.1177/1522637918823261; Krishnan Vasudevan, "Depth of Field," *Journalism Practice* 13, no. 2 (February 7, 2019): 229–46, https://doi.org/10.1080/17512786.2017.1419826.

100. Nicole Smith Dahmen, Natalia ˙Mielczarek, and David D. Perlmutter, "The Influence-Network Model of the Photojournalistic Icon," *Journalism & Communication Monographs* 20, no. 4 (December 1, 2018): 264–313, https://doi.org/10.1177/1522637918803351; Hariman and Lucaites, *No Caption Needed*; David D. Perlmutter, *Photojournalism and Foreign Policy: Icons of Outrage in International Crises* (Westport, CT: Praeger, 1998).

101. David Campbell, "Geopolitics and Visuality: Sighting the Darfur Conflict," *Political Geography* 26, no. 4 (May 2007): 357–82, https://doi.org/10.1016/j.polgeo.2006.11.005; Deborah Poole, *Vision, Race, and Modernity: A Visual Economy of the Andean Image World* (Princeton, NJ: Princeton University Press, 1997).

102. Marita Sturken and Lisa Cartwright, *Practices of Looking: An Introduction to Visual Culture* (Oxford: Oxford University Press, 2001).

103. "Logic as Semiotic," in Charles S. Peirce and Justus Buchler, *The Philosophy of Peirce: Selected Writings*, International Library of Psychology, Philosophy, and Scientific Method (London: Routledge & Kegan Paul, 1956).

104. Roland Barthes, *Image-Music-Text* (New York: Hill & Wang, 1977).

105. Allan Sekula, "On the Invention of Photographic Meaning," in *Photography against the Grain* (Halifax: Press of the Nova Scotia College of Art and Design, 1984), 5.

106. Sekula, 5–6.

107. Allan Sekula, "Traffic in Photographs," in *Photography against the Grain* (Halifax: Press of the Nova Scotia College of Art and Design, 1984), 77–101.

108. Errol Morris, "Not Every Picture Tells a Story," *New York Times*, November 20, 2004, sec. Opinion, https://www.nytimes.com/2004/11/20/opinion/not-every-picture-tells-a-story.html.

109. Mary Angela Bock, "Theorising Visual Framing: Contingency, Materiality, and Ideology," *Visual Studies* 35, no. 1 (January 1, 2020): 1–12, https://doi.org/10.1080/1472586X.2020.1715244.

110. Laura Silver, "Smartphone Ownership Is Growing Rapidly Around the World, but Not Always Equally," Global Attitudes and Trends, Pew Research Center, February 5, 2019, https://www.pewresearch.org/global/2019/02/05/smartphone-ownership-is-growing-rapidly-around-the-world-but-not-always-equally/; Hall, "Encoding/Decoding."

111. Alvin Toffler, *The Third Wave* (London: Pan Books, 1981).

112. Felix Tusa, "How Social Media Can Shape a Protest Movement: The Cases of Egypt in 2011 and Iran in 2009," *Arab Media and Society* 17 (Winter 2013): 1–9.

113. Keith Hampton and Barry Wellman, "Neighboring in Netville: How the Internet Supports Community and Social Capital in a Wired Suburb," *City & Community* 2 (2003): 277–311; Joe Trippi, *The Revolution Will Not Be Televised: Democracy, the Internet and the Overthrow of Everything* (New York: HarperCollins, 2004); Howard Rheingold, *Smart Mobs: The Next Social Revolution* (Cambridge, MA: Perseus, 2002).

114. Sadaf R. Ali and Shahira Fahmy, "Gatekeeping and Citizen Journalism: The Use of Social Media during the Recent Uprisings in Iran, Egypt, and Libya," *Media, War & Conflict* 6, no. 1 (April 1, 2013): 55–69, https://doi.org/10.1177/1750635212469906; Tony Harcup, "Alternative Journalism as Active Citizenship," *Journalism* 12, no. 1 (January 1, 2011): 15–31, https://doi.org/10.1177/1464884910385191; Mehdi Semati and Robert Alan Brookey, "Not for Neda: Digital Media, (Citizen) Journalism, and the Invention of a Postfeminist Martyr," *Communication, Culture & Critique* 7, no. 2 (June 1, 2014): 137–53, https://doi.org/10.1111/cccr.12042.

115. D. Jasun Carr et al., "Cynics and Skeptics: Evaluating the Credibility of Mainstream and Citizen Journalism," *Journalism & Mass Communication Quarterly* 91, no. 3 (September 1, 2014): 452–70, https://doi.org/10.1177/1077699014538828; David Domingo and Ari Heinonen, "Weblogs and Journalism: A Typology to Explore the Blurring Boundaries," *NORDICOM Review* 29, no. 1 (June 2008): 3–15; Jane B. Singer, "The Political J-Blogger: 'Normalizing' a New Media Form to Fit Old Norms and Practices," *Journalism* 6, no. 2 (2005): 173–98.

116. Mike Ananny and Carol Stohecker, "Sustained, Open Dialogue with Citizen Photojournalism," Proceedings of Development by Design Conference, Bangalore, India, December 1–2, 2002; Kari Andén-Papadopoulos, "Citizen Camera-Witnessing: Embodied Political Dissent in the Age of 'Mediated Mass Self-Communication,'" *New Media & Society*, May 31, 2013, 1461444813489863, https://doi.org/10.1177/1461444813489863; Claire Sloan Cooley, "The Citizen Viewer: Questioning the Democratic Authority of the Camera Phone Image" (Master's thesis: University of Texas, 2015).

117. Stuart Allan, *Citizen Witnessing*, Key Concepts in Journalism (Cambridge: Polity Press, 2013); Stuart Allan and Chris Peters, "Visual Truths of Citizen Reportage: Four Research Problematics," *Information, Communication & Society* 18, no. 11 (July 9, 2015): 1–14, https://doi.org/10.1080/1369118X.2015.1061576; Mary Angela Bock, "Citizen Video Journalists and Truthful Authority: Reviving the Role of the Witness," *Journalism: Theory, Practice & Criticism* 13, no. 5 (2012): 639–53.

118. Jon Durham Peters, "Witnessing," *Media, Culture & Society* 23, no. 6 (2001): 707–23.

119. Nick Couldry, "Alternative Media and Voice," in *The Routledge Companion to Alternative and Community Media*, ed. Chris Atton (New York: Routledge, 2015), 45.

120. Dan Berger, "'We Are the Revolutionaries': Visibility, Protest, and Racial Formation in 1970s Prison Radicalism," *Publicly Accessible Penn Dissertations*, December 22, 2010, https://repository.upenn.edu/edissertations/250; Victoria J. Gallagher and Kenneth S. Zagacki, "Visibility and Rhetoric: Epiphanies and Transformations in the *Life* Photographs of the Selma Marches of 1965," *Rhetoric Society Quarterly* 37, no. 2 (March 29, 2007): 113–35, https://doi.org/10.1080/02773940601016056; Christina Neumayer and Luca Rossi, "Images of Protest in Social Media: Struggle over Visibility and Visual Narratives," *New Media & Society* 20, no. 11 (November 1, 2018): 4293–310, https://doi.org/10.1177/1461444818770602.

121. Ariella Azoulay, *The Civil Contract of Photography* (New York: Zone Books, 2008); Couldry, "Alternative Media and Voice," 45; Hariman and Lucaites, *No Caption Needed*.

122. Whitney Phillips, *This Is Why We Can't Have Nice Things: Mapping the Relationship between Online Trolling and Mainstream Culture* (Cambridge, MA: MIT Press, 2015).

123. Imran Awan, "Cyber-Extremism: ISIS and the Power of Social Media," *Society* 54, no. 2 (April 1, 2017): 138–49, https://doi.org/10.1007/s12115-017-0114-0.

124. Joseph Turow, Michael Hennessy, and Nora Draper, "Persistent Misperceptions: Americans' Misplaced Confidence in Privacy Policies, 2003–2015," *Journal of Broadcasting & Electronic Media* 62, no. 3 (July 3, 2018): 461–78, https://doi.org/10.1080/08838151.2018.1451867.

125. Troy Duster, "Ancestry Testing and DNA: Uses, Limits—and Caveat Emptor," in *Genetics as Social Practice: Transdisciplinary Views on Science and Culture*, ed. Barbara Prainsak, Silke Schicktanz, and Gabriele Werner-Felmayer, Theory, Technology and Society (London: Routledge, 2014), 59–73, https://doi.org/10.4324/9781315584300-10; Zeynep Tufekci, *Twitter and Tear Gas: The Power and Fragility of Networked Protest* (New Haven, CT: Yale University Press, 2017).

126. Zizi Papacharissi, "The Virtual Sphere: The Internet as a Public Sphere," *New Media & Society* 4, no. 1 (February 1, 2002): 9–27, https://doi.org/10.1177/14614440222226244; Zizi Papacharissi, *A Private Sphere: Democracy in a Digital Age* (Cambridge: Polity, 2010).

127. Amartya Sen, "Human Rights and Capabilities," *Journal of Human Development* 6, no. 2 (July 1, 2005): 151–66, https://doi.org/10.1080/14649880500120491; Martha C. Nussbaum, "Education and Democratic Citizenship: Capabilities and Quality Education," *Journal of Human Development* 7, no. 3 (November 1, 2006): 385–95, https://doi.org/10.1080/14649880600815974.

128. Nussbaum, "Education and Democratic Citizenship"; Lorella Terzi, "Capability Approach: Martha Nussbaum and Amartya Sen," in *Encyclopedia of Educational Theory and Philosophy*, ed. D. C. Phillips (Thousand Oaks, CA: Sage, 2014), 97–99.

129. Renee Hobbs, *Create to Learn: Introduction to Digital Literacy* (Hoboken, NJ: John Wiley & Sons, 2017), 15.

130. Lady Elizabeth Eastlake, "Photography," in *Classic Essays on Photography*, ed. Alan Trachtenberg (New Haven, CT: Leete's Island Books, 1857), 40.

131. Barney G. Glaser and Anselm Strauss, *The Discovery of Grounded Theory* (Chicago: Aldine, 1967).

132. Klaus Krippendorff, *Content Analysis: An Introduction to Its Methodology* (Thousand Oaks, CA: Sage, 2004).

133. Norman Fairclough, *Critical Discourse Analysis: The Critical Study of Language* (London: Routledge, 2013).

134. Ruth Wodak and Michael Meyer, *Methods of Critical Discourse Analysis* (London: SAGE, 2001), 2, https://doi.org/10.4135/9780857028020.

Chapter 2

1. See, for example, James Allen, ed., *Without Sanctuary: Lynching Photography in America* (Santa Fe, NM: Twin Palms, 2000); Amy Louise Wood, *Lynching and Spectacle: Witnessing Racial Violence in America, 1890–1940* (Chapel Hill: University of North Carolina Press, 2011).

2. American Civil Liberties Union, "Race and the Death Penalty," https://www.aclu.org/other/race-and-death-penalty (accessed January 30, 2021); US Census Bureau, "QuickFacts," https://www.census.gov/quickfacts/ (accessed January 30, 2021).

3. John J. Donohue, "Empirical Analysis and the Fate of Capital Punishment," *Duke Journal of Constitutional Law and Public Policy* 11 (2016): 51–106.

4. Death Penalty Information Center, "Facts about the Death Penalty," May 3, 2019, www.deathpenaltyinfo.org.

5. Mark Berman, "Most States Have the Death Penalty. Few Actually Carry Out Executions," *Washington Post*, March 14, 2019, https://www.washingtonpost.com/national/most-states-have-the-death-penalty-few-actually-carry-out-executions/2019/03/14/208e443a-45b1-11e9-8aab-95b8d80a1e4f_story.html.

6. Donohue, "Empirical Analysis and the Fate of Capital Punishment."

7. *Furman v. Georgia*, 408 U.S. 238 (1972), 369–70.

8. Marwan M. Kraidy, "The Projectilic Image: Islamic State's Digital Visual Warfare and Global Networked Affect," *Media, Culture and Society* 39, no. 8 (November 1, 2017): 1194–209, https://doi.org/10.1177/0163443717725575.

9. Allen, *Without Sanctuary*; Dora Apel, *Imagery of Lynching: Black Men, White Women, and the Mob* (Piscataway, NJ: Rutgers University Press, 2004).

10. Jessica M. Fishman, *Death Makes the News: How the Media Censor and Display the Dead* (New York: New York University Press, 2017).

11. See, for example, Michael Griffin and Jongsoo Lee, "Picturing the Gulf War: Constructing an Image of War in *Time, Newsweek*, and *U.S. News & World Report*," *Journalism and Mass Communication Quarterly* 72, no. 4 (1995): 813–25; F. Hanusch, *Representing Death in the News: Journalism, Media, and Mortality* (New York: Palgrave Macmillan, 2010).

12. John Taylor, *Body Horror* (Manchester: Manchester University Press, 1998).

13. Jeannene M. Przyblyski, "Revolution at a Standstill: Photography and the Paris Commune of 1871," *Yale French Studies*, no. 101 (2001): 54–78, https://doi.org/10.2307/3090606.

    Historic images of death were not only used for social control. During the Victorian era, when portraits were expensive, death photographs were popular, especially for children. See, for example, Patricia Jalland, *Death in the Victorian Family* (New York: Oxford University Press, 1996).

14. Barbie Zelizer, *About to Die: How News Images Move the Public* (Oxford: Oxford University Press, 2010).

15. Zelizer, 323.

16. "Three Americans," *LIFE*, September 20, 1943.

17. Susan D. Moeller, "Pictures of the Enemy: Fifty Years of Images of Japan in the American Press, 1941–1992," *Journal of American Culture* 19, no. 1 (1996): 29.

18. Christine Harold and Kevin Michael DeLuca, "Behold the Corpse: Violent Images and the Case of Emmett Till," *Rhetoric and Public Affairs* 8, no. 2 (November 7, 2005): 263–86, https://doi.org/10.1353/rap.2005.0075; Stephen J. Whitfield, *A Death in the Delta: The Story of Emmett Till* (Baltimore: Johns Hopkins University Press, 1991).

19. Serge F. Kovaleski, "George Zimmerman Freed on $1 Million Bond in Trayvon Martin Shooting," *New York Times*, July 6, 2012, sec. U.S., https://www.nytimes.com/2012/07/07/us/george-zimmerman-freed-on-1-million-bond-in-trayvon-martin-shooting.html.

20. The Martin/Zimmerman is discussed in greater detail in Chapters 4 and 5.

21. Michel Foucault, *Discipline and Punish: The Birth of the Prison*, Vintage Books ed. (New York: Vintage Books, 1979).

22. Lynchings during the Jim Crow era often resembled the very sort of slow, painful cruelty Foucault described. See Allen, *Without Sanctuary*.

23. Foucault, *Discipline and Punish*; Michel Foucault, *The Spectacle of the Scaffold* (London: Penguin, 2008); David Garland, "The Cultural Uses of Capital Punishment," *Punishment & Society* 4, no. 4 (2002): 459–87, https://doi.org/10.1177/1462474502004004050; Lorna Hutson, "Rethinking the 'Spectacle of the Scaffold': Juridical Epistemologies and English Revenge Tragedy," *Representations* 89, no. 1 (February 2005): 30–58, https://doi.org/10.1525/rep.2005.89.1.30; Annulla Linders, "'What Daughters, What Wives, What Mothers, Think You, They Are?' Gender and the Transformation of Executions in the United States," *Journal of Historical Sociology* 28, no. 2 (June 2015): 135–65, https://doi.org/10.1111/johs.12048.

24. Karen Halttunen, "Humanitarianism and the Pornography of Pain in Anglo-American Culture," *American Historical Review* 100, no. 2 (1995): 303–34.

25. The roping images exemplify the liminality of an "about to die" image identified by Zelizer, *About to Die*.

26. Michael Ruane, "One of the Last Grim Scenes of the Civil War Was Caught on Camera," *Washington Post*, July 4, 2015, https://www.washingtonpost.com/local/four-people-were-hanged-for-lincolns-assassination--and-it-was-caught-on-camera/2015/07/03/377614d4-1905-11e5-ab92-c75ae6ab94b5_story.html.

27. Women are far less likely to face the death penalty in the United States, and their involvement with executions, as the Bethea case shows, is treated as an oddity in the news, in keeping with masculinity's place in American judicial ideology.

28. Kevin G. Barnhurst and John Nerone, *The Form of News*, Guilford Communication Series (New York: Guilford Press, 2001).

29. Jessie Ramey, "The Bloody Blonde and the Marble Woman: Gender and Power in the Case of Ruth Snyder," *Journal of Social History* 37, no. 3 (2004): 625–50.

30. *Pensacola News Journal*, January 8, 1928, 21.

31. "As Bad as Hanging," *San Francisco Daily Examiner*, July 8, 1888, 10.

32. "Guitau's Gallows," *Bloomington Daily Pantagraph*, July 1, 1882, 1.

33. Andrew Hochstetler, "Reporting of Executions in US Newspapers," *Journal of Crime and Justice* 24, no. 1 (2001): 1–13; Austin Sarat, *Gruesome Spectacles: Botched Executions and America's Death Penalty* (Stanford, CA: Stanford University Press, 2014).

34. Sarat, *Gruesome Spectacles*.

35. Bill Richardson, "Sensational Story Missed by U.S. Newspapers in 1861," *Carlsbad (NM) Current-Argus*.

36. Devon Abbott Mihesuah, *Choctaw Crime and Punishment, 1884–1907* (Norman: University of Oklahoma Press, 2012).

37. *"Only Real War in Recent History of Choctaw Nation Ended in Tragic Execution," The Daily Oklahoman*, November 30, 1919, 19.

38. Jackie Hallifax, "Bloody Execution Photos Draw Gamut of Responses," *South Florida Sun Sentinel*, October 7, 1999, sec. B.

39. Associated Press, "Florida Execution Is Called Torture," *New York Times*, June 1, 1990, sec. U.S.

40. Associated Press, "Condemned Man's Mask Bursts into Flame During Execution," *New York Times*, March 26, 1997, sec. U.S., https://www.nytimes.com/1997/03/26/us/condemned-man-s-mask-bursts-into-flame-during-execution.html.

41. Roger Roy and David Cox, "Bloody Execution Helps Inmate Win Stay," *South Florida Sun Sentinel*, July 9, 1999, Broward Metro edition, sec. A.

42. Hallifax, "Bloody Execution Photos Draw Gamut of Responses."

43. Rick Bragg, "Florida's Messy Executions Put the Electric Chair on Trial," *New York Times*, November 18, 1999, sec. U.S., https://www.nytimes.com/1999/11/18/us/florida-s-messy-executions-put-the-electric-chair-on-trial.html.

44. Leslie Clark, "Bush Signs Death Orders," *Tallahassee Democrat*, January 27, 2000, sec. A.

45. Linders, " 'What Daughters, What Wives, What Mothers, Think You, They Are?' "

46. Garland, "The Cultural Uses of Capital Punishment." Lynchings continued well past the Jim Crow South. Michael A. Donald was lynched in 1981, and the 1998 dragging of James Byrd Jr. in Texas is considered to be a modern lynching.

   Claire Z. Cardona and Associated Press, "Racist Killer Executed Decades after Dragging James Byrd Jr. to His Death near Jasper," *Dallas Morning News*, April 24, 2019, https://www.dallasnews.com/news/crime/2019/04/24/racist-killer-faces-execution-tonight-decades-after-dragging-james-byrd-jr-death-jasper; Daniel M. Gold, "On the Discovery Channel, the Bad Old Days (Just a Few Years Ago)," *New York Times*, October 12, 2008, sec. Television, https://www.nytimes.com/2008/10/13/arts/television/13lynch.html.

   The execution of the man considered to be the "ringleader" in Byrd's death inspired a new Texas regulation against releasing to the public a condemned inmate's last words.

   Andrew Weber, "Texas Will No Longer Share the Written Last Words of Executed Inmates," kut.org, April 30, 2019, https://www.kut.org/post/texas-will-no-longer-share-written-last-words-executed-inmates.

47. Garland, "The Cultural Uses of Capital Punishment," 456.

48. Marylyn Underwood, "Rodriguez, Josefa (Chipita)," Texas State Historical Association, June 15, 2010, https://tshaonline.org/handbook/online/articles/fro50.

49. Ramey, "The Bloody Blonde and the Marble Woman."

50. Melanie Deziel, "Women Inmates Separate but Not Equal (Paid Post by Netflix from NYTimes.Com)," *New York Times*, October 1, 2018, sec. T Brand, https://www.nytimes.com/paidpost/netflix/women-inmates-separate-but-not-equal.html.

51. Michael Robert Chavez, "Representing Us All? Race, Gender, and Sexuality in *Orange Is the New Black*" (MA thesis, Minnesota State University–Mankato, 2015).

52. Christina Belcher, "There Is No Such Thing as a Post-Racial Prison: Neoliberal Multiculturalism and the White Savior Complex on *Orange Is the New Black*," *Television and New Media* 17, no. 6 (September 1, 2016): 491–503, https://doi.org/10.1177/1527476416647498; Chavez, "Representing Us All?"; Suzanne M. Enck and Megan E. Morrissey, "If Orange Is the New Black, I Must Be Color Blind: Comic Framings of Post-Racism in the Prison-Industrial Complex," *Critical Studies in Media Communication* 32, no. 5 (October 20, 2015): 303–17, https://doi.org/10.1080/15295036.2015.1086489.

53. Kathleen McHugh, "Giving Credit to Paratexts and Parafeminism in *Top of the Lake* and *Orange Is the New Black* on JSTOR," *Film Quarterly* 68, no. 3 (2015): 17–25; Anne Schwan, "Postfeminism Meets the Women in Prison Genre: Privilege and Spectatorship in *Orange Is the New Black*," *Television and New Media* 17, no. 6 (September 1, 2016): 473–90, https://doi.org/10.1177/1527476416647497.

54. Perry Thomas Ryan, *The Last Public Execution in America* (Kentucky: P. T. Ryan, 1992).

55. Ryan, *The Last Public Execution in America*.

56. Anton Kaes, "A Stranger in the House: Fritz Lang's 'Fury' and the Cinema of Exile," *New German Critique*, no. 89 (2003): 33–58, https://doi.org/10.2307/3211144.

57. Joe Wilson, played by Spencer Tracy in *Fury* (dir. Lang, 1936).

58. F. S. Nugent, "'Fury,' a Dramatic Indictment of Lynch Law, Opens at the Capitol—Other New Pictures," *New York Times*, June 6, 1936. See also *Fury* at IMDB.com, https://www.imdb.com/find?s=all&q=%22fury%22+spencer+tracy.
   Fury also presciently depicts the use of newsfilm as evidence during a trial, well ahead of the era of smartphone video evidence.

59. "Mother of 4 to Hang Slayer" *New York Daily News*, July 7, 1936, 36.

60. "Noose Conference," *New York Daily News*, August 14, 1936, 148.

61. *Owensboro Messenger*, June 26, 1936, 1, 6.

62. "Rainey Bethea Sentenced to Hang," *Owensboro Messenger*, June 26, 1936, 6.

63. Gerald Duncan, "10,000 May See Woman Sheriff Spring Trap at Bethea Hanging," *Owensboro Messenger*, July 5, 1936, 9.

64. Ryan, *The Last Public Execution in America*.

65. Ryan, *The Last Public Execution in America*.

66. Keith Lawrence, phone interview with author, September 26, 2018.

67. Ryan, *The Last Public Execution in America*, 169.

68. Ryan, *The Last Public Execution in America*.

69. Keith Lawrence, phone interview with author, September 26, 2018.

70. *New York Daily News*, August 15, 1936, 16–17.

71. Beckham Robinson, "The Hanging of Bethea," *The Courier Journal*, Louisville Kentucky, August 20, 1936, 6. *Owensboro Messenger* editorial page.

72. David Wolfe II, phone interview with author, October 2, 2018.

73. Gerald Duncan, "20,000 Picnic at Public Hanging," *New York Daily News*, August 15, 1936, 2.

74. Ryan, *The Last Public Execution in America*. Also: Robert Kirtley, defense attorney's son, personal communication with author, May 21, 2019.

75. David Wolfe II, phone interview with author, October 2, 2018.

76. Keith Lawrence, phone interview with author, September 26, 2018.

77. Ryan, *The Last Public Execution in America*.

78. Keith Lawrence, phone interview with author, September 26, 2018.

79. Death Penalty Information Center.

80. He granted permission to publish his name (phone interview with author, September 24, 2018).

81. Three of the reporters interviewed for this chapter have been given pseudonyms. "Greg" is a wire reporter, now retired, who worked in Florida. "Amy" is a wire service reporter in Florida, and "Gina" is a television reporter in Texas.

82. This is not an unusual practice for journalists generally, given deadline pressure and story genre. In fact, as I found in previous research, it's standard practice for visual journalists who must preconceive a story before they start production.

83. Juan A. Lozano and Michael Graczyk, "Chaos Erupts, 2 Arrested during Texas Execution," *Austin American Statesman*, March 1, 2019, https://www.statesman.com/news/20190301/chaos-erupts-2-arrested-during-texas-execution/1.

84. Lozano and Graczyk, "Chaos Erupts, 2 Arrested during Texas Execution."

85. Peters, "Witnessing."

86. U.S. Department of Justice, 2019. Ann E. Carson, "Prisoners in 2019" U.S. Department of Justice, Office of Justice Programs, Bureau of Justice Statistics, October 2020.

87. Nicole Lewis and Beatrix Lockwood, "The Hidden Cost of Incarceration," Marshall Project, December 17, 2019, https://www.themarshallproject.org/2019/12/17/the-hidden-cost-of-incarceration.

88. Dan Berger, " 'We Are the Revolutionaries': Visibility, Protest, and Racial Formation in 1970s Prison Radicalism" (PhD dissertation, University of Pennsylvania, 2010), 7.

89. Annie Correal, "No Heat for Days at a Jail in Brooklyn Where Hundreds of Inmates Are Sick and 'Frantic,'" *New York Times*, February 3, 2019, sec. New York, https://www.nytimes.com/2019/02/01/nyregion/mdc-brooklyn-jail-heat.html.

90. Annie Correal and Joseph Goldstein, " 'It's Cold as Hell': Inside a Brooklyn Jail's Weeklong Collapse," *New York Times*, February 9, 2019, sec. New York, https://www.nytimes.com/2019/02/09/nyregion/brooklyn-jail-no-heat-inmates.html.

91. Rachel Quester, Theo Balcomb, and Annie Brown, "No Heat, No Power: How a Federal Jail Failed Its Inmates," *New York Times*, February 13, 2019, sec. Podcasts, https://www.nytimes.com/2019/02/13/podcasts/the-daily/federal-jail-heat-power-brooklyn.html.

92. Shane Bauer, *American Prison: A Reporter's Undercover Journey into the Business of Punishment* (New York: Penguin, 2018); Donna Selman and Paul Leighton, *Punishment for Sale: Private Prisons, Big Business, and the Incarceration Binge* (Lanham, MD: Rowman and Littlefield, 2010).

93. Victoria Law, "How Companies Make Millions Charging Prisoners to Send an Email," *Wired*, August 3, 2018, https://www.wired.com/story/jpay-securus-prison-email-charging-millions/; Selman and Leighton, *Punishment for Sale*.

94. Bernadette Rabuy and Daniel Kopf, "Separation by Bars and Miles: Visitation in State Prisons," Prison Policy Initiative, October 20, 2015), https://www.prisonpolicy.org/reports/prisonvisits.html.

95. I covered one such story in the women's prison in Iowa, after my assignment editor spent a considerable amount of time arranging access. As an assignment editor in Philadelphia, I occasionally arranged to cover stories at the Graterford Prison, but because it was twenty-nine miles away, this happened infrequently.

96. *Pell v. Precunier*, 417 U.S. 817 (1974); *Saxbe v. Washington Post Co.*, 73 U.S. 1265 (1974); *Houchins v. KQED, Inc.*, 438 U.S. 1 (1978).

97. Caitlin Dickerson, "'There Is a Stench': Soiled Clothes and No Baths for Migrant Children at a Texas Center," *New York Times*, June 21, 2019, sec. U.S., https://www.nytimes.com/2019/06/21/us/migrant-children-border-soap.html.

98. Sean Sullivan, "Democrats Enraged after Touring Texas Immigration Detention Facility," chicagotribune.com, June 17, 2018, https://www.chicagotribune.com/news/nationworld/ct-democrats-tour-detention-facility-20180617-story.html.

99. Vanessa Yurkevich and Priscilla Alvarez, "Exclusive Photos Reveal Children Sleeping on the Ground at Border Patrol Station," CNN, May 14, 2019, https://www.cnn.com/2019/05/14/politics/border-patrol-mcallen-texas-pictures/index.html.

100. Donica Phifer, "Joaquin Castro Smuggles Device into Migrant Detention Facility, Captures Photos of 'Prison-Like' Cell," *Newsweek*, July 1, 2019, https://www.newsweek.com/joaquin-castro-smuggles-device-migrant-detention-facility-captures-photos-prison-like-cell-1447025.

101. Shane Bauer, phone interview with author, April 15, 2019.

102. Jessica Pupovac, "Freedom of Information, Prison Access Policies," Society of Professional Journalists, https://www.spj.org/prisonaccess.asp. Accessed September 6, 2019.

103. Shaila Dewan, "Inside America's Black Box: A Rare Look at the Violence of Incarceration," *New York Times*, April 4, 2019, sec. U.S., https://www.nytimes.com/2019/03/30/us/inside-americas-black-box.html.

104. Olivia Extrum, "New Photos Show the Cruelty of Alabama Prisons. Should They Be Published?," *Mother Jones* (blog), April 19, 2019, https://www.motherjones.com/crime-justice/2019/04/2000-leaked-photos-show-the-cruelty-of-an-alabama-prison-should-they-be-published/.

105. See Dan Berger (@dnbrgr), Twitter, March 31, 2019. Berger is also cited earlier in this chapter for his dissertation, "We Are the Revolutionaries."

106. Michael McLaughlin et al., "The Economic Burden of Incarceration in the U.S." (St. Louis: Institute for Advancing Justice Research and Innovation, October 2016). Assuming twenty-five thousand dollars a year for four years, or one hundred thousand dollars per person, educating two million people would cost two hundred billion dollars, a fifth of the price of incarceration.

107. David Garland, "The Peculiar Forms of American Capital Punishment," *Social Research* 74, no. 2 (2007): 447.

108. Foucault, *Discipline and Punish*.

Chapter 3

1. Kenneth Pins, "Voters Not Swayed by Mingo Stag Party, Iowa Poll Discovers," *Des Moines Register*, June 8, 1986, B1; Ken Fuson, "Exotic Dancer Tells of Party at Mingo Bar," *Des Moines Register*, June 13, 1986, A1.

2. Blaine Harden, "Parading of Suspects Is Evolving Tradition; Halted After a Judge's Ruling, 'Perp Walks' Are Likely to Be Revived—in Some Form." *New York Times*, February 27, 1999, sec. New York. https://www.nytimes.com/1999/02/27/nyregion/parading-suspects-evolving-tradition-halted-after-judge-s-ruling-perp-walks-are.html. Maureen Dowd, "Tab Talk," *New York Times*, March 13, 1994, sec. Arts & Leisure. William Safire, "On Language: Perp Walk." *New York Times*, September 15, 2002, sec. Magazine. https://www.nytimes.com/2002/09/15/magazine/the-way-we-live-now-9-15-02-on-language-perp-walk.html.

3. William Safire, "On Language: Perp Walk." *New York Times*, September 15, 2002, sec. Magazine. https://www.nytimes.com/2002/09/15/magazine/the-way-we-live-now-9-15-02-on-language-perp-walk.html.

4. Allie Yang, "'The View' Weighs In on Lori Loughlin Greeting Fans before Court Appearance," ABC News, April 5, 2019, https://abcnews.go.com/US/view-weighs-lori-loughlin-greeting-fans-court-appearance/story?id=62199891.

5. Nick Couldry, *Media Rituals: A Critical Approach* (London: Routledge, 2003).

6. Mary Angela Bock, "Framing the Accused: The Perp Walk as Media Ritual," *Visual Communication Quarterly* 22, no. 4 (October 2, 2015): 206–20, https://doi.org/10.1080/15551393.2015.1105104; Mary Angela Bock and José Andrés Araiza, "Facing the Death Penalty While Facing the Cameras," *Journalism Practice* 9, no. 3 (2014): 1–18, https://doi.org/10.1080/17512786.2014.964496.

7. Dan Clark, "Pennsylvania AG Kathleen Kane's Twin Sister Acts as Media Decoy for Preliminary Hearing," *Main Line Media News*, August 24, 2015, http://www.mainlinemedianews.com/kingofprussiacourier/news/pennsylvania-ag-kathleen-kane-s-twin-sister-acts-as-media/article_2e8dcee4-3c8a-53bc-917c-2ff2f399be71.html; Paul Vigna, "Kathleen Kane's Twin Sister Bounced from AG's Office: Report," pennlive.com, January 22, 2017, https://www.pennlive.com/politics/2017/01/kathleen_kanes_twin_sister_bou.html.

8. Sandrine Boudana, "Shaming Rituals in the Age of Global Media: How DSK's Perp Walk Generated Estrangement," *European Journal of Communication* 29, no. 1 (2014): 50–67, https://doi.org/10.1177/0267323113509361.

9. Adam Martin, "Inevitable Perp Walk Backlash Follows DSK Prosecution Failure," *The Atlantic*, July 5, 2011, https://www.theatlantic.com/international/archive/2011/07/inevitable-perp-walk-backlash-follows-dsk-prosecution-failure/352498/.

10. Capeci, "Perp Walk," in *Encyclopedia of Law Enforcement*, vol. 1, *State and Local*, ed. L. E. Sullivan, M. R. Haberfeld, M. S. Rosen, and D. M. Schulz (Thousand Oaks, CA: Sage, 2005), 328–29.

11. Sheila Livingstone, *Confess and Be Hanged: Scottish Crime and Punishment through the Ages* (Edinburgh: Birlinn, 2000).

12. Claude Cookman, *A Voice Is Born: The Founding and Early Years of the National Press Photographers Association under the Leadership of Joseph Costa* (Durham, NC: National Press Photographers Association, 1985).

13. Capeci, "Perp Walk."

14. Jim Ruiz and D. F. Treadwell, "The Perp Walk: Due Process v. Freedom of the Press," *Criminal Justice Ethics* 21, no. 2 (2002): 44–56.

15. Ruiz and Treadwell, "The Perp Walk"; Stephen Grafman, "End an Ignoble Spectacle," *National Law Journal* 25, no. 50 (2003): 31.

16. *Lauro v. City of New York* (U.S. Southern District of New York, 1999); R. Hagglund, "Constitutional Protections against the Harms to Suspects in Custody Stemming from Perp Walks," *Mississippi Law Journal* 7 (2011): 1757–908.

17. Palma Paciocco, "Pilloried in the Press: Rethinking the Constitutional Status of the American Perp Walk." *New Criminal Law Review: An International and Interdisciplinary Journal* 16, no. 1 (2013): 50–103. https://doi.org/10.1525/nclr.2013.16.1.50.

18. Julianne H. Newton, *The Burden of Visual Truth: The Role of Photojournalism in Mediating Reality* (Mahwah, NJ: Erlbaum, 2001), 138.

19. Kim McNamara, "Publicising Private Lives: Celebrities, Image Control, and the Reconfiguration of Public Space," *Social & Cultural Geography* 10, no. 1 (2009): 9–23; Kim McNamara, "The Paparazzi Industry and New Media: The Evolving Production and Consumption of Celebrity News and Gossip Websites," *International Journal of Cultural Studies* 14, no. 5 (2011): 515–30; Andrew L. Mendelson, "On the Function of the United States Paparazzi: Mosquito Swarm or Watchdogs of Celebrity Image Control and Power," *Visual Studies* 22, no. 2 (September 2007): 169–83.

20. McNamara, *Paparazzi*; Mendelson, "On the Function of the United States Paparazzi."

21. Capeci, "Perp Walk"; Ruiz and Treadwell, "The Perp Walk." See also Grafman, "End an Ignoble Spectacle."

22. Brooke Barnett, "Guilty and Threatening: Visual Bias in Television News Crime Stories," *Journalism Communication Monographs* 5, no. 3 (2003): 103–55.

23. Gray Cavender, Kishonna Gray, and Kenneth W. Miller, "Enron's Perp Walk: Status Degradation Ceremonies as Narrative," *Crime, Media, Culture* 6, no. 3 (December 1, 2010): 251–66, https://doi.org/10.1177/1741659010382329; Harold Garfinkel, "Conditions of Successful Degradation Ceremonies," *American Journal of Sociology* 61, no. 5 (1956): 420–24.

24. Barry Kirsh, interview with author, January 15, 2019.

25. Gaye Tuchman, *Making News: A Study in the Construction of Reality* (London: Free Press, 1978).

26. Lisa Henderson, "Access and Consent in Public Photography," *Image Ethics: The Moral Rights of Subjects in Photographs, Film and Television*, ed. Larry Gross, John Stuart Katz, and Jay Ruby (New York: Oxford University Press, 1988): 91–407. .

27. Robert M. Steele, "Video Ethics: The Dilemma of Value Balancing," *Journal of Mass Media Ethics* 2, no. 2 (1987): 7–17.

28. Stephen D. Reese, "Understanding the Global Journalist: A Hierarchy of Influences Approach," *Journalism Studies* 2, no. 2 (2010): 173–87.

29. Clark, "Pennsylvania AG Kathleen Kane's Twin Sister Acts as Media Decoy for Preliminary Hearing"; Vigna, "Kathleen Kane's Twin Sister Bounced from AG's Office."

30. It is against generally court rules for defendants to be seen in cuffs in front of jurors. Barnett found that such images of people in handcuffs inspire higher assessments of guilt. Barnett, "Guilty and Threatening."

31. Channel numbers for local television stations.

32. He has since sent a copy to me, but I don't print it here in order to protect his anonymity.

33. Mary Angela Bock, "Who's Minding the Gate? Pool Feeds, Video Subsidies, and Political Images," *International Journal of Press & Politics* 14, no. 2 (2009): 257–78; Mary Angela Bock, "Together in the Scrum: Practicing News Photography for Print, Television, and Broadband," *Visual Communication Quarterly* 15, no. 3 (2008): 169–79, https://doi.org/10.1080/15551390802235511; Tuchman, *Making News*.

34. For a discussion of ethnographic interpretation of interview data, see Martyn Hammersley and Paul Atkinson, *Ethnography, Principles in Practice*, vol. 2 (London: Routledge, 1983).

35. Michel Foucault, *Discipline and Punish: The Birth of the Prison*, Vintage Books ed. (New York: Vintage Books, 1979).

36. Gaye Tuchman, "Objectivity as Strategic Ritual: An Examination of Newsmen's Notions of Objectivity," *American Journal of Sociology* 77, no. 4 (1972): 660–79.

37. Although he had to wait several days for the top district attorney to return from vacation to hold the news conference.

38. Another veteran shooter has remarked to me, outside of this research project, that "these are not good days for anyone."

39. Cookman, *A Voice Is Born*.

40. J. M. Jennings, "Is Chandler a Final Rewrite of Estes?" *Journalism Quarterly* 59, no. 1 (1982): 66–73. *Chandler v. Florida*, 449 U.S. 560 (1981).

41. S. L. Alexander, *Covering the Courts: A Handbook for Journalists* (Lanham, MD: Rowman and Littlefield, 2003).

42. Tuchman, *Making News*, 4.

43. Wall, "Perp Walks Serve Legitimate Government Purposes"; *Caldarola v. County of Westchester*, U.S. Court of Appeals, Second Circuit, 7457 (2003).

44. Susan Sontag, *Regarding the Pain of Others* (New York: Farrar, Straus and Giroux, 2003).

45. Bock, "Framing the Accused."

46. Steele, "Video Ethics."

Chapter 4

1. Jean Baudrillard, *Simulacra and Simulation*, trans. Sheila Faria Glaser (Ann Arbor: University of Michigan Press, 1981); Guy Debord, *Society of the Spectacle* (n.p.: Bread and Circuses Publishing, 2012).

2. See Chapter 1 for a discussion of the ideological state apparatus and semiotic myth. Louis Althusser, "Ideology and Ideological State Apparatuses," in *Cultural Theory and Popular Culture: A Reader*, ed. John Storey, 2nd ed. (Harlow, UK: Pearson / Prentice Hall, 1998), 153–64; Roland Barthes, *Mythologies* (New York: Hill and Wang, 1972).

3. Bartholomew H. Sparrow, *Uncertain Guardians: The News Media as a Political Institution* (Baltimore, MD: Johns Hopkins University Press, 1999).

4. David L. Altheide, "Media Logic, Social Control, and Fear," *Communication Theory* 23, no. 3 (August 1, 2013): 223–38, https://doi.org/10.1111/comt.12017; David L. Altheide and Robert P. Snow, *Media Logic*, Sage Library of Social Research (Beverly Hills, CA: Sage, 1979).

5. Sandra F. Chance, "Considering Cameras in the Courtroom," *Journal of Broadcasting and Electronic Media* 39, no. 4 (1995): 555–61; Gilbert Geis and Robert E. L. Talley, "Cameras in the Courtroom," *Journal of Criminal Law, Criminology, and Police Science* 47, no. 5 (1957): 546–60, https://doi.org/10.2307/1139022; Stephen A. Metz, "Justice through the Eye of a Camera: Cameras in the Courtrooms in the United States, Canada, England, and Scotland," *Penn State International Law Review* 14 (1996): 673–702.

6. Ralph Blumenthal, "Courtroom Confidential - The New York Times," *New York Times*, November 24, 2017.

7. Elizabeth Williams and Sue Russell, *The Illustrated Courtroom: 50 Years of Court Art* (New York: CUNY Journalism Press, 2014).

8. Debord, *Society of the Spectacle*.

9. Barthes, "Myth Today" in *Mythologies* 217–274.

10. Chance, "Considering Cameras in the Courtroom"; Geis and Talley, "Cameras in the Courtroom"; Metz, "Justice through the Eye of a Camera."

11. David Shaw, "The Simpson Legacy: Obsession: Did the Media Overfeed a Starving Public?," *Los Angeles Times*, October 9, 1995, sec. Special Section.

12. Claude Cookman, *A Voice Is Born: The Founding and Early Years of the National Press Photographers Association under the Leadership of Joseph Costa* (Durham, NC: National Press Photographers Association, 1985). Claude Cookman, *American Photojournalism: Motivations and Meanings* (Chicago: Northwestern University Press, 2009).

13. Ruth Ann Strickland and Richter H. Moore Jr., "Cameras in State Courts: A Historical Perspective," *Judicature*, no. 3 (1994): 128–35.

14. John R. Vile, "Estes v. Texas (1965)," in *Encyclopedia of the First Amendment*, ed. John R. Vile, David L. Hudson Jr., and David Schultz, vol. 1 (Washington, DC: CQ Press, 2009), 425–26, http://go.galegroup.com/ps/i.do?id=GALE%7CCX2143300482&v=2.1&u=tx shracd2598&it=r&p=GVRL&sw=w&asid=e0f006348314d80b2c59edb1cc03beab.

15. J. M. Jennings, "Is Chandler a Final Rewrite of Estes?" *Journalism Quarterly 59*, no. 1 (1982): 66–73.

16. Shaw, "The Simpson Legacy."

17. RTDNA.org. Formerly the Radio, Television News Directors Association, it has since rebranded itself as the Radio, Television Digital News Association. See https://www.rtdna.org/content/cameras_in_court.

18. David L. Altheide, "Media Logic, Social Control, and Fear," *Communication Theory* 23, no. 3 (August 1, 2013): 223–38.

19. Walter R. Fisher, "The Narrative Paradigm: An Elaboration," *Communication Monographs* 52, no. 4 (December 1985): 347–67; Walter R. Fisher, "Narration as a Human Communication Paradigm: The Case of Public Moral Argument," *Communication Monographs* 51, no. 1 (March 1984): 1–22.
20. Althusser, "Ideology and Ideological State Apparatuses."
21. Baudrillard, *Simulacra and Simulation*; Debord, *Society of the Spectacle*.

Chapter 5

1. Noam Cohen, "How the Media Wrestle with the Web," *New York Times*, July 12, 2009; Meagan Flynn, "Voters Remove Judge Who Sentenced Brock Turner to Six Months in Stanford Sexual Assault Case," *Washington Post*, June 6, 2018, sec. Morning Mix, https://www.washingtonpost.com/news/morning-mix/wp/2018/06/06/voters-remove-judge-who-sentenced-brock-turner-to-six-months-in-stanford-rape-case/.
2. Jeannene M. Przyblyski, "Revolution at a Standstill: Photography and the Paris Commune of 1871," *Yale French Studies*, no. 101 (2001): 54–78.
3. Jens Jager, "Crime, Histoire et Sociétés, 2001/1," *Crime, History, and Societies* 5, no. 1 (2001): 27–52.
4. Josh Ellenbogen, *Reasoned and Unreasoned Images: The Photography of Bertillon, Galton, and Marey* (University Park: Pennsylvania State University Press, 2012); Zachary R. Hagins, "Fashioning the 'Born Criminal' on the Beat: Juridical Photography and the Police Municipale in Fin-de-Siècle Paris," *Modern and Contemporary France* 21, no. 3 (August 1, 2013): 281–96, https://doi.org/10.1080/09639489.2013.781143; Raynal Pellicer, *Mug Shots: An Archive of the Famous, Infamous, and Most Wanted* (New York: Abrams, 2008).
5. Elizabeth Edwards, "Photographic 'Types': The Pursuit of Method," *Visual Anthropology* 3, nos. 2–3 (January 1, 1990): 235–58, https://doi.org/10.1080/08949468.1990.9966534; John Tagg, "Evidence, Truth and Order: A Means of Surveillance," in *Visual Culture: The Reader*, ed. Stuart Hall and Jessica Evans (Thousand Oaks, CA: Sage, 1999), 244–73; Allan Sekula, "The Body and the Archive," *October* 39 (1986): 3–64.
6. Ellenbogen, *Reasoned and Unreasoned Images*. Allan Sekula, "The Body and the Archive."
7. Ellenbogen, *Reasoned and Unreasoned Images*.
8. Jonathan Mathew Finn, *Capturing the Criminal Image: From Mug Shot to Surveillance Society* (Minneapolis: University of Minnesota Press, 2009); Rachel Hall, *Wanted: The Outlaw in American Visual Culture, Cultural Frames, Framing Culture* (Charlottesville: University of Virginia Press, 2009); Peter Hamilton and Roger Hargreaves, *The Beautiful and the Damned: The Creation of Identity in Nineteenth-Century Photography* (Aldershot, UK: Lund Humphries, in association with the National Portrait Gallery, 2001); Tagg, "Evidence, Truth and Order."
9. Hamilton and Hargreaves, *Beautiful and the Damned*.

10. Hall, *Wanted*.

11. Paul Lashmar, "How to Humiliate and Shame: A Reporter's Guide to the Power of the Mugshot," *Social Semiotics* 24, no. 1 (January 1, 2014): 56–87, https://doi.org/10.1080/10350330.2013.827358.

12. Edwards, "Photographic 'Types'"; Richard Twine, "Physiognomy, Phrenology, and the Temporality of the Body," *Body and Society* 8, no. 1 (March 1, 2002): 67–88, https://doi.org/10.1177/1357034X02008001004.

13. Harold Garfinkel, "Conditions of Successful Degradation Ceremonies," *American Journal of Sociology 61*, no. 5 (1956): 420–24.

14. Steven Cohan and Ina Rae Hark, *The Road Movie Book* (London: Routledge, 1997).

15. Paul Ekman and Wallace V. Friesen, *Unmasking the Face: A Guide to Recognizing Emotions from Facial Clues* (Los Altos, CA: Malor Books, 2003).

16. Hall, *Wanted*.

17. Darnell M. Hunt, *O. J. Simpson Facts and Fictions: News Rituals in the Construction of Reality* (Cambridge: Cambridge University Press, 1999).

18. Debbie Elliott, "The Newest Magazine Fad: The Mug Shot Tabloid," NPR.org, November 23, 2011, http://www.npr.org/2011/11/23/142701001/the-newest-magazine-fad-the-mug-shot-tabloid.

19. Tim Stelloh, "Innocent until Your Mug Shot Is on the Internet," *New York Times*, June 3, 2017, https://www.nytimes.com/2017/06/03/opinion/sunday/innocent-until-your-mug-shot-is-on-the-internet.html.

20. Linda Mulcahy, "Docile Suffragettes? Resistance to Police Photography and the Possibility of Object-Subject Transformation," *Feminist Legal Studies* 23, no. 1 (April 7, 2015): 79–99, https://doi.org/10.1007/s10691-015-9280-x; Cameron T. Norris, "Your Right to Look Like an Ugly Criminal: Resolving the Circuit Split over Mug Shots and the Freedom of Information Act Note," *Vanderbilt Law Review* 66, no. 5 (2013): 1573–608; Allen Rostron, "The Mugshot Industry: Freedom of Speech, Rights of Publicity, and the Controversy Sparked by an Unusual New Type of Business," SSRN Scholarly Paper (Rochester, NY: Social Science Research Network, January 20, 2013), http://papers.ssrn.com/abstract=2337214.

21. Lashmar, "How to Humiliate and Shame"; Cassandra Batchelder, "Busted Mugs and Bad Lighting: Balancing First Amendment Interests against Claims for Control of One's Identity," MA Thesis, University of Minnesota, May 2014, http://conservancy.umn.edu/handle/11299/165422.

22. Megan Abbott, "Opinion | Our Love Affair with the Mug Shot," *New York Times*, July 19, 2014, sec. Opinion, https://www.nytimes.com/2014/07/20/opinion/sunday/why-we-cant-resist-mug-shots.html; Stelloh, "Innocent until Your Mug Shot Is on the Internet."

23. Note: Both charges have been since been dropped. Chuck Lindell, "Appeals Court Dismisses Rick Perry's Criminal Case," Statesman.com, February 24, 2016, http://www.mystatesman.com/news/news/appeals-court-dismisses-rick-perrys-criminal-case/nqXG5/.

24. Michael A. Lindenberger, "Can Perry Case Stick?" *Dallas Morning News*, August 18, 2014, 2A.

25. Omar L. Gallaga, "Perry Mugshot Tips: Rest, Ditch Glasses, Wear Blue," *Austin American Statesman*, August 19, 2014, A7.

26. GoPro is the brand name of a very small, wireless digital camera that is easily worn or mounted on everyday objects.

27. Rachel E. Morgan and Grace Kena, "Criminal Victimization, 2016: Revised," U.S. Department of Justice Office of Justice Programs Bureau of Justice Statistics, October 2018. Report no. NCJ 252121.

28. Sexual assault statistics are available at https://www.rainn.org/statistics/campus-sexual-violence.

29. Jessica Glenza and Rory Carroll, "Stanford, the Swimmer, and Yik Yak: Can Talk of Campus Rape Go beyond Secrets?," *The Guardian*, February 8, 2015, sec. Society, https://www.theguardian.com/society/2015/feb/08/stanford-swimmer-yik-yak-campus-rape.

30. Elena Kadvany, "Brock Turner Sentenced to Six Months in County Jail, Three-Year Probation," *Palo Alto Weekly*, June 2, 2016, https://www.paloaltoonline.com/news/2016/06/02/brock-turner-sentenced-to-six-months-in-county-jail-three-year-probation; Nick Anderson and Susan Svrluga, "In Stanford Sexual Assault Case, Probation Officer Recommended 'Moderate' Jail Term," *Washington Post*, June 10, 2016, sec. Grade Point, https://www.washingtonpost.com/news/grade-point/wp/2016/06/10/probation-officers-report-for-brock-turners-sentencing/.

31. Nick Anderson and Susan Svrluga, "Prosecutors Urged 'Substantial Prison Term' in Stanford Sexual Assault Case, Records Show," *Washington Post*, June 11, 2016, sec. Grade Point, https://www.washingtonpost.com/news/grade-point/wp/2016/06/11/prosecutors-urged-substantial-prison-term-in-stanford-sexual-assault-case-records-show/; Flynn, "Voters Remove Judge Who Sentenced Brock Turner to Six Months in Stanford Sexual Assault Case."

32. Amy Graff, "Brock Turner's Mom Blocks Cameras as Her Son Signs Sex Registry," *SFGate*, September 6, 2016, https://www.sfgate.com/bayarea/article/Brock-Turner-mom-shields-son-signs-sex-registry-9205224.php.

33. Emily Bazelon, "Have We Learned Anything from the Columbia Rape Case?," *New York Times*, December 21, 2017, sec. Magazine, https://www.nytimes.com/2015/05/29/magazine/have-we-learned-anything-from-the-columbia-rape-case.html; Manohla Dargis, "Review: 'The Hunting Ground' Documentary, a Searing Look at Campus Rape," *New York Times*, February 26, 2015, sec. Movies, https://www.nytimes.com/2015/02/27/movies/review-the-hunting-ground-documentary-a-searing-look-at-campus-rape.html.

34. Lindsey Bever, "'You Took Away My Worth': A Sexual Assault Victim's Powerful Message to Her Stanford Attacker," *Washington Post*, June 4, 2016, sec. Sports, https://www.washingtonpost.com/news/early-lead/wp/2016/06/04/you-took-away-my-worth-a-rape-victim-delivers-powerful-message-to-a-former-stanford-swimmer/; Lauren Duca, "The Stanford Rapist's Father Says His Son's Life Was Ruined Because He Raped Someone for 20 Minutes," *Teen Vogue*, June 6, 2016, https://www.teenvogue.com/story/stanford-rape-father-letter.

35. Michael E. Miller, "All-American Swimmer Found Guilty of Sexually Assaulting Unconscious Woman on Stanford Campus," *Washington Post*, March 31, 2016, sec. Morning Mix, https://www.washingtonpost.com/news/morning-mix/wp/2016/03/31/all-american-swimmer-found-guilty-of-sexually-assaulting-unconscious-woman-on-stanford-campus/.

36. Diana Pritchard, phone interview with author, January 18, 2019.

37. Mug shot releases by the sheriff's office are at the discretion of the sheriff, according to Lynne Martin, Law Enforcement Records Technician, Records Division.

38. Lauren O'Neil, "Brock Turner's Mug Shot: How Race Factors into the Stanford Rape Case," CBC, June 11, 2016, https://www.cbc.ca/news/trending/brock-turner-mugshot-stanford-rape-case-images-sex-assault-1.3629147.

39. Callie Marie Rennison, "I'm the Professor Who Made Brock Turner the 'Textbook Definition' of a Rapist," Vox, November 17, 2017, https://www.vox.com/first-person/2017/11/17/16666290/brock-turner-rape.

40. Rennison, "I'm the Professor Who Made Brock Turner the 'Textbook Definition' of a Rapist."

41. Meghan Keneally, "Textbook Showing Brock Turner's Mug Shot Next to Section on Rape Will Be Revised, Publisher Says," ABCNews.com, September 15, 2017, https://abcnews.go.com/US/textbook-showing-brock-turners-mug-shot-section-rape/story?id=49845886.

42. Amy Graff, "Brock Turner's Mom Blocks Cameras as Her Son Signs Sex Registry." News. SFGate, September 6, 2016. https://www.sfgate.com/bayarea/article/Brock-Turner-mom-shields-son-signs-sex-registry-9205224.php.

43. Mary Angela Bock and José Andrés Araiza, "Facing the Death Penalty While Facing the Cameras," *Journalism Practice* 9, no. 3 (2014): 1–18, https://doi.org/10.1080/17512786.2014.964496.

44. USA Today Network and The Cincinnati Enquirer, "Media Blasted for Racial Bias in Cincinnati Shooting Coverage," *USA Today*, July 30, 2015, https://www.usatoday.com/story/news/nation-now/2015/07/30/ohio-police-shooting-victim/30872955/; Kate Murphy and Mark Curnutte, "University of Cincinnati Pays $250k to Ex-Cop Who Killed Sam DuBose," Cincinnati.com, March 22, 2018, https://www.cincinnati.com/story/news/2018/03/22/university-cincinnati-pays-cop-who-killed-sam-dubose/450587002/.

45. Niraj Chokshi, "Teenagers Recorded a Drowning Man and Laughed," *New York Times*. July 21, 2017, https://www.nytimes.com/2017/07/21/us/video-drowning-teens-florida.html.

46. The story has since been removed from the internet. "Florida Police: Teens Watched Man Drown in Retention Pond," time.com, http://time.com/4868014/florida-teens-watch-man-drown/ (accessed July 26, 2017).

47. Lizette Alvarez and Cara Buckley, "Zimmerman Is Acquitted in Killing of Trayvon Martin," *New York Times*, July 14, 2013, sec. U.S., https://www.nytimes.com/2013/07/15/us/george-zimmerman-verdict-trayvon-martin.html.

48. Allan Sekula, "On the Invention of Photographic Meaning," in *Photography against the Grain* (Halifax: Press of the Nova Scotia College of Art and Design, 1984), 5–6.

49. Mark Di Ionno, "Ex-Superintendent in Pooping Case Speaks Out: 'I Was Used for Click-Bait,'" nj.com, October 28, 2018, https://www.nj.com/news/2018/10/superin-tendent_in_pooping_scandal_speaks_out_says.html.

50. Di Ionno, "Ex-Superintendent in Pooping Case Speaks Out."

51. Alex N. Gecan, "Kenilworth Ex-Superintendent Sues Holmdel over Defecation Incident," *Asbury Park Press*, May 1, 2019, https://www.app.com/story/news/local/courts/2019/05/01/thomas-w-tramaglini-kenilworth-superintendent-holmdel-high-school-track-public-defecation/3637923002/.

52. Keneally, "Textbook Showing Brock Turner's Mug Shot Next to Section on Rape Will Be Revised, Publisher Says."

53. Ellenbogen, *Reasoned and Unreasoned Images*.

54. Corey Hutchins, "Mugshot Galleries Might Be a Web-Traffic Magnet. Does That Justify Publishing Them?," *Columbia Journalism Review*, October 24, 2018, https://www.cjr.org/united_states_project/mugshots-ethics.php.

55. Matt Brown, "Why We Shut Down the 'Mugshots' Page," WTXL, May 23, 2019, https://www.wtxl.com/news/local-news/why-we-shut-down-the-mugshots-page.

56. Brown, "Why We Shut Down the 'Mugshots' Page."

57. Phone interview with author, June 20, 2019.

58. USA Today Network and the *Cincinnati Enquirer*, "Media Blasted for Racial Bias in Cincinnati Shooting Coverage." The officer involved, Raymond Tensing, was charged with murder, but two trials ended in a mistrial and he won a financial settlement from his employer, the University of Cincinnati, which had fired him. Murphy and Curnutte, "University of Cincinnati Pays $250k to Ex-Cop Who Killed Sam DuBose."

Chapter 6

1. Todd Spangler, "Jordan Peele Teams with BuzzFeed for Obama Fake-News Awareness Video," *Variety* (blog), April 17, 2018, https://variety.com/2018/digital/news/jordan-peele-obama-fake-news-video-buzzfeed-1202755517/.

2. The video is available at https://variety.com/2018/digital/news/jordan-peele-obama-fake-news-video-buzzfeed-1202755517/ (accessed January 30, 2021).

3. D. Afchar et al., "MesoNet: A Compact Facial Video Forgery Detection Network," *2018 IEEE International Workshop on Information Forensics and Security (WIFS)*, 2018, 1–7, https://doi.org/10.1109/WIFS.2018.8630761; F. Matern, C. Riess, and M. Stamminger, "Exploiting Visual Artifacts to Expose Deepfakes and Face Manipulations," *2019 IEEE Winter Applications of Computer Vision Workshops (WACVW)*, 2019, 83–92, https://doi.org/10.1109/WACVW.2019.00020; X. Yang, Y. Li, and S. Lyu, "Exposing Deep Fakes Using Inconsistent Head Poses," in *ICASSP 2019—2019 IEEE International Conference on Acoustics, Speech and Signal Processing (ICASSP)*, 2019, 8261–65, https://doi.org/10.1109/ICASSP.2019.8683164.

4. X. Kang and S. Wei, "Identifying Tampered Regions Using Singular Value Decomposition in Digital Image Forensics," in *2008 International Conference*

on Computer Science and Software Engineering, vol. 3, 2008, 926–30, https://doi.
org/10.1109/CSSE.2008.876; James F. O'Brien and Hany Farid, "Exposing Photo
Manipulation with Inconsistent Reflections," *ACM Transactions on Graphics* 31, no. 1
(2012): 1–11.

5. Robert Chesney and Danielle Keats Citron, "Deep Fakes: A Looming Challenge for
Privacy, Democracy, and National Security," *California Law Review* 107, no. 1753
(2019), U of Texas Law, Public Law Research Paper No. 692, U of Maryland Legal
Studies Research Paper No. 2018-21 (July 14, 2018), https://papers.ssrn.com/ab-
stract=3213954; Dawn Stover, "Garlin Gilchrist: Fighting Fake News and the
Information Apocalypse," *Bulletin of the Atomic Scientists* 74, no. 4 (July 4, 2018): 283–
88, https://doi.org/10.1080/00963402.2018.1486618.

6. Michela Del Vicario et al., "The Spreading of Misinformation Online," *Proceedings of
the National Academy of Sciences* 113, no. 3 (January 19, 2016): 554–59, https://doi.
org/10.1073/pnas.1517441113; David M. J. Lazer et al., "The Science of Fake News,"
Science 359, no. 6380 (March 9, 2018): 1094–96, https://doi.org/10.1126/science.
aao2998.

7. Jennifer L. Mnookin, "The Image of Truth: Photographic Evidence and the Power of
Analogy," *Yale Journal of Law and the Humanities* 10 (1998): 1–74.

8. Mnookin, "Image of Truth," 4.

9. Mnookin, "Image of Truth."

10. Victor E. Bianchini and Harvey Bass, "A Paradigm for the Authentication of
Photographic Evidence in the Digital Age Perspective," *Thomas Jefferson Law Review*
20 (1998): 303–22; Mnookin, "Image of Truth."

11. Bianchini and Bass, "A Paradigm for the Authentication of Photographic Evidence in
the Digital Age Perspective."

12. Walter R. Fisher, "Narration as a Human Communication Paradigm: The Case of Public
Moral Argument," *Communication Monographs* 51, no. 1 (March 1984): 1–22; Walter
R. Fisher, "The Narrative Paradigm: An Elaboration," *Communication Monographs*
52, no. 4 (December 1985): 347–67.

13. S. Elizabeth Bird and Robert W. Dardenne, "Myth, Chronicle, and Story: Exploring
the Narrative Qualities of News," in *Social Meanings of News*, ed. Dan Berkowitz
(Thousand Oaks, CA: Sage, 1988), 333–50; Marcel Machill, Sebastian Kibler, and
Markus Waldhauser, "The Use of Narrative Structure in Television News," *European
Journal of Communication* 22, no. 2 (2007): 185–205; Peter White, "Narrative Impulse
in Mass-Media 'Hard News' Reporting," in *Genre and Institutions: Social Processes in
the Workplace and School*, ed. Frances Christie and J. R. Martin (London: Bloomsbury,
2005), 101–23.

14. J. Christopher Rideout, "Storytelling, Narrative Rationality, and Legal Persuasion,"
Legal Writing: The Journal of the Legal Writing Institute 14 (2008): 53.

15. Robert P. Burns, *A Theory of the Trial* (Princeton, NJ: Princeton University Press,
2001), 159.

16. W. Lance Bennett, *Reconstructing Reality in the Courtroom: Justice and Judgment in
American Culture*, Crime, Law, and Deviance Series (New Brunswick, NJ: Rutgers
University Press, 1981).

17. Rideout, "Storytelling, Narrative Rationality, and Legal Persuasion."

18. Rideout; Roland Barthes, *Image-Music-Text* (New York: Hill & Wang, 1977).

19. Louis-Georges Schwartz, *Mechanical Witness: A History of Motion Picture Evidence in U.S. Courts* (Oxford: Oxford University Press, 2009).

20. Schwartz, *Mechanical Witness*.

21. Schwartz, *Mechanical Witness*.

22. Neal Feigenson and Christina Spiesel, *Law on Display: The Digital Transformation of Legal Persuasion and Judgment* (New York: New York University Press, 2011).

23. Robert Deitz, *Willful Injustice: A Post-O.J. Look at Rodney King, American Justice, and Trial by Race* (Washington, DC: Regnery, 1996); Robert Gooding-Williams, *Reading Rodney King/Reading Urban Uprising* (New York: Routledge, 1993).

24. Michel Foucault, "Truth and Power," in *Power/Knowledge: Selected Interviews and Other Writings, 1972–1977* (New York: Pantheon Books, 1980), 133.

25. Chase Hoffberger, "Seale and Balko Visit Peaceful Streets," August 16, 2013, http://www.austinchronicle.com/news/2013-08-16/seale-and-balko-visit-peaceful-streets/.

26. Bennett, *Reconstructing Reality in the Courtroom*; Le Cheng and Winnie Cheng, "Documentary Evidence as Hegemonic Reconstruction," *Semiotica* 2014, no. 200 (June 2014): 165–84, https://doi.org/10.1515/sem-2014-0009; Roberta Entner, "Encoding the Image of the American Judiciary Institution: A Semiotic Analysis of Broadcast Trials to Ascertain Its Definition of the Court System" (PhD dissertation, New York University, 1993), OCLC ID: ocm 30772701.

27. Bennett, *Reconstructing Reality in the Courtroom*; Cheng and Cheng, "Documentary Evidence as Hegemonic Reconstruction."

28. Denis J. Brion, "The Criminal Trial as Theater: The Semiotic Power of the Image," in *Law, Culture and Visual Studies*, ed. Anne Wagner and Richard K. Sherwin (Dordrecht: Springer, 2014), 329–59.

29. Brion; Cheng and Cheng, "Documentary Evidence as Hegemonic Reconstruction"; Sarah Kember, "The Shadow of the Object: Photography and Realism," in *The Photography Reader*, ed. Liz Wells (London: Routledge, 2003), 466.

30. Mnookin, "Image of Truth"; Richard K. Sherwin, Neal Feigenson, and Christina Spiesel, "What Is Visual Knowledge, and What Is It Good For? Potential Ethnographic Lessons from the Field of Legal Practice," *Visual Anthropology* 20, nos. 2–3 (February 22, 2007): 143–78, https://doi.org/10.1080/08949460601152799.

31. Charles Goodwin and Marjorie Harness Goodwin, "Contested Vision: The Discursive Constitution of Rodney King," in *The Construction of Professional Discourse*, ed. B. L. Gunnarsson, Per Linell, and Bengt Nordberg (New York: Routledge, 1997), 292–316.

32. Allen Feldman, "On Cultural Anesthesia: From Desert Storm to Rodney King," *American Ethnologist* 21, no. 2 (May 1, 1994): 404–18.

33. John Tagg, "Evidence, Truth, and Order: A Means of Surveillance," in *Visual Culture: The Reader*, ed. Stuart Hall and Jessica Evans (Thousand Oaks, CA: Sage, 1999), 244–73; Tyler Wall and Travis Linnemann, "Staring Down the State: Police Power, Visual Economies, and the 'War on Cameras,'" *Crime, Media, Culture* 10, no. 2 (August 1, 2014): 133–49, https://doi.org/10.1177/1741659014531424.

34. Jiri Benovsky, "Three Kinds of Realism about Photographs," *Journal of Speculative Philosophy* 25, no. 4 (2011): 375–95; J. Anthony Blair, "The Rhetoric of Visual Arguments," in *Groundwork in the Theory of Argumentation*, ed. Christopher W. Tindale, Argumentation Library 21 (Dordrecht: Springer Netherlands, 2012), 261–79, http://link.springer.com/chapter/10.1007/978-94-007-2363-4_19; Debra Hawhee and Paul Messaris, "Review Essay: What's Visual about 'Visual Rhetoric'?," *Quarterly Journal of Speech* 95, no. 2 (May 1, 2009): 210–23, https://doi.org/10.1080/00335630902842095; Paul Messaris, *Visual Persuasion: The Role of Images in Advertising* (Thousand Oaks, CA: Sage, 1997).

35. Anne Marie Seward Barry, *Visual Intelligence: Perception, Image and Manipulation in Visual Communication* (Albany: State University of New York Press, 1997); Renita Coleman, "The Effects of Visuals on Ethical Reasoning: What's a Photograph Worth to Journalists Making Moral Decisions?," *Journalism and Mass Communication Quarterly* 83, no. 4 (Winter 2006): 835–50; Bettina Fabos, "The Trouble with Iconic Images: Historical Timelines and Public Memory," *Visual Communication Quarterly* 21, no. 4 (October 2, 2014): 223–35, https://doi.org/10.1080/15551393.2014.987282; Rick Williams and Julianne Newton, *Visual Communication: Integrating Media, Art, and Science* (New York: Erlbaum, 2007); Barbie Zelizer, "What's Untransportable about the Transport of Photographic Images?," *Popular Communication* 4, no. 1 (2006): 3–20.

36. Paul Ricoeur, "Narrative Time," *Critical Inquiry* 7, no. 1 (October 1, 1980): 169–90.

37. Fisher, "Narration as a Human Communication Paradigm"; Fisher, "The Narrative Paradigm"; Rideout, "Storytelling, Narrative Rationality, and Legal Persuasion."

38. Jon Durham Peters, "Witnessing," *Media, Culture, and Society* 23, no. 6 (2001): 707–23.

39. Nick Couldry, *Why Voice Matters: Culture and Politics after Neoliberalism* (London: SAGE, 2010).

40. Bryce Clayton Newell, "Crossing Lenses: Policing's New Visibility and the Role of Smartphone Journalism as a Form of Freedom-Preserving Reciprocal Surveillance," *University of Illinois Journal of Law, Technology & Policy* 2014, no. 1 (2014): 59–104.

41. Kimberly Kindy, "Some U.S. Police Departments Dump Body-Camera Programs amid High Costs," *Washington Post*, January 21, 2019, sec. National, https://www.washingtonpost.com/national/some-us-police-departments-dump-body-camera-programs-amid-high-costs/2019/01/21/991f0e66-03ad-11e9-b6a9-0aa5c2fcc9e4_story.html.

42. Eugene Volokh, "Opinion | A First Amendment Right to Record the Police," *Washington Post*, July 7, 2017, sec. The Volokh Conspiracy, https://www.washingtonpost.com/news/volokh-conspiracy/wp/2017/07/07/a-first-amendment-right-to-record-the-police/.

43. Monica Anderson, "Mobile Technology and Home Broadband 2019," Internet and Technology. Washington D.C.: Pew Research Center, June 13, 2019. https://www.pewresearch.org/internet/2019/06/13/mobile-technology-and-home-broadband-2019/; Laura Silver, "Smartphone Ownership Is Growing Rapidly Around the World, but Not Always Equally." Global Attitudes and Trends. Washington D.C.: Pew Research Center, February 5, 2019. https://www.pewresearch.org/global/2019/02/

05/smartphone-ownership-is-growing-rapidly-around-the-world-but-not-always-equally/.

44. E. G. "Gerry Morris," phone interview with author, March 4, 2019.

45. Allan Sekula, "On the Invention of Photographic Meaning," in *Photography against the Grain* (Halifax: Press of the Nova Scotia College of Art and Design, 1984), 5.

46. Lucia Walinchus and Richard Pérez-Peña, "White Tulsa Officer Is Acquitted in Fatal Shooting of Black Driver," *New York Times*, May 17, 2017, https://www.nytimes.com/2017/05/17/us/white-tulsa-officer-is-acquitted-in-fatal-shooting-of-black-driver.html.

47. Walinchus and Pérez-Peña.

48. German Lopez, "Was the Sandra Bland Arrest Video Edited? Here's Why the Media Is Suspicious," Vox, July 23, 2015, https://www.vox.com/2015/7/22/9013647/sandra-bland-arrest-video-edited.

49. Abby Ohlheiser and Abby Phillip, "'I Will Light You Up!': Texas Officer Threatened Sandra Bland with Taser during Traffic Stop," *Washington Post*, July 22, 2015, https://www.washingtonpost.com/news/morning-mix/wp/2015/07/21/much-too-early-to-call-jail-cell-hanging-death-of-sandra-bland-suicide-da-says/?utm_term=.0f9a6a19abf7.

50. Feigenson and Spiesel, *Law on Display*.

51. Feigenson and Spiesel, *Law on Display*.

Chapter 7

1. Scott Bauer and Morry Gash, "Protests Erupt Overnight after Kenosha Police Shoot Man in Back in Incident Caught on Video," chicagotribune.com, August 24, 2020, https://www.chicagotribune.com/nation-world/ct-nw-wisconsin-police-shooting-20200824-cabsib77hve3xgtrrrh5lpixom-story.html.

2. Geoff Herbert, "Video of Daniel Prude's Fatal Arrest Sparks Protests in Rochester; 9 Arrested," syracuse.com, https://www.syracuse.com/state/2020/09/video-of-daniel-prudes-fatal-arrest-sparks-protests-in-rochester-9-arrested.html (accessed September 4, 2020).

3. Jane Rhodes, *Framing the Black Panthers: The Spectacular Rise of a Black Power Icon* (Urbana: University of Illinois Press, 2017).

4. Andrea Pritchett, personal communication with author, July 11, 2018. Suzanne Pegas, personal communication with author, August 1, 2018.

5. Victoria J. Gallagher and Kenneth S. Zagacki, "Visibility and Rhetoric: Epiphanies and Transformations in the *Life* Photographs of the Selma Marches of 1965," *Rhetoric Society Quarterly* 37, no. 2 (March 29, 2007): 113–35. Kari Andén-Papadopoulos, "Citizen Camera-Witnessing: Embodied Political Dissent in the Age of 'Mediated Mass Self-Communication,'" *New Media and Society* (May 31, 2013): 1461444813489863, https://doi.org/10.1177/1461444813489863.

6. Michel Foucault, *Discipline and Punish: The Birth of the Prison*, Vintage Books ed. (New York: Vintage Books, 1979); Michel Foucault, *The History of Sexuality*, Vol. 1: *An Introduction*, Reissue ed. (New York: Vintage, 1990) .

7. Foucault, *Discipline and Punish*; Michel Foucault, "Truth and Power," in *Power/ Knowledge: Selected Interviews and Other Writings, 1972–1977* (New York: Pantheon Books, 1980).

8. Mary Angela Bock, "Film the Police! Cop-Watching and Its Embodied Narratives," *Journal of Communication* 66, no. 1 (February 1, 2016): 13–34, https://doi.org/ 10.1111/jcom.12204; Hans Toch, *Cop Watch: Spectators, Social Media, and Police Reform* (Washington, DC: American Psychological Association, 2012).

9. Robert Gooding-Williams, *Reading Rodney King / Reading Urban Uprising* (New York: Routledge, 1993).

10. Stuart Allan, Citizen Witnessing, Key Concepts in Journalism (Cambridge: Polity Press, 2013); Andén-Papadopoulos, "Citizen Camera-Witnessing"; Jon Durham Peters, "Witnessing," *Media, Culture, and Society* 23, no. 6 (2001): 707–23.

11. Susan Bordo, "Feminism, Foucault and the Politics of the Body," in *Feminist Theory and the Body*, ed. Janet Price and Margrit Shildrick (New York: Routledge, 1999), 246–57, https://doi.org/10.4324/9781315094106-29; Foucault, *Discipline and Punish*; Margaret A. McLaren, Feminism, Foucault, and Embodied Subjectivity, SUNY Series in Contemporary Continental Philosophy (Albany: State University of New York Press, 2002); Jana Sawicki, *Disciplining Foucault: Feminism, Power, and the Body* (New York: Routledge, 1991) .

12. Kimberlé Crenshaw, ed., *Critical Race Theory: The Key Writings That Formed the Movement* (New York: New Press, 1995); Michael Omi and Howard Winant, *Racial Formation in the United States* (London: Routledge, 2014); Kristian Williams, *Our Enemies in Blue: Police and Power in America* (Chico, CA: AK Press, 2015).

13. Christopher J. Schneider, *Policing and Social Media: Social Control in an Era of New Media* (Lanham, MD: Lexington Books, 2016).

14. Sam Gregory, "Transnational Storytelling: Human Rights, WITNESS, and Video Advocacy," *American Anthropologist* 108, no. 1 (March 2006): 195–204, https://doi.org/10.1525/aa.2006.108.1.195; Lindsey N. Kingston and Kathryn R. Stam, "Online Advocacy: Analysis of Human Rights NGO Websites," *Journal of Human Rights Practice* 5, no. 1 (March 1, 2013): 75–95, https://doi.org/10.1093/ jhuman/hus036; Sandra Ristovska, "The Rise of Eyewitness Video and Its Implications for Human Rights: Conceptual and Methodological Approaches," *Journal of Human Rights* 15, no. 3 (July 2, 2016): 347–60, https://doi.org/ 10.1080/14754835.2015.1132157; Sandra Ristovska, "Strategic Witnessing in an Age of Video Activism," *Media, Culture, and Society* 38, no. 7 (October 1, 2016): 1034–47, https://doi.org/10.1177/0163443716635866; Sandra Ristovska and Monroe Price, *Visual Imagery and Human Rights Practice* (Cham, Switzerland: Springer, 2018).

15. Barbie Zelizer, *Remembering to Forget: Holocaust Memory through the Camera's Eye* (Chicago: University of Chicago Press, 1998).

16. Christian Delage, *Caught on Camera: Film in the Courtroom from the Nuremberg Trials to the Trials of the Khmer Rouge* (Philadelphia: University of Pennsylvania Press, 2013); Lawrence Douglas, *The Memory of Judgment: Making Law and History in the Trials of the Holocaust* (New Haven, CT: Yale University Press, 2005).

17. Sean Captain. "In Less Than Five Years, 45 Billion Cameras Will Be Watching Us." *Fast Company*, August 9, 2017, https://www.fastcompany.com/40450867/in-less-than-five-years-45-billion-cameras-will-be-watching-us; Laura Silver, "Smartphone Ownership Is Growing Rapidly Around the World, but Not Always Equally." Global Attitudes and Trends. Washington D.C.: Pew Research Center, February 5, 2019, https://www.pewresearch.org/global/2019/02/05/smartphone-ownership-is-growing-rapidly-around-the-world-but-not-always-equally/.

18. Matthew Powers, "The Structural Organization of NGO Publicity Work: Explaining Divergent Publicity Strategies at Humanitarian and Human Rights Organizations," *International Journal of Communication* 8, no. 1 (January 2, 2014): 90–107.

19. Yvette Alberdingk Thijm as recorded video from *The Atlantic*'s coverage of the Aspen Institute, https://www.theatlantic.com/video/index/566792/bystander-video/

20. Andén-Papadopoulos, "Citizen Camera-Witnessing."

21. Allan, *Citizen Witnessing*; Peters, "Witnessing"; Kerstin Schankweiler, Verena Straub, and Tobias Wendl, *Image Testimonies: Witnessing in Times of Social Media* (London: Routledge, 2018).

22. Allan, *Citizen Witnessing*.

23. Donatella Della Ratta, "The Unbearable Lightness of the Image: Unfinished Thoughts on Filming in Contemporary Syria," *Middle East Journal of Culture and Communication* 10, nos. 2–3 (January 1, 2017): 109–32, https://doi.org/10.1163/18739865-01002003.

24. Madeleine Bair, "Navigating the Ethics of Citizen Video: The Case of a Sexual Assault in Egypt," *Araq Media and Society*, no. 19 (2014): 1–7.

25. Mette Mortensen, "When Citizen Photojournalism Sets the News Agenda: Neda Agha Soltan as a Web 2.0 Icon of Post-Election Unrest in Iran," *Global Media and Communication* 7, no. 1 (April 1, 2011): 4–16, https://doi.org/10.1177/1742766510397936.

26. Bock, "Film the Police!"

27. Larissa Wilson, "Ag-Gag Laws: A Shift in the Wrong Direction for Animal Welfare on Farms," *Golden Gate University Law Review* 44 (2014): 311.

28. Ann Luce, Daniel Jackson, and Einar Thorsen, "Citizen Journalism at the Margins," *Journalism Practice* 11, nos. 2–3 (March 16, 2017): 266–84, https://doi.org/10.1080/17512786.2016.1222883.

29. Eyal Weizman, *Forensic Architecture: Violence at the Threshold of Detectability* (Cambridge, MA: MIT Press, 2017).

30. Petter Bae Brandtzaeg et al., "Emerging Journalistic Verification Practices concerning Social Media," *Journalism Practice* 10, no. 3 (April 2, 2016): 323–42, https://doi.org/10.1080/17512786.2015.1020331.

31. Claire Wardle, "How Newsrooms Use Eyewitness Media," in *Visual Imagery and Human Rights Practice*, ed. Sandra Ristovska and Monroe Price, Global Transformations in Media and Communication Research (Cham, Switzerland: Palgrave Macmillan, 2018), 299–308.

32. Ristovska, "The Rise of Eyewitness Video and Its Implications for Human Rights."

33. Zeynep Tufekci, *Twitter and Tear Gas: The Power and Fragility of Networked Protest* (New Haven, CT: Yale University Press, 2017).

34. Richard V. Ericson and Kevin D. Haggerty, *The New Politics of Surveillance and Visibility* (Toronto: University of Toronto Press, 2006); Daniel Trottier, *Social Media as Surveillance: Rethinking Visibility in a Converging World* (London: Routledge, 2016), https://doi.org/10.4324/9781315609508.

35. John Tagg, "Evidence, Truth and Order: A Means of Surveillance," in *Visual Culture: The Reader*, ed. Stuart Hall and Jessica Evans (Thousand Oaks, CA: Sage, 1999), 244–73"; John Tagg, *The Disciplinary Frame: Photographic Truths and the Capture of Meaning* (Minneapolis: University of Minnesota Press, 2009).

36. Allissa V. Richardson, "Bearing Witness While Black," *Digital Journalism* 5, no. 6 (July 3, 2017): 673–98, https://doi.org/10.1080/21670811.2016.1193818; Jocelyn Simonson, "Copwatching," *California Law Review* 104, no. 2 (2016): 391–446.

37. Chapter 8 discusses the rhetorical strategies in greater detail.

38. Nick Couldry, "Rethinking the Politics of Voice," *Continuum: Journal of Media and Cultural Studies* 23, no. 4 (August 2009): 579–82, https://doi.org/10.1080/10304310903026594; Nick Couldry, *Why Voice Matters: Culture and Politics after Neoliberalism* (London: SAGE, 2010) .

39. Amartya Sen, "Human Rights and Capabilities," *Journal of Human Development* 6, no. 2 (July 1, 2005): 151–66, https://doi.org/10.1080/14649880500120491; Martha C. Nussbaum, "Education and Democratic Citizenship: Capabilities and Quality Education," *Journal of Human Development* 7, no. 3 (November 1, 2006): 385–95, https://doi.org/10.1080/14649880600815974.

40. Michael S. Schmidt and Matt Apuzzo, "South Carolina Officer Is Charged with Murder of Walter Scott," *New York Times*, April 7, 2015, http://www.nytimes.com/2015/04/08/us/south-carolina-officer-is-charged-with-murder-in-black-mans-death.html.

41. Marc Santora, "Eric Garner's Family to Sue New York City over Chokehold Case," *New York Times*, October 7, 2014, http://www.nytimes.com/2014/10/08/nyregion/eric-garners-family-to-sue-new-york-city-over-chokehold-case.html.

42. Regina Lawrence, *The Politics of Force: Media and the Construction of Police Brutality* (Berkeley: University of California Press, 2000), 96.

43. Kimberly Kindy, "Some U.S. Police Departments Dump Body-Camera Programs amid High Costs," *Washington Post*, January 21, 2019, sec. National, https://www.washingtonpost.com/national/some-us-police-departments-dump-body-camera-programs-amid-high-costs/2019/01/21/991f0e66-03ad-11e9-b6a9-0aa5c2fcc9e4_story.html.

44. Max Ehrenfreund, "Body Cameras for Cops Could Be the Biggest Change to Come Out of the Ferguson Protests," *Washington Post*, December 2, 2014, sec. Economic Policy, https://www.washingtonpost.com/news/wonk/wp/2014/12/02/body-cameras-for-cops-could-be-the-biggest-change-to-come-out-of-the-ferguson-protests/.

45. Kindy, "Some U.S. Police Departments Dump Body-Camera Programs amid High Costs."

46. Randall Stross, "Wearable Video Cameras, for Police Officers," *The New York Times*, April 6, 2013, sec. Business Day, http://www.nytimes.com/2013/04/07/business/wearable-video-cameras-for-police-officers.html.

Chapter 8

1. Hannah Knowles and Isaac Stanley-Becker, "Some Officers March and Kneel with Protesters, Creating Dissonant Images on Fraught Weekend of Uprisings," *Washington Post*, June 1, 2020, https://www.washingtonpost.com/nation/2020/06/01/some-officers-march-kneel-with-protesters-creating-dissonant-images-fraught-weekend-uprisings/.

2. Aaron Besecker, "Watch Now: Five Buffalo Police Officers Kneel with Protesters," Buffalo News, June 4, 2020, https://buffalonews.com/news/local/watch-now-five-buffalo-police-officers-kneel-with-protesters/article_f6c349f6-dee0-5ab4-a010-d3170222f471.html.

3. Ali Ingersoll, "Police Assault Injures Protester," *Investigative Post* (blog), June 4, 2020, https://www.investigativepost.org/2020/06/04/police-protesters-give-peace-a-chance/.

4. Chad Loder, "This Is Why You Don't Kneel with Cops," Twitter, *@chadloder*, June 4, 2020.

5. Steven Chermak and Alexander Weiss, "Maintaining Legitimacy Using External Communication Strategies: An Analysis of Police-Media Relations," *Journal of Criminal Justice* 33, no. 5 (September 2005): 502, https://doi.org/10.1016/j.jcrimjus.2005.06.001.

   See also: Alison Stateman, "LAPD Blues," *Public Relations Tactics* 4, no. 4 (April 1997): 1–3; Ray Surette and Alfredo Richard, "Public Information Officers: A Descriptive Study of Crime News Gatekeepers," *Journal of Criminal Justice* 23, no. 4 (1995): 325–36, https://doi.org/10.1016/0047-2352(95)00023-J; Ray Surette, "Public Information Officers: The Civilianization of a Criminal Justice Profession," *Journal of Criminal Justice* 29, no. 2 (March 2001): 107–17, https://doi.org/10.1016/S0047-2352(00)00086-6.

6. Markus D. Dubber, "The Power to Govern Men and Things: Patriarchal Origins of the Police Power in American Law," *Buffalo Law Review* 52 (2004): 1277–346.

7. Markus Dubber, *The Police Power: Patriarchy and the Foundations of American Government* (New York: Columbia University Press, 2005).

8. In our study of a Facebook page devoted to supporting police we found heavy use of Christian imagery, in particular depictions of Saint Michael the Archangel. Mary Angela Bock and Ever Josue Figueroa, "Faith and Reason: An Analysis of the Homologies of Black and Blue Lives Facebook Pages," *New Media and Society* (November 16, 2017): 1461444817740822, https://doi.org/10.1177/1461444817740822.

9. Janet Chan, "Police Culture: A Brief History of a Concept," in *The Critical Criminology Companion*, ed. Thalia Anthony and Chris Cunneen (Sydney: Hawkins Press, 2008), 218–25; Thomas Nolan, "Behind the Blue Wall of Silence: Essay," *Men and Masculinities* 12, no. 2 (October 2009): 250–57, https://doi.org/10.1177/1097184X09334700.

10. Anastasia Prokos and Irene Padavic, "'There Oughtta Be a Law against Bitches': Masculinity Lessons in Police Academy Training," *Gender, Work, and Organization* 9, no. 4 (2002): 439–59, https://doi.org/10.1111/1468-0432.00168.

11. Jennifer Ammons, "Batterers with Badges: Officer-Involved Domestic Violence," *Women Lawyers Journal* 90 (2004–5): 28–39; Testimony of Leanor Boulin Johnson, Arizona State University, in "On the Front Lines: Police Stress and Family Well-Being," a hearing before the House of Representatives, Select Committee on Children, Youth, and Families (1991); Leanor Boulin Johnson, Michael Todd, and Ganga Subramanian, "Violence in Police Families: Work-Family Spillover," *Journal of Family Violence* 20, no. 1 (February 1, 2005): 3–12, https://doi.org/10.1007/s10896-005-1504-4; Peter H. Neidig, Harold E. Russell, and Albert F. Seng, "Interspousal Aggression in Law Enforcement Families: A Preliminary Investigation," *Police Studies: The International Review of Police Development* 15, no. 1 (1992): 30–38.

12. Vida B. Johnson, "KKK in the PD: White Supremacist Police and What to Do about It," *Lewis and Clark Law Review* 23, no. 1 (2019): 205–62; Mike Winter, "KKK Membership Sinks 2 Florida Cops," *USA Today*, July 14, 2014, https://www.usatoday.com/story/news/nation/2014/07/14/florid-police-kkk/12645555/; Kristian Williams, *Our Enemies in Blue: Police and Power in America* (Chico, CA: AK Press, 2015).

13. Kayla Epstein, "Racist Posts from Police Officers' Social Media Accounts Trigger a Wave of Investigations," *Washington Post*, June 4, 2019, sec. National, https://www.washingtonpost.com/nation/2019/06/04/racist-posts-police-officers-social-media-accounts-trigger-wave-investigations/; Plain View Project, https://www.plainviewproject.org (accessed July 9, 2019).

14. Patrick Doreian and Norman Conti, "Creating the Thin Blue Line: Social Network Evolution within a Police Academy," *Social Networks* 50 (July 2017): 83–97, https://doi.org/10.1016/j.socnet.2017.03.011; Nolan, "Behind the Blue Wall of Silence"; Albert J. Reiss, *The Police and the Public*, Terry Lectures (New Haven, CT: Yale University Press, 1971).

15. Graham Campbell, "Why Cops Like Me Are Quiet," Buzzfeed, May 6, 2015, https://www.buzzfeednews.com/article/dreamworks/why-cops-like-me-stay-quiet-about-police-brutality.

16. Christopher P. Wilson, *Cop Knowledge: Police Power and Cultural Narrative in Twentieth-Century America* (Chicago: University of Chicago Press, 2000).

17. Mary Angela Bock and José Andrés Araiza, "Facing the Death Penalty While Facing the Cameras," *Journalism Practice* 9, no. 3 (2014): 1–18, https://doi.org/10.1080/17512786.2014.964496.Timothy E. Cook, *Governing the News: The News Media as a Political Institution* (Chicago: University of Chicago Press, 2005); Stuart Hall, ed., *Policing the Crisis: Mugging, the State, and Law and Order*, Critical Social Studies (London: Macmillan, 1978); Gaye Tuchman, *Making News: A Study in the Construction of Reality* (London: Free Press, 1978).

18. D. Berkowitz and J. V. TerKeurst, "Community as Interpretive Community: Rethinking the Journalist-Source Relationship," *Journal of Communication* 49, no. 3 (September 1, 1999): 125–36, https://doi.org/10.1111/j.1460-2466.1999.tb02808.x; Zvi Reich, "The Process Model of News Initiative," *Journalism Studies* 7, no. 4 (August 1, 2006): 497–514, https://doi.org/10.1080/14616700600757928; Leon Sigal, *Reporters and Officials: The Organization and Politics of Newsmaking* (Lexington, MA: D.

C. Heath & Co., 1973); Herb Strentz, *News Reporters and News Sources: What Happens before the Story Is Written* (Ames: Iowa State University Press, 1977).

19. David D. Perlmutter, *Policing the Media: Street Cops and Public Perceptions of Law Enforcement* (Thousand Oaks, CA: Sage, 2000).

20. Albert J. Reiss, *The Police and the Public*, Terry Lectures (New Haven, CT: Yale University Press, 1971).

21. Mary Angela Bock, Melissa Suran, and Laura Marina Boria González, "Badges? Who Needs Them? Police Press Credential Policies, Professionalism, and the New Media Environment," *Journalism* (September 6, 2016): 1464884916667655, https://doi.org/10.1177/1464884916667655.

22. Ted Chiricos, Kathy Padgett, and Marc Gertz, "Fear, TV News, and the Reality of Crime," *Criminology* 38, no. 3 (August 1, 2000): 755–86, https://doi.org/10.1111/j.1745-9125.2000.tb00905.x; Phyllis Kaniss, *Making Local News* (Chicago: University of Chicago Press, 1991); Jeremy Harris Lipschultz and Michael L. Hilt, *Crime and Local Television News: Dramatic, Breaking, and Live from the Scene*, LEA's Communication Series (Mahwah, NJ: L. Erlbaum Associates, 2002),

23. Pierre Bourdieu, *Distinction* (Cambridge, MA: Harvard University Press, 1984).

24. Erik Barnouw, *Documentary: A History of the Non-Fiction Film*, rev. ed. (1974; Oxford: Oxford University Press, 1983); Michael Pfau et al., "Embedding Journalists in Military Combat Units: How Embedding Alters Television News Stories," *Mass Communication and Society* 8, no. 3 (2005): 179–95.

25. Daniel Boorstin, *The Image: A Guide to Pseudo Events in America* (New York: Harper & Row, 1961).

26. Kiku Adatto, *Picture Perfect: Life in the Age of the Photo Op* (Princeton, NJ: Princeton University Press, 2008); Murray Edelman, *Constructing the Political Spectacle* (Chicago: University of Chicago Press, 1988).

27. Brandon Keefe, "Roswell Boots 11Alive Chief Investigator & Cameras from City Hall," 11 Alive WXIA, Atlanta, December 17, 2018.

28. FOP Lodge 7, Facebook Post, screen grab, November 28, 2018.

29. The badge-cam video of the officer playing basketball in Chapter 6 was one such release.

30. Philadelphia public information officer, personal communication with author, June 2016.

31. Daniel Kudla and Patrick Parnaby, "To Serve and to Tweet: An Examination of Police-Related Twitter Activity in Toronto," *Social Media + Society* 4, no. 3 (July 2018): 205630511878752, https://doi.org/10.1177/2056305118787520.

32. Fraternal Order of Police: Chicago Lodge No. 7 on Facebook, March 28, 2019; Megan Crepeau Meisner, Madeline Buckley, Jason, Madeline Buckley, and Jason Meisner, "In Latest Plot Twist, Cook County Prosecutors Abruptly Drop All Charges against Jussie Smollett," *Chicagotribune.com*. March 26, 2019, News, Breaking News, https://www.chicagotribune.com/news/breaking/ct-met-jussie-smollett-charges-dropped-20190326-story.html.

33. Mary Angela Bock and Ever Josue Figueroa, "Faith and Reason: An Analysis of the Homologies of Black and Blue Lives Facebook Pages," *New Media and*

Society (November 16, 2017): 1461444817740822, https://doi.org/10.1177/1461444817740822.

34. Mary Bowerman, "Detroit Police Challenge Cincy, Philly, Chicago to Running Man Challenge," *USA Today*, May 24, 2016, https://www.usatoday.com/story/news/nation-now/2016/05/24/detroit-police-department-cincinnati-philly-challenge-running-man/84850080/.

35. In fact, police dance with the skeleton to "Staying Alive" by the BeeGees: https://www.youtube.com/watch?v=28HIDZiHK2I.

36. Chris Best, "EXCLUSIVE: Mobile Police Drop Their Lip Sync Battle Video, and It's Epic!," *WKRG* (blog), July 27, 2018, https://www.wkrg.com/mobile-county/exclusive-mobile-police-drop-their-lip-sync-battle-video-and-its-epic/.

37. *Mobile Police Department's Lip Sync Challenge: Behind the Scenes*, November 16, 2018, https://www.youtube.com/watch?v=zuv_aM9X5vE. According to the Mobile Police Department public information office, Jones is no longer with the department.

38. Megan Smolenyak, "What Race Is Bruno Mars?," *Huffington Post* (blog), November 12, 2012, https://www.huffingtonpost.com/megan-smolenyak-smolenyak/what-race-is-bruno-mars_b_2116984.html.

39. *NBC Nightly News with Lester Holt*, July 13, 2018. Note: Appearing in a network news story talking about creating media moments because of the popularity of a media artifact may be a perfect twenty-first-century illustration of the simulacra.

40. Stuart Hall, "Encoding/Decoding," in *Culture, Media, Language: Working Papers in Cultural Studies, 1972–79*, ed. Stuart Hall et al. (London: Routledge, 2005), 117–27.

41. This is actually a somewhat unfair stereotype of officers, rooted in a time when very few options for food were open during an overnight shift.

42. Abby Ohlheiser and Abby Phillip, "'I Will Light You up!': Texas Officer Threatened Sandra Bland with Taser during Traffic Stop—The Washington Post," *The Washington Post*, July 22, 2015, https://www.washingtonpost.com/news/morning-mix/wp/2015/07/21/much-too-early-to-call-jail-cell-hanging-death-of-sandra-bland-suicide-da-says/?utm_term=.0f9a6a19abf7; A.J. Perez, "Police Officer Who Choked Ex-NFL Player Desmond Marrow Fired," *USA Today*, May 10, 2018, https://www.usatoday.com/story/sports/nfl/2018/05/10/police-officer-choked-nfl-player-desmond-marrow-fired/599050002/; Frances Robles and Jose A. Del Real, "Stephon Clark Was Shot 8 Times Primarily in His Back, Family-Ordered Autopsy Finds," *The New York Times*, March 30, 2018, sec. U.S., https://www.nytimes.com/2018/03/30/us/stephon-clark-independent-autopsy.html; Michael Schmidt and Matt Apuzzo, "South Carolina Officer Is Charged with Murder of Walter Scott," *The New York Times*, April 7, 2015, http://www.nytimes.com/2015/04/08/us/south-carolina-officer-is-charged-with-murder-in-blackmans-death.html.

43. Shane Bauer, *American Prison: A Reporter's Undercover Journey into the Business of Punishment* (New York: Penguin, 2018).

44. The incident happened October 20, 2014, and the tape was released November 24, 2015. Nausheen Husain, "Laquan McDonald Timeline: The Shooting, the Video, and the Fallout," chicagotribune.com, January 13, 2017, http://www.chicagotribune.

com/news/laquanmcdonald/ct-graphics-laquan-mcdonald-officers-fired-timeline-htmlstory.html.

45. Ashley Southall, "Reporter Who Forced Release of Laquan McDonald Video Is Barred from News Event," *New York Times*, November 25, 2015, http://www.nytimes.com/2015/11/26/us/reporter-who-forced-release-of-laquan-mcdonald-video-is-barred-from-news-event.html.

46. Eric Dexheimer, "Texas Police Withheld Records of Their Son's Death. Now They Know Why," *Austin American Statesman*, April 20, 2017, http://www.mystatesman.com/news/texas-police-withheld-records-their-son-death-now-they-know-why/MHJC1hWAbPhcN6gOtqOkyM/.

47. Chicago Tribune Staff, "Van Dyke Trial: Breaking Down All 44 Witnesses," chicagotribune.com, January 18, 2019, https://www.chicagotribune.com/news/ct-van-dyke-trial-witnesses-htmlstory.html; Megan Crepeau and Stacy St. Clair, "5 Takeaways from the First Day of the Jason Van Dyke Trial," chicagotribune.com, September 17, 2018, https://www.chicagotribune.com/news/laquan-mcdonald/ct-met-laquan-mcdonald-jason-van-dyke-trial-20180917-story.html.

48. Chicago Tribune Staff, "Van Dyke Trial."

49. Ryan Autullo and Tony Plohetsky, "Austin Officer's Stun Gun Video Sealed from Public, Judge Rules," Austin American-Statesman, January 4, 2019, https://www.statesman.com/news/20190104/austin-officers-stun-gun-video-sealed-from-public-judge-rules.

50. Christina Jedra, "Video Shows 'Egregious' Response to Dying Inmate. Delaware Says You Can't See It," delawareonline, March 15, 2019, https://www.delawareonline.com/story/news/2019/03/15/delaware-doesnt-want-you-see-video-connections-medical-response/3166564002/.

51. Associated Press, "Video Shows Dying Delaware Inmate's 'Incompetent' Care," Business Radio KDOW 1220 AM, May 22, 2019, http://kdow.biz/news/politics/video-shows-dying-delaware-inmates-incompetent-care.

52. WBOC16, "Video Shows Dying Delaware Inmate's 'Incompetent' Care," wboc.com, May 22, 2019, http://www.wboc.com/story/40517582/video-shows-dying-delaware-inmates-incompetent-care.

53. Palma Paciocco, "Pilloried in the Press: Rethinking the Constitutional Status of the American Perp Walk," *New Criminal Law Review: An International and Interdisciplinary Journal* 16, no. 1 (2013): 50–103, https://doi.org/10.1525/nclr.2013.16.1.50.

54. Norman Fairclough, *Critical Discourse Analysis: The Critical Study of Language* (London: Routledge, 2013); Teun van Dijk, *News as Discourse* (Hillsdale, NJ: Lawrence Erlbaum and Associates, 1988).

55. Yana Kunichoff and Sam Stecklow, "How Chicago's 'Fraternal Order of Propaganda' Shapes the Story of Fatal Police Shootings," *Chicago Reader*, February 3, 2016, https://www.chicagoreader.com/chicago/fraternal-order-of-police-shootings-propaganda-pat-camden/Content?oid=21092544.

56. Barak Ariel, William A. Farrar, and Alex Sutherland, "The Effect of Police Body-Worn Cameras on Use of Force and Citizens' Complaints against the Police: A Randomized

Controlled Trial," *Journal of Quantitative Criminology* 31, no. 3 (September 1, 2015): 509–35, https://doi.org/10.1007/s10940-014-9236-3.

57. Crepeau and St. Clair, "5 Takeaways from the First Day of the Jason Van Dyke Trial."

58. Stacy St. Clair, Christy Meisner, and Jason Gutowski, "Van Dyke's Partner, Testifying under Immunity, Says Shooting Video Doesn't Accurately Depict What He Saw," chicagotribune.com, September 18, 2018, https://www.chicagotribune.com/news/local/breaking/ct-met-laquan-mcdonald-jason-van-dyke-trial-a-20180912-story.html.

59. Chicago Tribune Staff, "Van Dyke Trial."

60. Chicago Tribune Staff, "Van Dyke Trial."

61. Chicago Tribune Staff, "Van Dyke Trial."

62. Jeremy Gorner, "4 Chicago Cops Fired for Alleged Cover-Up of Fatal Police Shooting of Laquan McDonald," chicagotribune.com, July 19, 2019, https://www.chicagotribune.com/news/criminal-justice/ct-laquan-mcdonald-chicago-cops-discipline-20190718-46q2fyuxh5eqfph4uhvm3kewsa-story.html; Chicago Tribune Staff, "Van Dyke Trial."

63. Chicago Tribune Staff, "Van Dyke Trial."

64. Megan Crepeau, Christy Gutowski, and Stacy St. Clair, "McDonald's Behavior the Focus of 4th Day of Defense Testimony at Van Dyke's Trial," chicagotribune.com, September 27, 2018, https://www.chicagotribune.com/news/breaking/ct-met-laquan-mcdonald-jason-van-dyke-trial-20180928-story.html.

65. Megan Crepeau, Stacy St. Clair, and Jason Meisner, "6 Takeaways from the Ninth Day of Testimony in the Jason Van Dyke Trial," chicagotribune.com, October 2, 2018, https://www.chicagotribune.com/news/breaking/ct-met-laquan-mcdonald-jason-van-dyke-trial-updates-20191002-story.html.

66. Crepeau, St. Clair, and Meisner, "6 Takeaways from the Ninth Day of Testimony in the Jason Van Dyke Trial."

67. Megan Crepeau, Stacy St. Clair, and Jason Meisner, "How the Day Unfolded: Inside the Courtroom for Former Chicago Police Officer Jason Van Dyke's Sentencing," chicagotribune.com, January 18, 2019, https://www.chicagotribune.com/news/breaking/ct-met-laquan-mcdonald-jason-van-dyke-sentencing-20190118-story.html.

68. Andy Grimm, "Van Dyke Wasn't Charming, Couldn't Win Over Jury, Lawyer Says," *Chicago Sun-Times*, April 11, 2019, https://chicago.suntimes.com/2019/4/11/18435828/van-dyke-wasn-t-charming-couldn-t-win-over-jury-lawyer-says.

69. Aaron C. Davis, "'YouTube Effect' Has Left Police Officers under Siege, Law Enforcement Leaders Say," *Washington Post*, October 8, 2015, https://www.washingtonpost.com/news/post-nation/wp/2015/10/08/youtube-effect-has-left-police-officers-under-siege-law-enforcement-leaders-say/.

70. Eric Lichtblau, "F.B.I. Director Says 'Viral Video Effect' Blunts Police Work," *New York Times*, May 11, 2016, http://www.nytimes.com/2016/05/12/us/comey-ferguson-effect-police-videos-fbi.html.

71. National Law Enforcement Officer Memorial Fund, "Preliminary 2019 Fallen Officer Fatalities," 2019, https://nleomf.org/preliminary-2018-law-enforcement-officer-fatalities).

72. Doreian and Conti, "Creating the Thin Blue Line"; Nolan, "Behind the Blue Wall of Silence"; Reiss, *The Police and the Public.*

73. Interview with author, June 2016.

74. Chao Xiong, "Police Officer Charged in Fatal Shooting of Philando Castile," *Star Tribune*, November 17, 2016, http://www.startribune.com/ramsey-county-attorney-choi-to-announce-update-in-castile-shooting/401484635/.

75. Dave Collins, "Police Release Footage after Shooting on Unarmed Black Couple in Connecticut," *PBS NewsHour*, April 26, 2019, https://www.pbs.org/newshour/nation/police-release-footage-after-shooting-on-unarmed-black-couple-in-connecticut.

76. Deanna Paul, "'Keep Your Hands Visible': Texas Teens Can't Graduate until They Watch This Video about Police," *Washington Post*, October 16, 2018, sec. Education, https://www.washingtonpost.com/education/2018/10/17/keep-your-hands-visible-texas-teens-cant-graduate-until-they-watch-this-video-about-police/.

77. Texas Commission on Law Enforcement, Civilian Interaction Training Program (SB30), August 15, 2018, https://www.youtube.com/watch?v=Fi60a-W0Qsc&feature=youtu.be

78. PoliceOneVideo, "Reality Training: Why Cops Should Stay Vigilant during Traffic Stops," October 23, 2015, https://www.youtube.com/watch?v=UCA-wVwq76g.

79. Illya D. Lichtenberg and Alisa Smith, "How Dangerous Are Routine Police-Citizen Traffic Stops? A Research Note," *Journal of Criminal Justice* 29, no. 5 (September 1, 2001): 419–28, https://doi.org/10.1016/S0047-2352(01)00106-4; Jordan Blair Woods, "Policing, Danger Narratives, and Routine Traffic Stops," *Michigan Law Review; Ann Arbor* 117, no. 4 (February 2019): 635–712.

80. Katie Rogers, "The Death of Sandra Bland: Questions and Answers," *New York Times*, July 23, 2015, sec. U.S., https://www.nytimes.com/interactive/2015/07/23/us/23blandlisty.html, https://www.nytimes.com/interactive/2015/07/23/us/23blandlisty.html.

81. David Montgomery, "The Death of Sandra Bland: Is There Anything Left to Investigate?," *New York Times*, May 8, 2019, sec. U.S., https://www.nytimes.com/2019/05/08/us/sandra-bland-texas-death.html.

82. David Montgomery, "Sandra Bland, It Turns Out, Filmed Traffic Stop Confrontation Herself," *New York Times*, May 7, 2019, sec. U.S., https://www.nytimes.com/2019/05/07/us/sandra-bland-video-brian-encinia.html.

83. Michael Baraja, "The Sandra Bland Act Was Stripped of the Provision That Could've Prevented Her Arrest. Now It Has a Chance," *Texas Observer*, April 5, 2019, https://www.texasobserver.org/the-sandra-bland-act-was-stripped-of-the-provision-that-couldve-prevented-her-arrest-now-it-has-a-chance/.

84. Dan Hinkel, "As Reform Gains Traction, Chicago Police Union Pushes Back," chicagotribune.com, October 5, 2018, https://www.chicagotribune.com/investigations/ct-met-chicago-police-union-fop-20181105-story.html.

85. Daniel Herbert, "In the Law of Public Opinion, Police Officers Are the Bad Guys," *FOP Magazine*, February 2019.

86. Not even when they neglect to read the syllabus.

87. Body Politic News, "Alabama Cop to Citizen: 'Fuck You Is My Name,'" May 31, 2019, https://www.youtube.com/watch?v=G2xJ-NJHB2M

The department issued a news release about a week later saying that the officer's behavior was "not acceptable," but that no other information about this personnel matter would be released: Emme Long, "Officer Video Response," press release, Decatur (AL) Police Department, June 5, 2019.

88. Rémi Boivin et al., "The Body-Worn Camera Perspective Bias," *Journal of Experimental Criminology* 13, no. 1 (March 1, 2017): 125–42, https://doi.org/10.1007/s11292-016-9270-2; Lindsey Nicole Sweeney, "Jurors' Ability to Judge the Reliability of Confessions and Denials: Effects of Camera Perspective during Interrogation" (MA thesis, University of Arkansas, 2011), https://search-proquest-com.ezproxy.lib.utexas.edu/docview/899719462/abstract/65DE243A55914CE7PQ/1.

Chapter 9

1. Sarah Maslin Nir, "White Woman Is Fired after Calling Police on Black Man in Central Park," *New York Times*, May 26, 2020, sec. New York, https://www.nytimes.com/2020/05/26/nyregion/amy-cooper-dog-central-park.html.

2. Jan Ransom, "Amy Cooper Faces Charges after Calling Police on Black Bird-Watcher," *New York Times*, July 6, 2020, sec. New York, https://www.nytimes.com/2020/07/06/nyregion/amy-cooper-false-report-charge.html.

3. Henry Goldblatt, "A Brief History of 'Karen,'" *New York Times*, July 31, 2020, sec. Style, https://www.nytimes.com/2020/07/31/style/karen-name-meme-history.html.

4. Samuel Woolley, *The Reality Game: A Gripping Investigation into Deepfake Videos, the Next Wave of Fake News, and What It Means for Democracy* (n.p.: Octopus, 2020).

5. Kate Ince, "Bringing Bodies Back In: For a Phenomenological and Psychoanalytic Film Criticism of Embodied Cultural Identity," *Film-Philosophy* 15, no. 1 (February 2011): 1–12, https://doi.org/10.3366/film.2011.0001; Vivian Sobchack, *The Address of the Eye: A Phenomenology of Film Experience* (Princeton, NJ: Princeton University Press, 1992).

6. Marco Iacoboni, *Mirroring People: The New Science of How We Connect with Others* (New York: Farrar, Straus and Giroux, 2009); Lori Landay, "The Mirror of Performance: Kinaesthetics, Subjectivity, and the Body in Film, Television, and Virtual Worlds," *Cinema Journal* 51, no. 3 (2012): 129–36.

7. Marco Iacoboni, "Imitation, Empathy, and Mirror Neurons," *Annual Review of Psychology* 60, no. 1 (January 2009): 653–70, https://doi.org/10.1146/annurev.psych.60.110707.163604; Dylan D. Wagner et al., "Spontaneous Action Representation in Smokers When Watching Movie Characters Smoke," *Journal of Neuroscience* 31, no. 3 (January 19, 2011): 894–98, https://doi.org/10.1523/JNEUROSCI.5174-10.2011.

8. Paul Ekman and Wallace V. Friesen, "Constants across Cultures in the Face and Emotion," *Journal of Personality and Social Psychology* 17, no. 2 (1971): 124–29, https://doi.org/10.1037/h0030377.

9. Deen Freelon et al., "How Black Twitter and Other Social Media Communities Interact with Mainstream News," SocArXiv, August 5, 2018, https://doi.org/10.31235/osf.io/nhsd9.

10. Freelon et al.

11. Meredith D. Clark, "To Tweet Our Own Cause: A Mixed-Methods Study of the Online Phenomenon 'Black Twitter'" (PhD dissertation, University of North Carolina at Chapel Hill, 2014), 83, https://search.proquest.com/docview/1648168732/abstract/94FEC6267BAB499BPQ/1.

12. Aisha Harris, "She Founded MeToo. Now She Wants to Move Past the Trauma," *New York Times*, October 15, 2018, sec. Arts, https://www.nytimes.com/2018/10/15/arts/tarana-burke-metoo-anniversary.html; Sarah Jaffe, "The Collective Power of #MeToo," *Dissent* 65, no. 2 (May 1, 2018): 80–87, https://doi.org/10.1353/dss.2018.0031.

13. Freelon et al., "How Black Twitter and Other Social Media Communities Interact with Mainstream News."

14. Malanie Eversley, "$32K Raised for Michael's Manager Subjected to Customer Tirade in Chicago," *USA Today*, November 30, 2016, https://www.usatoday.com/story/news/2016/11/30/thousands-raised-michaels-manager-subjected-customer-tirade-chicago/94646406/.

15. Snider's followup video appears at https://www.youtube.com/watch?v=COlsbNNZsTM.

16. Nancy Dillon, "New 911 Audio Reveals Dispatcher Questioned 'BBQ Becky's' Mental Health after She Called Cops on Group of Black People Enjoying Cookout in Calif. Park," nydailynews.com, August 31, 2018, https://www.nydailynews.com/news/ny-news-bbq-becky-emergency-calls-released-20180831-story.html.

17. Christina Zhao, "'BBQ Becky,' White Woman Who Called Cops on Black BBQ, 911 Audio Released: 'I'm Really Scared! Come Quick!,'" *Newsweek*, September 4, 2018.

18. Camila Hudson, phone interview with author, June 7, 2019.

19. Chapter 6 explores the power of multiple video perspectives over a matched timeline.

20. Camila Hudson, phone interview with author.

21. "Video Shows White Man Racially Profiling Black Woman, Son at Pool," ABC News, July 6, 2018, https://abcnews.go.com/WNT/video/video-shows-white-man-racially-profiling-black-woman-56415289. In contrast with the declarative nature of online headline, the broadcast story used a question in the graphic overlay, asking "Prejudice at the Pool?"

22. D'Arreion Nuriyah Toles' Facebook page, October 13, 2018.

23. Karen Mizoguchi, "Missouri Woman Who Blocked Her Black Neighbor from His Condo in Viral Video Defends Her Actions," People.com, October 17, 2018, https://people.com/human-interest/woman-who-blocked-black-neighbor-speaks-out/.

24. Haaziq Madyun, "Family Wants to Create Awareness after BBQ Confrontation at Lake Merritt," *KRON4* (blog), May 10, 2018, https://www.kron4.com/news/bay-area/family-wants-to-create-awareness-after-bbq-confrontation-at-lake-merritt/.

25. John Bacon, "Philadelphia Mayor 'Heartbroken' after Black Men Arrested at Starbucks," *USA Today*, April 14, 2018, https://www.usatoday.com/story/news/nation/2018/04/14/philadelphia-police-chief-officers-did-nothing-wrong-starbucks-arrest/518123002/.

26. Jessica Campisi et al., "After Internet Mockery, 'Permit Patty' Resigns as CEO of Cannabis-Products Company," CNN, June 26, 2018, https://www.cnn.com/2018/06/25/us/permit-patty-san-francisco-trnd/index.html.

27. St. Louis Post-Dispatch Staff, "Woman Seen in Viral Video Confronting Neighbor at St. Louis Lofts Says She Was Motivated by Safety, Not Racism," *St. Louis Post-Dispatch*, October 17, 2018, https://www.stltoday.com/news/local/metro/woman-seen-in-viral-video-confronting-neighbor-at-st-louis/article_db7c6cf5-80f2-51d0-a0b6-5038b485396c.html.

28. The hashtag campaign #CrimingWhileWhite made this point directly.

29. US Department of Justice, Civil Rights Division, *Investigation of the Ferguson Police Department*, March 4, 2015, Washington DC.

30. FBI data released in 2018 show that while Blacks are 13 percent of the US population they constitute 31 percent of the people killed by police.

   See German Lopez, "There Are Huge Racial Disparities in How US Police Use Force," Vox, August 13, 2016, https://www.vox.com/identities/2016/8/13/17938186/police-shootings-killings-racism-racial-disparities.

   Other factors, such as the crime involved or neighborhood poverty, complicate this picture, so the disparity cannot be simplistically blamed on racial bias, but the fact that more Black people are killed—and the fear this inspires—remains.

   See Joseph Cesario, David J. Johnson, and William Terrill, "Is There Evidence of Racial Disparity in Police Use of Deadly Force? Analyses of Officer-Involved Fatal Shootings in 2015–2016," *Social Psychological and Personality Science* 10, no. 5 (July 1, 2019): 586–95, https://doi.org/10.1177/1948550618775108; David J. Johnson et al., "Officer Characteristics and Racial Disparities in Fatal Officer-Involved Shootings," *Proceedings of the National Academy of Sciences* (July 17, 2019): 201903856, https://doi.org/10.1073/pnas.1903856116.

31. Dan Simon, "Woman in 'Permit Patty' Video Speaks out: I Feel Manipulated," CNN.com, June 26, 2018, https://www.youtube.com/watch?v=lyJOYzof9R4.

32. Justine Miller, "Woman Apologizes after Claiming to Call Police on Boy," October 12, 2018, http://brooklyn.news12.com/story/39279395/woman-apologizes-after-claiming-to-call-police-on-boy.

33. Victor Fiorillo, "Woman Who Shared Philadelphia Starbucks Arrest Video Tells Her Story," *Philadelphia Magazine* (blog), April 14, 2018, https://www.phillymag.com/news/2018/04/14/philadelphia-starbucks-arrest-video/.

34. Anna Orso, "One Year Later: A Timeline of Controversy and Progress since the Starbucks Arrests Seen 'round the World," inquirer.com, April 12, 2019, https://www.inquirer.com/news/starbucks-incident-philadelphia-racial-bias-one-year-anniversary-stutter-dilworth-park-homeless-tables-20190412.html.

35. Simon, "Woman in 'Permit Patty' Video Speaks Out."

36. Orso, "One Year Later."

37. Steven Tavares, "Kenzie Smith, Target of BBQ Becky, Is Running for Abel Guillén's Council Seat," *East Bay Citizen*, June 26, 2018, https://ebcitizen.com/2018/06/26/kenzie-smith-target-of-bbq-becky-is-running-for-abel-guillens-council-seat/.

38. Simon, "Woman in 'Permit Patty' Video Speaks Out."

39. Vic Faust, "Woman in Viral Video with Black Man Speaks Out after Being Fired, Defends Her Actions," fox2now.com, October 16, 2018, https://fox2now.com/2018/10/16/woman-in-viral-video-with-black-man-speaks-out-after-being-fired-defends-her-actions/.

40. Karen Zraick, "Man Labeled 'ID Adam' Is Fired after Calling the Police on a Black Woman at Pool," *New York Times*, July 9, 2018, sec. U.S., https://www.nytimes.com/2018/07/06/us/pool-racial-profiling-white-man.html; Matt Stevens, "CVS Fires 2 for Calling Police on Black Woman over Coupon," *New York Times*, July 18, 2018, sec. Business, https://www.nytimes.com/2018/07/16/business/cvs-coupon-manager-black-woman-police.html.

41. Jan Ransom, "Case against Amy Cooper Lacks Key Element: Victim's Cooperation," *New York Times*, July 7, 2020, sec. New York, https://www.nytimes.com/2020/07/07/nyregion/amy-cooper-central-park-false-report-charge.html.

42. Nicole R. Fleetwood, *Troubling Vision: Performance, Visuality, and Blackness* (Chicago: University of Chicago Press, 2011).

43. Stuart Hall, "The Spectacle of 'the Other,'" in *Representation: Cultural Representations, and Signifying Practices*, ed. Stuart Hall, Jessica Evans, and Sean Nixon (Thousand Oaks, CA: Sage, 1997), 225–79.

44. Camila Hudson, phone interview with author.

45. Max Londberg, "Nick Sandmann Lawsuit against Washington Post Dismissed by Judge," *USA Today*, July 26, 2019, https://www.usatoday.com/story/news/nation/2019/07/26/nick-sandmann-lawsuit-against-washington-post-dismissed-federal-judge-trump/1842030001/; Edmund Lee, "Washington Post Settles Lawsuit with Student in Viral Protest Video," *New York Times*, July 24, 2020, sec. Business, https://www.nytimes.com/2020/07/24/business/media/washington-post-lawsuit-covington-student.html.

46. Joseph A. Wulfsohn, "CNN Airs Nicholas Sandmann RNC Speech Months after Settling $250M Defamation Lawsuit," FoxNews.com, August 25, 2020, https://www.foxnews.com/media/cnn-airs-nicholas-sandmann-speech-republican-convention.

47. Eyn Kyung Kim, "Nick Sandmann Interview with TODAY Show's Savannah Guthrie on Encounter with Native American Nathan Phillips," today.com, January 23, 2019, https://www.today.com/news/nick-sandmann-interview-today-show-s-savannah-guthrie-encounter-native-t147242.

48. Mary Angela Bock, *Video Journalism: Beyond the One-Man Band* (New York: Peter Lang, 2012).

49. Bock; D. M. Lindekugel, *Shooters: TV News Photographers and Their Work* (Westport, CT: Praeger, 1994).

50. This can be heard most clearly in the *Duncan* video.

51. Kim, "Nick Sandmann Interview with TODAY Show's Savannah Guthrie on Encounter with Native American Nathan Phillips."

52. Estimates as to how much we learn by percentage vary, and are often hijacked by nonscholars wishing to make a point about "body language."

53. Maria Elizabeth Grabe and Erik Page Bucy, *Image Bite Politics: News and the Visual Framing of Elections* (Oxford: Oxford University Press, 2009).

54. As identified by Roger D. Masters et al., "Television Coverage of Candidates' Display Behavior during the 1984 Democratic Primaries in the United States," *International Political Science Review* 8, no. 2 (April 1, 1987): 121–30, https://doi.org/10.1177/019251218700800203.

55. Grabe and Bucy, *Image Bite Politics*, also noted that nonverbal information contributed to political knowledge and argued for increased attention to the role of visual communication in political research.

56. Lasse Laustsen and Michael Bang Petersen, "Winning Faces Vary by Ideology: How Nonverbal Source Cues Influence Election and Communication Success in Politics," *Political Communication* 33, no. 2 (April 2, 2016): 188–211, https://doi.org/10.1080/10584609.2015.1050565.

57. Paul Ekman and Wallace V. Friesen, "Felt, False, and Miserable Smiles," *Journal of Nonverbal Behavior* 6, no. 4 (June 1, 1982): 238–52, https://doi.org/10.1007/BF00987191.

58. Paul Ekman and Wallace V. Friesen, "Constants across Cultures in the Face and Emotion," *Journal of Personality and Social Psychology* 17, no. 2 (1971): 124–29, https://doi.org/10.1037/h0030377.

59. Zachary Witkower et al., "Two Signals of Social Rank: Prestige and Dominance Are Associated with Distinct Nonverbal Displays," *Journal of Personality and Social Psychology*, April 25, 2019, https://doi.org/10.1037/pspi0000181.

60. L. L. Wood, *Nick Sandmann: The Truth in 15 Minutes*, February 1, 2019, https://www.youtube.com/watch?v=lSkpPaiUF8s

61. Kim, "Nick Sandmann Interview with TODAY Show's Savannah Guthrie on Encounter with Native American Nathan Phillips."

62. Robert Silverman, "The History of the Covington MAGA Teens' Racist 'Tomahawk Chop,'" *Daily Beast*, January 23, 2019, sec. Entertainment, https://www.thedailybeast.com/the-history-of-the-covington-maga-teens-racist-tomahawk-chop.

63. Shannon Connellan, "Twitter Suspends Account Linked to Boosting MAGA Teens Controversy," Mashable, January 22, 2019, https://mashable.com/article/twitter-suspends-account-maga-teens-native-americans/.

64. Connellan, "Twitter Suspends Account Linked to Boosting MAGA Teens Controversy."

65. The page has since been edited, but the original headline read "Teens mock Native American elder on the Mall." The caption read "A group of high school teens surrounded and jeered at Native American elder Nathan Phillips on the steps of the Lincoln Memorial on January 18. National section, January 19, 2019 Screenshot, WashingtonPost.com, from January 19, 2019 Washingtonpost.com, accessed July 25, 2019.

66. Erik Wemple, "'Fuller Picture': How Major Media Outlets Handled Their Evolving Accounts of the Covington Story," *Washington Post*, January 22, 2019, sec. Opinions, https://www.washingtonpost.com/opinions/2019/01/23/fuller-picture-how-major-media-outlets-handled-their-evolving-accounts-covington-story/.

67. Wemple, "'Fuller Picture.'"

68. Sarah Mervosh and Emily S. Rueb, "Fuller Picture Emerges of Viral Video of Native American Man and Catholic Students," *New York Times*, January 20, 2019, https://www.nytimes.com/2019/01/20/us/nathan-phillips-covington.html.

69. Ian Bogost, "Stop Trusting Viral Videos," The Atlantic, January 21, 2019, https://www.theatlantic.com/technology/archive/2019/01/viral-clash-students-and-native-americans-explained/580906/; Elizabeth Jensen, "Unraveling a Washington Mall Confrontation, Frame by Frame," NPR.org, January 25, 2019, https://www.npr.org/sections/publiceditor/2019/01/25/688833473/unraveling-a-washington-mall-confrontation-frame-by-frame; Wemple, "'Fuller Picture.'"

70. Wulfsohn, "CNN Airs Nicholas Sandmann RNC Speech Months after Settling $250M Defamation Lawsuit."

71. Barbie Zelizer, Taking Journalism Seriously: News and the Academy (Thousand Oaks, CA: Sage, 2004), 217.

72. Zelizer, Taking Journalism Seriously.

73. Issues are now archived at the Annenberg School for Communication at the University of Pennsylvania.

74. Kevin G. Barnhurst, Michael Vari, and Ígor Rodríguez, "Mapping Visual Studies in Communication," Journal of Communication 54, no. 4 (2004): 616–44, https://doi.org/10.1111/j.1460-2466.2004.tb02648.x.

75. Alex Hern, "Google's Solution to Accidental Algorithmic Racism: Ban Gorillas," The Guardian, January 12, 2018, sec. Technology, https://www.theguardian.com/technology/2018/jan/12/google-racism-ban-gorilla-black-people.

Chapter 10

1. Alexander L. Curry and Natalie Jomini Stroud, "The Effects of Journalistic Transparency on Credibility Assessments and Engagement Intentions," Journalism (May 25, 2019): 1464884919850387, https://doi.org/10.1177/1464884919850387; Gina M. Masullo and Ori Tenenboim, "Gaining Trust in TV News," Center for Media Engagement, June 2020, https://mediaengagement.org/research/trust-in-tv-news/ accessed March 17, 2021.

2. I welcome any leads on such a story.

3. Howard Rheingold, Smart Mobs: The Next Social Revolution (Cambridge, MA: Perseus, 2002); James Bohman, "Expanding Dialogue: The Internet, the Public Sphere, and Prospects for Transnational Democracy," in After Habermas: New Perspectives on the Public Sphere, ed. Nick Crossley and John Michael Roberts, Sociological Review Monographs (Norwich, UK: Page Brothers, 2004), 184; Steve Mann and Joseph Ferenbok, "New Media and the Power Politics of Sousveillance in a Surveillance-Dominated World," Surveillance and Society 11, no. 1/2 (July 16, 2013): 18–34, https://doi.org/10.24908/ss.v11i1/2.4456; Meredith D. Clark, "To Tweet Our Own Cause: A Mixed-Methods Study of the Online Phenomenon 'Black Twitter'" (PhD dissertation, University of North Carolina at Chapel Hill, 2014), https://search.proquest.com/docview/1648168732/abstract/5184038F31174169PQ/1.

4. Zeynep Tufekci, Twitter and Tear Gas: The Power and Fragility of Networked Protest (New Haven, CT: Yale University Press, 2017); Roy Coleman, "Images from a

Neoliberal City: The State, Surveillance and Social Control," *Critical Criminology* 12, no. 1 (January 1, 2004): 38, https://doi.org/10.1023/B:CRIT.0000024443.08828. d8; Gino Canella, "Racialized Surveillance: Activist Media and the Policing of Black Bodies," *Communication, Culture and Critique* 11, no. 3 (September 1, 2018): 378–98, https://doi.org/10.1093/ccc/tcy013.

5. Amartya Sen, "Human Rights and Capabilities," *Journal of Human Development* 6, no. 2 (July 1, 2005): 151–66; Martha C. Nussbaum, "Women and Human Development: The Capabilities Approach," Cambridge Core (Cambridge University Press, March 2000), https://doi.org/10.1017/CBO9780511841286; Martha C. Nussbaum, "Education and Democratic Citizenship: Capabilities and Quality Education," *Journal of Human Development* 7, no. 3 (November 1, 2006): 385–95.

6. Jurgen Habermas, *The Structural Transformation of the Public Sphere: An Inquiry into a Category of Bourgeois Society*, ed. F. Lawrence (Cambridge: Polity Press, 1989); Douglas Kellner, "Habermas, the Public Sphere, and Democracy: A Critical Intervention," in *Perspectives on Habermas*, ed. Lewis E. Hahn (Chicago: Open Court, 2000), 26, http://www.gseis.ucla.edu/faculty/kellner/essays/habermaspublicspheredemocracy.pdf.

7. Nick Couldry, *Why Voice Matters: Culture and Politics after Neoliberalism* (London: SAGE, 2010).

8. Christina Neumayer and Luca Rossi, "Images of Protest in Social Media: Struggle over Visibility and Visual Narratives," *New Media and Society* 20, no. 11 (November 1, 2018): 4293–310.

9. Victoria J. Gallagher and Kenneth S. Zagacki, "Visibility and Rhetoric: Epiphanies and Transformations in the Life Photographs of the Selma Marches of 1965," *Rhetoric Society Quarterly* 37, no. 2 (March 29, 2007): 113–35.

10. Mann and Ferenbok, "New Media and the Power Politics of Sousveillance in a Surveillance-Dominated World."

11. Lauren Regan, "Policing the Police: Your Right to Record Law Enforcement," Civil Liberties Defense Center, April 22, 2015, https://cldc.org/policing-the-police/.

12. "Fatal Force: Police Shootings Database," *Washington Post*, September 24, 2020, https://www.washingtonpost.com/graphics/investigations/police-shootings-database/.

13. Sen, "Human Rights and Capabilities"; Lorella Terzi, "Capability Approach: Martha Nussbaum and Amartya Sen," in *Encyclopedia of Educational Theory and Philosophy*, ed. D. C. Phillips (Thousand Oaks, CA: Sage, 2014), 97–99.

14. Susan Sontag, *Regarding the Pain of Others* (New York: Farrar, Straus and Giroux, 2003); Susan Sontag, *On Photography* (New York: Picador, 1973).

15. Sontag, *On Photography*; Sontag, *Regarding the Pain of Others*.

16. Ariella Azoulay, *The Civil Contract of Photography* (New York: Zone Books, 2008), 145.

17. Lilie Chouliaraki, *The Spectatorship of Suffering* (London: SAGE, 2006).

18. Paul Messaris and Sandra Moriarty, "Visual Literacy Theory," in *Handbook of Visual Communication*, ed. Ken Smith et al. (Mahwah, NJ: Lawrence Erlbaum Associates, 2005), 481–502.

19. Renee Hobbs, *Create to Learn: Introduction to Digital Literacy* (Hoboken, NJ: John Wiley & Sons, 2017).

20. Maggie Rivas-Rodriguez, "Communities, Cultural Identity, and the News," in *Changing the News: The Forces Shaping Journalism in Uncertain Times*, ed. Wilson Lowrey and Peter J. Gade (New York: Routledge, 2012), 102 – 17; *The Kerner Report: The 1968 Report of the National Advisory Commission on Civil Disorders* (New York: Pantheon Books, 1988), catalog.hathitrust.org/Record/003173820.

21. Cristina Bodinger-de Uriarte and Gunnar Valgeirsson, "Institutional Disconnects as Obstacles to Diversity in Journalism in the United States," *Journalism Practice* 9, no. 3 (May 4, 2015): 399–417, https://doi.org/10.1080/17512786.2014.963367.

22. David Pritchard and Sarah Stonbely, "Racial Profiling in the Newsroom," *Journalism and Mass Communication Quarterly* 84, no. 2 (June 1, 2007): 231–48, https://doi.org/10.1177/107769900708400203.

23. Jennifer Vanasco, "Refocusing on Newsroom Diversity," *Columbia Journalism Review*, September 20, 2013, http://www.cjr.org/minority_reports/dori_maynard_diversity.php; Steve Buttry, "Dori Maynard Helped Journalists View Diversity as a Matter of Accuracy," *The Buttry Diary* (blog), February 25, 2015, https://stevebuttry.wordpress.com/2015/02/25/dori-maynard-helped-journalists-view-diversity-as-a-matter-of-accuracy/; Margalit Fox, "Dori J. Maynard, Who Sought Diversity in Journalism, Dies at 56," *The New York Times*, February 26, 2015, sec. Business, https://www.nytimes.com/2015/02/26/business/dori-j-maynard-who-sought-diversity-in-journalism-dies-at-56.html.

24. Preliminary research with my News as Culture group has found that digital native organizations record images from other media and repurpose them in online stories. We are designing a more systematic review.

25. Caitlin Nolan and Thomas Tracy, "NYPD Cops Receive Memo Reminding Them They Can Be Filmed While on Duty," nydailynews.com, August 10, 2014, https://www.nydailynews.com/new-york/nypd-cops-told-memo-filmed-article-1.1898379.

26. Antonia Noori Farzan, "An Arizona Cop Threatened to Arrest a 12-Year-Old Journalist. She Wasn't Backing Down," *Washington Post*, February 22, 2019, https://www.washingtonpost.com/nation/2019/02/22/an-arizona-cop-threatened-arrest-year-old-journalist-she-wasnt-backing-down/.

27. Joel M. Schumm, *Policing Body Cameras: Policies and Procedures to Safeguard the Rights of the Accused* (Washington, DC: National Association of Criminal Defense Lawyers, 2017).

28. Robert J. Smith, "Reducing Racially Disparate Policing Outcomes: Is Implicit Bias Training the Answer?," *University of Hawai'i Law Review* 37 (2015): 295–312.

29. See https://mappingpoliceviolence.org; https://www.theguardian.com/us-news/ng-interactive/2015/jun/01/the-counted-police-killings-us-database; or https://www.washingtonpost.com/graphics/2019/national/police-shootings-2019/?utm_term=.17027d38972d.

30. E. G. "Gerry" Morris, phone interview with author, March 4, 2019.

31. Oscar Schwartz, "You Thought Fake News Was Bad? Deep Fakes Are Where Truth Goes to Die," *The Guardian*, November 12, 2018, sec. Technology, https://www.theguardian.com/technology/2018/nov/12/deep-fakes-fake-news-truth.

32. Beatrice Dupuy, "Trump Fuels Spread of Altered Biden Video, Tweeting It Twice," *AP News*, September 16, 2020, https://apnews.com/b83c6017619eba4f92a3d033e5 0782f8.

33. Samuel Woolley, *The Reality Game: A Gripping Investigation into Deepfake Videos, the next Wave of Fake News and What It Means for Democracy* (n.p.: Octopus, 2020).

34. I used to joke with students to just watch for the use of saturated red and yellow, as the screaming colors frequently matched extremist screeds.

35. Andrew Guess, Jonathan Nagler, and Joshua Tucker, "Less Than You Think: Prevalence and Predictors of Fake News Dissemination on Facebook," *Science Advances* 5, no. 1 (January 1, 2019): eaau4586, https://doi.org/10.1126/sciadv.aau4586.

36. Alex Olshansky, "Conspiracy Theorizing and Religious Motivated Reasoning: Why the Earth 'Must' Be Flat" (Master's Thesis, Texas Tech University, 2018), https://ttu-ir.tdl.org/handle/2346/82666.

37. Barbie Zelizer, "Journalism through the Camera's Eye," in *Issues in Journalism*, ed. Stuart Allen (Maidenhead, Berkshire, UK: Open University Press, 2005), 167–76; Barbie Zelizer, "What's Untransportable about the Transport of Photographic Images?," *Popular Communication* 4, no. 1 (2006): 3–20.

38. M. J. Lazer et al., "The Science of Fake News," *Science* 359, no. 6380 (March 9, 2018): 1094–96, https://doi.org/10.1126/science.aao2998.

39. Guess, Nagler, and Tucker, "Less Than You Think."

40. Walt Kelly, *Pogo: We Have Met the Enemy and He Is Us*, 2nd ed. (New York: Simon & Schuster, 1987).

41. Mary Angela Bock and Ever Josue Figueroa, "Faith and Reason: An Analysis of the Homologies of Black and Blue Lives Facebook Pages," *New Media and Society* (November 16, 2017): 1461444817740822, https://doi.org/10.1177/1461444817740822; Ansgar Thiel et al., "Can Sport Be 'Un-Political'?," *European Journal for Sport and Society* 13, no. 4 (October 1, 2016): 253–55, https://doi.org/10.1080/16138171.2016.1253322.

Index

For the benefit of digital users, indexed terms that span two pages (e.g., 52–53) may, on occasion, appear on only one of those pages.

Tables and figures are indicated by *t* and *f* following the page number